Poetry & Peace

RICHARD RANKIN RUSSELL

Poetry & Peace

MICHAEL LONGLEY, SEAMUS HEANEY,
AND NORTHERN IRELAND

University of Notre Dame Press
Notre Dame, Indiana

Manufactured in the United States of America

"The Butchers," "The Ice-cream Man," "Ceasefire," "The Parting,"
"The Ghost Orchid," and "A Linen Handkerchief," from
Collected Poems by Michael Longley, published by Jonathan Cape.
Reprinted by permission of The Random House Group Ltd.

Library of Congress Cataloging-in-Publication Data

Russell, Richard Rankin.
    Poetry and peace : Michael Longley, Seamus Heaney, and
Northern Ireland / Richard Rankin Russell.
        p.   cm.
    Includes bibliographical references and index.
    ISBN-13: 978-0-268-04031-4 (pbk. : alk. paper)
    ISBN-10: 0-268-04031-1 (pbk. : alk. paper)
    1. Longley, Michael, 1939– —Criticism and interpretation.
2. Longley, Michael, 1939– —Aesthetics.   3. Heaney, Seamus,
1939– —Criticism and interpretation.   4. Heaney, Seamus, 1939– —
Aesthetics.   5. Belfast Group.   6. Political violence in literature.
7. Poets, Irish—20th century—Political and social views.   8. Northern
Ireland—In literature.   9. Reconciliation—Northern Ireland.   I. Title.
    PR6062.O515Z85   2010
    821'.914— dc22

                                                        2010024337

∞ *The paper in this book meets the guidelines for permanence and*
durability of the Committee on Production Guidelines for Book Longevity
of the Council on Library Resources.

To the memory of my mother, Diana Diggs Russell (1934 –1996),

and in honor of my father, Paul Lay Russell

Contents

Abbreviations

The following abbreviations are used for frequently cited sources. Other sources are given short-title citations in the endnotes. Full publication information for all sources is given in the bibliography.

CP	*Crediting Poetry*, by Seamus Heaney
CPL	*Collected Poems*, by Michael Longley
DC	*District and Circle*, by Seamus Heaney
DD	*Door into the Dark*, by Seamus Heaney
DN	*Death of a Naturalist*, by Seamus Heaney
EG	*The Echo Gate: Poems, 1975–1979*, by Michael Longley
EV	*An Exploded View: Poems, 1968–1972*, by Michael Longley
"FW"	"Feeling into Words," by Seamus Heaney
FW	*Field Work*, by Seamus Heaney
"I"	"Introduction" to *Causeway: The Arts in Ulster*, by Michael Longley
IP	*Irish Poetry after Joyce*, by Dillon Johnston
GO	*The Ghost Orchid*, by Michael Longley
GF	*Gorse Fires*, by Michael Longley
HL	*The Haw Lantern*, by Seamus Heaney
LCNI	*Literature and Culture in Northern Ireland since 1965: Moments of Danger*, by Richard Kirkland

MI	*Mistaken Identities: Poetry and Northern Ireland,* by Peter McDonald
N	*North,* by Seamus Heaney
NCC	*No Continuing City: Poems, 1963–68,* by Michael Longley
"P"	"Poetry," by Michael Longley
SHMP	*Seamus Heaney: The Making of the Poet,* by Michael Parker
SHPM	*Seamus Heaney: Poems and a Memoir*
SI	*Station Island,* by Seamus Heaney
SL	*The Spirit Level,* by Seamus Heaney
ST	*Seeing Things,* by Seamus Heaney
SW	*Snow Water,* by Michael Longley
TCAT	*The Cure at Troy,* by Seamus Heaney
TS	*Tuppenny Stung; Autobiographical Chapters,* by Michael Longley
WJ	*The Weather in Japan,* by Michael Longley
WO	*Wintering Out,* by Seamus Heaney

Preface

Because of the violence in Northern Ireland since 1969, much Northern Irish literature became a literature of exile, written mostly by authors living in the Republic of Ireland, Scotland, London, or, even further, America and Canada. Several stayed home, of course. Michael Longley was one of these, and his poetic journey bulks large in these pages both because of the personal poetic vision of his intimate, precise verse and because of his broader vision for reconciliation in the province. Seamus Heaney is a fully deserving winner of the Nobel Prize, but Longley deserves a peace prize of his own for his commitment to poetry in Northern Ireland. Edna Longley's prose has often been the critical correlative to his poetry, and some of the central ideas behind this book flow from her pioneering and courageous insights.

In this country, several wonderful people have played a part in helping me come to a meaningful understanding of the intersection of life and literature in Northern Ireland. This project began as a dissertation directed by my mentor, Weldon Thornton, at the University of North Carolina at Chapel Hill. Weldon alternately inspired and questioned me and, like all the great teachers, ultimately left the conclusions up to me. His generosity, warmth, and scholarly acumen will forever be a model for me and other generations of scholars in Irish literary studies. Marilynn J. Richtarik encouraged me to write on Michael Longley and has always greatly supported my scholarly work. Michael Valdez Moses has been encouraging, rigorous, and unfailingly kind, welcoming me to his seminars at Duke University, from which I profited greatly during my time in graduate school at Chapel Hill. His steadfast support of my work over the years has been a wonderful gift. Finally, without my wife Hannah's patient love and encouragement, this project would have never been published.

Warm gratitude is also due to the following:

— The Graduate School at the University of North Carolina at Chapel Hill for a Dissertation Research Fellowship to Belfast, Northern Ireland, for the spring semester of 2000.
— Ophelia Byrne at the Linen Hall Library in Belfast, Northern Ireland.
— The Institute for Irish Studies, Queen's University, Belfast, for providing me office space in the spring of 2000.
— Michael Longley, for our conversation in the spring of 2000 in Belfast.
— Libby Chenault at the Henry C. Pearson Collection of Seamus Heaney, Rare Book Collection, University of North Carolina at Chapel Hill.
— Staff at the Davis Library, UNC-Chapel Hill.
— Stephen Ennis and staff at the Special Collections Department, Robert W. Woodruff Library, Emory University.
— Grania McFadden at the BBC Northern Ireland Community Archive, Cultra, Northern Ireland.
— Staff at the Moody Library of Baylor University.
— The readers for the University of Notre Dame Press, whose suggestions greatly improved this book.
— Denis Donoghue for reading and commenting on a draft of the introduction; Margaret Mills Harper for general encouragement of the project.
— James E. Barcus, Clement Goode, J. R. LeMaster, Joe Fulton, and the late Ann Vardaman Miller, at Baylor University, for their friendship and enthusiasm for my work; George Lensing at UNC-Chapel Hill for consistent support of my scholarship; Bryan Giemza at Randolph-Macon College for friendship and encouragement beyond measure; the late Joan Jones and Ruby Krider of Paris, Tennessee, for believing in me; my sister, Marjorie Levy, my father, Paul Lay Russell, and my late mother, Diana Diggs Russell, for their love and encouragement.

— The former provost of Baylor University, David Lyle Jeffrey, and the former chair of the Department of English, Maurice Hunt, for a reduced teaching load starting in the fall of 2004, which enabled me to conduct more research and writing on this book during the academic year; and the former dean of Arts and Sciences at Baylor, Wallace Daniel, and the Committee on Summer Sabbaticals at Baylor for summer sabbaticals in 2002, 2003, and 2004.

— My graduate students in my "Yeats and Contemporary Irish Poetry" seminar at Baylor University in Fall 2008, who read and commented upon the entirety of this manuscript, for catching various errors at a late stage of this project. Teaching my undergraduate students in my Friel and Heaney class at Baylor in the spring of 2009 helped me think through and write the close reading of Heaney's "Anything Can Happen" in chapter 8.

— Michael Longley for permission to cite from holdings in the Michael Longley Papers at Emory University. Wake Forest University Press and Jonathan Cape/Random House, for permission to reprint several poems by Michael Longley.

— Permission from Faber and Faber to cite lines from Louis MacNeice's poem "Snow."

— Permission from AP Watt, Inc., to reproduce parts of several W. B. Yeats poems.

— Editors of *Carolina Quarterly, Colby Quarterly, Irish University Review,* and *New Hibernia Review* for permission to reprint portions of the reviews and essays published in those pages on Michael Longley. Palgrave Macmillan, for allowing me to republish part of my essay on Heaney that appeared in the collection *Seamus Heaney: Poet, Critic, Translator.*

— BBC Northern Ireland Community Archive, Cultra, Northern Ireland, for permission to quote from the broadcasts "The Artist's Conflict in Ulster," "Good Morning Ulster," "Seamus Heaney—Poetry International," "Creative Writing," "Michael Longley," "A Poet at Work," "Sketches of Britain—Letter from Ulster," "Thought for the Day: 'A Favourite Reading,'" "Radio Two Arts Programme," and "Whatever You Say Say Nothing."

— BBC Radio for permission to quote from the broadcast "Interview with Seamus Heaney."

— Neil Shawcross, for permission to reproduce his lovely paintings of Longley and Heaney that grace the cover of this book, and Chris Caldwell in Belfast for securing this permission.

— The staff of the University of Notre Dame Press, particularly Barbara Hanrahan, Margaret Gloster, Rebecca DeBoer, and Katie Lehman.

Northern Irish Poetry, Imagination, and Ethics

Society makes statements and sends forth instructions, edicts, laws,
definitions of reality. Literature makes counterstatements, Greek when
the official designations are Roman.

—Denis Donoghue

Taking poetry seriously can also mean taking poetry seriously as an
authority: the unique property of a real poem is its capacity to work against
the grain of opinion, or in complex and guarded relation to it, so as to create
an original order in which language overpowers the "weight of judgment
or opinion" through an individual (and essentially unrepeatable) form.

—Peter McDonald

Of course, reading a poem will never subdue a bigot or dissolve the political
divisions inherited from sectarian attitudes. It might, however, open the door
to look anew at history, the individual's place in it, the willing and frank
acknowledgement of what has been done in their name and the possibility
thereby of transforming this experience into a sustaining creative one.

—Gerald Dawe

I begin by recalling two moments, one personal, the other public, where the literature and politics of Northern Ireland intersected in fascinating ways. The first and more distant: In August of 1972, the poet Seamus Heaney left Northern Ireland and relocated himself and his family to County Wicklow, south of Dublin, not so much out of a fear of being killed in the so-called Troubles, although that was undoubtedly a factor, as because "I was . . . being interviewed as, more or less, a spokesman for the Catholic minority during this early stage of the troubles. I found the whole question of what was the status of art within my own life and the question of what is an artist to do in a political situation very urgent matters."[1] Heaney's refusal to be co-opted into being a spokesman for the Northern Irish Catholic community and his dedication to exploring both his art and its relationship to politics constitute a salutary response to a common set of anxieties manifested by writers who have emerged from Northern Ireland before and during the Northern Irish Troubles. Such a response should be construed, not as a retreat, as it was in some quarters upon Heaney's departure, but rather (for him) as a necessary act of artistic independence. On the other hand, Michael Longley, a little-appreciated poet of tremendous talent from the Protestant community, chose to stay in Belfast, where he remains today. Neither poet's decision was wrong, of course: the commitment to poetry expressed by one man in leaving Northern Ireland and the other in staying there exemplifies artistic faithfulness.

The second moment is of a much more recent vintage: On September 6, 2007, Michael Longley was appointed Professor of Poetry for Ireland Chair and was praised by the new Northern Ireland Assembly's deputy first minister Martin McGuinness of Sinn Fein:

> I believe that Michael, like previous holders of the chair, recognizes the responsibility that comes with having such a gift. The impact that poetry and literature have on people and society should never be underestimated. We have recently embarked on a new era of power-sharing here and the First Minister and I are firmly committed to building structures and institutions which will underpin a peaceful and prosperous future for all of us. Literature and the other arts have a crucial role to play in what we are trying to achieve. Participation and enjoyment of arts and culture promote imagination and can change our perceptions of events and each other. I believe that arts and culture will continue to play a crucial role in knitting together the fabric of our society.[2]

The establishment of the Professor of Poetry for Ireland Chair itself was a momentous cultural event because it was the first cross-border academic chair to be set up as a result of the 1998 Good Friday Agreement; perhaps more momentous was that McGuinness, an alleged former IRA member, allegedly holding at one time the title of commander of the IRA's Derry brigade, was praising a (nominally) Protestant Belfast poet! Additionally, McGuinness's recognition of the role of poetry particularly and the arts generally in promoting reconciliation and peace in the province indicates how literature's imaginative power enables sometimes startling discourses, whether public conversations or pronouncements like McGuinness's or the personal, silent dialogues set up between writer and reader.

Both born in 1939, the year of W. B. Yeats's death, Michael Longley and Seamus Heaney are linked biographically, critically, and in the mind of the public, especially in Northern Ireland and Ireland. They are the two best poets who emerged from Philip Hobsbaum's Belfast Group, both because of the quality of their literature and because of their commitment to their craft, the latter of which often conceives of their art in spiritual terms. They also were very close friends in the 1960s and early to mid-1970s as they participated in the Belfast Group together from 1963 to 1966, edited the literary journal *Northern Review* together from 1965 to 1969, marched for civil rights in the province together on at least one occasion, took part in a 1968 Northern Irish Arts Council traveling poetry and musical tour called *Room to Rhyme,* and dedicated poems to each other.

Yeats's profound influence upon both Longley and Heaney, one that has not always been salutary for all Irish poets, further connects them, and although this study attempts no systematic tracing of such an influence on each poet, Yeats's example—particularly his "two-mindedness," a quality of receptivity to multiple perspectives—has enabled both men to maintain the imaginative integrity of their poetry in a time of violent pressures on it to become propaganda or journalism. In *A Jovial Hullabaloo,* Longley's inaugural lecture as Professor of Poetry for Ireland Chair in 2008, Longley, having mentioned the pressures that Northern Irish poets such as Heaney faced because of the violence during the Troubles, warmly invoked Yeats, noting, "More than any other poet he helped us to find our way through the minefield," and further asserting that "we did not write in Yeats's shadow, as some would have it, but in the lighthouse beam of his huge accomplishment."[3]

Although Heaney came to Yeats much later than did Longley, only beginning to seriously study him in the 1970s, he nevertheless has long displayed a Yeatsian quality, as has Longley, that has strengthened their imaginative integrity—two-mindedness. Michael Cavanagh has recently argued, concerning Yeats's famous statement, "We make out of the quarrel with others, rhetoric, but of the quarrel with ourselves, poetry," that "there is perhaps no writer to whom Yeats's famous judgment has meant more than Heaney."[4] But as we shall see, Michael Longley has been similarly drawn to the positive two-mindedness that Yeats modeled. Fully recognizing that he and Heaney share this quality, Longley muses, in the last section of his sequence "Letters" entitled "To Seamus Heaney," originally published in *An Exploded View* (1973),

> And, since *both would have it both ways,*
> On the oily roll of calmer seas
> Launch *coffin-ship and life-boat,*
> Body with soul thus kept afloat,
> *Mind open like a half-door*
> To the speckled hill, the plovers' shore.
> (*CPL,* 61, emphasis mine)

These lines explicitly suggest that both Longley and Heaney are divided within themselves, torn between pessimism about Ireland's and the province's past and present troubles—the "coffin-ship"—and hope about such conflicts—"the life-boat." The poem has just invoked the conflict in its first four stanzas, the last of which concludes, "We sleepwalk through a No Man's Land / Lipreading to an Orange band" (60). "No Man's Land" is a phrase that always bespeaks in-betweenness to Longley, connoting sometimes the actual space between the trenches of opposing sides in World War I, as in his poem of that name honoring Isaac Rosenberg, and at other times doubt about his poetic enterprise, or an affirmation of Northern Irishness as a productive state between English and Irish cultures.[5] The condition thus is one of uneasiness but finally suggests hope tempered by reality as the mind surrounded by conflict looks toward nature. Longley's and Heaney's bicultural identities and their poetics—oscillating between an inward notion of lyric poetry as disinterested, even insouciant, and an outward desire to speak to and create community — have equipped them well to diagnose and offer tentative remedies for the ills of their divided society.

In 1999, each poet published his selected poetry: Heaney's *Opened Ground: Poems, 1966–1996* and Longley's *Selected Poems*. Writing on the two poets in 1999 and noting their very different strengths, Peter McDonald nonetheless makes a strong case for studying their work together because "both poets have passed the test of keeping faith with their own best strengths and instincts over these years"; he further holds that "the careers of both poets offer object lessons in fortitude."[6] While being appropriately cautious about literature's impact on "the real world," Longley and Heaney share a sense that poetry expresses values worth preserving and thus has an educational role to play in society. Heather Clark has argued that Longley, Heaney, and other Belfast poets who emerged from Philip Hobsbaum's creative group in the 1960s believed that "literature, while functioning autonomously, could serve a social purpose by encouraging and upholding humanist values. . . . It was not the politicians who would bring about peace, but the artists, the Arts Council, the museums, and the universities working together."[7] As we will see, such beliefs would be tested sorely as the Troubles raged for over two decades in Northern Ireland.

Longley, Heaney, and Derek Mahon were so associated with each other by the late 1960s in reality and in the mind of the public that Michael Foley sarcastically called them "the tight-assed trio."[8] Longley even wrote in an unsent long letter to Heaney's wife, Marie, that "my friendships, first with Mahon, then with Heaney, have been of central importance to me and contributed greatly to my own development as a man and poet: . . . my second book . . . explored the notion of an artistic community, a poetic sodality [with them]."[9] While Longley wrote "To Seamus Heaney" (along with "To Derek Mahon" and "To James Simmons" for his second volume, *An Exploded View*), Heaney dedicated "Personal Helicon," the last poem of his first full-length volume, *Death of a Naturalist* (1966), to Longley, its title suggesting something of Longley's personal inspiration to Heaney. Michael Parker has argued that Heaney may have learned to suppress his "angry Catholic voice" over injustices against Catholics in the province because of "his new friendships

with the Longleys and [David] Hammond, who were both *[sic]* of Protestant stock, and by that spirit of communality generated by the [Belfast]
Group" (*SHMP,* 55). Longley's and Heaney's place in Northern Irish culture is perhaps epitomized by the Neil Shawcross portraits that at one
time hung in Belfast's Linen Hall Library, reproductions of which grace
the cover of this book.

The Shawcross portraits suggest strongly the link between Heaney
and Longley in the public's mind as well, as does a telling article in the
Irish Times celebrating the surprise seventieth birthday party for Michael Longley held at Queen's University Belfast on June 25, 2009,
shortly before his actual birthday. The Northern Editor for the paper,
Gerry Moriarty, led the article with the phrase, "Seamus Heaney and
other literary figures assembled at Queen's University Belfast yesterday."
Moriarty also notes that "Heaney said Longley's friendship was of vital
importance to him and his wife, Marie, for well over 40 years, going back
to 1963 when the emerging Belfast-based poets such as Derek Mahon,
Eavan Boland and Edna gathered in Longley's flat on Malone Avenue
in Belfast." He then quotes Heaney about his "intense" friendship with
Longley in 1960s Belfast: "'It was certainly one of the centres of poetry
of these islands in the 1960s. It was sort of a high-voltage area,' Heaney
recalled. 'Friendships from the beginning are crucial and are never as intense again. So I have a deep connection and deep respect for Michael's
achievement.'"[10]

Despite my marked admiration for Derek Mahon's poetry as some
of the best written in English over the last four decades (along with that
of Longley and Heaney), I have chosen not to focus on him in this study
for several reasons: because he was not a member of the Belfast Group,
because he has not consistently explored the situation of Northern Ireland in his poetry as Longley and Heaney have, and because he has been
absent from the island for long periods, although he lives there now and
has off and on for years. Although, as Dillon Johnston notes, Mahon's
poetry is typically set "in an actual specified place, often Belfast, or, more
frequently, in some barren, primitive, or post-holocaust site" (*IP,* 225), it
has been repeatedly characterized as exilic and often is characterized by
its representations of distance, unlike much of the intimate particularity
of Longley's and Heaney's poetry. Significant exceptions to this charac-

terization thrust their way forward, of course, just as the clamoring, singularly rendered mushrooms do in Mahon's "A Disused Shed in Co. Wexford." Terence Brown may put it best when he notes that Mahon presents himself in his first collection of poetry, *Night-Crossing* (1968), as "a migratory imagination for which journeys away from and occasionally back to a native place would constitute a defining way of being in the world."[11] Mahon's ironic stance of independence is well articulated in Heaney's own observation that "Longley is Protestant and so is Derek Mahon—but Derek was never entangled with the Belfast faithful, as it were. I always think of Derek as the Stephen Dedalus of Belfast, the man who is an ironist and who refuses to serve that in which he no longer believes, whether that covers family, church, regional loyalty or whatever."[12]

The creative work of other remarkable, younger poets from Northern Ireland, such as Ciaran Carson, Paul Muldoon, and Medbh McGuckian, and of a still younger generation represented by the poet-critic Peter McDonald, is not explored here either. First, there is the matter of space: a proper attempt to do justice to their profound poetry would far exceed the size of an academic monograph. Moreover, their engagements with Yeats, one of many significant connections between Longley and Heaney, have been extraordinarily more vexed than have those of my two chosen poets and, in the case of McGuckian, are even mediated through Heaney.[13] More important, because they came of age during the Troubles, these younger poets' particular explorations of the Northern Irish conflict and the peace process are markedly different from those of Heaney and Longley, who had time to develop their poetic voices beginning in the late 1950s for roughly a decade before the contemporary conflict began.

This book explores how the nuanced poetry written by Longley and Heaney upholds a commitment to artistic integrity through their concerns with poetry's imaginative power and form. This faithful allegiance to poetry delights in the particular, the seemingly trivial, and the forgotten in its evocation and revelation of the transcendent. Although both poets emerged from particular Christian milieus—Longley from English Protestantism, Heaney from Irish Catholicism—their work's emphasis on the sacred draws not only on Christian conceptions but also on those of other religious traditions, such as Judaism and Buddhism in the case of Longley.

Writing in 1968, Vincent Buckley observed that "even in a desacralized society like our own, there are some poets who, *as a mode of life,* concern themselves with estimating, defining, and recreating manifestations of the sacred. In fact, in a heavily desacralised society there may be a few poets whose emphasis on this activity will be more intensive and exclusive than it would have been in a society more habitually open to the sacred dimensions of life."[14] Longley and Heaney are two such poets that have concerned themselves "with estimating, defining, and recreating manifestations of the sacred" in our "heavily desacralized society." Their faith in the imagination suggests their connection to the sacred: as Denis Donoghue has argued, "I think it only reasonable to admit that a theory of literature which takes imagination as its ground or point of departure lays claims to certain axioms: that art is the inspired work of a few rare souls, adepts of a sacred mystery; that while common minds slide upon the surface of things, artists search the depths."[15] Throughout their long and fruitful careers, Longley and Heaney have habitually rendered the sacred present in poems that often concern the beauty and fragility of the quotidian world. In so doing, their quiet insistence on poetry's ability to evoke and even create sacred spaces and objects through words has enabled them to maintain their primary allegiance to the imaginative autonomy of art, yet also to make secondary contributions to the long and arduous peace process in Northern Ireland. Their success is all the more remarkable because they have worked in a society where traditional religious practices and expressions often divide human beings across relatively homogeneous communities.

Perhaps the best articulation of the aesthetic/religious attitude toward poetry held by Longley and Heaney and other faithful artists can be found in George Steiner's *Real Presences,* where he suggests that "the making into being by the poet, artist and, in a way yet to be defined, by the composer, is *counter*-creation. The pulse of motive which relates the begetting of meaningful forms to the first act of creation, to the coming into being of being . . . is not mimetic in any neutral or obeissant sense. It is radically agonistic. It is rival."[16] As countercreators, poets and other

serious artists enact "a root-impulse of the human spirit to explore possibilities of meaning and of truth that lie outside empirical seizure or
proof."[17] In a little-cited interview, Heaney himself put the matter well
when he told Richard Kearney about the role of the poet in the Troubles,
"He or she can be the magical thinker; he or she can stand for values
that aren't utilitarian. The artist can refuse History as a category, can say
'No. I prefer to dream possibilities.'"[18] In their sacred attitude toward
their art, Longley and Heaney affirm with Steiner that "it is the enterprise and privilege of the aesthetic to quicken into lit presence the continuum between temporality and eternity, between matter and spirit,
between man and 'the other.'"[19]

Longley and Heaney both have explicitly articulated their essentially religious view of art as revealing real presences, a conception that is
grounded in the highest appreciation for art's integrity. Longley, for example, in discussing his translation of the Baucis and Philemon story,
pointed out that his favorite art "transforms the everyday and shows the
divine . . . in everyday objects."[20] Elsewhere, he noted, "I'm anti-clerical,
full stop. And I'm also an atheist, or certainly an agnostic," but went on
to suggest, "I am interested in what it could mean to write religious poetry, particularly at the end of this godawful century. . . . I like Horace's
phrase, 'Priest of the Muses.'"[21] Shortly after the publication of his *Poems,
1963–1983,* Longley told Robert Johnstone in an interview that "poetry, the effort to write it, reading it and living it, is, if you like, my religion. It gives me something akin to religious experience. Perhaps one of
the things an artist should do is suggest the sacerdotal values of life—in
a completely secular way, of course."[22]

In a review of Osip Mandelstam's *Selected Poems,* Heaney provoca-
tively holds that "art has a religious, a binding force, for the artist. Language is the poet's faith and the faith of his fathers and in order to go his
own way and do his proper work in an agnostic time, he has to bring
that faith to the point of arrogance and triumphalism."[23] Coming from
a poet who has spent a career, like Longley, writing against religious
triumphalism, this affirmation of poetry's power is revelatory. As Seamus Deane has argued, Heaney's attitude toward his art is analogous to
"the reverence of an acolyte before a mystery of which he knows he is
also the celebrant."[24] For Heaney, as traditional religious faith continues

to decline in Ireland and in other Western countries, its proper replacement is poetry, an exalted calling that pledges allegiance to the inward occurrence of the poem over the action of outer reality. In one of his major essays, "The Government of the Tongue," Heaney argues that "poetry is its own reality and no matter how much a poet may concede to the corrective pressures of social, moral, political and historical reality, the ultimate fidelity must be to the demands and promise of the artistic event."[25]

By inscribing their own poetry as a sort of sacred space, both rival to and continuous with the presence of the ineffable while being momentarily discontinuous with reality, Longley's and Heaney's imagining of poetry as a numinous zone accords with Mircea Eliade's compelling conception of how the manifestation of the sacred interrupts the normal time-space continuum: "When the sacred manifests itself in any hierophany, there is not only a break in the homogeneity of space; there is also revelation of an absolute reality, opposed to the nonreality of the vast surrounding expanse."[26]

These two great poets have sought and found art as a verifiably religious calling, one that seemingly ironically but appropriately opposes sectarian violence. Their particular poetry of the sacred constitutes both a linguistic escape from violent vengeance and an alternate reality that habitually exists in the present, waiting for our inhabitation. If, as René Girard has famously argued, "Vengeance . . . is an interminable, infinitely repetitive process," each enactment of which runs the risk of initiating "a chain reaction whose consequences will quickly prove fatal to any society of modest size," the sacred poetry of Longley and Heaney instead instantiates singularity, not repetition, and constitutes a force that values all life.[27] Heaney has explicitly suggested that the nuance and particularity of Northern Irish poetry penned by "the writers of my generation" contrasted with the brutal redundancies of sectarianism at the time: "The fact that a literary action was afoot was itself a new political condition, and the poets did not feel the need to address themselves to the specifics of politics because they assumed that the tolerances and subtleties of their art were precisely what they had to set against the repetitive intolerance of public life."[28]

Literary particularity is a vexed concept, one that is contaminated by criticism in the sense that generalizations almost always creep in when critics seek to elucidate it, as Jon Kertzer has pointed out in a compelling and provocative essay: "Although the specificity of a literary work may strike us forcefully on first reading, it is difficult to define because all the modes of definition at our disposal have the perverse effect of depriving a work of its particularity. Explanations inevitably generalize."[29] I believe that of all genres poetry is the most prone to generating particularity because of its verbal precision and also because of a process that Derek Attridge argues arises out of a reader's performance of verbal singularity when reading poetry, *"a sense of its real-time unfolding."*[30] How then, can we attempt to approach the poems of Longley and Heaney, which are supreme examples of particularity? Kertzer helpfully suggests that "the course of a particular comes into focus if we imagine it situated in a present that expires as soon as it occurs, and is only known when it haunts us afterwards."[31] As we shall see, much of the poetry explored in this study focuses on the fleeting and the terminal; imagining poetry's own expiration, as it were, may enable its haunting and revisiting of us later in a way that generates our ethical response and connects us to each other, a point taken up at the end of this introduction.

Salman Rushdie has made perhaps the most eloquent plea in the late twentieth century for art to occupy a middle ground "between the material and spiritual worlds" and, in the process, to "offer us something new—something that might even be called a secular definition of transcendence."[32] Transcendence, for Rushdie, includes events such as birth, lovemaking, joy, and the moment of death, spots of time in which one can experience a "soaring quality" and feel "the sense of being more than oneself, of being in some way joined to the whole of life." He believes that art's special role is to oscillate between the poles of religious fundamentalism and "secular, rationalist materialism" by capturing "that experience, to offer it to, in the case of literature, its readers; to be, for a secular materialist culture, some sort of replacement for what the love of god offers in the world of faith."[33]

Later in this essay, however, Rushdie backs away "from the idea of sacralizing literature" because he says he "cannot bear the idea of the writer as secular prophet" and because "all art," according to Samuel Beckett, "must end in failure." But, of course, as he further holds, "This is, clearly, no reason for surrender."[34] Rushdie finally settles upon the conceit of literature as "an unimportant-looking little room" in which "we can hear *voices talking about everything in every possible way.* . . . We do not need to call it sacred, but we do need to remember that it is necessary. . . . Wherever in the world the little room of literature has been closed, sooner or later the walls have come tumbling down."[35]

Longley and Heaney would likewise not worship literature, including poetry, but do approach it reverently, even sacredly, because of precisely its capacity to set up conversations about any possible subject, a capacity that Rushdie identifies as literature's life-giving quality, standing in opposition to deathly rhetoric and oppressive force. Longley has offered an analogous image to that of Rushdie, suggesting that "art in the community is like a small gland in the body, like the pituitary gland. It's so small it seems unimportant but when it's removed the body dies. It's the totalitarian forces that always want to remove it."[36] Heaney has argued that fidelity to art constitutes a consistent witness to conscience over against conscription of the artist by the state. Writing again of Osip Mandelstam, he observes that "for him, obedience to poetic impulse was obedience to conscience; lyric action constituted radical witness." Mandelstam thus bore "witness to the necessity of what he called 'breathing freely,' even at the price of his death; to the art of poetry as an unharnessed, non-didactic, non-party-inspired, inspired act."[37] Bearing witness—the phrase is borrowed from believers who testify to their faith. Consistently testifying to their faith in poetry's power, Longley and Heaney have shown how art constitutes an extraordinary reality in its own right, separate from yet inextricably tied to our ordinary world.

In holding this critical view of literature, I share Rita Felski's dismay at what she believes is the tendency of critics who value literature's otherness, alterity, and singularity to "overlook the equally salient realities of its connectedness." Such critics, according to Felski, by praising "the ineffable and enigmatic qualities of works of art," actually "fail to do justice to the specific ways in which such works infiltrate and inform our lives."[38] Thus I believe Longley's and Heaney's poetry articulates an imagined community through their particular poetic language that emphasizes our deep spirituality and need for each other. I realize that such a focus on the literary imagination will be regarded by some as passé, retrograde, even untenable, given developments in literary theory over the past several decades. Such disregard for the literary imagination is usually conjoined to a corresponding conception of those who profess such belief as bizarre creatures who think art operates in an hermetically sealed vacuum. No such caricature has ever existed to my knowledge, and I am happy to report I am no such critic, nor are the writers under consideration in this study. Nevertheless, because of the persistence of this critical suspicion of the literary imagination, I am led to conclude with Nathan Scott Jr., writing in 1985 about his own study of the poetic imagination, that "the entire project will no doubt by many be felt immediately to be something questionable. For in our own late phase of modernity the concept of the imagination has suffered so great a decline in prestige as to have lost very nearly altogether its admissibility into the lexicon normally controlling intellectual exchange."[39] And yet not altogether. There are hopeful signs that the study of the literary imagination is making a comeback, manifested in the recent upsurge of what Marjorie Levinson terms the "New Formalism," an admittedly lumpy description of a general movement consisting of at least two somewhat distinct critical turns toward form over recent years.[40] Suffice it to say that authors have faithfully maintained a belief in the literary imagination even as many critics over the last several decades have despised and denigrated it, preferring instead to treat the study of literature as sociology, history, or practically anything other than what it is by virtue of its form—a particular discipline with sufficient integrity in and of itself. Felski has succinctly identified what is lost in such narrowly ideological approaches: "To define literature as ideology is to have decided ahead of time that literary works can be objects of knowledge but never sources of knowledge. It is to rule out of court the eventuality that a literary text could know as much, or more, than a theory."[41] Perhaps nowhere in recent history has this authorial belief in the power of literature as a source of knowledge been so evident as in the particular case of Northern Ireland and the writers that emerged from that often benighted province in the second half of the twentieth century.

Fran Brearton has noted that although there are several problems with the flattened conception of a "Northern [Irish] Renaissance" in the 1960s, the poets from that era most often linked, Mahon, Heaney, and Longley, do "share the sense of art as an alternative spirituality; in varying degrees, this seemingly 'traditional' or romantic assumption makes it a mode of subversion all the more telling in a context where sectarianism is rife."[42] Longley himself has talked about poetry as a properly revolutionary activity, one occurring beyond the poet's control yet formally measured:

> Poetry is about something happening with words that is beyond that poet's personality, way beyond that poet's prejudices and beliefs in a way that is completely out of control but formally perfect. . . . I think that if poetry's not revolutionary it's lost. And by revolutionary I mean the Latinate sense of the word, of just turning things over. If you're not taking people's prejudices, our lazy ways of seeing and responding, and giving them a great shakeup so that we see the world and our circumstances anew, then it's not really poetry. That's what it's about, it's a revolution, and that's why it's dangerous.[43]

As chapter 1 will demonstrate, Longley's and Heaney's already deep regard for their craft was enhanced greatly by their participation in Philip Hobsbaum's Belfast Group in the early to mid-1960s. During that period their commitment to their art was already enabling them to form an ecumenical outlook that would become an implicit part of their revolutionary poetry, a revolution that would enable their subtle engagements with the turbulence on the streets of Northern Ireland after the initial successes of the Catholic civil rights movement.

Even deeply religious believers admit that they struggle with doubt; hence the common prayer spoken by the father of the demon-possessed child that Jesus goes on to heal in Mark's Gospel: "Oh Lord, I believe; help Thou my unbelief."[44] Poets, including Longley and Heaney, evince an analogous attitude toward their work in a quest for inspiration and creation. A significant portion of this study, including much of the opening chapter on Longley and almost all of the first chapter on Heaney, thus explores the ways in which these two wordsmiths have sought inspiration and corresponding postures from which they could write creatively. Longley has gone through two searching periods of writer's block—in the late 1960s and very early 1970s and then from 1979 to 1985 and from 1987 to 1988[45]—and a shy Heaney's early pen name was "Incertus." But this doubt is salutary for two reasons. First, as Buckley suggests,

"The very self-doubt of the poet is a testimony to, if not a proof of, his almost unwillingly persistent commitment to the writing of poetry as a sacred act and an aspiration to self-completion."[46] Additionally, such doubt creates a leavening effect in a society where, especially after the outbreak of the contemporary "Troubles," certainty became the province of the ideologically committed. Bigots employed "sureties" often based on nothing but hearsay or cliché to mobilize their followers. Poetry, of course, dwells in ambiguity and suggestion, seeking to evoke pleasure, not partisanship. As Longley has remarked about his artistic goals for his readers: "The main thing I want them to receive is pleasure . . . some sense of reverence for the physical world, and some sense of mystery beyond the physical world."[47]

And yet there is a way in which Longley and Heaney and all good poets are supremely concerned with the truthful particulars they seek to depict; their poetry's dwelling in specificity profoundly evokes the transcendent. Nathan Scott's conception of poetry's relationship to the sacred illuminates Longley's and Heaney's tendency to reverently gaze upon manifestations of worldly realities. Despite their differences, both poets share what Scott points out is Heidegger's conception, in his *Holzwege,* of poetry's truthful work: "Truth is at work because poetic art, by inviting an attitude of enthrallment before the various concrete realities of the world, prepares us to be laid hold of by that wherewith these things are inwardly constituted and enabled to be what they are—which is none other than Being itself."[48] Because of its compression and singularity, poetry, more than the other genres of literature, properly leads us into deep appreciation of the uniqueness of both our given world and what is beyond it. And because art generally, as Denis Donoghue has argued, "is sustained by the different form of attention it provokes" from the perceiver in comparison to other objects of perception, art becomes "'inexhaustible to meditation,'" a truth that is evidenced by the deep contemplation on display in many of the poems analyzed in this study.[49]

This truthful transcendence derived from the material world in the poetry of Longley and Heaney confounds and subverts the sectarian boundaries often drawn in the province through its subtle perspectives. Rather like the ancient Janus-faced statue on Boa Island in County

Fermanagh, these writers generally exhibit the kind of two-mindedness that Heaney identifies in his 1984 lecture *Place and Displacement: Recent Poetry of Northern Ireland* as manifesting the "strain of being in two places at once, of needing to accommodate two opposing conditions of truthfulness simultaneously."[50] Using *two-mindedness* as a term is potentially problematic, as it often suggests someone in a state of indecision and thus of "two minds" about an issue. Yet it is an enabling term for Longley and Heaney. Longley has spoken repeatedly about being "schizophrenic" in an enabling way through his love of ambiguity and through his joint Irishness and Britishness. For example, he has pointed out about his poem "Persephone" that it "might also explain the state of being in two minds, or more extremely, schizophrenia. This seems to be a twentieth-century complaint."[51] Speaking of his dual cultural allegiances, Heaney notes in his essay "Frontiers of Writing" that "there is nothing extraordinary about the challenge to be in two minds. If, for example, there was something exacerbating, there was still nothing deleterious to my sense of Irishness in the fact that I grew up in the minority in Northern Ireland and was educated within the dominant British culture. My identity was emphasized rather than eroded by being maintained in such circumstances."[52] And the contemporary Northern Irish novelist Glenn Patterson has similarly argued that the bifocal vision of the typical writer from the province creates authorial freedom and enhanced cultural understanding: "As writers we are often pulled in seemingly contrary directions, looking inwards and appealing outwards. In reality, though, there need be no contradiction, for . . . in trying to understand one place very well it might just be possible to understand many other places at least in part."[53]

   This outlook has enabled Heaney and Longley to thoughtfully critique both the cultural tradition into which they were born, as well as traditions less familiar to them. In so doing, they have written skillfully and deeply about local conditions in Northern Ireland in a parochial, not a provincial, manner, in Patrick Kavanagh's famous terms. As Kavanagh states in "The Parish and the Universe," "Parochialism and provincialism are opposites. The provincial has no mind of his own; he does not trust what his eyes see until he has heard what the metropolis — toward which his eyes are turned — has to say on any subject. . . . The parochial mentality on the other hand is never in any doubt about the social and artistic validity of his parish."[54] Kavanagh's decision to write about his local culture modeled this sort of positive parochialism for Longley and Heaney, and both poets have repeatedly mentioned him as an early exemplar. Kavanagh's concern with depicting much of the harshness of rural Irish life permitted Longley and Heaney to similarly depict static Northern Irish society along with their own immediate environments.

In its exploration of Longley and Heaney's faith in poetry's integrity, this study often tests that commitment by measuring their poetic "responses" to the Troubles in Northern Ireland, although such poems are usually filtered through their respective imaginations in such a way as to reaffirm their faith in poetry's capacity to create worlds of wonder and thus develop alternate realms of potential from the given realities on the ground, while sometimes secondarily drawing on those seemingly unyielding facts. Their poetry reaches toward such a potential while also being written out of their knowledge that, as the poet and critic James Longenbach has held, "the power of a poem inheres in the realization that we cannot count on it. Its ephemeral consolation depends precisely on its being ephemeral, open to the vicissitudes of self-doubt."[55] Much of Longley's and Heaney's poetry focuses upon the ephemeral, the fleeting—celebrating vivifying qualities of plant, animal, or human life while knowing their short life span. These two poets thus share a corollary regard toward their art with one of their exemplars, W. B. Yeats, as supremely expressed in his "Lapis Lazuli": "All things fall and are built again / And those that build them are gay."[56] As they are for religious believers, faith and doubt are essential components for poets. Doubt paradoxically strengthens faith or poetry and steels it in the fires of this world, just as untested faith or poetry is weakened and made brittle by being held only theoretically. Yet poetic or religious faith still has an elusive quality to it that we cannot fully articulate—if we could, why would we then believe? Some things are simply beyond our ken, and that should engender wonder and Yeatsian gaiety in us if nothing else.

Whether or not these poets even have an obligation to write about the Troubles warrants some investigation. As the discerning Northern Irish critic and poet Peter McDonald has argued, "Northern Ireland,

and its history during the last three decades, has been allowed to set the terms for almost all critical writing on poetry by Northern Irish poets. Inevitable as this must appear, there are senses in which it needs, and has long needed, to be resisted."[57] The present study, while engaging with the specificities of Northern Irish history over the last four decades, has attempted to maintain faith with poetry's particularities and pressures, with questions of diction, form, and the intersection of form with content—just as Longley and Heaney have.

The Troubles have thrust thoughtful Northern Irish authors into a recurring dilemma: whether they should warn of the implications of developing situations; comment immediately upon a development or atrocity; or wait until after the occurrence of an event—sometimes even years—to reflect upon it. Michael Longley discussed this dilemma when he attempted to articulate the role of the artist in 1971 in his introduction to *Causeway: The Arts in Ulster*:

> Too many critics seem to expect a harvest of paintings, poems, plays and novels to drop from the twisted branches of civil discord. They fail to realise that the artist needs time in which to allow the raw material of experience to settle to an imaginative depth where he can transform it and possibly even suggest solutions to current and very urgent problems by reframing them according to the dictates of his particular discipline. He is not some sort of super-journalist commenting with unfaltering spontaneity on events immediately after they have happened. Rather, as Wilfred Owen stated over fifty years ago, it is the artist's duty to warn, to be tuned in before anyone else to the implication of a situation. ("I," 8)

Longley's statement epitomizes the dilemma of the artist in Northern Ireland: on the one hand he wants a Wordsworthian reflection in tranquillity upon events so that he can properly write about them, but on the other he seems to feel that the artist should also act as an early warning system. He is correct to dismiss the third option—to act as a "sort of super-journalist commenting with unfaltering spontaneity on events immediately after they have happened."[58] He has consistently articulated this position, recalling in 2003, "From the beginning my friends and I resisted the temptation to hitch a ride on yesterday's headlines and write, to paraphrase John Hume, the poetry of the latest atrocity."[59] The artistic dilemma of whether to warn of the implications of a developing situation well in advance or simply to wait and reflect upon its repercussions is itself further complicated by the artist's attempt, not merely to be a mouthpiece for his "tribe," but to represent both his own community and "the other side." Despite this double dilemma, Longley and Heaney have generally had a measured, evenhanded approach to writing creatively about the conflict. Their poems about the subject have been imaginative and thoughtful; they have usually not written to the moment; and they often react in such a personal way as to render simplistic an attempt to link them or their positions with a received political identity.

The arts in Northern Ireland had reached enough of a critical ferment for Michael Longley's edited book *Causeway: The Arts in Ulster* to be published by the Arts Council of Northern Ireland in 1971. Published against a backdrop of rising violence in the North, the volume constitutes an important literary intervention at a time of increasing despair in the province. The variety of arts in the province is indicated by its contents: two chapters on architecture, one on Irish traditional music, one on jazz, one on classical music, and one on the Ulster Folk Museum, as well as chapters on painting and sculpture, poetry, prose, and drama. Longley points out in his introduction the diversity evidenced by the different arts in Ulster at the time and crucially notes that the current flowering occurred before the political upheaval of the late 1960s: "The range and depth of artistic activity in Ulster are in themselves symptoms of its continued liveliness—even though it is this very vitality which most creative people here would wish to qualify and refine, just as surely as they recognise it as one of the sources of their energy. The political explosion was preceded, as is so often the case, by an artistic efflorescence. The Sixties began and continued with a surge of creativity which might have prevented and certainly suggested the upheaval with which they were to end" ("I," 8). He is correct in pointing out that the arts in the province were flourishing before the outbreak of the current "Troubles"—an important assertion, given that some critics of this literature have assumed that contemporary Northern Irish literature is merely some sort of reaction to the fighting and dependent upon it for its creative vigor. Nothing could be further from the truth, although this literature has been probably given greater scrutiny in the eyes of the world because of the widespread media coverage given to the Troubles over the last several decades.

Elsewhere, Longley has emphasized that he and his other poet friends at the time "hated what we now call 'Troubles trash.' . . . We disliked the notion that civic unrest might be good for poetry, and poetry a solace for the bereaved and broken-hearted."[60] Seamus Deane has also perspicaciously warned of the danger of identifying Northern Irish literature with the Troubles:

> The beginning of the Northern troubles coincided with the emergence of the Northern poets as a clearly identifiable group. Although in retrospect it would seem to be one of those apparent coincidences which are really part of a recognizable pattern of related events, it is too easy and dangerous to stress this aspect. For, secreted within this attitude, is the view that there is an inevitable and even welcome connection between violence and art. The release of one and the efflorescence of the other are assumed to be simultaneous. The facts of Northern experience do not bear this out. Violence has often disfigured the society there, but art has not consistently flourished in its shadow. The twenties and thirties were particularly barren in the North as far as artistic productions were concerned. But violence, especially of the politically-directed, official kind, was frequent.[61]

Deane is not correct here, however, in suggesting that the emergence of the Northern poets and the Troubles coincided. The Belfast Group started in 1963, well before the outbreak of the current Troubles, and Longley, Heaney, and Mahon had all garnered critical recognition before 1969. More important, though, Deane's warning is a clear call to scholars to examine this period thoughtfully and not argue a simplistic causal relation between the literature and the conflict. In both its origins and its current complex manifestations, contemporary Northern Irish literature, while undeniably responsive to the current conflict, has emerged from a tradition that is rooted in a pervasive aesthetic emphasis on the power of the imagination and a rejection of monolithic categories and identities.

My exploration of the varying responses by Longley and Heaney to the contemporary Troubles and corresponding artistic issues is grounded in my understanding of the long existence of Northern Irish literature that predates the contemporary Troubles. My use of *Northern Irish literature* is not meant to be taken as a political statement recognizing the legitimacy of the province; I employ it because it is gradually becoming the accepted term to describe the literature written in and about the province, although there is still at times a studious reluctance to employ such terms, often for compelling political and cultural reasons.[62]

To be sure, literature from the province—especially that written since the start of the Troubles—is deeply marked by that conflict. But the writers under consideration view their primary artistic duty as being to the imagination—not, say, to the reintegration of the province with the Republic. Heaney, himself an admitted constitutional nationalist who desires a united Ireland, even has suggested that identification with a particular political stance compromises the writer's autonomy: "A constant fidelity to a political position makes you uninteresting. You are factored in to a party's calculations."[63] Once both of the poets in this study established a fidelity to the imagination, they engaged in an astonishing array of critiques of political, religious, and cultural identities, all the while maintaining that original and primary allegiance.

Some might suspect that literature issuing from a six-county, artificially drawn province cannot have an aesthetic or that any aesthetic it does have must be insignificant or limited. However, as I will show, the artistic projects undertaken by Michael Longley and Seamus Heaney demonstrate otherwise. Their common aesthetic project of fidelity to their art has resulted in some of the most carefully crafted literature over the last century in the English-speaking world and some of the most profound, nuanced critiques of identity in the province. The assiduous pursuit of their artistic vocation has enabled them both to be true to their own voices and to escape the cultural and political determinism of their environment. This pursuit has often come through a deep commitment to the form of their work, which allows them true artistic freedom.

Heaney argues in his 1984 lecture *Place and Displacement* that "the appeasement of the achieved poem" enabled the Northern Irish poet of the 1960s and afterwards a liberation from the entrapping ways in which one's cultural/religious group attempted to "confine the range of one's growth, to have one's sympathies determined and one's responses determined by it."[64] Note that Heaney reappropriates "appeasement" from the political realm and applies it to poetry, a necessary maneuver in those first violent days of the Troubles. Because thoughtful Northern Irish poets such as Heaney and Longley engaged in this move, they were then able to offer the beginnings of notions of reconciliation, far more long-lasting than the temporary (political) notion of appeasement. Poetry's appeasement, though seemingly temporally appeasing, if entered into enough times enacts a long-lasting appeasement that does not merely soothe the mind but reconditions it by enabling it to be supple, nimble, and contemplative, qualities that are necessary for true imaginative daring.

Heaney then claims that this intensification of personal being and detachment from immediate predicaments "lies behind the typical concern of Northern Irish poets with style, with formal finish, with linguistic relish and play."[65] His argument that form and style in Northern Irish poetry act as linguistic buttresses against the constraining pressures of received identities accords with Denis Donoghue's argument about form: "The beauty of literature seems to entail resistance to the official designations of reality. Even when it makes statements in ordinary language, a poem is not the sum of those statements. It maintains its autonomy—never absolute, however—by virtue of its form."[66] The autonomy of imaginative literature thus leads to artistic independence— a positive aesthetic variation on the oft-threatened Unilateral Declaration of Independence by hard-line Protestant loyalists—which is essential for establishing the autonomy of the Northern Irish writer, beckoned as he is by cultural, religious, and political loyalties.

As Heaney goes on to argue, this commitment to poetry does not preclude political engagement, but it ensures that this engagement is on the poet's home ground, his consciousness:

> It is a superficial response to the work of Northern Irish poets to conceive of their lyric stances as evasions of the actual conditions. Their concern with poetry itself wears well when we place it beside the protest poetry of the sixties: the density of their verbal worlds has held up, the purely poetic force of the words is the guarantee of

a commitment which need not apologise for not taking up the cudgels since it is raising a baton to attune discords which the cudgels
are creating. To attune it within the pit of their own consciousness, of
course, not in the arena of dustbin lids and shoot-to-kill operations.[67]

Heaney's concluding musical metaphor suggests that harmony in
all of its manifestations must start within the individual consciousness,
then spread out to the community, not the other way round. Literature
is capable of attending to the particular, embodying it and displaying
it in such a way that it becomes a riposte against cultural, political, and
religious abstractions and establishes a form of resistance that enables
realignments, different imaginings, new possibilities. Elmer Kennedy-
Andrews adumbrates this major strand of my argument in his book on
fiction and the Northern Ireland troubles since 1969 when he says, "The
most significant feature of the literature has been its resistance to, and
liberation from, orthodoxy and ideology, its commitment to the 'world
elsewhere' made possible by language."[68] Such an allegiance to the imagination enables a modeling of the order that could be instantiated into
the disordered world outside poetry, while preserving its own autonomy.
As Heaney puts it in his essay "The Government of the Tongue," "Just
as the poem, in the process of its own genesis, exemplifies a congruence
between impulse and right action, so in its repose the poem gives us a
premonition of harmonies desired and not inexpensively achieved. In
this way, the order of art becomes an achievement intimating a possible
order beyond itself, although its relation to that further order remains
promissory rather than obligatory."[69]

One of Michael Longley's most discerning readers, Fran Brearton,
has recently argued that the commitment to form by Longley and his fellow poets is itself a type of political maneuver: "The whole point of that
formal technique is to bring it into collision—and collusion—with a disruptive element: order meets impurity; the rewards are mutual. That encounter of like with unlike, the mingling of different elements, becomes
a paradigm of political responsibility. . . . The distinction drawn here is
between a form of political commitment in poetry that too easily becomes a one-dimensional, even propagandist taking of sides, and a commitment to poetry which, by default, is a political activity."[70] Brearton's

purposely provocative statement may well go too far for many readers, but she rightly stresses the commitment to poetry evinced by Longley and his contemporaries that is the foundation both for their art and for this study. Only art that is internally committed to itself as a work of art has even a chance of interacting thoughtfully with the conditions of the outer world. Heaney has recently argued, in response to an interviewer's question about Sartre's rejection of poetry as apolitical, that poetry's form enables preservation and makes it political in a certain sense: "Poetry, after all, can save the world! Just as form keeps, so poetry keeps, saves and stays."[71]

The focus on the specific conditions—physical, political, cultural, and religious—of Northern Ireland has led ineluctably to this literature transcending its specific location and often constraining identities and becoming truly universal in the way that all great literature that attends to the detailed and local does. The particularity of this literature, moreover, accords with what Cleanth Brooks has termed one of the major uses of literature, a function we might call the literary/epistemological: "The peculiar kind of knowledge that literature gives us is concrete—not a generalization about facts but a special kind of focusing upon the facts themselves—not the remedy for a problem but the special presentation of the problem itself."[72] As Brooks argues further, in a statement relevant to a central concern of this study to pay special attention to the formal qualities of Northern Irish literature and also to see the literature not as programmatic but as subtly exemplary, "In short, we oversimplify the way in which literature offers its characteristic knowledge if we see the form of literature as merely rhetorical and its method merely didactic."[73] Literature's knowledge may be fleeting or deeply visionary, but it exists finally for itself and unto itself. Because of this quality, only in its dynamic expression of artistic integrity can it offer help for the vexing problems of the human condition. Heaney's statement in an interview in the *Irish Times* in 1975 suggests as much: "I do believe that poetry is its own special action and that having its own mode of consciousness, its own mode of reality, has its own efficacy gradually."[74]

Longley and Heaney emerged from the Belfast Group, a coterie that influenced them to value the artistic allegiance above all other loyalties—the first major contention of this study, explored at some length in chapter 1. This first chapter also explores the early emergence of the writers from this group. My second argument about these writers — that they began laying the foundation for cultural, political, and even religious understanding in the province — hinges on the first. Artistic fidelity led to their significant contributions to imagining a new Northern Ireland, but this latter development was always subsumed by their first allegiance.

This study engages in significant explorations of poetic creativity, a necessary maneuver both because the poets themselves are so often concerned with this process and because creativity, with its refusal to be rushed, provides a striking analogy to reconciliation. The Mennonite peace scholar John Paul Lederach has pointed out in his engaging book *The Moral Imagination: The Art and Soul of Building Peace* that "the artistic process has its own sense of time and it is not chronological. When the creative process is forced or obligated, less than desirable and artificial outcomes emerge. People working with reconciliation need to rethink healing as a process paced by its own inner timing, which cannot be programmed or pushed to fit a project. People and communities have their own clocks."[75] Attending to the creative process with its own integrity of time thus can lead us to the realization that reconciliation cannot be accomplished overnight and is a process like writing or reading poetry, which demands deliberation and a willingness to put our own self-interests aside.

Moreover, creativity and reconciliation share a belief in the irrational. The beginning of this introduction argues for Longley and Heaney's pursuit of poetry as a spiritual search characterized by oscillating belief and doubt. Lederach suggests that just as "the artistic process initially breaks beyond what can be rationally understood and then returns to a place of understanding that may analyze, think it through, and attach meaning to it," such a movement "is much like the process of reconciliation. Brokenness wanders all over our souls. Healing requires a similar journey of wandering."[76] Poets who so strongly believe in the spiritual capacity of poetry are adept in expressing tentative belief in the long and complicated process of reconciliation. The arrival of the unexpected in the mind of the artist may prefigure political and cultural events that no one ever believed possible, such as the parleying of sworn enemies.

Writing within a year of the 1994 IRA Ceasefire and the Combined Loyalist Command Ceasefire, Heaney made probably the most explicit comparison between poetry making and peacemaking that anyone ever has. After commenting on the "inspiration" that had "happened in the public life" in Northern Ireland after the cease-fires, he went on to liken that inspiration to "the kind of excitement that starts a poet writing." Excitement, technique, persistence, sensitivity, and an ability to push the boundaries are all shared by poets and peacemakers, he suggests.

> And just as the work of poetry depends for successful completion upon turning that original excitement into a process of sustained and resourceful composition, so in the work of peacebuilding, the outcome will depend upon the ongoing alertness and thorough-going technique of the workers at every stage of the process. Quickness in responding, readiness to discard one draft for another, feeling out and fitting in, sensitivity to nuance, readiness to go beyond where you knew you could go with the approval of your inner censor, all of those things which are operative in bringing forth the dark embryo of the poem will have to be operative on all sides in the embryology of the new Northern Ireland.[77]

No strangers to disappointment about either the making of poetry or the lack of progress in resolving Northern Ireland's Troubles for many years, Heaney and Longley have nonetheless preserved their excitement, their inspirational power, and while they realize that making peace will be difficult, fragile, risky work, they are, as they always have been, committed to helping imagine the birth of a new province.

Reconciliation is an exceedingly difficult subject, one that this project, whose primary aim is to explore how the imaginative artistic integrity of Longley and Heaney models such a process, cannot hope to and does not try to fully plumb. The best single book on the subject is Graham Dawson's far-ranging and objective study *Making Peace with the Past? Memory, Trauma, and the Irish Troubles,* which studies the lingering presence of hundreds of years of past sectarian conflict in present Northern Ireland, the effects of the contemporary Troubles, particular atrocities such as Bloody Sunday and the Enniskillen Remembrance Day Bombing, the aftermath of the Good Friday Agreement, and the continuing problems for Catholics living in such areas as the Ardoyne neighborhood, which is nearly surrounded by loyalist areas of North Belfast, and for Protestants living in largely republican areas along the border with the Republic of Ireland. Dawson articulates the twofold process that Northern Ireland is currently going through: "the attempt to resolve the underlying causes of division and conflict by establishing the basis for peaceful co-operation and the securing of social justice; and . . . the attempt to address the damaging effects of violence inflicted and undergone in the course of conflict, whether through state repression and its resistance, war or civil strife."[78]

Norman Porter has pointed out that "the single greatest obstacle blocking receptiveness to an enthusiastic response in Northern Ireland is that reconciliation is hugely demanding: it potentially disturbs any number of our prejudices, self-understandings, priorities, and practices."[79] As Porter and any number of other commentators have noted, despite real progress in cultural dialogue in the province, significant problems remain: along with some citizens' genuine recalcitrance toward reconciliation, segregated housing, education, and endogamy impede opportunities for cultural exchange. Nevertheless, Porter, for example, has persuasively argued for the pursuit of reconciliation as a worthy goal, while observing that "a reconciled society, unlike a perfect one, is a reasonable possibility . . . that hangs on the realization of inclusive citizen belonging . . . in terms of recognition of individual, cultural and political modes of citizen dignity."[80] Porter argues that the foundational ground for reconciliation is a recognition of our "thick commonality," a notion that rejects various types of pluralism in favor of recognizing "that we share a dignity by virtue of being persons" and "by virtue of being citizens."[81] Longley and Heaney seem to apprehend this thick commonality and often promote it in their poetry.

At the same time, I fully acknowledge and agree with what Rita Felski cautions are the pitfalls of placing too much weight on literature to change the world. As she argues about the best and subtlest literature that literary critics enjoy reading, such works are often "stripped of any direct links to oppositional movements, marked by often uneasy relations to centers of power," while "their politics are revealed as oblique

and equivocal, lending themselves to alternative, even antithetical readings. Texts, furthermore, lack the power to legislate their own effects; the
internal features of a literary work tell us little about how it is received
and understood, let alone its impact, if any, on a larger social field. Political function cannot be deduced or derived from literary structure."[82]
Therefore, much of this study suggests that Longley's and Heaney's
poetry—by virtue of its imaginative vigor, nuanced language, and carefully crafted forms—can be exemplary for the long process of reconciliation in Northern Ireland (and by extension, elsewhere in the world),
but it does not often attempt to empirically prove their works' impact on
this process, with some significant exceptions such as Longley's "Ceasefire," explored in chapter 4, and Heaney's *The Cure at Troy,* examined in
the coda. The coda does, however, attempt to show how, in the dissemination of Longley's and Heaney's poetry through television, radio, and
school syllabi, the conciliatory aspect of that work and indeed the poets
themselves have been well received across the political divide(s) in Northern Ireland.

After exploring Longley's important and deliberate melding of form
and content, chapter 2 examines his search for remote places to literally
and figuratively inhabit, such as oceans and islands, and the exemplary
exotic qualities he could adopt—such as the verve and insouciance manifested in certain American jazz and blues singers like Fats Waller—in
his early poetry collected in *No Continuing City* (1969). The most important of these far-flung locations for him, in establishing an isolated
position in which to dwell and receive poetic inspiration, was the Hebridean Islands of Scotland. Longley's reclamation of a Scottish component to Northern Irish literature in both traditional geographic and cultural terms, along with his anticipation of the so-called "Scottish" mode
of history advanced by British historian J. G. A. Pocock in the 1970s, allowed him to suggest that this mode might be most appropriate for appreciating the liminal situation of the citizens in Northern Ireland, caught
between expressions of British and Irish cultural and religious identity,
and for enabling a mental dynamism that would move freely between
these zones. Chapter 3 explores Longley's carefully crafted poems about
the conflict in Northern Ireland and shows the development of his theory
of reconciliation through his particularized poetics and his readings in

contemporary theories of ceremony, ethics, and Christian forgiveness. Chapter 4 investigates Longley's urban poems set in Belfast, his pastoral poems set in Counties Clare and Mayo, his poems about the Holocaust, and his Asian poems, all of which affirm the fragility of human and animal life and their interrelatedness in such a way as to reject the life-crushing forces of sectarianism that have often operated in the province. Longley's poetry, especially his most recent work, finally imagines the world as a connected region with significant sites in America, Northern Ireland, Eastern Europe, China, and Japan.

Chapter 5 argues that Seamus Heaney's development of his artistic identity, highlighted in a series of metapoetic poems in *Death of a Naturalist* (1966) and *Door into the Dark* (1969), is indelibly influenced by his meditative worldview, which has enabled him to stay true to his poetic inner self. Chapter 6 explores linguistically significant poems from *Wintering Out* (1972) that attempted to recover a common language for Catholics and Protestants in the province, then shows how, despite Heaney's anger at the treatment of Northern Irish nationalists, significant poems from *North* (1975) suggest his embrace of his true north— the role of the poet. Chapter 7 offers readings of seminal poems from *Field Work* (1979), *Station Island* (1984), and *The Haw Lantern* (1987) that deal with the poet's continued development of his vocation, while also speculating about the conciliatory impulse behind Heaney's translation of *Sweeney Astray* (1983). Chapter 8 explains Heaney's full transition from his interest in creativity, often anchored in evocations of sacred physical spaces, to a later phase, in which his mind itself becomes a luminous space, an outlook central to the poems beginning with *Seeing Things* (1991) and continuing through important poems from *The Spirit Level* (1996), *Electric Light* (2001), and *District and Circle* (2006).

Heaney's move inward, in his later poetry, from the province to the country of his own mind thus stands in a chiastic relationship to Longley's move outward from the province to the entire world. Heaney's poetry increasingly draws upon a seemingly limitless state within his mind that he terms the "frontier of writing." This is a nonsolipsistic position from which he can remain ever more attentive to poetry's imaginative demands and secondarily imagine a new province of reconciliation. Heaney's superb ability to contemplate, sometimes shown within poems themselves, has allowed him to reach a higher plane of consciousness that radiates hope for the future of the province.

Close readings of particularly important (and often critically misread poems) anchor each chapter. Thus chapter 2 contains a long discussion of Longley's "Words for Jazz Perhaps" and "The Hebrides"; chapter 3, extended explorations of his "Wounds," "The Butchers," and "Ceasefire"; and chapter 4, forays into his "The Linen Industry," "The Ice-cream Man," and "All of These People," a suite of poems about the Holocaust, and a cluster of poems dealing with Asian themes. The chapters on Heaney's poetry similarly are grounded in readings of major poems—"Digging," "The Forge," and "Bogland" in chapter 5; "The Road to Derry," a series of philological poems from *Wintering Out,* and crucial metapoetic poems from *North* in chapter 6; "Casualty," "Station Island," and "From the Frontier of Writing" in chapter 7; and important later poems such as ones from the sequence "Lightenings," "'Poet's Chair,'" "Tollund," and "Anything Can Happen" in chapter 8.

The coda to this study compares and contrasts the poetics of Longley and Heaney, then explores their influence on the Northern Irish peace process through the incorporation of their poetry into the political, artistic, cultural, and popular discourse of Northern Ireland. In this respect, the realism but also tentative hope of Longley's 1994 poem "Ceasefire" and Heaney's 1990 translation of the Greek play originally named *Philoctetes* as *The Cure at Troy* have become part of the lexicon of peace and reconciliation in the province. Heaney has remarked about *The Cure at Troy* that it "seems to me not only a declaration of a need for the imagination to outface the expectations of the topical but also a proof that it can happily and 'relevantly' do so."[83] Indeed, the seemingly oracular powers of each poet are on display in both of these major works, demonstrating that, as Heaney suggests here, an allegiance to the imagination supersedes the pressures of topical events and can create new realities in art that exemplify the analogous need for the emergence of new thinking about political and religious divisions.

Despite my choosing Longley and Heaney on the basis of their clear artistic merit, their friendship, and their similar attitudes toward their art, this move may be seen as some sort of misguided attempt at egalitarianism since Longley hails from an English, Protestant background, and Heaney an Irish, Catholic milieu. More disturbing, featuring authors from seemingly opposed socioreligious groups may at first seem doomed to perpetuate preconceived binary notions of identity. But there are good reasons for this strategy. First, by showing how these writers were originally seen as linked closely to their respective communities, I am better able to chart how their work avoids simple representation of a "tribal" viewpoint. Second, while both of my chosen writers despise tribalism in any form, each retains a cultural tie to his original community that enables him both to speak to that community and, since the connection to that population is relatively loose now, also to converse with another community. Third, knowing a given author's cultural and religious milieu aids in understanding his work. For example, Longley's use of Ulster-Scots words does more than add a cultural veneer to his poetic translations and reimaginings of episodes from *The Iliad*: it injects this ancient literature with an updated meaning for Northern Irish culture and the role of the Protestant community in it.

This study has been preceded by several notable critical works on Northern Irish literature, for which I am grateful. One of these is Patrick Grant's book *Breaking Enmities: Religion, Literature, and Culture in Northern Ireland, 1967–97.* My study, however, differs from Grant's in an important regard. While he focuses on a variety of issues in Northern Irish culture, including education, gender, and imprisonment, I have restricted myself to exploring the ways literature from the province potentially unites seemingly disparate human beings by confounding and complicating, even making irrelevant, stereotypical notions of political identity. I too, though, want to "examine the embeddedness of literature in the culture that it mirrors, reproduces and criticizes," and I agree with his assertion, "I do not believe that literature can be reduced to or fully explained by the cultural circumstances of its production."[84] Grant goes on, "I am at pains to provide a sufficiently coherent sense of certain cultural issues in order to explain the problems some authors address, but without losing the distinctiveness of the literature they write as a result. As I have suggested, such distinctiveness is central to the contribution literature makes in resistance to the mechanisms keeping old enmities alive in the culture at large."[85] I share this view of literature's distinctiveness and its corresponding ability to resist calcified enmities.

Furthermore, I hope my own study implies that the cultural and political scenes in Northern Ireland and how they have evolved over the last several decades are important background for examining how two of its exemplary poets, when they so choose, can unravel and subtly explore identity in its many resonances.

At the same time, I fully agree with Peter McDonald's assertion that "any celebration of literature in terms of identity is finally prescriptive in nature, because it can only recognize things within strictly limited ranges, and cannot afford to put itself at the mercy of literature's actual unpredictability and variousness" (*MI*, 8). McDonald's argument is compelling, especially since human experience continues to be, in the words of the Northern Irish poet Louis MacNeice, "incorrigibly plural."[86] I want to expose preconceived and stultifying notions of identity in Northern Ireland to the imaginative force of its literature, not the other way round, as has sometimes been done in critical writing on this literature. While always asserting the primacy of literature over criticism or theory, I differ with McDonald on an important point: writers from Northern Ireland make an important and enduring contribution to conceptions of identity there, even if—and especially if—they end up exploding any stereotypical notions of identity. McDonald's own work, in *Mistaken Identities: Poetry and Northern Ireland,* and other books and essays, has been salutary for my own project.

After establishing these writers' commitment to their art above all else, I hope to suggest the ways in which imaginative literature in the province has opened the "cultural corridor" between republicans and unionists about which Edna Longley has written so perceptively.[87] I am aware of, but disagree with, Gerald Dawe's rejection of this illuminating phrase. Dawe has argued that "the suggestion of fluidity here . . . is appealing, but the notion of more boundaries *(corridor)* in some indistinct way, like a nervous tic, poses more problems than it can possibly hope to solve. After all, corridors must lead somewhere and what might be working in a poem (the translation of influences) is a totally different story when it comes to politics and the struggle for power."[88] I agree with Dawe that poetry and politics operate in different ways, but this entire study emphasizes the imaginative power of literature and shows how it can sometimes subtly effect cultural, even political change, precisely by not constantly seeking to do so but instead engaging in the pleasures of poetry. Edna Longley has further elucidated her image of the cultural corridor in "From Cathleen to Anorexia: The Breakdown of Irelands," where she suggests that Northern Ireland is a "frontier-region, a cultural corridor, a zone where Ireland and Britain permeate each other" and holds that if the Republic "face[s] up to difference and division" the province can "relax into a genuinely diverse sense of its own identity: to function, under whatever administrative format, as a shared region of these islands."[89] Because the Republic gave up its claim to Northern Ireland for the first time ever in the Good Friday Agreement, the province now has precisely this chance to culturally relax that Longley calls for in her essay.

I do not wish to argue that literature exists to serve a political end, but rather that it has always offered a richer and more subtle way of imagining the possibilities of dialogue between the disparate groups in Northern Ireland than has been offered by traditional political conceptions of Northern Irish identity. I do believe that poetry can make things happen; what it makes happen, though, is not so much definitive, measurable social change as an imaginative realignment and reconfiguration of our thinking on a given subject if we immerse ourselves in it fully. As Michael Longley told Paul Keen in 1999, "Imagination is one of the key ingredients for a lasting political settlement, along with tolerance and patience."[90]

Although reconciliation in Northern Ireland is a secondary but important concern of this project, I view the approaches to reconciliation as evinced by Longley and Heaney as exemplary for reconciliation there and in other war-torn communities and for understanding relationships between the living and the dead, the ultimate suprahistorical community. The third chapter on Longley, for example, attempts to show how he connects human beings and the environment, Ireland's evasion of fighting fascism in World War II with the burden we all share of the Holocaust, and Asian culture with Western art. Moreover, both Longley and Heaney have predilections for writing elegies dedicated to particular terrains, plants, animals, and people, and, taken collectively, much of their poetry seeks a reconciliation of the living and the dead across species. In collecting and commemorating such ecologies and organisms, their work quietly but insistently celebrates the living and the dead and gathers them into verbal "cemeteries" that can be continually visited. As Vincent Buckley has argued, poetry is both "an art and act" that sets "aside certain experiences or places or people or memories as representatively revealing ones—in however attenuated a form, sacred ones."[91] The sacred poetry of Longley and Heaney preserves the dead and instantiates a conversation of sorts with the living through what Renee Ashley has called the "dimensional" time of the poem, "in which all the poet's considered 'times' coexist—so that, in spite of our common perception, time is presented not as a merely linear, countable passage, is not unidirectional as we tend to assume, is, in fact, not directional at all, but is instead dimensional."[92]

In this elegiac preservation of the continuity of the living and the dead, Longley and Heaney are swimming against a dehumanizing current endemic in Western civilization, especially in Europe and increasingly in America—the tendency to eliminate graveyards and funerals as part of a general drift into atomic individualism and eventual nihilism. Speaking of this issue, Joseph Bottum recently has argued that three propositions about human association and culture are manifested in our attitudes toward death: first, that "the losses human beings suffer are the deepest reason for culture"; second, that "the fundamental pattern for any community is a congregation at a funeral"; and third, "that [a] healthy society requires a lively sense of the reality and continuing presence of the dead."[93] Reading the poetry of Longley and Heaney through Bottum's paradigm suggests their work's thorough and healthy immersion in culture and community. Northern Irish society still contains certain elements that have often commemorated the dead in unhealthy ways, manipulating their passing to promote sectarian division, often through murals or street songs. In contrast to this "celebration" of the dead, Longley's and Heaney's poetry shows how the death of any person, animal, or even plant diminishes culture because of our interconnectedness. It also enfolds the dead into an ongoing, elegiac conversation with the living, enriching all of our lives in the process.

Imaginative literature confirms and strengthens us in our individual and collective identity as human beings—not as members of political categories—while allowing us access, insight, to the essential humanity of others. One of our wisest literary critics, C. S. Lewis, himself from

Northern Ireland, has pointed out the way literature effects this change and insight: "Literary experience heals the wound, without undermining the privilege, of individuality. There are mass emotions which heal the wound; but they destroy the privilege. In them our separate selves are pooled and we sink back into sub-individuality. But in reading great literature I become a thousand men and yet remain myself. Like the night sky in the Greek poem, I see with a myriad eyes, but it is still I who see. Here, as in worship, in love, in moral action, and in knowing, I transcend myself; and am never more myself than when I do."[94] Transcendence is still not too much to expect from great literature, whether from Northern Ireland, the Republic, or anywhere else. And this transcendence, coming in the form of particularized, concrete language across a range of genres, is precisely what is needed to overcome monolithic, abstract notions of identity in Northern Ireland. As Edna Longley argues, literature can be a powerful resister and destroyer of these simplistic notions of identity: "Poetry possesses the semantic means, the metaphorical audacity, to press beyond existing categories, to prepare the ground where, in Derek Mahon's words, 'a thought might grow.' Certainly literature has helped to erode the compact majorities that came to power in Ireland after 1921 and the censorships they brought with them."[95] Poetry particularly, as Grant has concluded in his discussion of John Hewitt's and Heaney's poetry, "calls us to acknowledge the importance of a personal voice and of personal experience as a bulwark against sectarianism that feeds on stereotypes confirmed in turn by various kinds of over-simplified rhetoric."[96] Literature is not obliged to carry out this function because it is always sufficient unto itself, but it can provide points of connection between communities that all too often have set up rigid categories that admit no osmosis. Sometimes this process of connection is achieved through the creation of a sense of the sublime that penetrates quotidian life, suffuses it with moments of hope, and establishes, however temporarily, human community.

Seeing others—reading others through Lewis's concept of "a myriad eyes"—creates a plurality of experience for the careful reader, an invaluable lesson in an age in which tolerance is often superficially applied as a salve to societal problems and the individual is exalted. What Denis Donoghue has termed "the pleasure of reading literature" recalls Lewis's conception of reading as an outward-looking experience, an escape from self-absorption all too common to our culture, which is obsessed with improving ourselves. This pleasure "arises from the exercise of one's imagination, a going out from one's self toward other lives, other forms of life, past, present, and perhaps future. This denotes its relation to sympathy, fellowship, the spirituality and morality of being human."[97]

This sort of imaginative entry into other lives and other worlds, moreover, remains an ethical activity, in contrast to Donoghue's construction of a "recovered disinterestedness," in which we deny ourselves and our own values—at least temporarily. As he argues, "If we can't or won't sequester our immediately pressing interests, put them in parentheses for the time being, we have no hope of reading literature. If we read merely to have our political or other values endorsed, or to find them abused, by the work of literature, the situation is vain."[98] Citing George Levine's 1994 study *Aesthetics and Ideology,* Donoghue holds that such an aesthetic position offers "what Levine calls a 'space where the immediate pressures of ethical and political decisions are deferred.'"[99] My own reading of poems and other imaginative literature in this study, however, shows that aesthetic activity is ethical in the terms that the Russian formalist Mikhail Bakhtin and a particular strand of recent aesthetic criticism have articulated.

While I appreciate Donoghue's attempts to privilege literature's imaginative power as a response to the often reductive activities of much current "literary" criticism, I concur with Paisley Livingston, who convincingly suggests that aesthetic appreciation commonly involves not just intrinsic appreciation but also instrumental appreciation: "An important background assumption here, which is often overlooked in discussions of aesthetic disinterestedness, is that it is not only possible but quite common to value something both intrinsically and instrumentally at the same time. Aesthetic appreciation may, then, be accompanied by the pursuit of various practical or instrumental goals, so it is not a question of defending the ideal of a *purely* detached or disinterested attitude."[100] Livingston's "instrumental goals" include the pursuit of the ethical as part of proper, holistic aesthetic appreciation. Thus he later points out that "if . . . moral and political ideas are an intrinsic part of many literary works of art, their assessment would seem directly relevant to an evaluation of the work's overall merits," and he finally quotes Colin McGinn's stirring statement: "Ethical questions, I contend, are integral to the study of literature, and it can only impoverish literary study to try to bracket such questions."[101]

As Bakhtin writes in his classic essay "Discourse and the Novel," a discussion that begins with a general exploration of all literary genres, "The study of verbal art can and must overcome the divorce between an abstract 'formal' approach and an equally abstract 'ideological approach.' Form and content in discourse are one."[102] As he further claims, "More often than not, stylistics defines itself as a stylistics of 'private craftsmanship' and ignores the social life of discourse outside the author's study, discourse in the open spaces of public squares, streets, cities and villages, of social groups, generations, and epochs."[103] Although Bakhtin's contention about the marriage between form and content is confined to the novel in this portion of his essay, his point nonetheless applies to other genres such as poetry as well.

The author's needed attention to form and content articulated by Bakhtin suggests another fruitful understanding of the Northern Irish writer as "two-minded." Neil Corcoran has argued that "much of the . . . contemporary writing of Northern Ireland . . . is characteristically double-focused, turned in a Janus-faced way towards both form and event, prominently intertextual but vulnerably anxious about responsibility and obligation."[104] Corcoran's description aptly captures the position of strength from which the best Northern Irish writers operate: attuned to both the integrity stemming from the formal qualities of the work itself and their ethical responsibility to their role as artists in a culturally complex and divided society.

The present study largely concerns itself with the individual poetics of Longley and Heaney, a specific manifestation of what Bakhtin calls "private craftsmanship," yet also consistently attempts to show how poetic privacy and contemplation lead not only to the created poem but also to a real contribution to public discourse on such issues as sectarianism when the poem is read in its proper, though secondary, context. As Grant has argued, "Reconciliation alone can be shaped through a personal knowledge and mutual understanding of which literature is the harbinger and example, and from which political discourse still has much to learn."[105] Reconciliation is a long, difficult process, but it is the only real solution to centuries-long hatreds and prejudices in Northern Ireland. Literature, not politics, seems best able to unravel the cat's cradle of contradictions and confusions attendant upon identity in Northern Ireland and to weave a new design that explodes nativist and exclusivist ideas in all of the communities in the province.[106] The ethical aim of this project, as will become clear, is to articulate poetry's aesthetic enabling of a refined and civilized discourse in the context of what McDonald has called one of Northern Irish poetry's most profound achievements: a reinvigorated poetic imagination that has maintained its own integrity "by maintaining and insisting upon the privileges and properties of its own existence."[107]

Derek Mahon's stirring description of poetry's exemplary political power in 1970 is especially relevant to this concern:

> Battles have been lost, but a war remains to be won. The war I mean is not, of course, between Protestant and Catholic but between the fluidity of a possible life (poetry is a great lubricant) and the *rigor mortis* of archaic postures, political and cultural. The poets themselves have taken no part in political events, but they have contributed to that possible life, or to the possibility of the possible life; for the act of writing is itself political in the fullest sense. A good poem is a paradigm of good politics—of people talking to each other, with honest subtlety, at a profound level. It is a light to lighten the darkness, and we have had darkness enough, God knows, for a long time.[108]

In response to Dennis O'Driscoll's question about the meaning of this statement by Mahon, Heaney discussed the nature of poetry's truthfulness:

> I think Derek meant that a good poem holds as much of the truth as possible in one gaze. Can a good untrue poem be written? If you are an Israeli or Palestinian poet at this moment, what poetry ideally requires of you is a disinterested gaze at how you are situated, whereas your people will require passionate solidarity, and opposition to the Other. The same situation prevailed in Northern Ireland

in a diminished way: Protestants, Catholics, nationalists, Unionists, are you with us or against us? But what Mahon meant, and what I would mean, is that we in Northern Ireland qua poets were subject to that larger call to "hold in a single thought reality and justice."[109]

Heaney's approval of Mahon's statement indicates that he believes in an ethical notion of poetry as telling the truth by gazing on reality's starkness and yet keeping the poet's fidelity to poetry. In his brief essay on Japanese poetry's effect on English poetry, Heaney expounds on why poetry as a verbal art of particularity must be truthful: "In the course of the twentieth century, as empires and ideologies contended for supremacy, and atrocities were committed on a scale unprecedented in human history, poets became desperately aware of the dangers of rhetoric and abstraction. In these circumstances, the poet's duty to be truthful became more and more imperative."[110]

As I argued earlier in this introduction, poetry's particularity and especially the properties of Longley's and Heaney's precise poetry must be experienced ephemerally; moreover, and more startlingly, this ephemeral experience can effect an ethical response from us on an individual level that complements the theories of the intertwined nature of aesthetics and ethics articulated above by Lewis, Bakhtin, and Grant. Unfortunately, as J. Hillis Miller has argued, "Literary study hides the peculiarity of literary language by accounting for it, naturalizing it, turning it into the familiar. This usually means seeing in it as in one way or another a representation of the real world."[111] Because of Longley and Heaney's deep allegiance to the imagination, which in turn has enabled them to create viable other worlds in their poetry, their strange and angular poetry works against literary criticism that would attempt to smooth its contours. Jon Kertzer articulates how "a comparable ethical dilemma" corresponds with what he has already identified as critical attempts to grapple with "the paradox of literary singularity": "Ethical insights, like aesthetic ones, become intelligible only within a larger system framed by general principles and rules, but that very generality dispels the uniqueness of the insight and the urgency of the call."[112] Although Kertzer, following Emmanuel Levinas, rejects the traditional view of ethics as based on a universal system and embraces a Levinasian, individual, subjective ethics, I follow Kant in believing that ethical judgments must be read against communally held, universal norms and that such norms can be determined, however faintly, from carefully nuanced readings of literature.[113]

Both Heaney and Longley seem to believe in a more traditional ethical system as well. For example, John Desmond has recently argued that Heaney's criticism of deconstruction "makes clear his belief in a 'covenant' or community of meaning rooted in a shared understanding of words as the basis for ethical order in society and for ethical meaning in literature, a bond that is transgenerational, transnational, and ultimately transhistorical."[114] Longley, too, as I have argued elsewhere, rejects deconstruction and its relativity in favor of a shared plurality of difference that binds us together.[115]

How then, does the process of reading particular poems, such as those by Longley and Heaney, effect ethical responses from us? One way has been recently delineated by Derek Attridge in *The Singularity of Literature.* Attridge suggests that "what we experience in responding to the artwork . . . is not a generalized obligation but a call coming from the work itself—the work as singular staging of otherness."[116] If we "apprehend the other as other," we "register its resistance and irreducibility" as well as seeking to render it more familiar.[117] For Attridge, "A responsible response to an inventive work of art, science, or philosophy (to mention only a few possibilities) is one that brings it into being anew by allowing it, in a performance of its singularity for me, for my place and time, to refigure the ways in which I, and my culture, think and feel."[118] In this sense, thoughtfully experiencing the poetry of Longley and Heaney as singular events in our minds enables us to be confronted with an alterity beyond us that stretches us and leads us out of ourselves, even as it links us to values we share with others. Northern Irish readers and hearers of Longley's and Heaney's poetry have undoubtedly experienced this alterity over the decades, which may in turn have helped them to conceive more positively of "the other side."[119]

While experiencing the otherness engendered by literary singularity can spur ethical refigurings of how we think and feel, beholding literary particularity can create ethical responses through seeing ourselves

as similar—as generators or replicators in a lesser, though still powerful, sense of that process as it is practiced by our best writers. I have already argued, pace Steiner, that Longley and Heaney see themselves as
secondary or countercreators who struggle to bring into being secondary worlds that rival the original creation. Moreover, if we critics and
readers see ourselves as tertiary creators or replicators, in Elaine Scarry's
sense of the term, we may heighten our ethical agency. Scarry's study of
beauty rescues this supposedly Platonic concept from its traditional pas-
sivity and holds that perceiving beauty is a potentially ethical act. Interestingly, the press release of the Nobel Prize Committee in 1995 for
Heaney's award explicitly recognizes this link: the committee points out
that Heaney believes that "the task of the poet is to ensure the survival
of beauty, especially in times when tyrannical regimes threaten to destroy it."[120] My criticism of Longley's and Heaney's poetry in what follows takes for granted that critical perception is grounded not only in
singularity but also in beauty and wonder—at literature's capacity to inspire and awe us. Scarry argues that "there are attributes that are, without exception, present across different objects (faces, flowers, birdsongs,
men, horses, pots, and poems), one of which is this impulse toward
begetting." Replication, she says, "reminds us that the benign impulse
toward creation results not just in famous paintings but in everyday acts
of staring."[121]

Staring closely at the following poems is a perceptual and critical
necessity in order for us to recognize any ethical impulse that may arise
in us as a result of such regard for the particular. Scarry points out several
qualities of beauty relevant for my purposes: it is sacred, unprecedented,
and life affirming, and, most important, "it incites deliberation."[122] A
flower and a carefully crafted poem—not to mention Longley's carefully crafted poems about flowers—epitomize all these qualities but
especially invoke deliberation in us if we behold them deeply. Such attention to the aesthetic necessarily makes us more reflective and deliberate, qualities that are necessary prerequisites to undertaking ethical acts.
I will return to more specific ethical applications of Scarry's theory of
beauty in my discussion of Heaney's "Punishment" in chapter 6 and in
the coda, but for now I want to emphasize how the following poetry
readings implicitly assume they are dealing with the beautiful—not as

an abstract concept but as concrete examples—and accordingly linger over them, recognizing their sacred, unprecedented, life-affirming power and thus attempt to be thoughtful in an admittedly poor approximation of the deliberation that it took to create them in the first place. Beauty is linked to but separate from truth, as Scarry also propounds, and it is my hope that this study reveals unifying truths about the human condition such as our need for each other in a fragmented and fragmenting world.

To apprehend the truth of the poems that will be explored here, we need to put ourselves in the posture of the poets in a series of essentially Heideggerian maneuvers. Mark William Roche suggests that Heidegger's concept of truth as "*aletheia* or unconcealment has at least three moments": "First, poetic truth is not something that we can will or force. Instead, it happens to us. It finds us; we do not find it. As with grace, our primary action toward it must be openness of comportment. Second, because this concept of truth arises not from our intentions but from our alertness, our listening for it, we must be especially attentive as recipients. We must listen to the otherness of the other, quietly, patiently. . . . Third, the artwork not only reveals, it also conceals. The artwork cannot be exhausted by our conceptual analysis."[123] A receptive alertness, coupled with a humility that we will never completely plumb the depths of such profound poems, should enable us not only to experience the truths they offer us but also to realize that the poems are ultimately beyond our full ken.

Radically unlike the qualities of beauty grounded in perceptions of the particular—the sacred, the unprecedented, the life affirming, the deliberate—the terrible reality of life on the streets of Northern Ireland during the Troubles with its horrific violence offers a difficult challenge to properly read the literature written before, during, and now after that time period. Yet poetry itself is up to the challenge of being simultaneously alert to ugliness and beauty, as Michael Longley points out in the context of discussing Adorno's often-misunderstood statements about culture's role after the Holocaust: "Poetry has to face into awfulness as well as into beauty. I am struck by the fact that the people who were going into the gas chambers wrote poems, that poetry fulfills very deep needs in humanity, especially in extremis."[124] Longley has himself articulated a fascinating image of art's role in society, noting in his introduction to

Causeway: The Arts in Ulster that "in one of the dictionaries I consulted 'causeway' is defined as a path of stepping stones. This is, I think, a fair description of the role played by the arts in any society: it defines what should reasonably be expected of them in all civilised countries, but especially in a troubled community like our own" ("I," 9).[125]

I see my own role as a critic in these pages as laying down stepping stones of another sort from those in Longley's compelling description of art's role in society, in a critical maneuver akin to that advanced by Louis MacNeice in the introduction to his outstanding and still valuable 1941 study of Yeats. MacNeice convincingly argues that poetry and life are intertwined, which is a basic assumption of this study, but that poetry nevertheless has a life of its own; the job of the literary critic, he claims, is ultimately to point to the experience of the poem itself: "The background of a poem, its origin, its purpose, its ingredients, can be analysed but the poem itself can only be experienced. All that the critic can do is lay stepping stones over the river — stones which are better forgotten once the reader has reached a position where he is in touch with the subject of criticism."[126] The unique experience, pleasure, and mystery that poetry gives to a host of readers are finally what this book exalts. Paul Muldoon has recently suggested that critics should submit themselves to poetry in a way analogous to a poet's reception of a poem's visitation, arguing that "our only decent end is to let the poem have its way with us, just as the poet let it have its way with him or her."[127] In the gifted hands of Michael Longley and Seamus Heaney, the poem shines and shimmers with a life of its own, unrepeatable, mysterious, and other, yet always humane and self-delighting, truly an instructive soul music for our time.

CHAPTER ONE

Laying the Foundations

THE BELFAST GROUP AND MICHAEL LONGLEY'S
CONCILIATORY CULTURAL WORK

The Belfast Group

The cultural conditions enabling the Belfast Group, with its eclectic mix of students and workers, were greatly aided by the educational acts of the 1940s. Declan Kiberd directly links the creative renascence in Northern Ireland beginning in the early 1960s with these acts: "This latest artistic renaissance, like the Civil Rights movement among the Roman Catholic minority in the north, may owe more to the education acts of the 1940s than to any more immediately political cause—for these acts sent, in due time, a wholly new kind of student to university in the 1960s."[1] Kiberd does not describe this type of student, but presumably she was often Catholic. Cultural tensions in the province were still far from rosy at the time and would explode by the end of the decade. Strangely enough, it would take an Englishman—Philip Hobsbaum—to help bridge sectarian differences and formulate the idea of an inclusive Northern Irish aesthetic.

Hobsbaum had run other creative writing groups before—in Cambridge, Sheffield, and London—but was nervous about putting one together in Belfast, given its cultural conditions and relative lack of resources for writers, as he noted in a 1966 BBC radio program:

I must say here, I had to be very, very cautious. You see, I was under no illusions about Belfast; I had some knowledge of Northern Ireland beforehand and I did know that conditions here are probably unique within the British Isles. I didn't know either, how you found writers, and this is the important thing, because you must realize, you have to discover talent the whole time. How do you find them? Where do you meet them? What were the writing conditions in Northern Ireland? Well, frankly, I found them rather bad. There was one literary magazine, called *Threshold,* which kept a very high standard up and which came out very, very intermittently. There were one or two Queen's magazines in the university, but of course they catered for students mostly. So I had quite a job. It took me a whole year, in fact, to get a whole nucleus together. A very, very mixed bunch. No, there's no single social class or background. They're not all English; they're not all Irish. And I think to a great extent, this disparity has made for creative effort.[2]

The English Hobsbaum's courage in putting together such a diverse group of writers in the heart of such a divided city is striking, even given his opportunity to recruit from a broader range of students, thanks to the aforementioned educational acts. Although Hobsbaum is characterized as an exemplar of New Criticism with supposedly an attendant disregard for literature's effect on society, his statements suggest that he felt the broad mixture of students from different backgrounds and nationalities—"this disparity"—resulted in "creative effort."

Hobsbaum's concern with creating a community of writers implies his continuing interest in reading literature through communal experience. In this regard, he exemplifies his mentor F. R. Leavis's primary belief in imaginative literature's unifying power. Geoffrey Strickland cites Leavis's 1962 Richmond lecture on C. P. Snow as evidence of Leavis's belief in literature as a collaborative creation: "[English literature is a] living whole that can have its life only in the living present, in the creative response of individuals, who collaboratively renew and perpetuate what they participate in—a cultural community or consciousness."[3] Hobsbaum, after pointing out the shared approval of Wallace Stevens's "Sunday Morning" by two critics as different as R. P. Blackmur and

Ivor Winters, agrees with Leavis's approach to literature as a communal enterprise when he concludes, "A [critical] response is personal and . . . it may be shared. Every critic has his predilections, but only some poems can overcome these. But the poems that succeed in this have broken down psychological barriers; bridged the gulf between human beings; asserted that no man is an island."[4] Believing so strongly in literature's capacity to constantly be renewed and perpetuated through literary coteries, and, just as important, in its potential to connect radically dissimilar human beings, Hobsbaum eagerly awaited the results from his latest endeavor in the most culturally static society in which he had yet attempted to put together such a group.

With the exception of Heather Clark's *The Ulster Renaissance: Poetry in Belfast, 1962–1972,* criticism of the Belfast Group, which Hobsbaum ran from 1963 to 1966, has usually given its communal aspect and its diversity across sectarian divides little notice, preferring instead to articulate and often criticize Hobsbaum's role as an alternately fierce and cajoling formalist teacher of mainly poetry.[5] But Hobsbaum himself has noted the ecumenical thrust of the Belfast Group. As he recalls, when he came to the province in 1962, merely inviting Catholics and Protestants to meet together was a culturally fraught endeavor:

> It was curiously fragmented. This was a result of sectarianism in schooling, disparate communities, and loyalty of individuals to their various sects. To start any venture without paying regard to the several communities whose people might be involved seemed a virtual impossibility. I was told by more than one person that Catholics and Protestants would never meet under one roof—for any purpose. The Belfast Group, among its other achievements, proved these ill-wishers wrong. . . . [But] I had little idea of the ground I was breaking when I invited people from both Catholic and Protestant communities, or from no community at all, to take part.[6]

Along with Clark, Dillon Johnston is one of the few critics who has pointed out how the Belfast Group anticipated a softening of the sectarian divide in Northern Ireland: "The friendship of Catholic poets . . . and Protestant poets serves also as a political model for a new integrated society" (*IP,* 51). This ecumenical writing group and the continued staying power of its "graduates" indicate just how much Northern Irish literature has been able to transcend local and national politics.

An understanding of the Belfast Group's critical practices reveals much about its profound aesthetic and ethical legacy to the writers that emerged from it. Hobsbaum's typical procedure was to select several pieces from the work of one of the group's writers, then have those selections typed, copied, and distributed to members. The next week, the members would meet and hear the writer read his or her work. The first half of the meeting was always devoted to that reading and to other members' criticism of the pieces under consideration immediately afterward.[7] Hobsbaum forced each member to stand by every word he had uttered. As one member, Jack Pakenham, ruefully recalled, "Woe to any unsuspecting poet who could not stand over every word written."[8] After this session, there was a refreshment break followed by an "open session" where anything could be read without having been previously distributed.[9] Hobsbaum's insistence that every word tell made the writers carefully ponder diction, aural effects, and form. Arthur Terry, a poetry translator who was a seminal member, approvingly recalls "the attention given to the sound of a poem (all work was read aloud) and to the details of its verbal texture."[10]

Although these were often downplayed in subsequent recollections by members such as Michael Longley, the Belfast Group bequeathed several lasting characteristics to contemporary Northern Irish literature: a variety of formal control, a depth of imagination, a penchant for collaborative literary efforts, a marked emphasis on the individual artist's role in society, an intense regard for local surroundings and conditions, and a belief that literature could create connections among people.[11] This multifaceted approach toward their art on the part of both Longley and Heaney will be seen throughout the following chapters.

For two of the most thoughtful literary critics writing on Northern Irish poetry, Fran Brearton and Edna Longley, however, the very different voices already developed by Longley, Heaney, and Mahon in their first collections of the 1960s have tended to make less significant their sharing of the general aesthetic principles articulated in the preceding paragraph. Brearton has wrongly argued that any aesthetic classification of the Belfast Group's poetry, especially that of Heaney and Longley, is "disallow[ed]" by "the diversity of the[ir] collections published in the

1960s, the combative poetic environments in which they were forged, and the development of strong and distinctive poetic voices. . . ."[12] And Edna Longley argues that "most accounts of the Group over-stress a cosy fostering and ignore the aesthetic conflicts that pervaded its sessions."[13] While Longley's argument must be true (and she would know), she and Brearton seem to feel that the specific aesthetic conflicts that inevitably arose in the Belfast Group preclude any sort of shared, over-arching aesthetic assumptions, a view that is clearly disproved by close examination of these writers' works.

Of these aesthetic characteristics, perhaps most important was the Leavisite formalism with which Hobsbaum conducted Belfast Group meetings. This approach enabled an astonishing synergy between the group's writers and the ways they explored and developed their craft, although Michael Longley, as we will see later, claims it was singularly unhelpful in developing his own poetry. Hobsbaum's particular aesthetic repelled Longley, but his general emphasis on literature as craft, especially poetry, was enabling for Longley and indeed for all the Belfast Group writers, as Norman Dugdale, a group member, recalled in 1976: "The Group's chief merits lay in taking writing seriously as craft and expression; in providing an audience, however localised, which was prepared to listen; in creating conditions where newcomers could find (in both senses) their feet."[14]

Hobsbaum's precision in critiquing the diction and form of the group writers ineluctably led to their general appreciation for literature's imaginative and formal power. Hence, Longley and Heaney have experimented with a variety of verse forms throughout their careers (Longley more so than Heaney); the poet, then dramatist Stewart Parker attempted to invent a new type of drama; and Bernard Mac-Laverty has harnessed the specificity of the short story to his explorations of the lonely lives of his Northern Irish Protestant and Catholic characters.

Besides the Belfast Group's emphasis on literature's imaginative and formal power, another of its characteristics that is crucial to the present study was its emphasis on local conditions and culture. Taking their cue from Hobsbaum's insistence that they write out of what they knew, a demand that echoed Patrick Kavanagh's elevation of the parochial over the provincial, Belfast Group writers such as Heaney, Longley, Parker, and MacLaverty wrote about their local surroundings and situations. Heaney's approving recollection in 1978 of Hobsbaum, which directly employs Kavanagh's positive renovation of the term *parochial,* suggests that the English critic reinforced Kavanagh's influence on this genera-tion of Northern Irish writers to write about their immediate sur-roundings. Heaney further recalled, regarding the widespread critical acclaim for members of the Belfast Group, "It's easy to be blasé about all that now for now, of course, we're genuine parochials. Then we were craven provincials. Hobsbaum contributed much to that crucial trans-formation."[15] This "permission" to write about local conditions and cul-ture ensured that the members of the group would continue to devolve Northern Irish literature away from English literature and develop the self-confidence to conceive of Northern Ireland as a viable regional entity, inclusive and pluralistic, that had begun with its older writers such as John Hewitt. Heather Clark's formulation about the artistic in-tegrity and aesthetic principles shared by the Belfast Group members implicitly suggests as much: "By the 1970s, the tone of the conversa-tion would change as the term 'Ulster poetry' bore new burdens, yet it is important to recognize that the poets had already established a viable Northern identity—one centered around the idea of a local literary community which shared aesthetic principles and claimed kinship with Ulster poetic father figures—before the onset of violence."[16] Northern Irish literature was rapidly devolving, even as the province, just a few years later, would lose its relative political autonomy and would have direct rule from London imposed upon it.

At first, because Northern Irish literature had provided exemplary imaginative and ecumenical writers over the preceding decades, and later, because the rapidly deteriorating political conditions in the province warranted it, the Belfast Group writers looked inward to their own prov-ince in attempting to determine what contribution, if any, their work could make toward softening the hardening sectarian divide there. The work of the two major poets from the Belfast Group covered in this study always reveals the careful craftsmanship and extensive meditation of form first learned in that setting, even though Longley would ex-press indignation with Hobsbaum's particular aesthetic. Their long and continuing exploration of their genre and their overriding fidelity to the power of the imagination have been heightened and their poetic independence has been challenged by the crisis in Northern Ireland, which first accelerated in the late 1960s through Protestant loyalist violence in reaction to the Catholic civil rights movement and subsequent responses such as the brief reemergence of the moribund Irish Republican Army and the new, much more powerful Provisional Irish Republican Army.[17]

That a general Northern Irish aesthetic was developing in the 1960s is evident from Hobsbaum's central importance in formulating this aesthetic, the concerns of writers who emerged from his coterie, and the proliferation of periodicals and presses that tapped into and helped foster this movement. As Richard Kirkland admits, "The aesthetic principles he espoused, within a young and ambitious collection of poets, prose-writers and critics, have clearly been formative in establishing a distinctive Northern aesthetic to an extent which is comparable to the more often cited influences of MacNeice and Hewitt" (*LCNI,* 79). While Kirkland lauds the establishment of this aesthetic, he curiously refuses to describe it in detail, merely denigrating it for being based on close reading.

Both Kirkland and Brearton remain skeptical about whether the Belfast Group was a real literary movement, even in the mind of its star, Heaney. As supposed evidence that it was not, Kirkland cites a 1982 interview with Heaney conducted by Frank Kinahan, in which Heaney said of Hobsbaum, "He made the *Belfast Telegraph* believe that they had a literary movement on their hands. Well, those things generate their own power. And then we all got books published here and there; and there was your movement" (quoted in *LCNI,* 79). Kirkland reads this alleged "movement away from a group collective ethic" (as opposed to Heaney's full endorsement of the Belfast Group in his essay "Belfast" and in his contribution to "The Belfast Group: A Symposium") as a sign of Heaney's "growing reliance on the artistic paradigm of Joyce and a concomitant shift from that of Yeats" (*LCNI,* 79). As the chapters on Heaney demonstrate, though, he has never really chosen between Joyce and Yeats, and he turns to Yeats repeatedly in formulating his theories of poetic reception. Brearton cites the same 1982 interview with Kinahan as evidence that "Heaney himself has subsequently retreated from some of its [*Preoccupation*'s] judgments," particularly his wholehearted praise for Hobsbaum and the Group.[18] Heaney clearly still greatly values the Belfast Group, however, as evidenced in his remarks to Karl Miller in 1999 about the value he attached to the literary and intellectual community he joined at Harvard when he started teaching there: "It's a literary community I was lucky to meet, a second living poetry environment, after the first one I'd known in Belfast."[19]

The marked emphasis on the power of the imagination in the Belfast Group becomes even more compelling when its ethical mooring is understood. I noted earlier that the group modeled the future of Northern Ireland in its ecumenism, but just as salutary for Longley and Heaney was Hobsbaum's own conviction of poetry's connection to the world outside the poem and its liberating potential. Hobsbaum rejected a severely limited New Criticism, which takes into account nothing extraneous to the verbal world of the poem. For example, his discussion of Wallace Stevens's poems in the first chapter of his *Theory of Criticism* concludes by arguing, against R. P. Blackmur's view of Stevens as "no more than a creator of the beautiful and a purveyor of rhetoric," that "Stevens's poems do not exist merely as word-collocations, texture to be enjoyed for texture's sake."[20]

Both Longley and Heaney, as I have argued in the introduction and as indeed I hope this entire study shows, share such a view of poetry in general in their strong commitment to the imagination that includes poetry's ethical aims, indirect though they often may be. To return specifically to the example of Wallace Stevens, Longley shares with Hobsbaum an admiration for the American's poetry and more important, a sense that Stevens's poetry is not a rhetorical cul-de-sac but inextricably part of the outside world even as it affirms its own microcosmic reality— two points of connection between Longley and Hobsbaum in a relationship that was often vexed. In Longley's introduction to *A Jovial Hullabaloo*, which opens with his recitation of Stevens's "A High-Toned Old Christian Woman," he insists that in that poem Stevens "weighs in the scales religious belief and the life of the imagination. Although he clearly prefers the latter, he seems to compromise by suggesting that both end up creating the same thing: 'A jovial hullabaloo among the spheres.'"[21]

Thus the joy created by poetry's uproarious unsettling of us through its rattling of our convictions moves through us and the universe; because of our immersion in it as "the supreme fiction," to quote from the first line of Stevens's poem, which Longley mentions specifically in his lecture, it leads us out of quotidian reality and into a luminous higher reality that becomes at least temporarily true. Poet-prophets such as Longley and Heaney have returned from their excursions into poetry to show us what might be imagined out of poetry's "supreme fiction," including the possibility of a new thaw in frozen relations throughout Northern Ireland, although their poetry never has this potential as its main objective.

Michael Longley's Conciliatory Cultural Work

Although a great deal of critical consideration has been given to Seamus Heaney's efforts to deal with his own cultural heritage and that of his province, Michael Longley, with few exceptions, has yet to receive sustained attention for his own work in this regard. While Heaney long ago left Northern Ireland, living in County Wicklow and Dublin and teaching at Harvard and Oxford, Longley stayed in his native Belfast, committing himself to fostering local Northern Irish talent in an ecumenical manner. As Robert Johnstone has noted, "Successive waves of writers were encouraged into print by the ambience Michael did so much to create, through his job, but also by example, by being an excellent writer who stayed through the bombs and the bullshit and deserved to be taken seriously at the highest level internationally. . . . Just by being so thoroughly himself he changed the weather."[22] Longley initiated programs for literature, the arts in education, and the traditional arts in his role as combined arts director of the Arts Council of Northern Ireland. He was also a founding member of the Cultural Traditions Group, which aims to encourage acceptance and understanding of diversity in the province.

Poetry in the province, especially that poetry appearing from Hobsbaum's Belfast Group in the 1960s, gave a new sense of vitality to the entire literary scene in the North. Longley's early critical and community work also significantly advanced the notion of a contemporary Northern Irish literature that was inclusive and nonsectarian. An example of his early efforts is his essay "Poetry," written for *Causeway: The Arts in Ulster* (1971). This article asserts the existence of "Ulster poetry," delineates the influences upon contemporary Northern Irish poets, and recalls the cultural conditions that helped produce the current flowering of Northern poetry.

After discussing the short-lived ventures of the Ulster literary journals *Rann* and *Lagan* in the 1940s and 1950s, Longley approvingly notes the appearance of poems by John Montague, Richard Kell, James Simmons, and Padriac Fiacc, yet argues that "none of these was involved in the sort of local coterie or group which, whatever the originality of its individuals, can inspire its different members and help to extend the imaginative estate of the community to which it belongs" ("P," 95). This final phrase about extending "the imaginative estate of the community to which it belongs" is worth attending to, especially given the double entendre upon *estate*, which connotes both the realm of imaginative possibility envisioned by poetry and the localized, typical method of settlement in working-class areas of Northern Ireland—the housing estate. Housing estates are often notorious for their sectarianism and usually are composed of homogeneous, working-class populations known for fiercely defending their turf. Especially since he follows this paragraph with a discussion of Hobsbaum's group, Longley clearly has in mind here the transformations that coterie effected among an admittedly very small population of the Northern Irish community. These transformations involved both a sense of consolidation and coalescence for Northern Irish writing, especially in poetry, and a breaking down of sectarian walls among members of the Belfast Group, so that it served as a model for the pluralist society Northern Ireland might become.

Longley clearly dates this "new phase" of Northern Irish writing to the appearance of the *Festival Publications* pamphlets in 1965. These pamphlets published many members of the Belfast Group, including Longley himself, Heaney, Stewart Parker, and Hobsbaum. Both Longley's *Ten Poems* and Heaney's *Eleven Poems* were published in that year.[23] In reference to the Belfast Group Longley says, "Various talents may certainly have been emerging on their own, but Hobsbaum's enthusiasm and energy did much to accelerate the process" ("P," 96). Along with the appearance of the Belfast Group poets and new collections from older poets such as Hewitt, Fiacc, and McFadden, Longley mentions the wealth of literary journals in the province, including the *Honest Ulsterman* and *Threshold,* and the support given this upsurge in literary activity by the Arts Council: "Recognising this new vitality the Arts Council of Northern Ireland has increased its budget for literature. It granted a subvention to the Festival pamphlets series and continues to give subsidies to *Threshold* and *The Honest Ulsterman.* The Council has also promoted successful poetry reading tours—*Room to Rhyme* in 1968 with Seamus Heaney, the folk singer David Hammond, and myself, and in 1970 and 1971 *The Planter and the Gael* with John Hewitt and John Montague" ("P," 97). The editing of *Causeway* and the essay "Poetry" from that volume are early examples both of Longley's articulation of contemporary Northern Irish poetry and of his promotion of writing talent generally in the province. As Dillon Johnston has argued, "If Hobsbaum and then Simmons have fostered this poetic community through the Group and the *Honest Ulsterman,* Michael Longley's avuncular patronage and encouragement from his position as assistant director of the Arts Council have extended this spirit" (*IP,* 51).

The first of the poetry-reading tours Longley mentions in this essay, *Room to Rhyme,* conducted in the spring of 1968, has received little critical attention, perhaps because it has been largely overshadowed by the subsequent tour *The Planter and the Gael.* Kirkland has pointed out that this latter tour—which Longley, then officer in the Arts Council, promoted in good faith as his first community event—merely reinforced the simplistic idea of two opposing cultures in Northern Ireland: "In retrospect, it was this event which can serve as a suitable codification for tendencies that are now familiar as it demonstrated an early willingness on the part of the poets concerned to speak from a communal rather than individuated position. As the Arts Council Report for 1969–1970 noted, the selection of the poetry performed was intended 'to define the two main strands of Ulster culture which each poet represents and to illustrate how complementary and mutually enriching these can be'" (*LCNI,* 64). Kirkland goes on to cite David Hammond's harsh critique of the tour: "'The Planter and the Gael' tour reinforced 'some kind of crippled vision of what Ireland was. . . . It's to do with the feeling that all

Celts are Catholics and all Planters are Protestant'" (*LCNI,* 64). Hammond's comments explicitly identify the tendency toward identitarian politics in Northern Ireland that this tour undoubtedly recapitulated despite Longley's best intentions for using it to promote cultural and religious reconciliation.

In implying that there were only two communities in the province and by also downplaying the very real diversity across these two dominant communities, *The Planter and the Gael* starkly highlighted somewhat abstract cultural differences, although as Heaney points out, the mere use of the word *Gael* in its title "was an admission in the official language of Unionist Ulster that there was a Gaelic dimension to Ulsterness— something that would have been taboo in the six counties of Lord Brookborough where I grew up in the 1940s and 1950s."[24] This tour was so popular that it was conducted again the next year against a backdrop of increasing violence in the North. Although it gave new poetic life to the aging Hewitt and recast the American-born Montague (who had been living in the Republic of Ireland) as the representative of Northern Irish Catholics, it must be considered an artistic failure, both in its diminution of poetry's significance and in its too-neat bifurcation of identity in the North.

On the other hand, the earlier tour, *Room to Rhyme,* while attracting smaller audiences than *The Planter and the Gael,* modeled the dialogue between cultural "traditions" much better and allowed poetry to breathe, to be spoken, in an atmosphere not solely devoted to ameliorating political conditions. Its participants, Hammond, Heaney, and Longley, were ideally suited for such an endeavor. As Marilynn Richtarik has noted, Hammond was already well known by the late 1960s as a collector of folk music and singer in his own right, performing "under the auspices of Orange Lodges, Gaelic football clubs, and government departments."[25] Eschewing the idea of two clearly opposed cultures in the North, Hammond instead recognized its mixture of cultures and lauded the province's vernacular speech and song. Richtarik posits that "like [playwright Brian] Friel, Hammond is fascinated by the idea of language as the emblem for a whole culture, and the language he wants to capture in some lasting form is the language of 'the street and the kitchen' before it is 'driven out' by formal education."[26] His affection for vernacular songs colors the tunes in *Room to Rhyme,* such as "I Loved a Lass," "MacPherson's Farewell," "Farewell to Tarwathie," and the American folksong "John Henry."

The poems and songs from *Room to Rhyme* are divided into nine headings: love, heroes, birth, seasons, going away, animals, death, loneliness, and work. Heaney recited "For Marie," "The Diviner," "Elegy for a Still-born Child," "Requiem for the Croppies," "Digging," "Eel Returning," "Last Look," "The Peninsula," and "Churning Day" in each of these categories, respectively. Longley's contributions included "Epithalamion," "Dr Johnson on the Hebrides," "Christopher at Birth," "Freeze-up," "Leaving Inishmore," "The Osprey," "Remembrance Day," "Emily Dickinson," and "Elegy for Fats Waller." These themes and their poetic illustrations attend closely to everyday conditions in the life of any human being, following Kavanagh's and Hobsbaum's insistence on local culture, and are generally nonpolitical, with the exception of Heaney's "Requiem for the Croppies" and Longley's "Remembrance Day."

While implicitly providing a model of intercultural relations in the province (Heaney was already emerging as a voice of minority Northern Catholics) during 1968, the year of the founding of the Northern Ireland Civil Rights Association, this tour allowed both poets to showcase early work in a format designed to reach a wider audience than publication might achieve. It also signaled the early formalist emphasis of both poets—many of these poems feature perfect and slant rhyme. Finally, it suggested by its very title that the poet—poetry in general—needs room to rhyme, space in which to engage the imagination. Through this imaginative engagement, *Room to Rhyme* was also able, on the eve of the beginning of the Troubles, to make a small contribution to increasing the cross-cultural consciousness of citizens on both sides of the political and religious divide.

In a newspaper article written a week after the IRA declared a ceasefire on August 31, 1994, Heaney recalled that for him the *Room to Rhyme* tour marked a brief period of potential in the intellectual, political, and social life of the North, particularly for the nationalist minority:

> I remember in particular feeling empowered (although the word was not in vogue then) by a week on the road with David Ham-

mond and Michael Longley in May 1968 when we brought a programme of songs and poems to schools and hotels and libraries in
unionist and nationalist areas all over Northern Ireland. The programme was called *Room to Rhyme* and I thought about it too last
Wednesday [the date of the IRA cease-fire]. The title was taken
from the opening verse of a mummers' play that went "Room, room,
my gallant boys, and give us room to rhyme," a line that expressed
perfectly the eagerness and impatience that was in the air at the
time. As a member of the 11-Plus generation of Catholic scholarship boys, just recently appointed to the faculty of Queen's University, I knew myself to be symptomatic of a new confidence in the
nationalist minority; and on this particular trip, sponsored by the
Northern Irish Arts Council, with David Hammond singing "The
Boys of Mullaghbawn" and Michael Longley writing about "Leaving Inishmore" and myself reading "Requiem for the Croppies," I
was conscious that an Irish dimension was at last beginning to figure
in the official life of the North. Small changes of attitude, small rap-
prochements and readjustments were being made. Minimal shifts
in different areas—artistic, educational, political—were beginning
to effect new contacts and concessions.[27]

The *Room to Rhyme* tour suggests how public Longley's and
Heaney's concerns for poetry had become. As we will see in subsequent
chapters, the work of both poets is marked by emphases highlighted in
this tour and first developed in Hobsbaum's Belfast Group: a commitment to their art above all else and a profound interest in effecting cultural and political reconciliation in the province, the latter of which
could result only from a careful attentiveness to their respective poetic
projects.

In Longley's developing conception of Northern Irish writing—
increasingly promoted through his role as assistant director of literature
in the Northern Irish Arts Council and then through his role as combined arts director—all aesthetics and viewpoints were welcome and
contributed to this burgeoning literature's vigor. Thus he supported the
brilliant early work of Paul Muldoon as well as the work of more mature writers such as Heaney and James Simmons. Longley eschewed

promulgating a particular aesthetic in favor of both promoting reviews of Northern Irish writing across genres and dismissed critical attempts to portray this literature as utterly bound up with political and martial events in the province. At the same time, not long after having resigned from the Arts Council in 1991, he looked back fondly on his time spent as the Arts Council representative to the Cultural Traditions Group and clearly articulated his belief that the arts can ameliorate hatred and misunderstanding over time: "We are involved in cultural preparation, a constellation of conversions, gradual processes which short-term thinking by Government would abort. The redemptive powers of the arts must be given time to work."[28]

CHAPTER TWO

Lighting Out for the Unknown Territory

LONGLEY'S *NO CONTINUING CITY*

In this chapter, after briefly exploring Longley's early poetic and critical aesthetic, I explore his predilection for remote places, manifested by his poems set on and near oceans, his jazz and blues poems, and his poems set in the Scottish Hebrides; from these positions he can be receptive to poetic inspiration by occupying liminal positions between worlds and by trying on different identities. In the subsequent two chapters, I show how he develops his sacramental poetic aesthetic in his poems about transnational violence, his pastorals, his Holocaust poems, and his Asian works.

Longley's Poetic and Critical Aesthetic

The introduction and first chapter of this study noted the liberating effect of Kavanagh's elevation of the parochial over the provincial and Hobsbaum's similar emphasis on the parochial through his demand that the Belfast Group writers write out of what they knew. In his autobiography, however, Longley recalls his dislike for the particular ways in which Hobsbaum superimposed his specific aesthetic over the group members' urge to write about their local surroundings and situations:

Hobsbaum's aesthetic demanded gritty particularity, an unrhetorical utterance. Heaney's work fitted the bill especially well: at the second or third meeting which I attended a sheet of his poems was discussed—"Digging" and "Death of a Naturalist" (it was called "End of a Naturalist" then). By this time I was beginning to enjoy what was for me as a lapsed Classicist a new experience—practical criticism. But I didn't care much for The Group aesthetic or, to be honest, the average poem which won approval. I believed that poetry should be polished, metrical and rhymed; oblique rather than head-on; imagistic and symbolic rather than rawly factual; rhetorical rather than documentary. (*TS*, 40)

The vexed relationship between Longley and Hobsbaum comes through more clearly later in Longley's recollection of his time in the Belfast Group:

When my turn came I was expecting sharp criticism, but was rather surprised by the ferocity of Hobsbaum's attack and the incomprehension which my work seemed to inspire in everyone else. Just before Hobsbaum left Belfast for Glasgow he admitted that I was really quite good, but up until then I had been encouraged to think of myself as a degenerate sophisticate. This merely confirmed me in my ways—in fact I used to look forward masochistically to the seasonal maulings. I can honestly say that I did not alter one semicolon as the result of Group discussion. (*TS*, 41)

Longley's disdain for Hobsbaum's formal method is reflected in an interview with Jody Allen Randolph where he contrasted it with the influence of the avuncular Alec Reid upon his poetry and that of others at Trinity College, Dublin, in the 1960s: "Literary exchanges were *ad hoc* compared to the Belfast group under Philip Hobsbaum. Alec did not proselytize."[1] Besides the aesthetic disagreement between Hobsbaum and Longley, what is striking about this statement from Longley's autobiography is that Hobsbaum's aesthetic nonetheless influenced him—to further articulate his own particular aesthetic and be confirmed in it.

Fran Brearton has convincingly argued that "Hobsbaum's method of reading poetry struggles to accommodate the kind of disruptive aesthetic evident in Longley's early work," noting that the criticism practiced by Hobsbaum in the Belfast Group and summarized in his 1970 work *Theory of Criticism* privileges closure and coherence in poetry and assumes great poetry can have only one agreed-upon meaning.[2] For Brearton, Hobsbaum's preference for Heaney's poetry over Longley's can be explained by the critic's predilection for Heaney's seemingly more straightforward work in contrast to Longley's ambiguous verse.

Despite Michael Longley's assertions to the contrary, Hobsbaum has recently claimed that "there was no one school of thought in the Belfast Group"—a statement that seems suspect because, as Hobsbaum quickly admits, the major artistic disagreement between the two men had to do with rhyme.[3] In his recollection, Hobsbaum admiringly cites Longley's early poem "Dr Johnson on the Hebrides"—a poem dedicated to himself, no less! Yet he immediately attacks the poem as an example of "Michael's literariness" generally and then settles particularly on Longley's preference for rhyme in his early work as the prime debilitating factor at the beginning of his career:

> At the time it seemed to me that Michael's literariness, demonstrated in this poem, rather got in the way of his experience. . . . The inhibition, it appears now, was not literariness *per se* so much as a reliance on rhyme. The rhymes in themselves cannot be faulted, and the craft of the early poems seems on the surface to be most assured. But there has been a breakthrough, at a time well advanced in this poet's working life, with the remarkable collection *Gorse Fires*. This seems to me qualitatively superior to any of the previous books, and it cannot be a coincidence that the poems in *Gorse Fires* are on the whole unrhymed. There may have been in the past some inhibiting pressure that was later removed.[4]

This passage suggests that, contrary to Hobsbaum's protestations, there was a particular, restrictive, and divisive Belfast Group aesthetic that differed from the general, more expansive, and unifying aesthetic articulated in the previous chapter. This aesthetic, grounded in Hobsbaum's personal poetic inclinations, had to do mainly with a preference for the "gritty particularity" found in Heaney's "Digging" (think of "the squelch and slap / Of soggy peat" in that poem; *DN*, 2), an abhorrence of rhetoric, and a disdain for rhyme, though some of Heaney's early poems certainly features various rhymes and slant rhymes.[5] Longley's early poetry was much more imagistic, oblique, and rhymed than the poetry that received Hobsbaum's stamp of approval. He has said that Yeats's rhyming inspired the rhymes of the poems collected in his first volume, *No Continuing City*.[6] Longley's poetry from the 1960s promulgates a pleasing complementariness between form and content, an early expression of his marriage of aesthetic and ethical concerns, while delighting in formal playfulness.

In the introduction to his 1968 pamphlet *Secret Marriages*, published by Phoenix Pamphlets Poets Press, Longley makes his fullest statement on his early commitment to form and especially rhyme:

> "Secret Marriages" seems to be the logical conclusion of a long preoccupation with form, with stanzaic patterns and rhyme—pushing a shape as far as it will go, exploring its capacities to control and its tendencies to disintegrate. Six of these poems are in rhyming couplets which are usually something of a caretaker form, I think—a temporary address between more permanent lodgings. However, I think of the couplets in this pamphlet as tiny units, reduced stanzas, circuits which are almost closed, relying more on their own interrelationships than would the usual cursive and open-ended kind. These poems have an air of "end of the road" rather than "en route" about them. The next stage in logical progression would be a blank page and dead silence: they enjoy already the brevity of epitaphs.[7]

This Beckettian formal minimalism has gone largely unremarked until very recently in the scant commentary on Longley's early work.[8]

Although Brearton intriguingly argues in her discussion of *No Continuing City*, which includes the poems of *Secret Marriages*, that Longley, like Paul Muldoon, "suggests that form is its own form of accident and anarchy," Longley's own subject matter in the poems of *Secret Marriages* suggests otherwise and demonstrates how form and content, like aesthetics and ethics, are always closely and deliberately intertwined in his work, a tendency that will be examined in more detail in the succeeding chapters that deal with the later poetry.[9] For direct evidence of Longley's belief in purposely matching particular forms (even using them as guides) as they develop in the course of writing a poem to specific contents, we need look no further than his own declaration that "a poet on the track of the real thing will find himself in unknown territory, using the form of the poem (as it emerges) as an explorer uses a compass and sextant."[10]

After his discussion of the formal properties of *Secret Marriages,* Longley makes explicit the connection between form and content in the poems of the pamphlet: "As though to complement the rather extreme formalism, my subject matter in most of the pieces concentrates on extremes of experience or on remote notions. 'Persephone' and 'Narcissus,' for instance, are all that remains of an attempt to define schizophrenia, although 'Narcissus' also comments ironically on the poet and poetry."[11] This statement constitutes one of Longley's earliest references to schizophrenia, or to return to the term mentioned in the introduction to this study, two-mindedness. He almost always sees the condition positively, since from it one can explore both or multiple sides of a problem or situation, a posture that would serve him well as he promoted the various cultures in the province in his work at the Arts Council of Northern Ireland. I thus agree with Brearton, who has argued that the volume's "schizophrenia" can create "a rich poetic tapestry," as Yeats's oscillations did, and that "it has also proved a liberating aesthetic principle, one which underpins his poetic career and which serves to create, over time, a wholly distinctive voice."[12]

These early poems, then, in their purposefully subtle yokings of form and content, are themselves "secret marriages" performed by the poet as aesthetic priest, an inherently Joycean position, one shared with Seamus Heaney, as we shall see in chapter 5. Longley has even approvingly noted that "Horace calls the poet *musarum sacerdos,* priest of the muses," but quickly adds that "the Scottish word *makar* is a straight translation of the Greek *poetes.* The poet oscillates between notions of craft and vision."[13] Thus the poet must perceive abstractly but make concretely and never become lost in one mode or the other.

Remoteness and Buoyancy in *No Continuing City*

These "marital" exercises in aesthetics were important in developing Longley's independent poetic stance before the outbreak of the martial problems in the province by decade's end. They suggest that the poet already favored remote positions in which he could inhabit and experience freedom from particular pressures and receive images for his poetry, as in "Narcissus," where the poet's face is buoyant while gazing at sunken, ordinary objects that acquire an aura of the extraordinary:

> Unweatherbeaten as the moon my face
> Among the waterlogged, the commonplace,
>
> Old boots and kettles for inheritance
> Drifting into my head on the off-chance—
>
> A wide Sargasso where the names of things
> (Important guests at all such christenings)
>
> Submerge in mind and pool like treasuretrove.
> My face as sole survivor floats above.
>
> (*NCC*, 35)

This important early poem signals Longley's desire to sink quotidian objects into the depths of his mind and recover them later as poetic inspirations, a maneuver directly borrowed from the Romantic poets. However, the poem's couplets, use of parenthesis, and final two end-stopped lines suggest the poet's anxious desire to contain such memories, a strain that would largely disappear as he developed as a poet and learned to enjoy sudden visitations of various memories.

The epigraph to *No Continuing City* is taken from chapter 13, verse 14 of St. Paul's letter to the Hebrews, the King James translation: "For here we have no continuing city, [but we seek one to come]." Longley's epigraph signifies the "but" clause through points of ellipses, a punctuation that itself suggests continuation. On a historical level, the use of this half-verse may imply that Longley's native Belfast, sinking as it was into violence in 1969, simply could not continue on that course or would cease to exist as it had previously. And yet many of the poems from this collection were written and published before the onset of the civil rights marches and the consequent violence.[14] The title poem itself is intensely personal, comprising both a farewell to former lovers troped in terms of landscape and a welcome to his "wife-to-be" (*NCC,* 33).

More likely, Longley and his speakers in these poems about earthly isolation are pondering the general stance that Paul, in chapter 11, advises the Hebrews to take as he implicitly compares them to the great heroes of the Christian faith going back to Abel in Genesis. There, these believers are described by Paul as "strangers and pilgrims on the earth" (11:13). Current believers are told in 11:16 that "now they desire a better country, that is, an heavenly: wherefore God is not ashamed to be called their God: for he hath prepared for them a city." This city, or heaven, is the same city sought by believers and by Paul himself in 13:14. Paul often contrasts the earth and earthly things, which are ephemeral, a city that does not continue, with the city of God, which lasts forever. Longley sees himself as a poetic, not so much religious, pilgrim in this volume, however—as a wanderer among various islands and oceans that are not familiar to him. This psychic and geographic condition accords with his preferred form at this time: as we have seen in his introduction to *Secret Marriages,* he believes the rhyming couplets employed in a number of these poems to be "a temporary address between more permanent lodgings."[15] But unlike Paul, Longley and his speakers often take comfort in these far-flung locales, perceiving them as refuges from the pressing concerns of their homes. Finally, if baptism was for Paul the sign of Christianity, an outward proclamation to the world of being submissive to and set apart for God, immersion in deep waters—sometimes literal and at others figurative—signifies Longley's message that he has surrendered himself to poetry.

Appropriately, then, many poems from *No Continuing City* are oceanic, drawing on images of actual seas such as the "Sargasso" from "Narcissus" to connote a sense of the speaker's being figuratively adrift and alone, an ideal position for such a carefully observant poet as Longley. These include "The Osprey," "En Route," "Freeze-up," "The Hebrides," "Circe," "Nausicaa," "To Bessie Smith," "Dr Johnson on the Hebrides," "Dr Johnson Dying," "Leaving Inishmore," and "Man Friday."

"Man Friday" casts enabling solitude as Robinson Crusoe's faithful servant:

To lighthouse-keepers and their like I say—
Let solitude be named Man Friday:

Our folk may muster then, even the dead,
Footprint follow footprint through my head.
(NCC, 56)

These two couplets privilege solitude, remoteness, as conducive to raising not only memories of the living but "even the dead." Much of Longley's poetry attempts to recover from the past a whole stream of objects
and people that have passed away—to revivify them and make them
walk again. The footprints that these unidentified memories make render his head analogous to the "furthest strand" of the poem's first line
(56): figuratively windswept and smooth, the speaker's mind is a palimp-
sest upon which memories move and make tracks.

Footsteps, not footprints, feature at the end of "Persephone," a
poem that is not set on or near the sea but that shares the observational
reverence of others in the volume. Again, solitude is evoked—this time,
through the speaker's gazing upon a mole, swallows, a bat, a squirrel,
"weasel and ferret, the stoat and fox," which are all preparing for winter
(*NCC*, 34). From the point of view of Persephone in hell, whose time on
earth is limited to the warm spring and summer months of the year, winter's punishing cold leads some of the animals—the bat, the squirrel—
to a series of solitary retreats, while others, namely the weasel, ferret,
stoat, and fox, "Move hand in glove across the equinox. // I can tell how
softly their footsteps go— / Their footsteps borrow silence from the
snow" (34). The animals' borrowing of silence from the snow suggests
how connected they are to nature, whereas Persephone is cut off from
nature for a part of the year. Her sense of being on the outside looking
in, or looking out as it were here, also adumbrates a favored poetic position for many of Longley's speakers in later poems. Such poems recall the
wistful, solitary narrators of such Philip Larkin poems as "The Whitsun
Weddings" or "Church Going," although Longley's poems rarely feature
the simultaneous sarcasm of Larkin's poems in this mode.

Earlier poems in the volume such as "The Osprey," instead of offering a catalog of animals, focus intensely on one exemplary creature that

shows the poet how he might occupy simultaneous positions. Just as the speaker's face floats above the "waterlogged, the commonplace" in "Narcissus," so does this unusual bird "whom / No lake's waters water-log" (*NCC*, 22). Like that buoyant face, this bird gleans treasures from the water but floats above them. Instead, he "Regulates his liquid acre / From the sky, his proper element" (22). More important for Longley, who would himself attempt to live two lives as the conflict in Northern Ireland accelerated—the life of the mind and the life of the public citizen—this bird does so without apology: "He lives, without compromise, / His unamphibious two lives—" (22).

A final oceanic poem from *No Continuing City* that suggests the inspiring quality of remote places for Longley is "Leaving Inishmore," concerning the poet's trip to this most populated of the three Aran Islands. Those islands have long inspired Irish writers—most famously the playwright John Synge, who journeyed there on Yeats's advice and incorporated that milieu into his masterful play *Riders to the Sea* (1904). The poem's participial title suggests the ongoing allure of the island for the speaker and implies his hope that he might return again some day. On this same trip during the mid-1960s, Longley also traveled to the island of Inisheer with Derek Mahon "one Easter," as he recalls in "To Derek Mahon," published in his next volume, *An Exploded View* (*CPL*, 58). Considering along with his poems about the Hebrides in *No Continuing City*, these poems suggest a competition among islands for Longley's attention at this time: he was drawn to both the Aran Islands and the Scottish Hebridean Islands, probably because of their isolation and preservation of archaic languages and cultures. In her sustained book-length reading of Longley's work, Brearton argues that "Leaving Inishmore" "is really the first poem which suggests the importance of *[sic]* the West of Ireland—another 'elsewhere'—will have for Longley."[16] This observation is true in a general sense, but the importance of the poem in the specific context of the others in the volume lies in its evocation of the strange and exotic quality of the surging Atlantic Ocean that makes it an ideal location for poetic inspiration. In the second stanza, the speaker recalls

> Miles from the brimming enclave of the bay
> I hear again the Atlantic's voices,

The gulls above us as we pulled away—
So munificent their final noises
These are the broadcasts from our holiday.

(NCC, 52)

It is as if the boat trip back from the island exists in an eternal, liminal location for the speaker, poised between Inishmore and the mainland, hovering metaphorically in the swelling Atlantic, just as the speaker's face was buoyed above the flotsam in "Nausicaa." The boat is described as being in a "perfect standstill," while "The harbour wall of Inishmore" is "astern / Where the Atlantic waters overspill—" (52).

This seemingly ideal equipoise is threatened, however, by the fear of winter ice spreading figuratively over the sea, a concern broached in an earlier poem from the collection, "Freeze-up," in which the speaker fears the literal icing over of the ocean: "The freeze-up annexes the sea even, / Putting out over the waves its platform" (*NCC*, 25). Both the feared metaphorical freezing up of the sea at the end of "Leaving Inishmore" and the literal icing over of it in "Freeze-up" obliquely suggest Longley's fear of his own poetic faculties becoming rigid as his first extended writer's block, then accompanying depression, would begin in 1967, the year after the poem was written. In "Freeze-up," the speaker desires to "Release to its decay and true decline / The bittern whom this different weather / Cupboarded in ice like a specimen" (25). This frozen bird differs from the dynamically hovering osprey described in "The Osprey," which stays aloof and suspended between the elements, signifying Longley's vaunted ability to be in two minds and receptive to varying influences. At the end of "Leaving Inishmore," he fearfully invokes another wintry vision, metapoetically imagining writer's block as "Our ocean icebound":

I shall name this the point of no return

Lest that excursion out of light and heat
Take on a January idiom—
Our ocean icebound when the year is hurt,
Wintertime past cure—the curriculum
Vitae of sailors and the sick at heart.

(52)

Suspension between sea and land here signifies poetic receptivity, while the dynamism of the pounding ocean suggests poetic creativity, and the potential looming "ocean icebound" a proleptic failing of poetic powers and an onset of melancholy, being "sick at heart."[17]

These early poems of the largely positive aspects of solitude antici-pate the remoteness of later poems set in the Burren area of County Clare or the land around David Cabot's cottage in rural Carrigskeewaun, County Mayo, which Longley has often visited, and they imply his ap-proval of a seemingly divided mind. Perhaps because of his poetry's de-parture from the particularly personal Belfast Group aesthetic promul-gated by Philip Hobsbaum, Longley felt the need to begin articulating his own, more inclusive aesthetic, drawing on aspects of the Belfast Group's general aesthetic. His own early poetry took its cue from another Philip—Philip Larkin—and is highly influenced by the Movement poet's preference for rhyme, meter, and conversational voice, along with Louis MacNeice's colloquialism.[18] Larkin's own geographic dislocation in Hull and then, for five years in the 1950s, his sojourn in Belfast proved exemplary for Longley, who increasingly put himself in remote pos-tures both in his poetry and in his personal preferences for the isola-tion of Belfast and of rural western Ireland, often in order to gain poetic inspiration.

All That Jazz: The Example of an American Art Form

One of the largely unremarked ways in which Longley achieves such solitary, yet creative postures is through his deep interest in jazz and blues music, a concern he shares with Larkin that appears intermit-tently throughout Longley's oeuvre. These Atlantic voices from America are both continuous and discontinuous with the ocean sounds and bird cries of other oceanic poems in the volume such as "The Osprey." The jazz and blues poems from *No Continuing City*, together entitled "Words for Jazz Perhaps," are much more personal than the other poems set on the ocean, partly because of their focus upon identifiable human be-ings; yet they share with the other poems just discussed a similar em-phasis on buoyant freedom, achieved here by soaring sonic qualities and form.

Longley's specific fascination with jazz would continue with the suite of poems in his next collection, *An Exploded View,* which are collectively entitled "Doctor Jazz," and with his tribute to Larkin, "Jug Band," from *Gorse Fires,* but "Doctor Jazz" is much less formally interesting than "Words for Jazz Perhaps," featuring a series of four short quatrains with variations of *abba* rhymes. "Jug Band," however, pays homage to Larkin's nuanced rhymes with an initial quatrain that riffs on the *abab* rhyme scheme with "band" and "behind" linked together in lines 1 and 3 and "time" and "theme" chiming against each other in lines 2 and 4 (*GF,* 16), recalling one of the major themes of "Words for Jazz Perhaps," improvisation. The speaker of "Jug Band," whom I take to be Longley himself, notes that

> . . . we have left clarinet and drums behind
> And make up the instruments, and then the theme,
>
> And the theme is the making up of instruments,
> Jugs and kazoos for us to improvise our souls,
> Thimbles for keeping time with and making sense
> On a washboard of our uncomplicated roles.
>
> (16)

Thoroughly at home in their soulful improvisations, Larkin and Longley march along disdaining to use anything but the most common instruments for their jazz. This sense of comfortableness, however, is missing from the jazz poems of *No Continuing City,* which were written by a much younger Longley, one who was still experimenting with poetic techniques and much enamored of the exotic elements he heard in many jazz performances in Belfast.

Written out of deep admiration for music played on more traditional instruments than that soulful music would be years later in "Jug Band," "Words for Jazz Perhaps" exemplifies Longley's penchant for the catalog, a strategy that will be examined in more detail in subsequent chapters; models artistic creativity; affirms Longley's formally compressed poetry at that time; and becomes an exotic elsewhere desired by Longley as a middle-class young man growing up in a relatively static cultural environment in the Belfast and Dublin of the 1950s. Longley thinks so highly of jazz that despite its relatively late appearance in the North, he commissioned an essay on it from his close friend and record shop owner, Solly Lipsitz, for *Causeway: The Arts in Ulster*. Lipsitz's piece is valuable in its own right as a record of jazz's immigration to Ulster, particularly through the arrival of American servicemen in World War II, and also makes helpful though only glancing connections between the Irish and African Americans.[19]

"Words for Jazz Perhaps" is dedicated to Lipsitz and, taken as a series of portraits of three famous jazz musicians and one blues singer, exemplifies Longley's favorite poetic device, the catalog. "Elegy for Fats Waller," "Bud Freeman in Belfast," and "To Bix Beiderbecke" together limn a trio of important jazz artists, while "To Bessie Smith" admires that blues singer's majestic voice but finally edges away from her as too powerful and exotic.

Longley recalls in his essay on jazz and poetry "the exact moment when the wonders of jazz first grabbed me as a young boy," going on to recall that "The English Number One tennis player, Tony Mottram, chose as one of his Desert Island discs Fats Waller's 'Alligator Crawl.' I was standing in our kitchen at the time (early nineteen fifties?) and thrilled to the rolling boogie base of the great stride pianist."[20] Longley fell in love with Waller all over again when he was twenty-five and married and had just moved back to Belfast. Upon discovering Lipsitz's record shop, Longley purchased two LPs from him, *Fats on the Air*. His description of these compilations suggests the example jazz provided him for his own poetry: "I loved the drive, the warmth, the apparent spontaneity, the insouciance, the dizzy humour, the hilarious demolition of sentimental material, but I also sensed a dark and unsettling aspect, as though behind the twinkle Wallers is issuing a challenge: 'Yes, I'll make you laugh and tap your feet, folks, but not until you've kissed my fat black ass!' Waller seamlessly combines sunniness and subversion. Undermining not only the inane Tin Pan Alley lyrics, but our racial and artistic preconceptions as well, he can be very complicated indeed."[21]

Waller's blend of warmth, spontaneity, and insouciance with complex subversion was salutary to Longley as he was casting around for his own poetic voice in the 1960s and has continued to provide him a model for his later work as well. To take the second part of the dialectic first, Waller's challenge to authority and preconceived notions can be seen in Longley's own embrace of a fluctuating series of national identities— English, Scottish, Irish—and his desire not to be pinned down or appropriated by any political cause. These fruitful complications of state identity are distilled in Northern Ireland in such a way as to make artistic creativity possible out of tension, as we will see in the latter part of this chapter.

Waller's more appealing qualities—his energy, great emotion, spontaneity, and insouciance—likewise proved enabling for Longley and gave him a sort of permission to write passionately and yet do it with lighthearted unconcern. "Elegy for Fats Waller" employs two memorable phrases about Waller's playing that blend his focused energy and unconcern: "The maker of immaculate slapstick," and "with such precise rampage," in lines 5 and 6, respectively (*NCC,* 39). How can slapstick, an inherently improvisational comedic gambit, be made and made immaculately? How can anyone rampage precisely? This balance, between great intensity and seeming disinterest, has been identified by Longley as a central creative tension in his own work: "Poetry is like a mote in the eye. If you try to focus on it too hard, it disappears. If you desire it too urgently, it may well reject you. No matter how intense the concentration or lofty the ambition, insouciance seems to be a necessary ingredient."[22] Artistic creativity for him thus dwells in the wavering balance between focus and insouciance, a necessary dynamism that Waller occupied superbly. Longley suggests that "Elegy for Fats Waller" tries "to convey the weightless artistry of this hugely overweight man,"[23] and, as we have seen, his emphasis on the musician's buoyancy resonates with the similarly buoyant properties valorized in poems such as "Narcissus," "The Osprey," and "Leaving Inishmore." Treading lightly, floating figuratively above the waterlogged or oppressing world, epitomizes artistic receptivity and creativity.

Longley has remarked in an interview that he enjoys the strain of American art that is largely invented, a quality epitomized, to his mind, by jazz: "I like the D. I. Y., the do-it-yourself quality in American art. The greatest example of that, really, is jazz, where the black slaves picked up the musical instruments abandoned on the battlefields of the Civil

War, taught themselves to play saxophones and trombones, took their own work songs and took hymns from the missionary churches, took a bit of opera from the New Orleans opera house—dozens of strands—and improvised and just did it themselves, and produced out of their spontaneity, out of degradation and terror, this life-enhancing music that has taken over the world."[24] That sort of borrowing and improvising from traditional arts to make something new must have encouraged Longley generally to continue exploring various poetic traditions yet still create his own inimitable poetry. Moreover, since most jazz instruments are played through techniques of inspiration and respiration, the jazz musician figuratively stands for the poet in important ways for Longley. He has said, "I believe in the old-fashioned notion of inspiration, the breathing into the mind of some idea, the suggestion of an emotion or impulse from outside the confines of your own body and personality."[25] Longley blows his own inspired music through breathing in such outside emotions and impulses.

Traditional jazz, which was played in the 1920s and 1930s and again in the so-called "traditional revival" of the 1950s by the New Orleans- and Chicago-influenced artists (save Beiderbecke, who died in 1931) that Longley profiles in "Words for Jazz Perhaps," often is concentrated in a way that later jazz, such as that played by Miles Davis or John Coltrane, with their long, ruminative runs and melodic wandering, is not, and this brevity also influenced Longley's formal compression in *No Continuing City*. In discussing his own attraction to particular forms like the couplet or sonnet, Longley told Meg Harper in an interview that the three-minute recordings of jazz music necessary for fitting songs on the old 78 shellac or vinyl records (before the advent of the long-playing album, or LP) not only enabled jazz's rapid spread but also raised a whole series of artistic questions necessary for making music fit into that time slot: "The three minutes in the shellac record—I don't think jazz would have developed so potently and swiftly if it hadn't been forced to concentrate and compress itself. . . . But when they went into a studio to record, they had to decide, what are we going to say? how are we going to say it? and how are we going to bring it to an end? And that raised all the artistic questions which had to be solved, which is one of the main reasons for the vitality and the paradox, the freedom, of that music."[26]

The brevity of much of the jazz and blues Longley enjoyed (not Waller's *Fats on the Air*, which were on LPs) therefore confirmed his sense that great art could be wrought in miniature forms and that the brevity of such forms actually imparted to them a paradoxical freedom in which the mind could wander contentedly.

Bessie Smith's blues have such a distilled quality to them if Waller's jazz does not. For example, Longley recalls having once heard the following triplet sung by Smith: "It's raining and it's storming on the sea, / It's raining, it's storming on the sea; / I feel like somebody had shipwrecked poor me." He points out that "the three minute span of those early pre-electric recordings clearly helped to concentrate an already potent brew."[27] So does Smith's use of a traditional blues device, the repetition or near-replication of the first line, employed by blues singers as a way of inscribing their music in the minds of their listeners.

The two six-line stanzas of "To Bessie Smith" achieve some of their concentration through five end-stopped lines and a consistent rhyme scheme—*abacbcdedfef*—a rhyme scheme that the more loosely rhymed quintets (combining full, half, and quarter rhymes) of "Elegy for Fats Waller" do not display. As B. J. Leggett has pointed out in his study of the blues intertext in Philip Larkin's poetry, "In the typical three-line blues stanza, each line is a complete sentence or clause,"[28] and "To Bessie Smith" attempts to mimic this completeness through its own compression of four typically three-line blues stanzas into two six-line stanzas and through its use of end-stopped lines. Of the full rhymes, five of the six end rhymes in the first stanza are masculine, starting with line 2 and running through line 6—"mind," "sea," "stay," "find," and "day" (*NCC*, 40)—imparting a clear, hard-edged sound to the lines and, by extension, to Smith's music itself. Clearly, Longley is sonically endeavoring to represent Smith's "huge voice" as something analogous to scavenged treasures—"like sea shells salvaged from the sea / As bright reminders of a few weeks' stay" (40). Smith's voice is so powerful and unusual that the speaker ends the first stanza by admitting, "I couldn't play your records every day" (40). Stanza 2 even contrasts the landscapes of "Tra-na-rossan, Inisheer, / Of Harris," which Longley describes as "landscapes I must visit year by year," with Smith's even stranger voice: "I do not live with sounds so seasonal / Nor set up house for good. Your blues contain / Each longed-for holiday, each terminal" (40).

As the poem's compass narrows from "Chattanooga Tennessee" in line 1 to the Irish and Scottish landscapes—still exotic—of lines 7 and 8, Smith's blues are characterized as imagined holidays, in contrast to the real holidays Longley has taken to these remote locales in the Irish and Scottish archipelago. Thus he can "think of" these landscapes closer to home as a panoramic whole but can paradoxically describe Smith's huge voice only in diminutive terms—as "sea shells" and "random notes" he must search for (*NCC*, 40). Just as making the blues, which takes its name from the often miserable lives of their early practitioners, is difficult, so is listening to it, Longley implies. Unlike the more sprightly traditional jazz evoked in the other three poems in "Words for Jazz Perhaps," the prescribed aspect of the blues and its quality of lament may have made a poet looking for models of artistic spontaneity and joy decide to look elsewhere, although the practice of handling the end-stopped lines and full rhymes of the blues genre was helpful in his early explorations of form.

Formally, "Words for Jazz Perhaps" displays full, half, and quarter rhymes and free verse that adorn a variety of stanza lengths: "Elegy for Fats Waller" is written in quintets, "Bud Freeman in Belfast" in triplets, "To Bessie Smith" in sextets, "To Bix Beiderbecke" in triplets, and an epitaph for Billie Holiday (omitted from the sequence) in a single couplet.[29]

"To Bix Beiderbecke" celebrates the career of that white jazz cornetist and pianist through three triplets and a concluding single-line stanza, the latter of which emphasizes Beiderbecke's singularity as an artist. Although Beiderbecke died young, the poem revels in his joyful artistry, unlike "To Bessie Smith," in which the poet cannot simply enjoy Smith's downtrodden music. Beiderbecke survives in the mind's eye of the speaker, playing a "perpetual one night stand," forever young and frenetic: "The havoc there, and the manoeuvrings!—" He could "improvise with the best of them // That parabola from blues to barrelhouse" (*NCC*, 40). Beiderbecke's ability to play a whole series of musical subgenres, his exuberant energy, coupled with his improvisational style, which is signaled by the appearance of only two sets of partial end rhymes ("school" and "skull" in lines 1 and 3 and "terminus" and "barrelhouse" in lines 8 and 10), together suggest Longley's desire to learn a variety of poetic types, to sing them with gusto, and to begin experimenting with free verse, as he does briefly here and much more fully later in his career.

Finally, understanding the often emotionally driven, energetic poems of "Words for Jazz Perhaps" may seem unhelpful for grasping Longley's overall poetic concerns in *No Continuing City*, brimming as it is with poems set in remote, sometimes cold locales. And yet Longley's jazz poems in this and his next volume can be read as musical masks the poet slips on for a time to experience both the pain (the active persecution and exclusion) and the pleasure (the warmth and humor) of being black—for example, in "Fats Waller" and "Bessie Smith"—and of isolation, in "To Bix Beiderbecke" (Beiderbecke died alone of alcoholism). In this same volume, after all, he enters the mind of Circe, briefly assumes the identity of Persephone, and imagines Emily Dickinson at home in seclusion in Amherst, Massachusetts.

In citing "To Bix Beiderbecke," Longley has compared himself to that great musician as a fellow interloper into previously homogenous worlds: just as Beiderbecke "was the first white man to play great jazz," Longley, when writing that poem, "wondered if I might be the first Englishman to write Irish poetry."[30] Beiderbecke's example gave Longley courage to walk onto the stage of Irish poetry, which is often vexed by questions of nationality, and make his own music that was transnational and trans-Atlantic. White jazz players such as Bud Freeman and Beiderbecke were experiments of a sort as they crashed the gates of a party that had long been all-black. Although they consistently played the same music (Freeman played into his eighties), Longley has continued exploring different forms and content. In an interview, he describes earlier periods of his writing life as times of experimentation—"I wouldn't want to disown the earlier 'me's,' the earlier versions of me"—then suggests he was "trying on faces and . . . trying things out."[31] What better way to metapoetically represent the search for a true poetic self than to write a series of poems about great experimental artists?

A continuing legacy of Longley's interest in jazz is his ongoing concern for the oppressed. He began to apprehend the black struggle for equality in America through listening to jazz records and attending live performances, and he has remarked how astonishing it is that "the suffering and degradation of slavery should bring forth so much redemptive beauty."[32] His jazz poems remained a touchstone that, as the Catholic civil rights movement in Northern Ireland began, served to remind him of similarities between the African American and Catholic struggles for equality. Moreover, as he started writing poems about the Holocaust, jazz and its playful freedoms signified the possibilities that well-rendered art, whether his own poetry or that done by concentration camp prisoners, retains in the face of authoritarianism. The subsequent two chapters explore how Longley increasingly trusted in the integrity of his developing art while being assailed with images of violence during the Troubles and while expanding his poetic range into western Ireland, eastern Europe, and Asia.

Longley's Two-Mindedness, Scotland, the Limbo of "The Hebrides," and Scottish Historiography

Longley believes, like Heaney, that his two-mindedness (his depiction of being caught between land and sea in "Leaving Inishmore" manifests this ideal position well) actually enriches his poetic and personal imagination. As part of his development of a theory of reconciliation, Longley has transcended the sectarian politics of his province by evolving the cultural duality or two-mindedness that marks his poetry and personal philosophy. This duality has enabled him to establish himself as a veritable spokesman for understanding between Catholics and Protestants in Northern Ireland. His preoccupation with dualities has led him to embrace aspects of each and find an enabling, not disabling, position that borrows from these binaries and dwells in them, often transcending them. After one of his poetry readings, Longley explicitly affirmed this condition, noting, "My mother and father moved to Belfast in 1927. I was born in Belfast in 1939. In as much as Ireland has provided me with most of the data out of which I try to make sense of experience, I am *Irish*. But there is bound to be an English tinge to the way I see things. I feel rather ill at ease on both islands. I like to believe this is a healthy condition."[33] This dual identity explains both Longley's ecumenical political position and the way he represents elements of British and Irish culture in his poetry.

The emergence of this dynamic outlook is rooted in his upbringing in Belfast. Although he is a middle-class Protestant, his family experienced economic decline, and he was sent to a local primary school attended almost entirely by lower-class Protestants. To fit in, Longley began acquiring their accent while at school during the day, dropping some syllables and elongating others. But upon returning home every afternoon, he had to switch back into a middle-class Protestant accent. As he notes in his memoir, "By the age of six or seven I was beginning to lead a double life, learning how to recreate myself daily" (*TS*, 25). Slipping back and forth between dialects would prove a fertile early exercise for a poet dedicated to seeing issues from multiple sides.

Longley's varied use of both Lallans (the proper name for the Scots dialect) and Irish words such as *machair* and *duach* in his poetry is a linguistic manifestation of his duality and deserves further exploration elsewhere. He also scatters Northern Irish dialect words such as *duncher* (the Ulster term for a flat cap) throughout his poetry (see, for example, "Laertes" in *GF,* 33). A starting point would be to examine his rendering of parts of the *Iliad* rendered in Lallans in poems like "The Parting," which I reproduce here in its entirety: "He: 'Leave it to the big boys, Andromache.' / 'Hector, my darling husband, och, och,' she" (*GO*, 38). He also uses Scots to humorous effect in "The Mad Poet" and in "Phemios and Medon" (*GO*, 6, 44).

Such dialectical dynamism energizes Longley, as does the daily experience of living in such a cross-cultural milieu. For example, in an extended interview in September 1987 for BBC Northern Ireland Radio, Longley pointed out both the difficulty and excitement inherent in living in the province:

> I find other societies two-dimensional by comparison. Away from Ulster, I can get by without having to tune into all the wavelengths simultaneously. My antennae aren't continuously twitching. And I miss the cat's cradle which is conversation between Ulstermen. Knotted and twisted it may often be, but there is usually an intricate pattern waiting to reveal itself. Among the main strands of the cat's cradle are class, caste, regional affiliation, cultural background, and of course, religion and politics. Although the construction may be fatally ruptured by the last two, it will lose its tautness if, in the interests of misguided liberalism, they are denied their place. I would not want this to happen, and I count myself one of the liberals. Indeed if an attribute of liberalism is being curious and informed about the other side, then the game of cat's cradle becomes a neces-

sary educational exercise. . . . So let me quote two lines by the great English poet, W. H. Auden—"All real unity commences in / consciousness of differences. / Loving is wanting to know."[34]

Longley's emphasis on true diversity here is perfectly in keeping with his healthy two-mindedness that I have discussed throughout this chapter. He is right to point out the necessary tautness that religious and political affiliation gives to this cat's cradle of conversation that is enacted daily among inhabitants in the province.

However, he quickly notes that this precarious balance can easily be tipped toward outright war:

> The nightmare result of a breakdown in the game of cat's cradle is sectarian violence and civil war. When ignorance and superstition replace curiosity and information, the consciousness of differences, like a diseased essential organ, produces a cancerous and mocking version of itself. As the deadly inheritance of a colonial strategy, the sticks and stones of an antique European struggle continue to fly and break bones in the streets of Belfast, Derry, Portadown. The apartheid that precludes mixed schools and mixed marriages furnishes the unchanging backcloth. . . . A walk or a drive anywhere in the province is punctuated by memories of a shooting here, a bombing there. Normality is ambushed—land-marks, death-marks.[35]

Longley's recognition of the terrible legacy of British colonization of Ireland and its lingering presence in Northern Ireland tempers his recognition of himself as variously British and Irish. While certainly not implicating himself in colonial strategy in Ireland or the province, Longley realizes and perspicaciously points out the lasting inheritance of colonization: bloodshed between the descendants of those colonizers and colonized. This violence has created a catalog of murderous *dinn-seanchas,* or place lore, in the province that evokes specific atrocities committed in particular places.

At the same time, he notes a positive, even offsetting legacy of colonization—a mixed cultural heritage that inhabitants of Northern Ireland should draw on in an attempt to end binary thinking:

Imagine that if Ulstermen and by extension Irishmen, could be the beneficiaries of a unique cultural confluence which embraces the qualities of the Irish, the English, the Scottish, and the Anglo-Irish. Those who seek to describe or alter the relationship between our two islands, tend to undervalue, or even ignore, the Scottish horizon, the Mull of Kintyre visible from the Glens of Antrim. Presbyterians used to row across the sea to worship in Scotland on Sundays. Ian Paisley may look and sound out of place in London, but in Glasgow, he is perfectly comprehensible. In America, they refer to the Scots-Irish, a usage that refers to the still-partial nature of the sea-change. Years ago the Ulster poet and erstwhile Presbyterian minister W. R. Rodgers wrote about the creative wave of self-consciousness which occurs wherever two racial patterns meet. By comparison, the concept of a purely green Ireland and an orange Ulster seem impoverished, especially since you can't have one without the other. . . . Both cultures should be able to define themselves by a profound and patient scrutiny of each other.[36]

Longley's recognition of the mixed cultural heritage of Northern Ireland's inhabitants is a crucial plank of his platform in promoting reconciliation in Northern Ireland. Thus he spent twenty years at the Arts Council of Northern Ireland promoting the literature and culture of both of the major groups in the province.[37] At the same time, he rightly insists that any political solution must include the nearly one million Protestants in the province; their settlement in this corner of Ireland over several hundred years cannot be ignored or dismissed. In asserting the constant geographical presence of Scotland, Longley recognizes the very real presence of the northern part of Britain and the cultural implications for Northern Ireland, especially its Protestant citizens. The relative lack of poems he has written set in Scotland should not be construed as an absence of this influence in his poetry generally; Scots phrases pepper his poetry, as do Irish ones, enacting an ongoing linguistic example of the "cat's cradle" of conversation he discusses above.

In *No Continuing City*, Longley explicitly invokes Scotland, particularly the Hebridean Islands, in several poems: briefly and specifically in "To Bessie Smith," in "Dr Johnson on the Hebrides," in "Dr Johnson

Dying," and, in what is one of the longest poems in his canon, "The Hebrides." The Hebrides had long been on his mind: one of his poetic exemplars, Louis MacNeice, wrote a poem entitled "Leaving Barra," which Longley cites approvingly in an essay on MacNeice to show how "in his search for Atlantis MacNeice was never able to align himself wholeheartedly with any aesthetic, political or religious creed, to borrow somebody else's map and compass."[38] MacNeice's yearning for Atlantis and wandering spirit were influential for Longley, as was his transnationalism—MacNeice was neither fully Irish nor English but hailed from Northern Ireland, which "is a limbo between two (three?) cultures."[39] After vicariously trying on other identities elsewhere in the volume, such as the jazz and blues in "Words for Jazz Perhaps," Longley eases into the limbo of identity symbolized by the Hebridean Islands and finds himself both lost and fully at home there.

In "To Bessie Smith," when hearing the singer's voice, the speaker thinks "Of Harris drenched by horizontal rain—" (*NCC*, 40). "Dr Johnson on the Hebrides," dedicated to Philip Hobsbaum, and "Dr Johnson Dying" (both combined into one poem dedicated to Hobsbaum called "Homage to Dr Johnson" in *Poems, 1963–1983,* in *Selected Poems,* and in *Collected Poems*) speculate about Johnson's fascination with etymology. "Dr Johnson on the Hebrides" signifies Longley's early recognition of the Hebrides as a remote place, one where philosophical and linguistic meditation can naturally occur away from the charged atmosphere of Belfast. The lonely, "unsinkable lexicographer" (50) who is Johnson in this poem follows another lonely figure in "The Hebrides"—Longley himself.

"The Hebrides" features the islands as a refuge for the poet from his "no continuing city," which suggests the political and economic stasis endemic in Belfast during much of the 1960s. In the opening stanzas, the poet has "lost my way at last, / So far from home. // In whom the city is continuing" (*NCC*, 26). Longley notes how the stagnancy and dreariness of Belfast continue to surge in him even on the desolate Hebridean islands. After he pauses to look around him, he finds his feet still rooted and a sky shimmering with birds overhead: "To find my feet among the ling / And bracken—over me / The bright continuum of gulls, a rook / Occasionally" (26).

The next section of the poem gradually embeds Longley in the landscape and seascape around him, and he gains an enlarged sense of the natural world of wind, water, and soil. For example, in the opening stanza of this section, Longley gradually is able to change his vision from one preoccupied with the narrow streets and lanes of his native Belfast to a more panoramic one—a broad vision that seems as much metaphorical as literal:

> My eyes, slowly accepting panorama,
> 　　Try to include
> 　In my original idea
> 　　The total effect
> Of air and ocean—waterlogged all wood—
> 　　All harbours wrecked—
> 　　　　　　　　　　(*NCC*, 26)

The lineation of this stanza clearly echoes Longley's struggle to acquire this panoramic vision. It begins with a long line that echoes his eyes' slow acceptance of "panorama," then features three short lines that recall his relatively narrow original vision of this vast landscape. Then his original idea and his current view coalesce and expand into the long line "Of air and ocean—waterlogged all wood—": a typically horizontal Longley list (a maneuver that chapter 4 fully explores) that functions here as an echo of the wide world immediately around him.

The next stanza speaks of the poet having "dead-lights latched by whelk and barnacle," waiting "By the sea wall of the time I kill—" (*NCC*, 27). This dawdling image is strengthened in the third stanza, which features him in a psychographically liminal position, obviously influenced by his geographically liminal position, between mainland Britain and Ireland, betwixt water and land:

> Between wind and wave this holiday
> 　　The cormorant,
> 　The oyster-catcher and osprey
> 　　Proceed and keep in line
> While I, hands in my pockets, hesitant,
> 　　Am in two minds.
> 　　　　　　　　　　(27)

This articulation of his two-mindedness here is perfectly in keeping with Longley's penchant for ambiguity generally and with his particular unease in the stanzas that follow about the conditions in his native city.

As we see in the third section, Longley is preoccupied with "Old neighbours" who "People my brain—" (*NCC*, 27). These people march in his mind's eye out to sea, clad in raincoats, and evoke heartfelt sorrow from the poet at their passing:

> And I feel them
>   Put on their raincoats for ever
>   And walk out in the sea.
> I am, though each one waves a phantom limb,
>   The amputee,
>
> For these are my sailors, these my drowned—
>   In their heart of hearts,
>   In their city I ran aground.
>   Along my arteries
> Sluice those homewaters petroleum hurts.
>   Dry dock, gantries,
>
> Dykes of apparatus educate my bones
>   To track the buoys
>   Up sea lanes love emblazons
>   To streets where shall conclude
> My journey back from flux to poise, from poise
>   To attitude.
>   (27–28)

This collective weight of troubles gives Longley's poetic ship too much ballast, leading it to run aground "In their city." He, too, has been maimed by their loss, amputated, numbed by their shared, troubled city of Belfast—troped here by the images of the shipyards on Belfast Lough and in the streets where he is quickly led from the "sea lanes love emblazons" (28).

The last stanza in this third section finds Longley "at the edge of my experience," watching "Another tide / Along the broken shore [which] extends / A lifetime's wrack and ruin—" (*NCC*, 28). Being literally on the edge of Britain leads Longley to speculate about the fringes of his experience. He finds that "No flotsam I may beachcomb now can hide / That water line" (28). "That water line" connects him back to Belfast and his disturbed province, and in the next section he successively "discern[s] / My sea levels" and "Remove[s] upstream" to see "the salmon, risking fastest waters—" (28–29).

The fifth and final section finds him literally waterlogged, recalling this similar condition in "Narcissus," peering into his own past:

> Now, buttoned up, with water in my shoes,
>   Clouds around me,
>   I can, through mist that misconstrues,
>   Read like a palimpsest
> My past—those landmarks and that scenery
>   I dare resist.
>
>   (*NCC*, 29)

Longley has now fully become part of his surroundings: his own "water line" is presumably up to his ankles, and his head is swathed in mist. He has come full circle from his physical position in the first stanza, where his feet are "among the ling / And bracken" and gulls and rooks that soar overhead (26). Even though he has mentally scrubbed the slate of much of his past life clean, his literal immersion in water evokes memories of "those landmarks and that scenery / I dare resist." Then these images "fade away—" in the next stanza, as they roil in his "mind's unsympathetic trough" (29).

As he gazes out to sea, Longley envies the literal weightiness of the fishing trawlers and fights for balance in his thinking, even as he craves vertigo:

> Granting the trawlers far below their stance,
>   Their anchorage,
>   I fight all the way for balance—
>   In the mountain's shadow
> Losing foothold, covet the privilege
>   Of vertigo.
>
>   (29)

Longley's gaze throughout the poem has been focused on the natural world of the Hebrides, its birds, fish, waves, and wind. Now he seems to pull back from this world, to draw away from the sea, which "grow[s] old," and focus instead on the trawlers. Longley obviously desires mental focus, a psychic anchorage at this point; his mental dissolution into the natural world has clearly exhausted him. His sporadic rhyming in the poem evidently served to anchor him as he reflected on his musings in the wide-open spaces of the Hebrides. This rhyme scheme is evidence that, while he covets "the privilege of vertigo," he knows that his duty as poet and human being is to draw upon his sensory and philosophical experience and make an ordered contribution to his art and to his world.[40] While his outlook seems continuous with his surroundings, he recognizes, as he will later in his "Aubade" (*CPL,* 178), his clear difference from the natural world and his ethical burden as a human being and an artist to make a difference in others' lives.

The unsettling personal journey into unknown areas of himself undertaken by Longley in "The Hebrides" indirectly promotes cultural understanding in the province by implicitly suggesting the necessity of movement away from certainties into strange territories. Terence Brown has pointed out how the varying geographical settings such as the Hebrides and other locales function in *No Continuing City* "as metaphors of possible states of consciousness explored by a poet inventing himself in his art."[41] In this regard, Brown sees "The Hebrides" as "a key early poem . . . [which] ponders a region of the mind for which a wild, rocky Atlantic world is appropriate metaphor."[42]

More concretely, Longley's evident fascination with the Outer Hebridean islands is an early indication of how his reflections upon the natural world have informed his thinking about identity in Northern Ireland.[43] The subtext of "The Hebrides" is important for a clearer understanding of the "cultural confluences" of Northern Ireland that he remarks upon above. These islands have always featured a continuum of religious identities, running as they do from fundamentalist Protestant Lewis and Harris in the north down to Catholic Barra in the south. In their religious makeup, they are a literal microcosm of religion in Ireland. The northern Hebrides thus can be thought of as an analogue to majority-Protestant Northern Ireland, while the middle and southern

Hebrides can be thought of as representing the still overwhelmingly Catholic Republic of Ireland. Longley's immersion in this mixed cultural and religious milieu as the province was poised on the brink of martial conflict suggests his need to obtain a distance from the overheated rhetoric of Northern Ireland but also to dwell upon its problems in an atmosphere that uncannily replicated its religious and cultural mixture. At the same time, Longley's Hebridean affinity is much more than mere recognition of a society that somewhat mirrors his own: on a transnational level, it reflects his realization of the archipelagic nature of England, Scotland, and Ireland.

He had already evinced an interest in the culture of the various islands that together make up Great Britain and Ireland through his work with the Arts Council of Northern Ireland. For example, in his autobiography, Longley sketches out an archipelagic map of the various Arts Councils across Ireland and Britain: "There are five Arts Councils on the archipelago: one in Belfast, one in Dublin and, across the water, the Scottish and Welsh Arts Councils which are funded by the fifth and largest body, the Arts Council of Great Britain" (*TS*, 49). This archipelagic configuration is possible, Longley suggests, through regional affiliations similar to John Hewitt's formulation. Longley cites the regionalist philosophy of E. Estyn Evans and Hewitt as instrumental in providing a sense of continuity and inspiration for his early programming in the Arts Council of Northern Ireland: "They inspired my thinking, and gave me a sense of continuity. Thanks to them, the programmes for literature and the traditional arts began to overlap and provide shelter for modest but timely explorations. Hewitt had already written my script: 'Out of that loyalty to our own place, rooted in honest history, in familiar folkways and knowledge, phrased in our own dialect, there should emerge a culture and an attitude individual and distinctive, a fine contribution to the European inheritance and no mere echo of the thought and imagination of another land'" (*TS*, 51–52). In pursuing a series of programs that reflected his own ecumenical version of this regionalist philosophy, Longley was enacting a process by which the traditional cultures of two of the original subnational groups on the island—the Scots-Irish and the Catholic Irish (the Anglo-Irish being the other)—were recognized in a dynamic relationship. In this model, the relation of the metropole of London to the province becomes increasingly marginal, and the real emphasis is placed, as it ought to be, on the interactions between sub-national groups.

Longley's pursuit of a reconfigured notion of the cultural dynamics across the islands shares certain similarities with the historian J. G. A. Pocock's attempt to establish a new "British" history beginning in the mid-1970s. Pocock argued in a series of articles starting in 1975 that British history should be construed not as "the simple narrative of a monolithic empire's interactions with its external proletariats" but rather as "the interrelations of a number of advanced and sophisticated provinces."[44] Pocock rejects the term *British isles* as the site of this history and instead terms it *the Atlantic archipelago.* This, he defines as "a large—dare I say a sub-subcontinental?—island group lying off the northwestern coasts of geographic Europe, partly within and partly without the oceanic limits of the Roman empire and of what is usually called 'Europe' in the sense of the latter's successor states."[45] He goes on to argue that both the "marcher lordships" such as the Earldom of Orkney and "a diversity of intermediate and counterreactive societies" across this archipelago created "the political and cultural pluralism of the early and middle phases of 'British history.'"[46]

These phases are distinguished from the later phase of British history (dominated increasingly by England) by the constant absorption and creation of subnations, especially in Ireland:

> The *locus classicus* of this sort of process is of course Ireland, where by the end of the seventeenth century one subnation, the Catholic Old English, has been partly extinguished and there have emerged three subnations in a single island: the Protestant Anglo-Irish or New English, a garrison landholding class who generate a high culture without becoming a nation; the Scots-Irish, who survive into our own times as a classic example, along with the Afrikaners of South Africa, of the settler nation which is at the same time an antination; and the Catholic "old," "mere," or "native" Irish, undergoing a social transformation as violent as any in the history of colonization and for that reason evolving toward the presentation in the nineteenth and twentieth centuries of a revolutionary nationalism of an East European or Third World type, situated however within the confines of the history of the Atlantic archipelago.[47]

Pocock goes on to elucidate three modes of historical consciousness that have emerged in the most recent phase of "British" history: English, Scottish, and Irish. He argues that the English mode "rests upon a sense of identity so secure as to be unreflective and almost unconscious; Irish historiography affirms and records a romantic crisis of identity, and Scottish a tangential identity consisting in a continuous movement between alternative roles."[48] At the same time, he insists that inhabitants of each of these areas should not pursue their own history in isolation, then examine British history, which is really English history. Rather, archipelagic history should replace "the image of a monolithic 'parent society' with that of an expanding zone of cultural conflict and creation."[49]

Viewed through Pocock's conception of the British and Irish archipelago, the cultural (and political) conflict in Northern Ireland can be thought of historically as the interaction between the settler Scots-Irish, who constitute an antination, and the Catholic Irish, who share much of the typical Irish crisis of romantic identity. Yet this configuration is limited and doomed to replicating binary thinking. In an unpublished essay from the early 1970s, Longley rejected the claims of both nationalism and unionism on Northern Ireland, while sympathizing with the concerns of both of these ideologies:

> The "man lying on the wall" *does* see and feel for both sides, but rejects both a "green" Ireland and an "orange" Ulster as inadequate concepts. In the long terms I hope for a united *island,* but see the need for a gradual and profound *cultural* preparation before *political* solutions can even be contemplated. . . . I am frightened by the fascist undertow of much Green and Orange thinking and rhetoric — the former an Hibernian equivalent of the nightmarish Aryan programme and the latter as bad but compounded by an Afrikaaner-like belief in "the chosen race," "the last bastion of European Protestantism," as Paisley would have it. Art can help to subvert, very slowly, such death-dealing certainties.[50]

The poet identifies himself with this figure in several letters from the same period. The image is a striking one: the man on the wall can literally see on both sides of the wall—and symbolically on both sides of an issue—a position in which Longley undoubtedly found himself in his role promoting literature across cultures for the Arts Council at this time.

Because these two subnational groups share a relatively small land mass and provincial status, perhaps they could find unity in a shared mode of historiography, which would still permit differences within it. The Scottish mode of historiography, as outlined by Pocock, may be the most elastic and helpful for both dominant cultural groups in the province in achieving unity, since it is "a tangential identity consisting in a continuous movement between alternative roles." This, after all, is a daily exercise for many, if not all, of the province's inhabitants. The Scottish mode as Pocock envisioned it no longer corresponds very closely to a newly devolved Scotland, but the province of Northern Ireland remains torn between British and Irish notions of identity. Adoption of Pocock's Scottish mode of history seems invaluable for continued efforts toward reconciliation in the province: in this mode political, cultural, and religious allegiances can be tentatively advanced, suspended, or withdrawn as the situation demands. Longley's early conception—on both a poetic, personal level and a province-wide, professional level—of cultural relations in the province within an archipelagic context constitutes a signal and dynamic contribution to Northern Irish culture and literature.

CHAPTER THREE

Longley's Poetry of War and Peace

Despite Longley's preoccupation with events in the outer world during his time on the Arts Council of Northern Ireland, he maintained a fidelity to his own imaginative work that is worth briefly exploring. Although he has written far less about the creative process than has Seamus Heaney, as we will see in those chapters of this study dealing with Heaney, he nonetheless has made several remarks about poetic reception and composition that display his commitment to his work, an artistic faith that would stand him in good stead in the face of the growing violence in the province starting in 1969.[1] In the summer of that year, Longley published a brief essay in Harry Chambers's regional journal *Phoenix* that explained the process of composition in terms of patient gestation:

> Up until now I have written very slowly, waiting for a poem to accumulate. It's a question of being prepared throughout the period of composition to receive the lines whenever they choose to present themselves—. . . . The state of preparation is maintained by scribbling over a lot of paper, following false trails, driving up and reversing down cul-de-sacs. The miles of scrawl are a kind of "placenta previa" which is not always fatal, rather than imperfect versions of the final object. With this method of composition a failure is stillborn rather than deformed.[2]

Longley's patient waiting on poems to present themselves to him indicates his contemplative mind-set and belief in poetry's autonomy and agency. After confessing with some relief to Peter McDonald in the late 1990s that his departure from the Arts Council of Northern Ireland gave him more time for poetry, he clarified how his full-time commitment to writing had enabled his work: "I do feel that a poem needs not just a space, but ideally, space around that space — space for meditation, reverie, subliminal link-ups. I sense that poetry happens at a level above or below intelligence. . . . For me, now, poems sometimes occur in clusters, in a way that they never used to."[3] Longley's very reluctance to pin down how poems emerge from his consciousness suggests further his belief in poetry writing as a reverential mystery, one unable to be quantified. As he has noted elsewhere, "Writing a poem is an experiment, an exploration. You do not know beforehand what you are going to say. If you do, you are merely versifying opinion."[4]

The closest he has come to explaining this process is through comparisons to human fertilization and religious experience. In 1998, he would tell Sarah Broom in an interview that "I don't go to myths looking for poems. A poem has to be there. I believe that the poet's mind is like a woman's ovaries. There are only so many poems and that they're waiting to be fertilized, as it were."[5] In a 2000 interview with Mike Murphy, Longley explicitly equates the poetic process to a religious experience, saying, "What makes a poem is something quite mysterious. The writing of a poem is akin to what I imagine a religious experience might be. Poetry is the way I make sense of the world. It's an exploration."[6] This inward gaze has enabled Longley to resist outside pressures to produce immediate verse, poetry that is bound to the moment, and instead to write lovingly crafted, meditative poetry that is particular but timeless.

Longley's own personal aesthetic of poetry as patient exploration would be challenged by events taking place in Northern Ireland during the civil rights movement, yet he still evinced an interest in articulating the responsibility to the integrity of the artistic endeavor in times of unrest. In 1969, he argued in a seminal essay, "Strife and the Ulster Poet," that the primary duty of the artist at such a time is to his imagination, adumbrating concerns about the artist's role in a conflicted society that he would articulate more fully in his introduction to *Causeway*, which was examined in the introduction to this study. This duty does not preclude political or cultural engagement with the problems brought on by unrest; indeed, if sufficient attention is given to the imagination, it can also positively affect the political situation. Longley concludes this essay by noting that he no longer has a "life which is my own entirely. However, as a poet I insist that the imagination has a life of *its* own, a life that has to be saved: if it isn't, everything else will be lost."[7] His urgent declaration about the autonomy of the imagination might seem out of place at such a crucial time in the short history of the province, but it remains the most striking statement to be issued about the relevance of art to the conflict at the time. If art will have any significant role to play in responding to the violence, Longley suggests, it must stay faithful to the imagination, not to the headlines of the newspaper on any given day.[8]

And yet Longley's aesthetic fidelity to the imagination is inextricably tied to his ethical interest in effecting harmony between opposing cultures in Northern Ireland, often divided by religion. Something of this concern is expressed in his wonderful phrase "sodality of the imagination,"[9] implying that those artists who uphold the imagination are members of a brotherhood or fellowship or, in a more specifically Catholic context, members of a religious guild committed to a particular devotion. His insistence on imaginative allegiance to art, which approaches reverence toward a sacred mystery, while under social and political duress shares the central aim of Heaney's poetry, as the chapters on that poet will show. Every Northern Irish poet writing in the last three decades has had to address the conflict in the province; only a small handful, among them Longley, Heaney, Mahon, and Muldoon, have done so appropriately. Longley's work toward reconciliation, however, especially in his poetry, has been relatively overlooked.[10] The present chapter seeks to redress this imbalance and delineate Longley's unique contribution to political and cultural understanding in the province through his articulation of an aesthetic and spiritual theory of reconciliation, grounded in his semantically precise poetry, which is constantly attuned to the interaction between the material and spiritual worlds, and also expressed in penetrating essays.

Longley has written many poems that do not deal directly or indirectly with the conflict at all. In fact, his poetic range, both stylistically and in subject matter, is easily one of the broadest of any poet today writing in English. As I argue in the next chapter, his nature poetry does, however, need to be read in the context of his humanitarian concerns about the Northern Irish conflict. Reading these poems in this manner does not politicize them but does suggest the way his concerns about the fragility of life emerge in both his urban poems about the violence and his rural poems about the possibility of violence being visited upon the natural world. Occasionally, as in the poem "The Ice-cream Man," the two different milieus are brought together seamlessly.

Despite clear evidence to the contrary, there is a disturbing trend in some of the extant criticism of Longley's work to accord him no real engagement with the province's violence in his poetry before *Gorse Fires* (1991). Jonathan Hufstader, for example, claims in his recent book on Northern Irish poetry and social violence that Longley's early poetry dealing with the Troubles is bewildered and too distanced from the violence. Hufstader strangely attempts to separate Longley the Arts Council worker from Longley the poet, arguing that until the publication of *Gorse Fires* "Longley the poet" refused to get involved in or even comment upon the conflict in Northern Ireland:

> Longley the poet distinguishes himself from all the other poets in this study, even Medbh McGuckian, by his apparent refusal—one which finally proves deceptive—to admit or accept any personal involvement in the Troubles. . . . For Longley the poet . . . this rigorous absence of personal involvement in any pattern of violence separates him from his colleagues. . . . An exception must be made, however, for some of Longley's most recent work, written after a long period during which he published no books of poetry. Now, having relinquished his public work, he has produced two books of poetry which use the perspectives of Greek mythology (as Heaney has done) to develop new ideas and feelings about social violence. These latest works implicitly call into question the authorial attitudes of Longley's best-known poems.[11]

Throughout the first part of his chapter dedicated to Longley's early poetry, Hufstader presents Longley as "Fleance, as a voice separated from action and therefore as an almost victimized observer . . . a bewildered spectator of a violence which he does not understand and with whose proponents he has no sympathy."[12] Hufstader's misapprehension of Longley's consistent poetic engagement with the violence in the province — this is not even to comment on his bizarre bifurcation of Longley into concerned public official and diffident private poet — continues a strain of Longley criticism that includes earlier critics such as Stan Smith.[13]

My own analysis of Longley's poems about the conflict from the 1970s demonstrates the critical misapprehension of both Smith's and Hufstader's appraisals of Longley's early poetry. These poems register the shock from the violence endemic in the province in the very late 1960s and 1970s and establish connections with violence in other times and places, achieving a powerful multitemporality.

For example, the famous poem "Wounds" from *An Exploded View* (1972) not only recognizes the contribution of Ulster Protestants to the Battle of the Somme in World War I but also acknowledges contemporary victims of political violence in the province. The poem opens with "two pictures from my father's head — ":

> First, the Ulster Division at the Somme
> Going over the top with "Fuck the Pope!"
> "No Surrender!": a boy about to die,
> Screaming "Give 'em one for the Shankill!"
> "Wilder than Gurkhas" were my father's words
> Of admiration and bewilderment.
>
> (*EV*, 40)

The second picture is of "the London-Scottish padre / Resettling kilts with his swagger-stick, / With a stylish backhand and a prayer." The first section concludes with an image of Longley's father dying:

> At last, a belated casualty,
> He said — lead traces flaring until they hurt —
> "I am dying for King and Country, slowly."
> I touched his hand, his thin head I touched.
>
> (40)

In the second section of the poem, Longley mentally buries "Three teenage soldiers, bellies full of / Bullets and Irish beer, their flies undone"

(*EV*, 40) beside his father, an indication of his recognition of their joint service to an abstract idea of nation and the utter senselessness of war. His father has retained the idea of "dying for King and Country" ever since he served in the war, while the contemporary teenage soldiers here have been co-opted into serving a diminished British Empire. These lads are the three Scottish teenaged British Army soldiers killed by the IRA on March 9, 1971, and are connected in the poet's mind to his father, who fought in the London-Scottish regiment during World War I.[14] Longley's recognition of their joint military service indicates his recognition of the often confusing and inhumane nature of war. Another obvious connection between these contemporary British soldiers and those from World War I is their age; he decries their common lost youth, symbolized here by the image of the "heavy guns [which] put out / The night-light in a nursery for ever" (40).

Suggesting his belief in ceremony as one of the mainstays of civilization, Longley suggests that the soldiers had been urinating, as indeed they were, when they were gunned down. Micturition is a kind of habitual ceremony, of course, and being shot while urinating and relaxing violates that ceremony just as the ceremonies of the bus conductor's home are shattered by his murderer later in the poem. The poem finally becomes itself a kind of ceremony that gathers together the dead and their material remains and buries them in an effort to give the dead the honor and dignity that so often escaped them in life.

Longley goes on to associate (not equate) the "service" rendered by his father and the British soldiers with that of the bus conductor, since he throws the "bus-conductor's uniform—" into the grave as well. This bus conductor seems to be a victim of random, not sectarian violence, but Michael Parker has identified him as "Sydney Agnew, a forty-year-old Protestant father of three, who was due to give evidence in court against an IRA-man who had hijacked and set fire to his bus."[15] We are told that

He collapsed beside his carpet-slippers
Without a murmur, shot through the head
By a shivering boy who wandered in
Before they could turn the television down
Or tidy away the supper dishes.

To the children, to a bewildered wife,
I think "Sorry Missus" was what he said.
                              (*EV,* 40–41)

While Hufstader implicitly and mistakenly conflates what he perceives as Longley's own bewilderment with that of the poet's father and
the bus conductor's wife in the poem, Longley's elegy sharply perceives a
continuation among the ostensibly legitimized violence in the theater of
World War I and the violence in the province in the late 1960s and early
1970s.[16] The brilliance of this poem lies in the way in which he outlines
three different kinds of service—his father's World War I service, the
current service of the British soldiers, and the service of the bus conductor to the community—then shows how the dehumanizing nature of violence pervades both the moments of service and the moments when
that service is over. That this violence is committed in the name of religion becomes clear from the emphasis on the "London-Scottish padre"
that "My father followed" for "fifty years" in stanza 1 and from the IRA's
assassination of the soldiers and bus conductor in stanza 2 and their neglect of Christ's compassion, symbolized by "the Sacred Heart of Jesus /
Paralysed," which Longley significantly withholds from burying with the
other bodies and objects. In this regard, Fran Brearton has argued persuasively in her discussion of the poem and its exploration of the pervasive and continuing effects of war such as shell shock that "Longley's
elegies reveal not only the short-term, tangible damage caused by violence, but also the long-term effects not immediately, or possibly ever,
readily apparent."[17] Thus, even though "Wounds" elegizes the poet's father Richard Longley, the three teenage soldiers, and the bus conductor
on a microcosmic level, on a macrocosmic level it laments the wounds in
the fabric of civilized society created by the sorts of intimate killings that
its elegized are associated with: the hand-to-hand combat Longley's father engaged in at times (see his later poem, "The Kilt," which portrays
his father "stabbing a tubby German," from *GO,* 35), the befriending of
the teenage soldiers by the IRA members and then their slaying, the personal intrusion of the "shivering boy" who shoots the bus conductor.

The Irish poet Brendan Kennelly clearly appreciated Longley's
evenhandedness here. In a letter of November 23, 1973, he wrote Long-

ley, "Wounds . . . is a stunningly good piece of work, the best poem I know written about the troubles in Belfast. The problem with most of the poetry written about your city is that, to put it bluntly, the poems are sectarian and therefore crippled. Wounds knows no frontiers and its pity is unconfined."[18] In "Wounds," Longley seems to agree with World War I poet Wilfred Owen that "the poetry is in the pity." Hufstader churlishly argues, however, that "Longley's way of looking at and expressing social violence distorts both its topic and its poetic style in an excess of obvious emotion. The quaint tones which accompany the father's death and the tabloid 'snaps' of the bus-conductor's home end by compromising the poem's attempt to find a serious political voice."[19] Nothing seems quaint about Longley's dual critique of his father's dying "for King and Country" and his lament for him. Nothing is "tabloid" about the violent shattering of the domestic peace of the bus conductor's home. Hufstader misses the poem's critique of all types of violence, which marks the emergence of Longley as a major humanitarian, a stance that achieves yet transcends any perceived "attempt to find a serious political voice."

Owen's role in developing the duty of the artist in relation to violence has been instructive for Longley in other ways as well. As I noted in the Introduction, Longley has argued that the artist in Ulster shares with artists in the midst of conflict everywhere a duty to warn the community about the implications of the violence: "As Wilfred Owen stated over fifty years ago, it is the artist's duty to warn, to be tuned in before anyone else to the implications of a situation" ("I," 8). "Wounds" can thus be read as an early warning about the Troubles, while also suggesting that citizens of Northern Ireland recognize that their situation is not unique and that the violence there is part of a universal continuum of violence that has been ongoing for many years. At the same time, the poem intensely individualizes the violence through Longley's articulation of a real scenario about his father's war experience and an imagined burial of him, the slaying of the Scottish soldiers, and the murder of the bus conductor. Longley's refusal to distance himself from the violence in the province here is itself the best rebuttal of Hufstader's charge that in this poem he "sedulously maintain[s] his own bewilderment in the ordered cadences of blank verse."[20]

The volatile situation in the province at the time led the critic Douglas Dunn to write Longley on June 15, 1972, suggesting he change the title of the collection in which "Wounds" would shortly appear: "'An Exploded View' doesn't seem a bad title: but 'exploded' does have Ulster associations which might put an emphasis on the book you might not want. . . . What about 'Casualties'; or is that too reminiscent of someone else? You are a sort of war poet now, you know, like Seamus."[21] However, Dunn's title is especially inappropriate for a volume of poetry featuring only one poem, "Wounds," directly about the Troubles; most of the poems in this volume are about nature, except for the notorious "To Derek Mahon," which I will discuss shortly. Longley obviously resisted both Dunn's title (as too derivative of Wilfred Owen) and being called a "war poet." Such a label, as is evident from considering Longley's protest against Padraic Fiacc's poetry collection on the Troubles explored below, would create a perception of a school of poetry in the province being written merely as a response to the violence. The contents of *An Exploded View* suggest that instead of drawing on the explosive issue of the Troubles, Longley was trying to explode notions of a Northern Irish poetry based solely on reactions to the violence in the province; his other poems in the volume imply that quotidian life going on elsewhere during this period was just as important as registering or commenting on the violence.

Longley's position as assistant director for literature with the Arts Council of Northern Ireland gave him authority in his (often public) pronouncements on writing in the province and allowed him to shape public and critical perception of this literature indelibly. As the Troubles exploded across the province, critical firestorms flared up occasionally among former Group members and other writers and critics attempting to define Northern Irish literature and its features. A significant early instance of the concern over public perception of Northern literature among some of its most prominent poets occurred in an epistolary exchange between Longley and Derek Mahon in late 1971. The two had been fast friends since their undergraduate days at Trinity College and had often served as sounding boards for each other's work. The quarrel was over some lines in a poem Longley had written, "To Derek Mahon," which was published in the *New Statesman* on December 3, 1971. Gavin Drummond has shown that Longley's poem was written in response to an untitled, unpublished epistolary poem of Mahon's that desires art to "bring an ordered shape to the world, even if that orderliness is untrue to formless reality."[22] Drummond argues that this poem of Mahon's portrays the speaker, presumably Mahon himself, to be "bewildered by the outbreak of violence in the North" and "appealing for help from his implied reader, Michael Longley."[23] Longley's response-poem was later published in *An Exploded View,* his second volume of poetry.

Longley closely links himself and Mahon in the poem and characterizes them as Protestant outsiders, "poetic conservatives" who were alienated from the Catholic-minority population of Northern Ireland. I quote the first two stanzas here:

> And did we come into our own
> When, minus muse and lexicon,
> We traced in August sixty-nine
> Our imaginary Peace Line
> Around the burnt-out houses of
> The Catholics we'd scarcely loved,
> Two Sisyphuses come to budge
> The sticks and stones of an old grudge,
>
> Two poetic conservatives
> In the city of guns and long knives,
> Our ears receiving then and there
> The stereophonic nightmare
> Of the Shankill and the Falls,
> Our matches struck on crumbling walls
> To light us as we moved at last
> Through the back alleys of Belfast?
>   (*CPL,* 58)

Mahon's letter to the editor a few days later succinctly stated his objections:

> A casual reader of TWO LETTERS, [a reference to the two poems now titled "Letter to Derek Mahon" and "Letter to Seamus Heaney"] by my friend Michael Longley (*New Statesman,* Dec. 3d), might be

forgiven for drawing one or two erroneous conclusions. Mr. Longley, with the best will in the world, appears to attribute to me attitudes to which I do not, in fact, subscribe. I refer to lines 6 and 9 of
"To Derek Mahon"—"The Catholics we scarcely loved" and "Two
poetic conservatives." The implications of line 6, as it stands, are
frankly untrue, not to say damaging, and the overtones of line 9
tendentious and misleading. No-one likes to see his views misrepresented, however innocently. Mr. Longley may speak for himself;
he doesn't necessarily speak for me.[24]

Longley apparently held his ground and refused to change the lines,
since the controversy was still alive later in the month. Apparently, there
had been a private exchange of letters between the two poets.

In a response to Longley during that same month, Mahon goes
into greater detail about his objections to the lines in Longley's poems:

Micko,
Let's be quite clear about the letter/poem business. The reason I
wrote the letter to NS was because I felt my feelings/attitudes had
been misrepresented in yr poem. I still think that; my attitude to the
lines in question, and to my own action, is unchanged. I'm sorry that
you've been so hurt by this: to hurt you was not, needless to say, my
intention. Also, I would be happy to see the whole thing finished
with so that we can get back to normal relations—and so, I know,
would you. The only problem is that we don't yet see eye to eye on
how the thing can be finished with. From my point of view, since I
feel (rightly or wrongly) that I've been misrepresented, I can only repeat my request that the lines in question be changed. I have no intention of inserting a note, clarification, addendum or whatever, or
having you insert one, in NIGHT-SHIFT (Macmillan, 1973), to
the effect that I don't hold with To DM. If you won't change the
lines the poem must go in as it is, without comment. But I most particularly implore you to change the lines, preferably before it appears
again in PEN or whatever. This is not a matter of censorship. Seamus, here last week, put it like this: by dedicating a poem to someone you make him in a sense co-author of the piece; you associate

him, will he nill he, with the contents of the poem, thus giving him some measure of, yes, proprietary right. It's not something I would claim in the ordinary course of events (nor would anyone); but the circumstances are exceptional. So let's change the lines, like a good man: it's the only just solution.[25]

Mahon's argument, via Heaney, that he is "co-author" of Longley's poem seems tenuous at best. More interesting is his co-opting of the Catholic Heaney in an effort to impress upon Longley what Mahon and Heaney felt should be one of the primary concerns of their friendship— inclusiveness.[26] The implication is that Mahon and Heaney thought that Longley's poem, coming as it did from a public official of the Arts Council, could misrepresent the general perception of Northern Irish literature as ecumenical and balanced. This perception stemmed at least in part from the ecumenism that Hobsbaum's Belfast Group had fostered and from the cultural goodwill developed by the two previous Arts Council Tours—*Room to Rhyme* and *The Planter and the Gael*—that had promoted cultural communication between the two dominant cultures. Mahon may also have felt that he was being trotted out as a representative of the Protestant community in Northern Ireland, a position with which he felt extreme discomfort.[27]

Additionally, Mahon's anxiety about the exceptional circumstances he alluded to is probably twofold. First, he felt that their friendship and the fact that the poem was dedicated to him, along with his perception that he was misrepresented, entitled him to request the change. Second, Mahon was implying the dangerous effect of printing such a seemingly sectarian poem in the midst of the violence endemic in the province at the time. Unfortunately, Longley only slightly changed one line, leaving the other offending lines as they were, and the poem has become one of his most anthologized.[28] This lapse certainly does not characterize Longley's feelings toward Catholics in general, as he has consistently promoted cultural, religious, and political understanding in the province through a shared regional literature.

Longley's epistolary exchange with Mahon and his epistolary statement examined below should be read in the context of his Northern Irish Protestant cultural identity, a culture that often expresses itself, as

Tom Paulin has noted, through "forms of writing that are often dismissed as ephemeral or non-canonical—familiar letters, pieces of journalism, overtured addresses, the minutes of synodical and other meetings."[29] Just as the Northern Irish Protestant writers Paulin identifies as part of this culture, such as the eighteenth-century Belfast Presbyterian and republican William Drennan and the current preacher/politician Ian Paisley, are often marked by their fiery use of rhetoric in these noncanonical forms of writing, Longley employs a similarly angry and sometimes recalcitrant tone in the following letter but for a much more ecumenical purpose than the anti-Catholic Paisley.

On December 10, 1974, Longley wrote the editor of *Hibernia* protesting Padraic Fiacc's article "Violence and the Ulster Poet," which advertised for his anthology *The Wearing of the Black,* a collection of poems from seventy-three poets concerning violence in the province. In his letter, Longley condemned the idea of poetry as a mere response to violence and the attempt by Fiacc to collect poems on this subject:

Dear Sir,

I write to protest against Padraic Fiacc's sloppily written and presumptuous article "Violence and the Ulster Poet" (Hibernia, 6.12.74). Fiacc claims that I fought him about including a poem of mine on the assassination of my "grocer and friend." This is a personal matter which Fiacc has no right to report. The grocer was not my friend: I rather liked him, that's all. The poem seemed to me to be bad, or at least inadequate, and I asked that it should not be included in Fiacc's Encyclopedia of Tormented Ulster Poets. Imagine my surprise when, as our hero admits, he re-arranged it for me. Since Fiacc can scarcely write a coherent sentence, his re-arrangement did not amount to an improvement. Fiacc then presumes to read my thoughts on the subject. . . . Fiacc ends in grand style by referring to "the Ulster poet's tragic anguish." Selfregarding nonsense like this makes me feel ashamed of the journalistic tag "Ulster poet." (I am normally just embarrassed or irritated).

I wish to dissociate myself and my poetry from Fiacc's pathetic meanderings. He buzzes around the Ulster tragedy like a dazed bluebottle around an open wound.[30]

Longley's revulsion against Fiacc's collection coheres perfectly with the philosophy he had already articulated, in his introduction to *Causeway*, about the artist's responsibility in dealing with civil discord: "[The artist] is not some sort of super-journalist commenting with unfaltering spontaneity on events immediately after they have happened" ("I," 8). Additionally, this letter marks the moment at which Longley's real reason for disavowing the term *Ulster poet* emerges: he rightly feels that a regional poetry—especially one as varied as Northern Irish poetry—must be unified by something more deep-rooted than shared civil strife.[31]

Fiacc's anthology must have especially incensed Longley, who was himself trying to argue for a very different vision of Northern Irish writing: parochial (in Kavanagh's terms), yet universal, and attuned to the political situation in the North but not in a tabloid kind of way. Richard Kirkland shares Longley's conviction about Fiacc's ill-conceived project, arguing that *The Wearing of the Black* "proposes a Northern Ireland consisting solely of dark primal forces: fear-grips, notes of sudden panic are struck, and the province darkens for no apparent (other than atavistic) reason" (*LCNI*, 65). This letter about Fiacc's tabloid poetry collection of Northern Irish poetry relating to the Troubles also signals the convergence of Longley's epistolary articulations of his vision of Northern Irish writing with his own poetic attempts to reflect on the political and martial conflict in the province.

As Longley has argued, another duty of the artist, besides warning of the too-easy linkage between violence and poetry, is "to celebrate life in all its aspects, to commemorate normal human activities. Art is itself a normal human activity. The more normal it appears in the eyes of the artist and his audience, the more potent a force it becomes" ("I," 9). I explore Longley's commemoration of normal human and animal activity in the next chapter to show the continuum he develops between poems about urban violence and poems about the natural world, but for the sake of continuity I want to continue considering other poems about the Troubles Longley has written that commemorate normal human lives lost in Belfast. In a retrospective essay, "A Tongue at Play," Longley humbly remarks, "I have written a few inadequate elegies. I offer them as wreaths. That is all."[32] Typically for a poet who is so fascinated with flowers—their profusion and their fragility—he considers his elegies

for victims of the Troubles wreaths, with the implication that verbal tex-
tures surely cannot compensate for lives lost. Yet his elegies memorialize the dead in an effective, nonmaudlin manner by precisely painting
pictures of the very ordinariness of the dead.

The sparely beautiful and appropriately named poetic sequence
"Wreaths" comprises three poems examining the sectarian murders of
ordinary people in the North: "The Civil Servant," "The Greengrocer,"
and "The Linen Workers." "Wreaths" appeared in *The Echo Gate* (1979),
the last fully new volume of poetry Longley published before *Gorse Fires*
in 1991. A sharp focus on material remnants of the deceased unifies these
three poems. "The Civil Servant" emphasizes the man's private life: "The
books he had read, the music he could play." After he is killed, "his widow
took a hammer and chisel / And removed the black keys from his piano,"
both to demonstrate her brokenness and to remove the harsh tones his
death has injected into her life (*EG*, 12).

"The Greengrocer," the poem Fiacc wanted for his anthology, employs a wealth of detail, characteristically given through Longley's favorite poetic device — the list — to memorialize this man. The poem is
flooded with images of the greenery that abounded in the greengrocer's
shop: "holly wreaths for Christmas, / Fir trees on the pavement outside" (*EG*, 12). In the second stanza, Longley inserts the greengrocer
into the traditional Christmas story, giving it a contemporary Northern
Irish emphasis:

> Astrologers or three wise men
> Who may shortly be setting out
> For a small house up the Shankill
> Or the Falls, should pause on their way
> To buy gifts at Jim Gibson's shop,
> Dates and chestnuts and tangerines.
>
> (12)

Instead of gold, frankincense, and myrrh, we have "dates and chestnuts
and tangerines." McDonald has cleverly pointed out the soothing quality
of this concluding grocery list of items: "The focus on the particular at
the end of this poem is the very opposite of frivolous; it ensures the
maintenance of Longley's characteristic *gravitas,* which is essentially the

seriousness of a complete imaginative fidelity to the immediate. The nouns are meant to soothe, though they cannot (and do not) pretend to console" (*MI*, 136). In addition to the concluding "naming" in this poem, the victim is named, whereas he remained anonymous in the previous one. Perhaps most important, Longley's recognition of a possible solution to the conflict emerges in this updated vision of the journey of the magi who visit two of the sectarian ghettos of the city. He obviously sees the birth of the only One who can truly bring peace in the midst of this tragedy as still worth celebrating.

"The Linen Workers" continues the trajectory of this sequence toward the more personal because it combines a famous massacre from the Troubles with memories of Longley's father, while also connecting to other Longley poems past and future about material remains of the dead. The poem opens with Longley's image of another material remnant, Christ's teeth:

> Christ's teeth ascended with him into heaven:
> Through a cavity in one of his molars
> The wind whistles: he is fastened for ever
> By his exposed canines to a wintry sky.
>
> (*EG*, 13)

The first stanza, seemingly from a child's point of view, works both to suggest a motif of body parts that Longley will associate with other deceased people and to set the poem in a Christian context. In stanza 2, however, a mature Longley quickly conflates Christ's teeth with his father's false teeth:

> I am blinded by the blaze of that smile
> And by the memory of my father's false teeth
> Brimming in their tumbler: they wore bubbles
> And, outside of his body, a deadly grin.
>
> (13)

We have already seen Longley write his father's World War I experience into "Wounds," a poem that also laments victims of the contemporary Troubles. This poem achieves a similar success, for his father's dentures are quickly succeeded by another set of false teeth in stanza 3:

When they massacred the ten linen workers
There fell on the road beside them spectacles,
Wallets, small change, and a set of dentures:
Blood, food particles, the bread, the wine.

(13)

This massacre took place on January 5, 1976, when a van of linen
workers was stopped by the Provisional IRA in the North.[33] The masked
men killed all of the workers except for the lone Catholic in the group,
who reluctantly stepped forward when the murderers called all Catholics to do so (he and the ten victims thought he was about to be killed
by a Protestant paramilitary unit). Longley subtly evokes the outrageous nature of their deaths by the material, seemingly trivial objects
they leave behind: money, false teeth, blood, and food particles. Somehow, in the aftermath of this tragedy, Longley is able to see the symbols
of the Eucharist—the bread and the wine—in the blood and food particles on the pair of dentures. Recalling Christ's words at the Last Supper, "This do in remembrance of me," the poem envisions a continuum
of deaths that begins with Christ's sacrifice on the cross and includes
these contemporary Protestants, thus compelling us to remember their
sacrifices.[34] In thus evoking a sacrifice valued by Protestants and Catholics alike, this stanza suggests the possible Christian basis of a potential reconciliation between members of supposedly opposed cultures in
Northern Ireland.[35]

The poem ends with Longley preparing his father's body for burial
by employing the objects left from the linen workers' massacre:

Before I can bury my father once again
I must polish the spectacles, balance them
Upon his nose, fill his pockets with money
And into his dead mouth slip the set of teeth.

(*EG,* 13)

This concluding trope of preparing a body for the underworld that
Longley undoubtedly knew from his classics studies ends the poem in a
sacramental manner. By using the belongings of the dead workers to prepare his father for the journey of death, Longley memorializes the work-

ers by bodying bits of them forth in his father. This process effects a strange sort of transubstantiation that follows from the images of the food particles and blood in the previous stanza.[36] In that stanza, Longley suggests a theological, eternal memorialization of the linen workers for the community of believers; here, he renders significant parts of them in a sacramental present preparation of his father's body for reburial. The effect is both settling and unsettling, peaceful and gruesome.[37]

The emphasis on burial and particular objects in "The Linen Workers" is part of a larger continuum across Longley's poetry, functioning both analeptically and proleptically, looking back to the earlier "Wounds," in which Longley buries the three teenage Scottish soldiers beside his father, including "his badges, his medals like rainbows, / His spinning compass" (*EV,* 40), and forward to his later Troubles and Holocaust poems (examined in the next chapter), with their focus on material remains of those slain in the Northern Irish conflict and of murdered Jews. Anyone who has been to one of the preserved European concentration camps has seen the cases of spectacles, orthopedic devices, wallets, dentures, and other possessions that Nazis stripped from Jews headed to the gas chambers, and thus we cannot help remembering those victims from the past even as we mourn these contemporary victims.

Even though the bodies of the three teenaged soldiers in "Wounds" and those of the Protestant linen workers were recovered and given proper burials, many bodies of victims during the Troubles were hidden by their killers; therefore, the closure of the repeated preparation and pending burial of Longley's father in "Wounds" and "The Linen Workers" and the then-future funerals of the teenaged soldiers, bus conductor, and linen workers offers a chance for readers and the poet himself to have the satisfactions of the ceremony inherent in an orderly funeral and feel the emotional resonance of viewing their material effects. Such satisfactions were denied, of course, to many families of victims during the Northern Irish conflict. In Longley's later poem "On Slieve Gullion," for example, he mourns that the IRA men who murdered the British agent Robert Nairac (who had infiltrated the IRA) "left / Not even an eyelash under the leaves / Or a tooth for MacCecht the cupbearer / To rinse" (*CPL,* 158). In "Love Poet," written during the same period as "On Slieve Gullion," the speaker expresses his penchant for preserving material effects of the dead, noting,

I make my peace with murderers.
I lock pubic hair from victims
In an airtight tin, mummify
Angel feathers, tobacco shreds.
                    (*CPL*, 155)[38]

More specifically, I believe "The Linen Workers" may offer a tenta-tive, retrospective consolation—fleeting as it is—not only to the fami-lies of the murdered linen workers, but also to the family members and friends of those killed on July 21, 1972 (seven years before *The Echo Gate* was published), in the notorious "Bloody Friday" bombings in Belfast, in which a series of IRA bombs in the city center killed eleven citizens, maiming them so badly that the remnants of some bodies had to be scooped up off the pavement. Nothing, of course, can replace those human beings, or the murdered Jews of the 1930s and 1940s, or even the linen workers, and the poem does not attempt that, which would be offensive. Rather, it simply observes, particularizes, humanizes, and re-members those ten brave linen workers and in the process enables read-ers to imaginatively and more specifically remember their own dead. The nagging persistence of the particular possessions in "The Linen Work-ers" of Longley's father and the murdered men and their incorporation into a poem suggest something about poetry's persistence as well—despite its fragility because of its dependence on material publication and on finding a reading and/or hearing audience, poems like "The Linen Workers" linger lovingly over the dead, reminding us that verbal preci-sion through naming assures a continuing life for the subjects of poetry and poems themselves.

"Peace" is the longest poem in *The Echo Gate,* and its length and use of the long line enable Longley to more fully develop his thinking about war and peace generally than did the shorter poems composed of quat-rains or sextains from "Wreaths," which were all focused specifically on the conflict in the province. Longley wrote "Peace" at the request of the Northern Irish Peace People in the 1970s, but its compass is much wider than the contemporary conflict. This long poem suggests that the city is a site where war flourishes to the forced rhythms of a mechanized society, whereas the country and its natural rhythms engender a harmony between man and nature. The poem begins with a postlapsarian moment when the speaker wonders, "Who was responsible for the very first arms deal—?" (*EG*, 35). However killing entered the world, whether through a marketing ploy or through hunting wild animals, "Murder got into the bloodstream as gene or virus / So that now we give birth to wars, short cuts to death" (35). This theory is Longley's version of Adam's and Eve's curse—war becomes like original sin, passed on from generation to generation, and Eve, suffering in her labor, gives birth to war and bloodshed. The aptness of "short cuts to death" is remarkable, picking up as it does the opening image in line two of "marketing the sword" (35) and coupling that image to a shortened life span in which birth is quickly supplanted by death through the "short cuts" of the sword in both the literal sense and the figurative sense of an abbreviated passageway.

The last lines of the first stanza romanticize pastoral life, however, when the speaker states flatly, "Blame the affluent society: no killings when / The cup on the dinner table was made of beechwood" (*EG*, 35). This belief of the speaker does not seem to be satirized by the poet; rather, he endorses it when the speaker blandly and foolishly claims in the opening lines of the second stanza, "I would like to have been alive in the good old days / Before the horrors of modern warfare and warcries / Stepping up my pulse rate" (35). Since the context of the entire poem is postlapsarian in the specific sense established by the first stanza, "the good old days" are rendered not just banal but also delusory.

Understandably, however, the speaker longs for a time when he could commune with nature, "worship there with bunches of early grapes, / A wreath of whiskery wheat-ears" (*EG*, 35), away from the "barricades and ghettos" of contemporary Northern Ireland, mentioned in the first stanza. He yearns for an integration into the natural rhythms of rural life and desires "peace to be my partner on the farm, / Peace personified: oxen under the curved yoke; / Compost for the vines, grapejuice turning into wine" (36). The sword of the opening stanza has been transformed into sharp domestic tools like the "Hoe and ploughshare gleaming" (36), echoing the biblical saw about turning swords into ploughshares, "while in some dark corner / Rust keeps the soldier's grisly weapons in their place" (36).

Yet it is to Longley's great credit that despite his abstracted, idealized embrace of the bucolic as a site of peace in the poem, the last two stanzas finally admit conflict of a different sort into the poem from that with which it began. The martial conflict of the opening stanzas has now been replaced with the "skirmishes, guerilla tactics" of "lovers quarreling" (*EG*, 36). The wife-beater featured in this penultimate stanza clearly has committed "A crime against nature," just as the poet believes "the man of iron" does in his possible intent to use the sword "against wild animals" in the first stanza (35). Collapsing the distinction between killing wild game and beating one's wife, however, introduces a logical and moral strain to the poem: the former is legal around the world and often provides sustenance, where the latter is illegal in democratic societies and leads to a host of ills. Additionally, comparing the husband to presumably a Nazi who would "goose-step" seems facile and forced, while the speaker who quickly and thankfully distances himself from violence against women and depicts himself as wanting the female personification of peace "To come and fondle my ears of wheat and let apples / Overflow between her breasts" (37) also objectifies women, although not in the violent manner of the husband.

This disturbing tone is modified, though, by the sheer abundance and profusion of nature and the way in which the speaker sees himself as having "ears of wheat" and his wife, perhaps, having apples spilling out from her breasts. The harvest of martial and marital discord in urban and rural settings throughout the poem is now overwhelmed by the cornucopia image of the last lines. Touching, fondling, and caressing replace cutting, shooting, and hitting. The enjambment of the last two and a half lines smoothly incorporates the profusion of wheat and apples into the measured flow of the poem and sonically suggests the poet's wish for a continuity of peace in his world. The last half line "I shall call her Peace," (*EG*, 37) implies a desire for a return to a prelapsarian moment, as the speaker is briefly rendered like Adam in Genesis, naming plants, animals, and even his mate.

"Peace" itself establishes a continuity in Longley's poetry in more ways than the one just mooted. Its formal use of longer lines seems to have confirmed his desire to employ and even expand the poetic sentence in ways that echo the expansiveness of his content in later poems. It also establishes more fully than did earlier poems the poet's reverent outlook on the natural world, a viewpoint that becomes increasingly sacramental in subsequent environmental poems. But Longley would prove himself capable of modifying, even critiquing the rural landscape as a site of peace in one of the most significant poems in his oeuvre.

After a hiatus of twelve years in which he published no full volumes of poetry, Longley released *Gorse Fires* in 1991, featuring a long poem entitled "The Butchers," which ostensibly concerns Odysseus's return home after his journey but also obliquely critiques the gruesome murders of Catholics by the Shankill Butchers, as they came to be called, in Belfast during the mid-1970s, and sectarian violence generally. Most of the poem follows the storyline of this episode from book 22 of the *Odyssey*; its conclusion, however, is from the beginning of book 24, where Hermes leads the ghosts of the suitors into the underworld. This is a gory episode, and Longley's poem pulls no punches; if anything, his version is bloodier than Homer's:

> When he had made sure there were no survivors in his house
> And that all the suitors were dead, heaped in blood and dust
> Like fish that fishermen with fine-meshed nets have hauled
> Up gasping for salt water, evaporating in the sunshine,
> Odysseus, spattered with muck and like a lion dripping blood
> From his chest and cheeks after devouring a farmer's bullock,
> Ordered the disloyal housemaids to sponge down the armchairs
> And tables, while Telemachos, the oxherd and the swineherd
> Scraped the floor with shovels, and then between the portico
> And the roundhouse stretched a hawser and hanged the women
> So none touched the ground with her toes, like long-winged
>   thrushes
> Or doves trapped in a mist-net across the thicket where they
>   roost,
> Their heads bobbing in a row, their feet twitching but not for
>   long,
> And when they had dragged Melanthios's corpse into the
>   haggard
> And cut off his nose and ears and cock and balls, a dog's dinner,
> Odysseus, seeing the need for whitewash and disinfectant,
> Fumigated the house and the outhouses, so that Hermes

Like a clergyman might wave the supernatural baton
With which he resurrects or hypnotises those he chooses,
And waken and round up the suitors' souls, and the housemaids',
Like bats gibbering in the nooks of their mysterious cave
When out of the clusters that dangle from the rocky ceiling
One of them drops and squeaks, so their souls were bat-
    squeaks
As they flittered after Hermes, their deliverer, who led them
Along the clammy sheughs, then past the oceanic streams
And the white rock, the sun's gatepost in that dreamy region,
Until they came to a bog-meadow full of bog-asphodels
Where the residents are ghosts or images of the dead.

(*GF,* 51)

Part of the poem's continuous power derives from Longley's seam-less connection of the events toward the end of book 22 and those from the beginning of book 24 in *The Odyssey,* as Peter McDonald notes: "In an extraordinary feat of syntactical suppleness, Longley joins his two source passages together without a moment's sign of the surgery: the 28 long lines of the poem as a whole constitute one complete sentence, and the slaughter is made literally of a piece with its supernatural se-quel."[39] Longley's penchant for the long poetic sentence may well orig-inate in his great fondness for the poetry of Louis MacNeice, a favorite exemplar. Terence Brown has pointed out that "MacNeice, like [Long-ley] himself, is a master of the sentence, allowing it to weave down lines of verse to compose a poem that possesses a curious, block-like form on the page and in the mind."[40]

In the sweeping sentence that comprises "The Butchers," Longley also achieves something of the quality of epic style that according to C. S. Lewis marks Milton's epic style in *Paradise Lost.* Lewis points out Milton's "unremitting *manipulation* of his readers—how he sweeps us along as though we were attending an actual recitation and nowhere al-lows us to settle down and luxuriate on any one line." Lewis also argues that "Milton avoids [epic] discontinuity by an avoidance of what gram-marians call the simple sentence."[41] Longley himself has approvingly re-marked upon Milton's lengthy poetic lines in *Paradise Lost.* He argues strongly against the "staccato" quality of contemporary verse and for the variety of possibilities in longer lines, invoking the opening sentence of *Paradise Lost* as an example: "So much contemporary verse lacks propulsion. It's a tedium of staccato stutters—oblivious to the complexities that can be created by angled clauses. In poetry a sentence can be made to do far more than in prose. A long sentence need not be a mere container. Rather, its facets and angles imply everything that cannot be contained. . . . The resplendent opening sentence of *Paradise Lost* should be inhaled regularly as an antidote to much contemporary practice."[42] The connection in Longley's mind between form and content could not be clearer. In "The Butchers," as we will see, he uses the long sentence as a formal strategy to incorporate a series of correspondences and "complexities" between the atrocities at the conclusion of *The Odyssey* and those in 1970s Northern Ireland, suggesting in the sweeping and continuous qualities of the line the connection between vengeful violence in the past and present.

Although McDonald, one of Longley's most discerning critics, argues that Longley's title "courts (but does not exactly lay claim to) parallels with the shorthand of Northern Irish atrocities," the changes Longley makes to this crucial section of the epic suggest otherwise.[43] For example, while Homer portrays Odysseus and his men only pulling Melanthios's genitals off and then cutting off his nose and ears, Longley significantly has "his nose and ears and cock and balls" *all cut off* in line 15 (*GF,* 51). And where Homer has Odysseus fumigate the house to purify it from both the past presence of the suitors and their amorous desires for Penelope and to cleanse the present gore from their bodies on the walls and floors, Longley has Odysseus fumigate the house because he sees "the need for whitewash and disinfectant" in line 16 (51). Finally, and most crucially, Longley's poem argues in lines 16 through 18 that only when this fumigation is performed can "Hermes / Like a clergyman . . . wave the supernatural baton / With which he resurrects or hypnotises those he chooses" (51). Why are Melanthios's body parts *only* cut off; why are they not both torn off and cut? Why does Longley use the modern word *whitewash,* with its simultaneously soothing and negative connotations? And why is Hermes compared to a clergyman using a baton? Finally, why end the poem with images of a Hibernicized meadow and Hibernicized flowers if it is mainly about events from *The Odyssey*?[44] The poem's title and the accretive power of these images suggest a specific parallel with a particularly disturbing period in the province's recent history. Read in the context of Longley's ongoing concern with ethical responses to violence generally, his specific aesthetic choices in translating these two sections of the poem can be properly understood.

This array of images he inserted into the poem would have had special resonance for residents of Northern Ireland in the early 1990s. The gruesome and lingering image of the dismembering of Melanthios's body accomplished *solely through cutting*, not cutting and tearing, coupled with the poem's title, specifically suggests Longley's comparison of this action with the violent killings committed by the Shankill Butchers in the mid-1970s. These killers were members of the Protestant paramilitary group the Ulster Volunteer Force, led by Lenny Murphy. Starting in late 1975, eleven members of the Shankill Butchers killed nineteen people, mostly Catholics, by stabbing them with butcher knives; they then dismembered them and abandoned the bodies. Even after Murphy was arrested in March 1976 and sent to the Maze prison, which housed paramilitary prisoners in the province until recently, he continued to direct his gang from inside until the remaining "Butchers" were arrested the next year. The leaders of the UVF at the time of the Shankill Road killings in the 1970s disturbingly allowed the killings to continue although they probably could have stopped them.[45] These crimes outraged the citizens of Northern Ireland and signified an all-time low point in the Troubles.

Longley has admitted in an interview the strong connection he had in his mind when writing the poem between the Shankill murders and the awful murders and dismemberings committed toward the end of *The Odyssey*:

> We were in Mayo, in this very remote cottage which we go to in Co. Mayo, which is sandy and remote. And the little smallholdings, and outhouses . . . it seemed to me that Odysseus would feel perfectly at home there—if slightly cold and damp—in that sort of an Irish scene—the smallholdings, the outhouses and the whitewashed walls. . . . And that was my feeling—and at that time one of the things people were talking about was the Shankill Road murders. There'd been some dreadful killings and torturings in outhouses, very remote places like that.[46]

The rural setting of some of the murders seems to have struck a nerve with Longley, who may have thought he had escaped the violence in the province by periodically visiting a cottage in rural County Mayo. A close reading of his particular translation of these lines demonstrates again his penchant for critiquing violence in multitemporal contexts.

The most interesting way in which he carries out this critique is through obliquely linking the Shankill Butchers, the Royal Ulster Constabulary, and the Reverend Ian Paisley in lines 17 through 19, when he writes that "Hermes / Like a clergyman might wave the supernatural baton / With which he resurrects or hypnotises those he chooses" (*GF*, 51). If Odysseus and his men are taken to be analogues for the Shankill Butchers, then Hermes, who is significantly described as being "Like a clergyman," could easily be the outrageous Paisley, who has allegedly urged violence against Catholics from his pulpit but has never himself been linked to any crimes. Paisley's alleged exhortations may have been taken literally by a number of Protestant paramilitary members in the province; thus the suggestion that Hermes is directing the subsequent action, much as a conductor does a musical score by using his baton, is certainly plausible. The beginning of the clause that follows the fumigation of "the house and outhouses"—"so that Hermes" might lead the suitors away—suggests that the whitewashing undertaken is a sanitization process by which Hermes keeps his own hands clean, much as Paisley has managed to keep his own hands clean during the decades of the conflict, despite his rhetoric against Catholics. Strengthening the connotation that Hermes signifies Paisley, the god is portrayed as using his baton "With which he resurrects or hypnotises those he chooses." Paisley's political power carries similar implications: he can make anyone's political career and also mesmerizes his followers with his fiery religious oratory. Hermes' "baton" also evokes images of the Royal Ulster Constabulary, now the Police Service of Northern Ireland, whose officers still carry batons. If Longley had wanted to suggest a more traditional image of Hermes, he probably would have chosen *wand*, with its more enchanting or comforting connotations.[47]

Finally, Longley cleverly evokes western Ireland with its majority-Catholic population in the concluding image of the "bog-meadow full of bog-asphodels." Because the suitors are led to this area, this image heightens the analogue with the Catholics murdered by the Shankill

Butchers, some of whose bodies were left in remote rural areas. Thus Longley evinces his clear revulsion toward the murders both in *The Odyssey* and in 1970s Northern Ireland, despite the poem's seemingly peaceful pastoral setting in its conclusion. Both the ghosts of the suitors, in the concluding lines of the poem, and the memories of those Catholics killed by the Shankill Butchers linger on in the minds of their friends and relatives, troubling reminders of the worst kind of atrocities.

While his distancing of himself from fellow Protestants who murdered purely for sectarian reasons reflects his general humanitarian views and his continued sympathy for members of the nationalist community, Longley is implicitly arguing as well that murder for vengeance is always wrong. This point too has multiple implications. Just as Odysseus's righteous anger over the suitors' pursuit of Penelope became immoral when he and his men slaughtered the suitors, so, Longley suggests, did the righteous anger of Northern Irish Protestants become immoral when members of their own community began killing Catholics on and around the Shankill Road in Belfast in the 1970s as a response to an upsurge of IRA violence in the province. Both the Protestants who did not speak out against the murders and the murderers themselves are condemned since all are ultimately culpable.

But despite all the links that the poem develops with the Shankill Butchers, Longley's point about vengeance applies to republicans as well. It is possible to extrapolate from this poem and read it as a condemnation of the sort of nationalist violence represented by the IRA, whose members reinvigorated the dormant movement in the late 1960s and early 1970s in response to Protestant loyalist attacks on fellow Catholic civil rights demonstrators, particularly in Derry. Longley has lamented the way in which the civil rights movement was quickly taken over by the IRA and its propagandists, recalling, for example, "in the late 60s joining a civil rights demonstration in Belfast, and then leaving it in despair when the crowd started to use the Nazi salute and shout at the police 'SS-RUC! SS-RUC!'"[48] Thus the poem's condemnation of not just murder but specifically murder for the purpose of vengeance has several valid applications derived from recognizing in the details of its original setting its connections with a contemporary situation in Northern Ireland.[49]

In 1995, Longley published *The Ghost Orchid,* a volume of poetry with perhaps his most famous poem about the Troubles, the sonnet "Ceasefire." This poem, originally published in the *Irish Times,* borrows its narrative frame from the incident, in the midst of the Trojan War, when the Greek warrior Achilles and the Trojan king Priam mourn together, but its title and date of composition (shortly before the 1994 IRA cease-fire) suggest the path to eventual reconciliation for those on both sides of the conflict in Northern Ireland. I quote it in full here:

> I
> Put in mind of his own father and moved to tears
> Achilles took him by the hand and pushed the old king
> Gently away, but Priam curled up at his feet and
> Wept with him until their sadness filled the building.
>
> II
> Taking Hector's corpse into his own hands Achilles
> Made sure it was washed and, for the old king's sake,
> Laid out in uniform, ready for Priam to carry
> Wrapped like a present home to Troy at daybreak.
>
> III
> When they had eaten together, it pleased them both
> To stare at each other's beauty as lovers might,
> Achilles built like a god, Priam good-looking still
> And full of conversation, who earlier had sighed:
>
> IV
> "I get down on my knees and do what must be done
> And kiss Achilles' hand, the killer of my son."
>
> (*GO*, 39)

This is a companion poem to "The Butchers": both poems are set against the backdrop of an ancient conflict but comment incisively on two significant moments in the Troubles through their titles and their artful recapturing of violence and peace, respectively. If "The Butchers" represents one of the most horrific moments of the Troubles, then "Ceasefire" represents one of the most difficult, yet potentially unifying moments—the declaration of a cessation of military activity by the IRA in 1994.

In his interview with Sarah Broom, Longley discussed how he hoped the poem would make a contribution, however slight, to the IRA cease-fire that was rumored at the time of the poem's composition:

> When I was writing it, it was at the time when there were rumours of an IRA ceasefire, and I wrote it partly because I do have some sense of the magic of poetry in the world—hoping that it would make some tiny, tiny, miniscule, unimportant contribution to the drift towards a ceasefire. And I sent it to *The Irish Times* and hoped that they would print it, in the hope that if they did print it somebody might read it and it might change the mind of one ditherer on the IRA Council. And by coincidence the IRA did declare a ceasefire—I think it was a Thursday, and then on the Saturday the poem appeared, which was a coincidence. The coincidence struck people, and the poem . . . had some kind of public life in as much as priests and politicians picked it up. I found that a refreshment. I was asked to read it when I went here and there, and what I should have said when I read the poem—but I didn't, you see, because I didn't want to put a jinx on the peace process—I should have said, of course, this is only a twelve-day ceasefire and the Trojan war resumes. And Achilles himself gets killed.[50]

By its publication two days after the IRA cease-fire, the poem seems to violate Longley's own rule that the poet shouldn't be "a super-journalist commenting with unfaltering spontaneity on events immediately after they have happened" ("I," 8). As he points out, however, he wrote the poem as an attempt to actually influence the cease-fire, an attempt that conforms more to his theory that the poet should, in Owen's words, warn about the implications of an event. Longley's political prescience lies not so much in anticipating the cease-fire, which was in the air anyway, as in realizing that "cease-fire," with its implications of a possible resumption of violence, was more appropriate to the situation than a poem about the final end of an armed struggle. After all, the IRA had declared lengthy cease-fires before and often had declared short ones around Christmas. Longley obviously did not want to get his or his readers' hopes up. At the same time, the poem suggests that this was a moment rich with potential for a future permanent end to the past violence between the Greeks and the Trojans and to the present violence among the IRA, the Protestant paramilitaries, and the British Army.

The opening phrase of the first line of the poem suggests the possibility that generations of violence can be stopped by the wrenching process of ceremonial forgiveness. Longley's focus on the ritual undertaken by this unrelated, yet linked father and son suggests his belief that ceremony deflates hatred and violence, a position that accords with Yeats's similar belief in "A Prayer for My Daughter." Yeats wishes that his daughter's "bridegroom" will "bring her to a house / Where all's accustomed, ceremonious" and asks rhetorically, "How but in custom and in ceremony / Are innocence and beauty born?"[51] Although Yeats may have been wishing a sort of naive innocence for his daughter in that poem, Longley clearly wishes a tough-minded innocence for Achilles and Priam, a state in which the disturbing particular violence of the immediate past can be recognized, forgiven, and finally rejected, but not forgotten.

Longley has explicitly stated his belief in Yeatsian ceremony and decorum, saying that he feels "form in poetry is a kind of decorum" and that peace is "the absence of war," and further explaining that "the opposite of war is custom, customs, and civilization. Civilization is custom and manners and ceremony, the things that Yeats says in 'A Prayer for My Daughter.'"[52] The ceremonial content of "Ceasefire" is heightened by Longley's use of the Shakespearean sonnet form. The first three quatrains show the brokenness of both Achilles and Priam in their departure from this sonnet's normal rhyme scheme, rhyming *abcb defe ghih* instead of *abab cdcd efef.* Yet Longley preserves the typical concluding couplet of the Shakespearean sonnet, and its retention establishes a sonic harmony through its masculine end rhymes that echo the pleasing content of these lines.

Sarah Broom has thoughtfully criticized the poem for its too-rigid adherence to the sonnet form, however, arguing that "the divisions seem unnecessary and clumsy in such a short poem, only succeeding in breaking up the poem's flow. They reflect, in fact, a resistance to narrative, a need to break down the flow of events into static moments. . . . The qualities of order, balance and, most especially, timelessness are not the most appropriate descriptors of a political process which must be dynamic, must model itself on narrative rather than portraiture; a process that must take place in and through the chaos and turbulence of ordinary life and daily conflicts."[53] But the formal dynamism of "Ceasefire," in its rejection in each quatrain of the consoling typical fixed rhymes of the traditional Shakespearean sonnet, goes some way toward obviating Broom's concern that the sonnet's formal divisions are not appropriate to a peace process predicated on fluidity.

Ritualized mourning unites the two warriors, as Achilles is significantly "Put in mind of his own father" upon seeing Priam's utter despair at his son Hector's death. The two men, one a displaced father, the other the battle-hardened son of another father, end up weeping together at the end of this stanza, lamenting Hector and presumably all the men who have died in the Trojan War. Their joint weeping seems to lead them to an honesty that was not present between them previously, for in the next stanza Achilles' presentation to Priam of Hector's cleansed body, "wrapped like a gift" and dressed in his uniform, suggests a straightforwardness in their new relationship to each other. This new rapport between the two leaders of their respective countries signifies just how much has changed in their formerly suspicious attitudes toward the other; this gift engenders trust, whereas the Greeks' earlier deceptive gift of the Trojan horse created mutual distrust. In stanza 3, the two men break bread together and admire each other's rugged good looks.

Despite the sonic neatness of the concluding couplet that constitutes stanza 4, Priam's words urge forgiveness of a most unqualified sort: "I get down on my knees and do what must be done / And kiss Achilles' hand, the killer of my son." That "must" has three possible meanings. First, Priam may be expressing the martial and societal obligation of the term, in that he is expected as a representative of the defeated Trojan army to kiss Achilles' hand. At the same time, it could be argued that the old king feels he must go through this process for himself—to avoid being destroyed with anger and hatred toward Achilles. Finally, Priam could be humbling himself out of societal and martial duty but in the process could experience a change of heart such that he really could forgive Achilles. Whatever the particular intended meaning of the gesture, the point seems to be that private verbal declarations of forgiveness must be accompanied by something like a public and honest announcement of the change of heart, while fully acknowledging the extent of the sin committed against the forgiver.

The poem's public life that it acquired after its publication in the *Irish Times* suggests that its specific image of forgiveness resonated for a number of individuals in the province. Susan McKay notes that it "informed difficult debates about reconciliation, the disappeared, and prisoner releases."[54] The American senator Edward Kennedy cited the concluding couplet of "Ceasefire" in his 1998 Tip O'Neill Memorial Lecture in Derry and then suggested that people in the province must heed Priam's words: "The two communities in Northern Ireland must reach out and do what must be done—and join hands across centuries and chasms of killing and pain."[55] Longley has since read the poem at a number of public occasions, two of which are worth noting here for their role in promoting reconciliation in the province.

The first of these was the invited reading of it he gave at the opening of the Mediation Northern Ireland Centre in Belfast. The presence of the Dalai Lama at this opening gave it an international flavor and signaled how well known the peace movement in the North is worldwide. One attendee at Longley's reading, Pauline Peters from Belfast, remarked that "it was a sobering but extremely moving moment as he concluded—"I get down on my knees and do what must be done / and kiss Achilles [sic] hand, the killer of my son."[56]

The second occasion when Longley read "Ceasefire" that I would like to discuss came at the daylong conference entitled "Digging Deeper: Sharing Our Past, Sharing Our Future," sponsored by the Heritage Lottery Fund and held at the Odyssey Pavilion in Belfast on November 15, 2007. On its Web site link about the conference, the Fund notes that it is working to "ensure that the stories from our past are told in a way that others can access, understand and learn from them. It is a process that allows many voices, a process that, on the one hand, acknowledges the differences in our identities, but on the other hand, moves to establish that there are more ways we are alike."[57] Longley's videotaped presentation, one of his first public acts as the new Ireland Professor of Poetry Chair, concluded with a reading of "Ceasefire" but is notable also for what he said in remarks leading up to the reading of the sonnet. He pointed out that the best poetry from Northern Ireland had been essentially two-minded and thus was "about not ignoring the dark present and at the same time imagining different futures." Such poems had been faithful to "our multifarious literary traditions" that offered "profound ways" to understand the cultural, religious, and political complications of Northern Ireland.[58]

This poem and Longley's other poems about the conflict in Northern Ireland suggest that the hard work of peacemaking must be conducted by individual victims and their attackers, literally or figuratively kneeling. Just as important, "Ceasefire" implies imaginative literature's ability to open the "cultural corridor" between nationalists and unionists about which the critic Edna Longley has written so perceptively. As she has argued, literature can provide a space in which ecumenism on the individual and societal levels can flourish: "The literature produced by Ulster people suggests that, instead of brooding on Celtic and Orange dawns, its inhabitants might accept this province-in-two-contexts as a cultural corridor. Unionists want to block the corridor at one end, republicans at the other. Culture, like common sense, insists it can't be done. Ulster Irishness and Ulster Britishness are bound to each other and to Britain and Ireland."[59] Edna Longley's contention speculates how Northern Irish literature might transcend traditional political boundaries—while simultaneously recognizing them—and create a corridor of communication between the most intransigent factions of the province. This process would be a crucial step toward reconciliation.

Michael Longley has had a continuing interest in promoting such cultural understanding through his poetry and through his work with the Arts Council of Northern Ireland. He has often drawn on contemporary theological theories about reconciliation that have their origin in work done by the late Hannah Arendt. In her book *The Human Condition: A Study of the Central Questions Facing Modern Man* (1959), Arendt argues that there is a political importance to two religious traits—the capacity to forgive and the capacity to make promises—both of which have a special resonance for the modern world:

> The possible redemption from the predicament of irreversibility—
> of being unable to undo what one has done though one did not, and

could not, have known what he was doing — is the faculty of forgiving. The remedy for unpredictability, for the chaotic uncertainty of the future, is contained in the faculty to make and keep promises. The two faculties belong together in so far as one of them, forgiving, serves to undo the deeds of the past, whose "sins" hang like Damocles' sword over every new generation; and the other, binding oneself through promises, serves to set up in the ocean of uncertainty, which the future is by definition, islands of security without which not even continuity, let alone durability of any kind, would be possible in relationships.[60]

Arendt's theory, applied to the ongoing conversation on forgiveness in Northern Ireland, suggests that forgiveness can release both the sinner and the sinned against from the pernicious binding power of past crimes and their effect, while promise making might effect a new province controlled, not by security forces, but by a secure sense of relationships based on trust. Arendt's articulation of the "islands of security" that would result from this process recalls Longley's theory of stepping-stones that he has argued are the artist's duty to establish in troubled societies ("I," 9). At the same time, her sense that forgiveness can actually "undo the deeds of the past" is ill founded and does victims of political violence anywhere a disservice.

Donald Shriver's theory of reconciliation has also specifically influenced Longley's thinking on forgiveness and reconciliation. Shriver has extended Arendt's theory of reconciliation and imbued it with Christian theology. As he argues in his book *An Ethic for Enemies,* political forgiveness begins with a collective memory "suffused with moral judgment." He cannot subscribe to the maxim "Forgive and forget," arguing instead that true forgiveness is possible only if we remember the crime committed. Since forgiveness on any level necessitates a forgiveness of a specific injury, it is important to recall the injury to effect the full, efficacious power of this process. Shriver also believes that forgiveness can still involve punishment for the perpetrators but that Christians must reject vengeance if they seek legal justice. Additionally, he argues that Christians must develop an empathy for the enemy's humanity as a step toward creating a future, workable, ecumenical community.[61] It is important to point out the distinction between forgiveness and reconciliation: "Forgiveness begins the process of which reconciliation is the end; reconciliation must combine repentance and justice with forgiveness."[62]

Longley's "Ceasefire" thus articulates a heart-rending, complex process of Christian forgiveness in which the pagan Priam swallows his urge for vengeance and kisses the hand of his son's killer as a step toward future reconciliation. An actual example of the process Longley writes so eloquently about in his poem was manifested several years earlier in Gordon Wilson's public forgiveness of the IRA after his daughter Maire died from wounds received in the IRA's bombing of Enniskillen on Remembrance Day in 1987. Wilson conducted two interviews with the BBC in the wake of the bombing and his daughter's death. In the first one, he said unequivocally, "My wife Joan and I do not bear any grudges. We don't feel any ill-will to those who were responsible for this. We see it as God's plan, although we do not understand it. I shall pray for those who did it. May God forgive them."[63] Despite their confusion and shock, the Wilsons managed to forgive the killers while not forgetting their crime. The appropriateness of this process of forgiving while not forgetting this Remembrance Day bombing is profound.

Longley's poems dealing with the Troubles accord with the outlook he developed while working on the Arts Council of Northern Ireland and later in the Cultural Traditions Group. They are crucial to understanding how literature and culture have been effective, nondidactic tools for cultural communication in Northern Ireland. As he notes in the conclusion to his autobiography:

> In Ulster, cultural apartheid is sustained to their mutual impoverishment by both communities. W. R. Rodgers referred to the "creative wave of self-consciousness" which can result from a confluence of cultures. In Ulster this confluence pools historical contributions from the Irish, the Scots, the English and the Anglo-Irish. Reconciliation does not mean all the colors of the spectrum running so wetly together that they blur into muddy uniformity. Nor does it mean denying political differences. . . . The Cultural Traditions approach involves a mixture of affirmation, self-interrogation and mutual curiosity. To bring to light all that has been repressed can be a painful

process; but, to quote the American theologian Don Shriver: "The cure and the remembrance are co-terminous." (*TS, 75–76*)

Longley's image of a spectrum here suggests the efforts of this group to prismatically include the different traditions in the province, affirm each individually, and stress affinities and differences among them. His recognition and incorporation of Shriver's thinking into his approach toward cultural education suggests the real potential for gradual reconciliation—not token, empty tolerance—effected through the coalescence of imaginative literature and Christian forgiveness.[64]

Longley has more fully articulated his convictions about forgiveness in his essay "Memory and Acknowledgement," originally given as a talk to a symposium entitled "Reconciliation and Community: The Future of Peace in Northern Ireland," at the University of Ulster in June 1995. Longley's lecture ranges widely over Buchenwald, the harsh treatment given to returning Irish veterans of World War I, Catholic expulsions from shipyards and streets in Belfast, and Protestant expulsions from West Cork. He recalls reading elegies for victims of the Troubles at the seventy-fifth anniversary of the Easter Rising in 1991, noting that "coming from Belfast, I felt Irish sometimes and sometimes I felt British. I sensed that the large crowd took little or no exception to what I was saying. Indeed, they seemed quite sympathetic to what amounted to my declaration of dual allegiance."[65] As he goes on to point out, he feels even more justified in his dual allegiance to both Britain and Ireland in the wake of (then Irish Taoiseach) John Bruton's acknowledgment of Ireland's debt to Britain and the other Allies, including the thousands of Irishmen who fought with Britain to defeat fascism. This acknowledgment is crucial for understanding the true story of Ireland's history, Longley implies. History must be a full record of the events, not a monolithic nationalistic narrative that privileges the story of an emergent nation above all else.

Longley's final story in this lecture deals with a service he attended earlier that year in Tullamore, a small town in the Irish Midlands, for victims of the Troubles. He recalls seeing a procession of locals carrying a number of placards down the aisle of the church where the event was being held. A woman from Dungannon had written out on these placards the names of every victim in the Troubles. Greatly moved by this procession, Longley extrapolates an argument about forgiveness that coheres with his reading of Shriver's theory cited above:

> The long list of names should become a litany—a litany of the dead. The word itself—"litany"—suggests three things: enumeration, repetition, penitence. Concepts such as "a clean slate" or "drawing a line" are offensive. If we are not ever to know who bombed Enniskillen and Birmingham, Dublin and Monaghan, we can at least go on asking "Where are all the missing bodies of the last twenty-five years? Where have they been buried?" In the ghastly paramilitary argot these are the "bog jobs." Amnesty does not mean amnesia.
>
> We Irish are good at claiming a monopoly on human suffering. We are good at resurrecting and distorting the past in order to evade the present. In Ireland we must break the mythic cycles and resist unexamined, ritualistic forms of commemoration. If we don't, it will all happen again.[66]

These references have particular resonance for the families of the victims in Northern Ireland, given the IRA's current refusal to tell where it buried many of its victims and given the amnesty granted to almost all paramilitary prisoners according to the terms of the Good Friday Agreement three years after this talk.

It is particularly ecumenical of the Protestant Longley to articulate his theory of forgiveness through discussing the concept of "litany," a term usually associated with the rituals of Catholicism, such as reciting the rosary. Longley's litany, however, resists the static, perfunctory quality that any litany can easily acquire; instead his theory of litany moves progressively forward through an enumeration of sins committed, a repetition or dwelling on these in realizing their full significance, then penitence for the sins. This kind of litany, taken as both a symbol of the process of forgiveness in the province and an actual device enabling forgiveness, rejects "amnesia" and invites "amnesty" to be given. Longley's advice to his audience to resist unexamined ritualized forms of commemoration is especially important in effecting the long process of true reconciliation and in rejecting static rituals such as paramilitary funerals as unhealthy repetitions, incapable of breaking out of preconceived notions of identity.

In his thoughtful and comprehensive book *Making Peace with the Past? Memory, Trauma, and the Irish Troubles,* Graham Dawson distinguishes between two types of remembering of atrocities from the Troubles, defensive and reparative remembering, and he privileges reparative remembering, the latter of which "involves opening emotionally to the disavowed past, connecting and integrating traumatic histories, and engaging with the memory world of the other."[67] The litany that Longley recommends is a type of reparative remembering because it lingers on the past—unlike defensive remembering, which disavows the past—and enables connections between various instances of traumatic histories to be established. Two highly successful print versions commemorating the dead of the Troubles have now been published and bear out Longley's conviction that reparative remembering is worth undergoing: the simpler and shorter *Bear in Mind These Dead* (1994) and the voluminous *Lost Lives: The Stories of the Men, Women, and Children Who Died through the Northern Ireland Troubles* (2005). At the same time, as Dawson notes, some relatives have been upset by these two books: "Protests have been made about these publications by those who do not wish (and did not sanction) the loss of their loved one to be linked or equated with the deaths of their enemies; or who objected to the greater weight of detail provided about certain cases in comparison to the meagerness of others; or who were upset at mistakes, or the repetition of unsubstantiated rumors or of the claims (of membership of a paramilitary organization, for example) originally used to justify a killing."[68] Clearly, even publication of all these deaths has proven controversial, but the conversations engendered by such controversy seem essential to the ongoing process of reconciliation.

While Longley is not an orthodox Christian, his search for patterns and paradigms for forgiveness and renewal sometimes embraces essentially Christian images that prove enabling for his articulation of his theory of reconciliation. For example, toward the end of his interview with Sarah Broom, in response to the question "Do you believe in God or any kind of spirituality?" Longley responded with a lengthy story about his response to the recent death of a dear friend. He spoke of a trip with his wife, Edna, to World War I battlefields and how that made him feel reverent, then of a visit to Sweden on that same trip. At the Lutheran church in Lund, a communion service was going on when the Longleys arrived. While Edna refused to take part, he did:

> I went up and took the sacraments, for the first time in about 35 years. And that was because of the First World War, and it was because a dear friend of mine had just died—she died of terrible bowel cancer. And another friend of mine who's a Methodist minister had stayed up with her for hours on end. She was a non-believer, but he was telling her how marvelous she was, how good a schoolteacher she was, how much she was appreciated, and he was reciting this over and over again. I heard from her husband that my friend was on his knees, for hours and hours on end. And that seemed to me Christ-like, and made me think that Christ was just the most perfect man—most perfect human—who's ever lived. . . . And he suggested that we should do this, you know, the bread and the wine. And since it was his suggestion it's worth doing.[69]

Longley's approval of his friend's use of litany, coupled with his recognition of the power of the Lord's Supper, is perfectly in keeping both with his theory of political and personal forgiveness and with his continued emphasis on the quotidian and concrete in his poetry. Images of bread and wine are sprinkled throughout his poetry, from "The Linen Workers" in *The Echo Gate* ("Blood, food particles, the bread, the wine," 13) to his free translation from Ovid, "Baucis and Philemon," in *The Ghost Orchid*. These concrete elements comfort our bodies and prepare our hearts and souls for his transcendent vision of peace and forgiveness.

At the same time, Longley's recognition of the healing, unifying force of the Eucharist suggests his own unified view of reality and mysticism and helps us understand the commingling of quotidian and spiritual qualities in his own poetry. Gregory Post and Charles Turner point out the philosophical application and the theological significance of the Christian elements in their study of the Eucharist in literature and scripture. Post and Turner note that Eastern Orthodoxy's view of this sacrament bridges the seemingly opposed views of the Eucharist taken by

Catholics and Protestants. Orthodoxy "sees the miracle of the Eucharist not so much as a change per se but as the actualization in bread and wine of that which is indeed true."[70] They cite Orthodox spokesman Alexander Schmemann's definition of the Eucharist as "an entrance into a fourth dimension which allows us to see the ultimate reality of life. It is not an escape from the world, rather it is the arrival at a vantage point from which we can see more deeply into the reality of the world."[71] Longley certainly seems to have broken through into this fourth dimension in poems such as "The Linen Workers." Dwelling on the significance of the Eucharist has enlarged his imagination to value truth as the commingling of the material and the spiritual.

His powerful poetic imagination thus has remained attuned to the material conditions of life in Northern Ireland and the Republic and registers the way in which the spiritual world influences and infuses this material world with moments of transcendence. In the next chapter, we will see how his detailed poetic observations of the pastoral world of Counties Mayo and Clare and beyond attain a different sort of sacramental quality from the more traditional Christian connotation that pervades poems like "The Linen Workers." This sacramental view of nature has in turn led to a newly enlarged conception of our planet in his Holocaust poems and poems about Japan, one that finally views the world as an interconnected region of fragile human beings, animals, and plants. Such a view is a necessary precondition for peace on a provincewide or indeed global level.

CHAPTER FOUR

Fragility and Ceremony

LONGLEY'S PASTORALS, HOLOCAUST ELEGIES,

AND ASIAN MINIATURES

As chapters 2 and 3 showed, Longley has often evinced a penchant for being "in two minds" or drawing upon multiple aspects of his identity. His healthy two-mindedness manifests itself in his poetic settings: while some poems are set in urban Belfast, even more of them focus upon the rural landscapes of Counties Clare and Mayo in Ireland. His claim on both landscapes is manifested in his biography. In a 1995 interview, Longley explained the rural attractions of his suburban childhood:

> [I was born] in a suburb. The Balmoral/Malone district of darkest South Belfast. 1930s ribbon development, but plenty of fields around the houses—playing fields, a field where a riding school trotted horses, a golf course, the remnants of ancient hedges, crab-apple trees like huge cradles, enough space in which to create your own wilderness. And a couple of miles away there was Barnett's Park, which sloped down to the Lagan and the towpath—and, a bit further west, the Minnowburn with its lanky, elegant beech trees; and then up a hilly road to the Giant's Ring, a dolmen set perfectly in a vast, circular grassy arena. I learned to love the countryside in South Belfast.[1]

Longley's immersion in this slice of countryside south of Belfast ineluctably led him to appreciate the particular beauties of nature, an interest that was later more fully manifested in his poems set in western Ireland. As he has recalled, "My English parents introduced me to the western seaboard of Ireland when I was twelve. That changed my life. They too loved Donegal and Connemara."[2] In his embrace of both urban areas of Northern Ireland dominated by Protestants, such as South Belfast, and rural, traditionally Catholic western Ireland, he is partially following in the footsteps of a Protestant predecessor, Louis MacNeice, another Belfast poet whose mythologized vision of the west of Ireland figures prominently in his later work. But while MacNeice's landscape is distant and expressed largely in terms of ethereal light, Longley's terrain is present in its quotidian, close-up qualities, such as the flowers of the Burren in County Clare that often appear in his poems. Moreover, his incorporation of his Catholic neighbors and the rural west of Ireland into his work represents an expansion of poetic terrain into an even wider locale.

Longley's Pastorals: Fragility, the Catalog, and the Troubles

In a previously unnoticed but important way, Longley's environmental ethic, which is part of his holistic sense of the world's interconnectedness, derives from his conception of poetry itself. He has claimed that "a poem is an organism in which relationships on many levels between words fuse various orders of experience into a unique perception."[3] His conception of poetry as alive thus recalls Angus Fletcher's theory of the "environment-poem," which "does not merely suggest or indicate an environment as part of its thematic meaning, but actually gets the reader to enter into the poem as if it were the reader's environment of living."[4] Such poetry has powerful appeal for readers as it immerses them thoroughly in its concerns, which in turn can lead them to ponder both the natural world's fragility and the fragility of human bodies in war-torn areas such as Northern Ireland, and perhaps can inspire their protection of such worlds. Yet there is a resilient quality to Longley's equation of poetry with living organisms, even a revolutionary one. For example, he has argued that "poetry is like a beautiful and rare orchid growing up through the tar macadam in a car park. That's what poetry does: there's nothing consolatory about that: a little plant creating its own revolution."[5]

Poetry's independence and hardiness even as it struggles to flourish in a world that largely disregards it are qualities that draw poets such as Longley to keep writing it, to keep faith with it.

The continuity between Longley's poetic worlds and the natural milieus they often lovingly perceive recalls Gerard Manley Hopkins's purpose in designing his unique poetry to evoke the experience of his singular observations for his readers and to preserve elements of the natural world that no longer exist, as he does in "Binsey Poplars." But their work differs in an important respect: Longley's nature poetry seems less labored than Hopkins's often arduously constructed verse. For example, where Hopkins's jagged syntax and elaborate punctuation slow the reader's attention to a crawl, Longley's sinuous lines can sweep us along (as we have seen in the previous chapter's analysis of "The Butchers") into something like a complete apprehension of the whole, giving us a panoramic view of a given natural scene in which particular elements are nonetheless enhanced, often through the poem's form or formal devices such as his characteristic catalogs.[6]

Longley thus perceives poetry's formal properties as analogous to the intricacies of biological entities, and he knows the natural world as intimately as the world of poetry. For example, his friend, the naturalist David Cabot, at whose cottage in Carrigskeewaun, County Mayo, Longley and his family have stayed annually since 1970, has even pointed out how "for a non-naturalist, his knowledge and understanding of nature is remarkable and deep."[7] Another close friend who often visits Carrigskeewaun with the Longleys, Michael Viney, himself a natural historian and author of *Ireland, A Smithsonian Natural History,* has recently noted about Longley that "his curiosity has the energy of Belfast's nineteenth-century naturalists; his botany puts me to shame."[8]

Resorting to a natural metaphor that raises two of the central concerns of this and previous chapters, Longley has argued that "poetry has its roots in ceremony and in celebration, but part of that is the shape of the poem. A poem has an almost biological cellular inevitability. . . . A poem has to be well-made. It can be free in its style or richly formal, but to talk about a well-made poem is as tautological as to talk about a well-made chrysanthemum or a well-made snowflake."[9] Real poetry, then, is rooted in ceremony and in celebration, which are themselves derived from its radical (in both the biological and usual sense) form that leads ineluctably to its carefully rendered, unique being. Despite his avowed agnosticism, Longley implicitly affirms that just as a creator expended great care in forming natural organisms and even inanimate things, so does the poet in shaping his intricate verbal worlds.

Longley's poetic representations of western Ireland's teeming ecology superbly manifest his belief in the inherent likenesses between poetry and the natural world. Spending time at Cabot's Carrigskeewaun cottage (Longley's spiritual home) inspired him to break his relative poetic silence in the mid-1980s. Though he did not publish *Gorse Fires* until 1991, Longley actually began writing again at the cottage in 1986, as he observes in some reading notes from around 1991: "My silence was properly broken in 1986 when I went to stay on my own in a remote cottage in County Mayo on Ireland's Atlantic seaboard. There, a cluster of short poems presented themselves."[10] These poems include "Insomnia," "Washing," "Migrations," and "Madame Butterfly," all published later in *Gorse Fires*.

Longley employs a device I have already discussed in the context of his thinking and writing on reconciliation, the litany, to write this delicate landscape onto his and his readers' hearts and suggest how it is analogous to his native cityscape of Belfast in its particularized fragility. John Lyon has noted that Longley's literary lists hearken back to Ovid, Homer, even Ben Jonson, but also are rooted in the poet's own early life, during which he would ask his mother repeatedly the names of the plants in their garden and later, when he would watch and name birds.[11] Longley's lists of townlands such as "Cloonaghmanagh and Claggan and Carrigskeewaun" in "Between Hovers" and of flowers such as primroses "And celandines and white may and gorse flowers" in "Gorse Fires" indicate his continuing penchant for cataloguing as a sort of personal solace and way of understanding the distinctiveness of the landscape around him (*GF,* 5, 10). At the same time, the inclusion of the gorse flowers, a part of the undesirable plant that is burned in winter, along with the celandines and white may, suggests that good plants are destroyed along with the bad ones in these fires. These rural catalogs suggesting the fragility of the delicate natural western Irish landscape form a continuum with his litany of urban atrocities committed against vulnerable human beings in "Wounds," "Wreaths," and "The Butchers."

The last chapter concluded by referencing the religious aspects of Longley's "The Linen Workers" from *The Echo Gate*. Another poem about linen from that volume, "The Linen Industry," suggests how he views nature in a sacramental fashion and implies a specific way in which he has managed to connect the natural and the urban in his poetry. The poem is framed in natural and artificial flowers, respectively: the opening line depicts the speaker and others "Pulling up flax after the blue flowers have fallen," while the last line images the bow on the bodice of the speaker's lover as "A butterfly attending the embroidered flowers" (*EG*, 45). The fallen "blue flowers" of the opening line linger in the background of the poem, decorous remnants of the stalks of flax, while the embroidered flowers of the last line adorn the woman's dress in such a way to connect her to those original blue flowers. Her fragility is underscored by the dainty embroidery work.

As the speaker and the other flax gatherers "become a part of the linen industry," they "follow its processes to the grubby town" (*EG*, 45). The city is a site of mechanical containment, if not outright violence as in "Peace," a poem discussed in the previous chapter. But the poet achieves a naturally rendered world within the linen factory, featuring his speaker making love "on a bleach green, the whole meadow / Draped with material turning white in the sun / As though snow reluctant to melt were our attire" (45). The presumably dirty conditions of the factory are supplanted by the overwhelming whiteness of the nature imagery in these lines, signifying the purity and naturalness of the couple's love. But flax and white linen are also sartorially suited for death, and the speaker finally links lovemaking and dying, stating, "Let flax be our matchmaker, our undertaker, / The provider of sheets for whatever the bed—" (45). The final stanza pictures the speaker's beloved "in the presence of death" (45), covered in white linen. It is not a static image, since that bodice is dynamically pictured as a "butterfly attending the embroidered flowers," and we are left with the peaceful sense that death is natural and the fluttering suggestion that even in death lie the seeds of life.

If Longley evinces a striking fascination with the local in his poems of western Ireland, his decided interest in the wildflowers of this area particularly stands out. While Longley usually stays at Mayo, he has spent a great deal of time in the Burren area of County Clare. This karst limestone area has very little soil or trees but bursts into bloom for a brief period every year. Its profusion and variety of flowers and their almost magical annual appearance are fitting for a poet who is so attuned to both the quotidian and the spiritual.[12]

The urban culture of majority Protestant Belfast and the rural culture of traditionally Catholic western Ireland coalesce in "The Ice-cream Man." Longley has claimed that "naming anything well is a poetic act,"[13] and this poem enacts that theory, naming the flowers of the Burren as a temporary verbal solace for and replacement of the flavors the murdered ice cream man in Belfast used to recite to customers:

> Rum and raisin, vanilla, butter-scotch, walnut, peach:
> You would rhyme off the flavours. That was before
> They murdered the ice-cream man on the Lisburn Road
> And you bought carnations to lay outside his shop.
> I named for you all the wild flowers of the Burren
> I had seen in one day: thyme, valerian, loosestrife,
> Meadowsweet, tway blade, crowfoot, ling, angelica,
> Herb robert, marjoram, cow parsley, sundew, vetch,
> Mountain avens, wood sage, ragged robin, stitchwort,
> Yarrow, lady's bedstraw, bindweed, bog pimpernel.
>
> (GF, 49)

The poem is framed by lists of ice cream flavors and flowers from the Burren and turns on another flower image: the carnations laid "outside his shop." This domesticated flower of respect obviously triggered a connection between the flavors of the ice cream and the flowers of the Burren that Longley had seen so many times. His abundance of flowers listed here more than compensates for the relatively spare list of ice cream flavors and seems in danger of tipping the poem too far toward the other, rural landscape.[14] But the point is precisely that the sheer variety and profusion of the wildflowers both offers a glimpse of a natural repository that the urban ice cream man vaguely mimicked in his celebratory recitation of flavors (whether he knew it or not) and acts as a beautifully intricate metaphorical wreath of flowers with which Longley adorns the man's memory.[15] In this latter sense, "The Ice-cream Man" returns to the concerns Longley adumbrated in the earlier sequence "Wreaths," explored in the previous chapter.

Reading "The Ice-cream Man" and its lists with the catalogs of "Wreaths" reveals to us another way in which Longley's imagination has created a unified body of work dealing with victims of the Troubles through the years. Robert Belknap's study of lists has special relevance for my argument here. Belknap notes that lists are both accretive and discontinuous, simultaneously maintaining both their individuality and collective meaning: "By accretion, the separate units cohere to fulfill some function as a combined whole, and by discontinuity each unit maintains its individuality as a particular instance, a particular attribute, a particular object or person. In this way, each unit of a list possesses an individual discrete significance but also a specific meaning for the collective by virtue of its membership with the other units in the compilation."[16]

Extrapolating from Belknap's argument, we can see how reading "The Ice-cream Man" with the sequence "Wreaths" produces both individual readings of each constituent poem and its featured victims (the discontinuous function of listing) and a collective understanding of how the lists in the four poems accrete into an aggregate list of victims of the Troubles. The effect is startling: individual victims are commemorated and elegized even as the human scope of the conflict is given something approaching its real horror because of the relative length of this "megalist." In this reading of Longley's poems about the Troubles, we can see how he has applied practically his theory of litany that he discussed at some length in the essay "Memory and Acknowledgement" (see chapter 3). Through these poems, Longley enacts a litany that underscores his admonition that we should strive for "amnesty, not amnesia" in that essay: the fallen stand out as in gold lettering, a permanent but dynamic written litany for the victims of the Troubles.

That Longley intended something like this reading of his "listing" poems about the Troubles is clear. For example, he reorganized the order of "The Butchers" and "The Ice-cream Man" from their separated appearance in *Gorse Fires* to their sequential appearance in *Selected Poems* (101, 102), demonstrating his desire to group poems about the conflict. In *Gorse Fires,* "The Ice-cream Man" appears as one of the last poems of the book and is followed by another poem composed almost exclusively of lists: "Trade Winds," a four-quatrain piece that enumerates the cargoes of various ships on Lough Neagh. Only then does "The Butchers" appear, a grim ending to a volume that began with poems listing aspects of the natural world in Mayo. This frame of "naming" poems effectively opens and closes the volume and implicitly links poems about the fragility of the natural world with those concerning the fragility of human beings exposed to violence, one of Longley's recurring concerns.

However, in *Selected Poems,* he chose to have "The Butchers" immediately precede the more elegiac "The Ice-cream Man." Both of these poems display lists having what Belknap terms "a horizontal orientation," with "one item directly follow[ing] another" across a given line of poetry.[17] The other orientation, he notes, is to vertically list single items line by line. The horizontal orientation of "his nose and ears and cock and balls" that have been cut off from Melanthios's corpse in "The Butchers" creates a very different effect from vertically listing these body parts. In the latter case, each constituent part would receive too much readerly attention, decreasing the effect of the overall, almost leisurely, creeping sense of horror created by the horizontal orientation of the list of these parts Longley chose. The same horizontally oriented type of list in "The Ice-cream Man," however, creates a comforting, meandering litany of sorts that effectively elegizes the man in his rhythmic, unhurried recitation of ice cream flavors, although this comfort may well be fleeting because it is grounded in the intimate immediacy of its environment, as McDonald has argued.[18] Equally important is the sense of relative optimism that results from reordering the appearance of these two poems in *Selected Poems.* All the horror of "The Butchers" *does* accrete with the senseless killing of the ice cream man, but the relative discontinuity in both the specific lists employed and the general tonal shift between the poems suggests a sort of aesthetic, achieved peace on the part of the poet in dealing with the violence. As John Lyon has convincingly argued, Longley's lists "register . . . a characteristic and conservative pursuit of *sense* and order, serving as a still point in, and a small defence against, a world which can appear, on occasion, bafflingly disordered."[19]

Longley's gradual move toward the ceremonial, as evidenced by these ordered listing poems about the Troubles, provides a helpful link between those poems about largely urban violence and his thoughtful meditations on the natural world in Counties Clare and Mayo. As he noted in a recent interview, "Poetry's origins are in ceremony. Poetry commemorates. At memorial services after September Eleven the heart of each ceremony was the recitation of victims' names. I've sensed this in Ireland too. Names are what we're left with. The whole story is one catalogue and then another."[20] Longley's lists of flowers and animals in the Burren and other rural areas of western Ireland are ceremonial in the quasi-sacramental sense he articulates here.

Despite the tendency toward order and rootedness in Longley's inherently ceremonial nature poetry, he has demonstrated his slight unease in adapting to rural life, even on a temporary basis.[21] As his fellow Northern Irish poet Medbh McGuckian has remarked about the poem "Lares," from Longley's *An Exploded View,* in which the poet eats a "broken / Oatmeal farl," in a rural Irish setting (*CPL,* 41), "What is really being eased is his sense of not belonging, or the tension of feeling critical about a way of life one can only marginally accept, yet instinctively, or with one part of one's self, find nourishing."[22] His unease is less present than in his fellow Ulster Protestant, John Hewitt, but nevertheless there. There is a certain sense in which Longley may be talking about himself in his following remarks on Hewitt in the same way he does in "Lares":

> In his protracted search for a community to which he might belong, Hewitt reflects the predicament of his fellow Ulstermen. Even beneath the calm surfaces of his nature poems, we sense an unease which is social as well as psychological. As a city man drawn to the countryside, he finds there that he is both fulfilled and excluded, that the poet is defined by the landscape, while to the people who live in it, the man is an outsider. . . . The city man's feelings of exclusion in the countryside modulate with some pain into the Protestant planter's uneasy desire to be assimilated into Celtic Ireland and yet remain true to himself. Private loneliness shades into the larger historical isolation.[23]

There is something of this "Protestant planter's desire to be assimilated into Celtic Ireland and yet remain true to himself" in Longley's poems set on the Irish west coast. This is not to say that Longley's immersion in this western landscape is artificial but rather that his recognition of an echo of the concrete landscape of his native Belfast in these ostensibly rural poems reflects the persistent influence of his native milieu and his slight apprehension at being in such a relatively depopulated landscape.[24]

We see this anxiety in the poem "Detour" as well. In describing his funeral, Longley tries to incorporate himself into the local community:

> Reflected in the slow sequence of shop windows
> I shall be part of the action when his wife
> Draining the potatoes into a steamy sink
> Calls to the butcher to get ready for dinner
> And the publican descends to change a barrel.
>
> (*GF,* 7)

The most striking aspect of this poem is Longley's detachment from these cozy domestic scenes that he simultaneously yearns to inhabit. This is the same sort of private loneliness he associates with Hewitt's struggles to fit into rural Ulster.

Perhaps another source for this relative unease—and I would stress that it is only relative, since Longley clearly feels fairly comfortable most of the time in this environment—stems from his continuing exploration of the pastoral poem. McDonald has argued in a comparison of Longley's pastoral mode to Heaney's that Longley's "has continued to deepen and complicate . . . in ways that Heaney's pastoral modes have not really kept pace with: Heaney's remembered County Derry remains in thrall to one (comparatively narrow) mode of writing, whereas Longley's West of Ireland has become more strange as it has accrued more detail, and it continues to challenge, rather than confirm, the poet's sense of his own place in things."[25] McDonald's observation is especially valid as one reads the poetry in retrospect. Early poems such as "Carrigskeewaun" largely focus on the wider geographic contours of the townland, such as the nearby mountain, a local path, the beach, a dry-stone wall, and a lake. While this early poem from *An Exploded View* includes specifically re-called animal inhabitants of the landscape such as "mallards," "kittiwakes," "lapwings," "curlews," and "snipe" (*CPL,* 68), they do not seem to obtain the autonomy and, yes, strangeness that Longley's animals possess in later volumes. Moreover, the poet himself intrudes into the poem a bit too much with his persistent first-person voice, and while he clearly is seeking to integrate himself into the landscape, the overall effect results in a slight narrative detachment from its creatures.

Paradoxically, as McDonald points out, the intensity of focus in the later pastorals leads to an even further distancing of the poet from the landscape in a sense, yet I would argue that Longley has finally so successfully effected his full integration into Carrigskeewaun and areas of the Burren in these later works that he virtually disappears from the poems altogether. This disappearance suggests a full measure of confidence in his poetic abilities to describe the landscape and its flora and fauna well and allow them to live and breathe and simply be. In this sense, Longley's relaxed but carefully controlled later rural poetry displays the quality he has ascribed to the artist Felim Egan's paintings and sculptures, which he says "come into being according to their own laws of growth. . . . Layers of different colours are applied in a way that allows each colour to insinuate itself and contribute to a complicated glow."[26]

Although Alan Peacock claims in his discussion of Longley's poems set in the west of Ireland that "questions of identity in the geo-political and cultural sense (which complicate, for instance, MacNeice's view of the West), do not seem relevant within Longley's elemental identification," Longley has seamlessly integrated these western landscape poems into his ethical aesthetic that rejects violence.[27] He has argued explicitly that "the most urgent political problems are ecological: how we share the planet with the plants and the other animals. My nature writing is my most political. In my Mayo poems I am not trying to escape from political violence. I want the light from Carrigskeewaun to irradiate the northern darkness. Describing the world in a meticulous way is a consecration and a stay against damaging dogmatism."[28] Longley's ascription of a sacramental quality to the semantic particularity of his pastoral poems that acts as a "stay against damaging dogmatism" suggests that precise poetic language can provide a linguistic buttress against the rhetorical dogmatism still common, for example, in fundamentalist Protestant preaching in the province.

Another aspect of Longley's interest in the Burren ecosystem that relates it to his interest in achieving harmony among the various cul-

tures in Northern Ireland concerns its fragility and the necessity for various groups to work well together to ensure its preservation. "The Ice-
cream Man" amply evidences his belief that daily life in Belfast during
the Troubles had an inherently provisional quality and links it with his
fascination with the ephemerality of nature, especially in the West of
Ireland in fragile ecosystems such as the Burren area of County Clare. In
an unidentified book review, Longley discusses the Burren and its unique
geological aspects extensively. At one point, he notes the destructive aspect of one type of human intervention in the Burren: "We are still tam-
pering with the Burren. The most visible changes in recent years have
been the removal of walls and eradication of small meadows, and their
replacement by much larger fields containing an artificial pasture of sown
grasses; undoubtedly such transformations bring benefits to farmers and
allow more efficient farming, but *grey pavements, walls* and wildflowers
are essential to the Burren."[29] Anyone who has visited the Burren knows
these "grey pavements" and "walls" that define much of the area. On a
cloudy or rainy day, driving through the Burren can create an almost
overwhelming experience of constant rockiness seemingly devoid of life,
like that of driving through a deserted, darkened city at dusk. Longley's
Burren poetry has both brilliantly rendered its rocky landscape and in-
fused it with overtones of city life in Belfast, in the process suggesting the
fleeting quality of rural animal and plant life and of urban human life,
respectively.[30]

Patricia Craig argues that even Carrigskeewaun "hasn't struck as
deep in the Longley subconscious as rainy old Belfast, Belfast with all its
cargo of dissension, violence, bloody-mindedness, aesthetic inadequacy
and protracted internecine tantrums," immediately adding that her own
characterization of Belfast is incomplete and indeed that Longley's poetry celebrates many positive qualities of Belfast.[31] Yet Longley himself
told Robert Johnstone in a 1985 interview about his collection *Poems,
1963–1983* that "when I was putting together the book and reading the
proofs it occurred to me that I hadn't written enough about Belfast. I
think that is a gap in the book. . . . Somehow . . . I find I'm moved by
trees in a way I'm not moved by lampposts and telegraph poles, and I'm
moved by birds in a way I'm not moved by aeroplanes and helicopters."[32]
In a sense, Longley has become so immersed in his native city that it

almost disappears in his work, except for street names such as the Malone, Lisburn, Falls, and Shankill roads. These four street names actually do delineate a rough grid of significant areas of the city: the Malone Road suggests its beautiful university district in the southern part of the city, while the Lisburn Road connects working-class Protestant areas with more upscale ones. The Falls and Shankill roads, of course, suggest the vast urban ghettos of west Belfast. Strangely enough, Belfast as city of conflict, as concrete and material, appears most significantly in Longley's work in what should be the most rural area of all—the Burren.

Longley has explicitly connected the fragility of unique human beings—a characteristic that has been especially exposed during the Troubles—with unique fragile objects of the natural world such as the wildflowers found in the Burren. For example, in a February 1989 interview with BBC Northern Ireland he pointed out this relationship by reference to his nature poetry:

> A bad poem about the hydrogen bomb will tell us far less about the human condition than a good poem about a blackbird. If we stop caring about blackbirds and the yellow mountain saxifrage, we become less human and more likely to damage or destroy each other. I hope it doesn't sound self-important, but perhaps my poems might be read as a reflection of life in Northern Ireland even when, or especially when they do not deal directly with The Troubles. Even if I'm writing about a butterfly's wing only, or a bird's egg, between the lines can be read my concern firstly, for the fragility of experience— the vulnerability of the human body to bullets and bombs—and secondly, my concern not to intrude on the suffering of fellow citizens, not to be an impertinent nosy Parker.[33]

The first of these concerns coheres perfectly with Longley's intertwining of the fragile, fleeting flowers of the Burren with the death of the shop owner in poems such as "The Ice-cream Man." This emphasis remains important to the poet in later volumes such as *The Ghost Orchid* and *The Weather in Japan.*

As an example of this continuing fascination with floral fragility and its relationship to the conflict in Northern Ireland, consider a later poem such as "The Ghost Orchid":

Added to its few remaining sites will be the stanza
I compose about leaves like flakes of skin, a colour
Dithering between pink and yellow, and then the root
That grows like coral among shadows and leaf-litter.
Just touching the petals bruises them into darkness.

(GO, 52)

Despite its abrupt opening, this poem is perfectly balanced, alternating between thirteen- and twelve-syllable lines. The center of the poem comes appropriately in the third line, which portrays a liminal flower caught between colors. Finally, the unexpectedness but rightness of comparing the flower's root with coral growing among shadows and leaf litter is remarkable, and the last line makes us want to reapproach the poem with the exquisite care the ghost orchid demands. Additionally, the appropriateness of publishing a volume with this title in the midst of the first IRA cease-fire establishes another connection between the fragility of humans and the natural world.

In both cultural reconciliation and environmental preservation, efforts across local communities are essential to promoting peace and preserving unique vegetation and animal life. Longley's comments in this regard about preserving the Burren share striking elements with his comments on peace and reconciliation and display his growing sense of what it means to be a responsible citizen in both urban and rural environments: "When we accept that the present-day Burren is worth conserving, the status quo will be maintained only by active management with political backing at local, national and international levels."[34]

In another book review relating to the Burren, Longley recites a typical litany of flowers he observed on a trip to the Burren and how they led to a prayer for its continued life and flourishing: "On my most recent visit to the Burren I wrote the names of the plants into my notebook as usual, a fresh page for each location. This time the names arranged themselves rhythmically, as though to release their power into prayers or spells. Campion, samphire, milkwort, lavender—these at Poll Salach. And on Black Head crowberry, juniper, saxifrage, willow. Prayers for what is irreplaceable. Spells muttered in the shadow of exploitation and destruction. At Corcomroe Abbey on my way home to Belfast this line came into my head: *Protect the Burren, Our Lady of the Fertile Rocks.*"[35]

He would incorporate this litany into his brief poem, "Burren Prayer," from his 2000 collection, *The Weather in Japan*. The opening of "Burren Prayer" recapitulates yet reconfigures the concluding image of the "embroidered flowers" adorning the bodice of the speaker's lover in "The Linen Industry" (*EG*, 45). Now those artificial manmade flowers are replaced with actual ones from the Burren: "Gentians and lady's bedstraw embroider her frock" (*WJ*, 9). Whereas flax provides the bed for both lovemaking and death and adorns the bodice in "The Linen Industry," the flower named "bedstraw" decorates this later feminine frock. Whose frock it is remains unclear until the concluding litany: *"Our Lady of the Fertile Rocks, protect the Burren. / Protect the Burren, Our Lady of the Fertile Rocks"* (9). By virtue of its mirrored syntax, this chiastic couplet frames the repetitious prayer for the Burren with its invocation to an invented ecological Marian personage.

This Longley litany quickly becomes a prayer, this time for the environment. This litany serves a similar purpose as he explains the litany of victims of the Troubles in his essay "Memory and Acknowledgement": it continually keeps names, here of flowers, in front of us, creating a sort of perpetual embodiment and remembrance of them and of the fragility of natural life. Longley's playfulness with a Catholic tradition of protective intercessory figures is perfectly in keeping with his recourses to a traditionally Catholic device, the litany, and displays his ability to borrow from the religious practices of a culture sometimes thought diametrically opposed to the one in which he was raised.

In his 2004 interview with Margaret Mills Harper, after invoking Yeats's concept of civilization in poems as "A Prayer for My Daughter," Longley further suggests that being truly civilized as a human being involves avoiding typically human self-absorption and opening ourselves to harmony with animals:

> [We have] to avoid being parochial in a human way, thinking only in terms of ourselves. The huge issue facing us as a species is how we get on with the other animals. I write about them, I hope, with reverence and wonder as a way of giving them space in my poems. . . . We're not civilized unless we look after them, the animals, which is why I like to write about them and celebrate them. I think we can

judge a culture by how it deals with the vulnerable, those creatures and those people who are indeed less fortunate than we are, children and animals. . . . I would hope, that in my poems . . . I am encouraging people to feel reverence and wonder in the natural world.[36]

At the same time, Longley clearly believes in a hierarchy of creation, privileging humans over nature in the sense that we are caretakers of it and as such must exercise our agency and moral responsibility to sustain the environment and civilization generally.

Longley's "Aubade," from *Gorse Fires,* translated from the original Irish of Nuala ni Dhomhnaill, makes clear that nature's indifference must be countered by humans' deep obligation to be involved healers in the world. While the opening lines of the first two stanzas flatly state, "It's all the same to morning what it dawns on—" and "It's all the same to the sun what it rises on—", the beginning of the third stanza emphatically observes,

> But it isn't all the same to us that night-time
> Runs out; that we must make do with today's
> Happenings, and stoop and somehow glue together
> The silly little shards of our lives, so that
> Our children can drink water from broken bowls,
> Not from cupped hands. It isn't the same at all.
>
> (*GF,* 23)

The tough-mindedness of this last stanza strikes a note seldom heard in Longley's verse, but its straightforward tone suggests the poet's endorsement of this realistic antiaubade. Nature's relative lack of agency and mankind's possession of accountability create an urgency heightened by the succession of dutiful phrases: "we must make"; [we must] stoop"; [we must] somehow glue together." Patching and piecing bowls for children to drink water from places the responsibility for the burden of facing life's problems on adults. Those "broken bowls" imply our joint vulnerability as humans and our need to help one another. Read in the context of Longley's abiding respect for and reverence of nature, "Aubade" suggests that we need to answer the pressing realities of the world not by escaping into anthropomorphizing and romanticizing nature, as in "Peace," but by acting responsibly so that future generations can "drink water" at all.[37]

Along with his remarkable connection of human and animal life through an emphasis on our joint fragility, Longley has often incorporated the dead into the community of the living. Many examples occur in his World War I poems, especially those about his father, whose fighting in that war, as we have seen in my analysis of "Wounds" in the previous chapter, Longley has returned to often in his poetry. His first major published World War I poem (from *No Continuing City*), "In Memoriam," inspired by a recording of Joan Littlewood's *O What a Lovely War* lent him by Seamus and Marie Heaney in the 1960s, exemplifies this penchant for forming a community of the living with the dead:[38] Wilfred Owen is rendered still present through the variation Longley plays on particular lines by the World War I poet, and Longley's father is pictured as surrounded by teasing women (*NCC*, 42). "In Memoriam" owes much to Owen's poetry and its general emphasis on pity, especially in lines 12 and 13: "The cracked and splintered dead for pity's sake / Each dismal evening predecease the sun" (41). More specifically, these two lines, taken together with the lines that resurrect the "chorus girls and countesses" whom his father had pursued after the war into a procession "who packed at last and went / Underground with you. Their souls again on hire" (42), draws on both the consoling girls and the image of darkness at the end of Owen's well-known poem "Anthem for Doomed Youth." The twelfth line of Owen's sonnet suggests that the dead young soldiers of the war will be given only "The pallor of girls' brows" as "their pall" and concludes in its fourteenth line by noting that at "each slow dusk" there will be "a drawing-down of blinds."[39] Longley's much longer poem (five stanzas of ten lines each) substitutes "Each dismal evening" on line 13 for Owen's partial line 14, "each slow dusk," and only at the end of Longley's poem does he return to Owen's image of darkness, ingeniously depicting the women his father had pursued after the war in an eternal present: they "lift their skirts like blinds across your eyes" (42). Whereas in Owen's poem the war widows draw down literal blinds, an inescapably dark image, in Longley's poem flirtatious women draw their skirts in the opposite direction, up, in a sexually suggestive way across his father's eyes, and are pictured as being "On the verge of light and happy legend" (42). In Longley's poem, both Owen and Longley's father live on in a sense, the former in Longley's intertextual variations on lines from "Anthem for Doomed Youth," and the latter like a Greek hero descended to the underworld for a time.

Decades later, in "January 12, 1996," the poet writes to his father on what would have been his hundredth birthday, and his father again is rendered eternally—this time in the trenches, as he "lifts with tongs from the brazier an ember / And in its glow reads my words and sets them aside" (*WJ*, 25). The recourse to the image of light, as in "In Memoriam," bathes the dead man in a luminous glow of activity and suggests he still is in contact with his son somehow. Other instances of this penchant for viewing the dead as being in community with the living occur in recent poems about Carrigskeewaun and some of its departed inhabitants. The simply titled "Ceilidh," from *Snow Water*, features a *ceilidh* or Irish dancing party listened to by "The ghost of Joe O'Toole at ease on his hummock / The far side of Corragaun Lake" (*SW*, 9). O'Toole hears "The O'Tooles from Inishdeigil who settled here / Eighty years ago," as does the ghost of the speaker "at the duach's sheepbitten edge" (9).[40]

"All of These People" from *The Weather in Japan* is a striking instance of Longley's insistence on ceremony and acts as a *summa* of his views on the necessity of recognizing the constitutive matrix of human civilization for both the living and the dead. The opening rhetorical question, "Who was it who suggested that the opposite of war / Is not so much peace as civilisation?" (*WJ*, 16), revises the argument of "Peace" from *The Echo Gate*. The somewhat simplistic rhetoric of "Peace" suggested that an abstracted version of peacefulness, grounded in a rural ideal, acts as the opposite of war. The wiser speaker of "All of These People," whom I take to be the poet himself, has realized through his long immersion in the rural culture of Carrigskeewaun in Mayo that violence is endemic in the countryside as well—indeed, that the relative simplicity of life there highlights violence's nature more starkly than the frenetic lifestyle of the city might. This speaker correctly views civilization, predicated on courtesy, ceremony, and custom, again in a Yeatsian sense, as the opposite of war.

"All of These People" is a supralitany, enfolding victims of sectarian violence such as "Our assassinated Catholic greengrocer" from "Wreaths" in *The Echo Gate* and "our ice-cream man," the latter from the well-known poem in *Gorse Fires*, into its elegiac list of the dead (*WJ*, 16).

Now, however, these men achieve an elevated status in death that they did not attain in their first appearance in Longley's poetry. Before, their very quotidian qualities and humanity were celebrated; here, they have become extraordinary. The greengrocer is described as having "died / At Christmas in the arms of our Methodist minister," while the ice-cream man's recitation of flavors in the original poem has now become a "continuing requiem" (16). These dead businessmen from the past are shown to form a community of the living and the dead with the contemporary cobbler "who mends shoes for everybody," the butcher who "Blends into his best sausages leeks, garlic, honey," and the shopkeeper who operates the "cornershop" that "sells everything from bread to kindling" (16). As the poet concludes, "All of these people, alive or dead, are civilised" (16).

Alan Peacock's recent assessment of Longley's continuing fascination with Carrigskeewaun anticipates my argument about the poet's increasing penchant for stitching together a community composed of both the living and the dead. As Peacock makes clear, in a poem such as "The Fox" from *The Weather in Japan,* Longley both acknowledges the death and decay endemic among animal life in this rural environment and rejoices in death's active persistence: "Transience, decay and ecological threat are given due acknowledgement, but in the precise, observant celebration and evocation of the dead creature's distinctive living presence there persists . . . the lyrical, unsentimental, impulse to elegize and celebrate simultaneously—to turn death on its head."[41] The dead fox, which is portrayed as "foxtrotting upside down / Against the camber of the Milky Way" (*WJ,* 52), is earthbound yet ethereal, nearly rendered a constellation. The death of one fox among all the creatures in the area may not seem to matter, but as Longley has made clear in "The Flock," in which he lovingly points out the seals frolicking in the water and rescues "one lamb from the seaweedy tangle," he feels like "a shepherd among his sheep / Going over them all and counting his flock by fives" (*WJ,* 5). Counting and cataloguing the plants, creatures, and human beings of rural Carrigskeewaun, Clare, and urban Belfast, naming them and celebrating their loves with tender care and affection, has enabled Longley to incorporate these denizens into a timeless community of plant, animal, and human life, a fragile ecosystem in which one death sends shock waves through the entire population.

Longley has become increasingly committed to exploring a widening world beyond the bounds of Northern Ireland. Gerald Dawe notes this quality in his poetry when he contrasts the constricted terrain of Derek Mahon's poems in the mid-1980s with Longley's more expansive compass: "Longley's amazement, interest, love and need to detail such a world literally knows no bounds."[42] The issue of Longley's cultural, religious, and political allegiances may be best answered by John Montague in a letter he wrote to Longley in May 1980: "And where, pray, is Michael's parish? Where his imagination rests; Rome, The First World War, Mayo!"[43] Paradoxically, the broadened scope of Longley's regionalism has enabled him to focus even more on the particular, as his fascination with the material remnants of the Holocaust and miniature objects from Asian culture demonstrates.

At the same time, Longley's focus on the specific marks him as a parochial writer, in the best sense of this term. In this regard his penchant for naming, for listing, acquires a fuller political and cultural significance. Longley's often microscopic examinations of the rural landscape of the Burren might seem the worst kind of narrowness in a poet interested in promoting cultural understanding on a subnational level. But his intensely filtered poems of the particular are inherently linked to his urge to understand his native ground on a broader level. As he remarks toward the end of his autobiography, parochialism, in Patrick Kavanagh's sense, is essential for unionists especially to understand who they are, separate from Britain: "Patrick Kavanagh's famous distinction between the provincial cast of mind—abstract, imitative, sterile—and the parochial—close, familiar, teeming with life—applies to Northern Ireland in a particular and urgent sense. Terrified of Irishness—the cultural ideology of the Free State and then of the Republic—Unionists have clung to what after 1968 has increasingly become known as 'the Mainland,' and to cultural importation. Those who depend on imports run the risk of themselves becoming exports" (*TS*, 74). Longley's interest in a positive kind of parochialism is thus closely tied to his desire for Protestants across the province to reinstate themselves in its cultural life rather than looking to London for their identity. This is perhaps the most striking example of the coalescence of Longley's poetic and cultural concerns.

Other instances of Longley's fascination with Kavanagh abound. For example, in his introduction to *Causeway* he describes the Ulster Folk Museum as an example of Kavanagh's parochialism.[44] His praise of Medbh McGuckian's poetry suggests his own continuing concern with the parochial: "McGuckian is a perfect example of how a true poet can mine for gold in the back yard. Her subject matter tends to be domestic, but her treatment of it is so intense, concentrated and versatile, that somehow she manages to imply the whole world which extends beyond."[45] For Longley, Kavanagh's emphasis on the ordinary acquires an extraordinary, even otherworldly and divine quality, as he said in a 1970 reading on BBC Northern Ireland radio in which he discussed Kavanagh's poem "A Christmas Childhood": "Kavanagh reminds me that ordinary objects can have a divine aspect."[46]

Because Longley is a parochial poet in this expansive sense, it is not sufficient to term him merely an Ulster or a Northern Irish poet. Longley's own staggering range of classical and contemporary allusions does suggest a universal voice. Influences on his work range from Herbert, Yeats, Kavanagh, MacNeice, Hewitt, and Larkin to Sibelius, jazz music, Greek literature and mythology, and Asian culture. In another poet, these influences might be dizzying or jarring, but Longley's kaleidoscopic interests are rendered in a poetic style that is structured, lyrical, and achingly beautiful. Unlike his evanescent ghost orchid, however, Longley's poetry has a long-term staying power that has already assured him a place in a poetic tradition that transcends the boundaries of the six counties of Northern Ireland.

Longley's expanding poetic terrain finally encompasses all human, plant, and animal life through his continuing exploration of their interrelatedness—a trajectory that in many ways moves in the opposite direction from that of Seamus Heaney, who has, with some significant exceptions, burrowed inwards into a limitless country of the mind, as we will see in subsequent chapters.

Longley's Holocaust Elegies

Longley's writing about the European concentration camps in which German Nazis imprisoned and murdered Jews and other minorities during the 1930s and 1940s accords with his interest in articulating the fragility of specific human lives snuffed out during the Troubles and with his passion for preserving in poetry the ephemeral flora and fauna of western Ireland. Longley has said in an interview that "Auschwitz is what poetry, even if it doesn't deal with it directly, has to face. . . . I think we're duty bound to try and work out how we got there."⁴⁷ His poems about the Holocaust spring from a series of personal connections he felt to that cataclysmic series of events, as we shall see shortly, and also from his long-standing concern with human rights in Northern Ireland and elsewhere, which stems from his conviction that a fanatical sense of superiority, whether racial, cultural, political, or religious, always results in a suppression of humanity. His belief was obliquely signaled in "Words for Jazz Perhaps" from *No Continuing City*. In his discussion of his interest in jazz, Longley makes clear a pressing humanitarian concern of these early jazz and blues poems and suggests jazz's spontaneous possibilities act as remedies to the authoritarianism he would critique in his later Holocaust poems: "The spontaneity of jazz is one of the best antidotes against authoritarianism, totalitarianism. That's why its emergence in the century of the jackboot is of the greatest cultural importance. I would suggest that jazz is the twentieth century's most significant contribution to the culture of the world. The Nazis hated it. They were frightened of swing. Syncopation is the opposite of the goose-step. 'The natural noise of good'—to quote Larkin."⁴⁸ Jazz's improvisational alchemy transmutes rigidity into looseness and fun, just as the Jewish children's artwork does in "Ghetto," analyzed below. Read in the context of Longley's belief in the restorative powers of spontaneous music, however, the silences of several of his other Holocaust poems may seem profoundly bleak.

The difficulty of writing about the Holocaust, especially for a non-survivor of the concentration camps and for a non-Jew, is profound. Many Holocaust narratives, such as Elie Wiesel's *Night*, have been written by Jewish survivors and are thus suffused with an aura of authenticity. Longley's challenge in writing about these atrocities has been to overcome suspicion of his distance from these nearly unspeakable events and to render the victims human even as he depicts the inhumanity of the systematic murders committed by the Nazis.⁴⁹ Additionally, as Scott Brewster has put it, his elegiac poetry, despite its attraction to ceremony and commemoration, "acknowledges the dangers of what Lyotard terms 'memorial history,' a discursive strategy that attempts to order and sanitize events that remain irreducibly alien and unassimilable."[50] Yet again, Longley's fidelity to the imagination above all else has enabled him to write powerful poetry about the Holocaust. As Daniel R. Schwarz has pointed out, imaginative literature about the Holocaust reverses, to some degree, the transmutation of hateful rhetoric into broken, often dematerialized bodily remains: "If the Nazis succeeded in turning words into charred bone and flesh, skeletons that survived in terror, bodies almost completely deprived of their materiality, then writing about the Holocaust paradoxically restores the uniqueness of the human spirit by restoring the imaginative to its proper place and breathes new life into the materiality of victims and survivors. Were the victims to remain numb and mute, they would remain *material* without soul as well as participate in an amnesia that protected the culprits."[51] Writing earlier poems about the bodily remnants of victims of sectarian violence such as "The Linen Workers," discussed previously, prepared Longley to cautiously and reverently attempt to breathe "new life into the materiality of victims and survivors" by gazing so deeply at ordinary remains as to render them extraordinary, in the process restoring spiritual dignity to them.

Contrasting Longley's Holocaust poems to those he has written about World War I, in which his father fought, April Warman misleadingly claims that "he has no such personal or familial relation to the Holocaust."[52] While no one in his family was a victim of the Holocaust, Longley clearly feels several deep personal connections to the Jewish culture generally and to the Holocaust specifically. First, his maternal grandmother was Jewish, and that fact, coupled with the knowledge that giving their children Irish first names would sound "so phony against my very Anglo-Saxon surname," led he and his wife, Edna, to use "Old Testament names, which are very hard to beat," for their children.[53] Warman's claim is countered most directly by Longley's close friendship with Helen Lewis of Belfast, herself a survivor of a Nazi concentration camp, whose memoir, *A Time to Dance*, Longley strongly recommended for publication to Blackstaff Press.[54] But more indirectly but nonetheless tellingly, Longley's interest in the Holocaust may have been inspired by the abrupt disappearance of his soldier uncle in World War I and by Longley's own discovery that he and his twin brother Peter had survived their mother's botched attempt at aborting them. Longley has recalled, "My mother's mentally retarded brother disappeared in the trenches—and from family conversation. His vanishing act haunted my childhood much more than the vast catastrophe ever did."[55] The disappearance of this uncle who simply vanished one day may well have enabled Longley to sympathize to some degree with the survivors of the Holocaust, many of whose friends and relatives similarly disappeared into the abyss of history when they were murdered by Nazis. Finally, the birth of Longley and his twin brother on the eve of World War II while many other children were being exterminated under the Nazi regime on the European continent is a miracle of survival against all odds and has led him to mourn the potential of the many Jewish children's lives lost.

A final reason Longley has become so interested in the Holocaust concerns his own disgust at the Irish Republic's policy of neutrality during World War II and their turning away of Jewish refugees from Irish shores. He has approvingly recalled former Irish Taoiseach John Bruton's public acknowledgment of "Ireland's great debt not only to Britain and the other Allies for doing the fighting, but also the thousands of Irishmen and women (Catholic and Protestant) who donned British uniforms to defeat Fascism."[56] He also has cited a speech given by Gerard Delanty at University College, Cork, who stirringly remarked in 1995, on the 150th anniversary of the beginning of the Great Famine in Ireland, "It is a matter of great regret that this country has not participated in the collective remembering of the Holocaust and the defeat of fascism."[57]

Longley's earliest Holocaust poem, "Kindertotenlieder," was published in his second volume, *An Exploded View*, a volume more recognized for its poetic attempts to begin responding to the Northern Irish Troubles. Many of Longley's Holocaust poems are characterized by their terrible silences, both in their content and in their compressed form, and "Kindertotenlieder" is no exception, bravely undertaking a fascinating formal exploration of gruesome content. The speaker of the six-line poem says, "There can be no songs for dead children / Near the crazy circle of explosions," suggesting that the high-pitched harmonies of the children are drowned by the din and dissonance of explosions (*CPL*, 61). Instead of voices, the children leave their "fingerprints / Everywhere, teethmarks on this and that" (61). These marks anticipate the remnants found among the bodies of the ten men whose murders are depicted in the later poem "The Linen Workers," yet they are rendered more ethereal and less substantial than those personal effects are in the later poem.

In the later poem "No Man's Land," which is dedicated to the memory of the World War I poet-soldier and Jew Isaac Rosenberg, an absence of the material Jewish body persists while manmade markers linger. Because of this absence, the speaker instead attempts to take consolation in random buttons from uniforms that he sees as identity discs Jews would have been forced to wear in the 1930s and 1940s: "Because your body was not recovered either / I try to read the constellations of brass buttons, / Identity discs that catch the light a little" (*CPL*, 157). Long interested in the material remnants of World War I soldiers (both "In Memoriam" and "Remembrance Day" from *No Continuing City* mention the medals of the poet's father and Great War veterans, respectively, while "Wounds" from the next volume, *An Exploded View,* also mentions his father's badges, medals, and spinning compass), Longley now turns his keen eyes to the degrading brass identity discs to read and then reinscribe Rosenberg into a record of the war dead. The poem simultaneously laments the loss of such a great poet and employs his death as a symbol of the looming disappearance of Jews throughout Europe under Hitler's reign of terror.

"On Slieve Gullion," which originally appeared immediately before "No Man's Land" in *Poems, 1963–1983,* laments the absence of any material effects from another soldier of sorts, Robert Nairac, who Longley notes was "officially described as an 'undercover liaison officer' between the army and police" and who "disappeared in May 1977. . . . His body has yet to be found."[58] Read alongside each other, "No Man's Land" and "On Slieve Gullion" mourn the loss of two British soldiers in two different landscapes scarred by the vicissitudes of war. The link among World War I, the Holocaust, and the Troubles in Northern Ireland could not be clearer: particular human beings simply disappeared in all three instances, mowed down by faceless killers, never to be seen again.

Fran Brearton has argued that Longley's Holocaust poems work so well because his voice is tender, yet not maudlin, and focuses on the particular in such a way as to stave off abstraction: "The success of

Longley's poems about the Holocaust lies in the use of a compassionate yet unsentimental voice, and an attention to detail which restores
specificity at a point in history when it is most in danger of being lost in
abstraction—numbers, dates, death-tolls counted beyond comprehen-
sion."[59] "No Man's Land" exemplifies this formulation, as do other poems
about the mass murders of Jews in this time period, as we will see.

Longley's "compassionate yet unsentimental voice" in these poems
is all the more remarkable because his return to writing about this historical atrocity in his later poetry stemmed from a personal revelation his
mother told him shortly before she died. In *Tuppenny Stung*, Longley recalls his mother's confession "that in the early days of the pregnancy she
had attempted in an amateurish way to abort us—or 'it' as we then were"
(*TS*, 29). This discovery, coupled with his mother's gift of "X-ray pictures
in which the shadowy shapes of Peter [Longley's twin] and me curl up
and tangle about five months after conception," led Longley to realize
just how close he had come to literally not existing shortly before Jewish
children would be killed in great numbers as World War II dragged on
(29).[60] "Love Poem," written before Longley's great burst of poetry in the
1990s, even employs the language of twins to make clear the connection
he felt to Jews in the Holocaust after his mother's revelation about her
attempted abortion when the speaker mentions "an orphan squatting" in
a "barbed wire" enclosure, then muses, "It is nineteen forty, forty-one /
Which makes him a sort of twin" (*CPL*, 154, 155).

"X-ray," the poem inspired by Longley's mother's dying revelation,
indirectly introduces a suite of Holocaust poems in *Gorse Fires*. The very
materiality of the embryos that are Longley and his brother, "two skulls
in a basket, / Two sets of bones that show no abnormalities" (*GF*, 37),
stands in stark but relieved contrast to the absent bodies of Holocaust
victims that follow and the "bare bottom" of Eva Braun in the poem
named after her (38).

In "Terezin," the formal compression of this two-line poem bespeaks its utter muteness: "No room has ever been as silent as the room /
Where hundreds of violins are hung in unison" (39). Although the
material violins are depicted in this poem, its reduced shape calls attention to the absence of the young Jewish musicians who would have
played these instruments.[61] The poet, thankful for his own life, attempts

to sing the life of those who have been rendered voiceless in "Ghetto," the following sequence about the Nazi school for Jewish children at Terezin.

"Ghetto" employs to remarkable effect Longley's penchant for listing, as a way both of recollecting and imaging these vanished, starving Jewish children through their personal belongings in stanza 1 and of offering a catalog of Irish potato names to other Jews as nominal sustenance in stanza 5. The horizontal list of items in the first stanza is pitiful, not plentiful: "Photographs, medicines, a change of underwear, a book, / A candlestick, a loaf, sardines, needle and thread" (*GF,* 40). Their "last belonging" is fittingly, "a list of your belongings" (40). The "needle and thread" of this stanza reappear in stanza 5, as we are given another list—this one of Jewish workers in a Nazi concentration camp. Included are "Those who suffer in sewing-machine repair shops" and "the leather-stitchers / Who are boiling leather so that their children may eat" (42). To them, the poet delivers another catalog: "Irish Peace, Beauty of Hebron, Home / Guard, Arran Banners, Kerr's Pinks, resistant to eelworm, / Resignation, common scab, terror, frost, potato-blight" (42). As one still haunted by his island's history of national hunger during the nineteenth-century Potato Famine, Longley offers this veritable cornucopia of potato names as verbal food of sorts, food that is seemingly imperishable to those who soon will perish. The sheer variety and liveliness of names offer a temporary respite from the daily drudgery pictured in the labor taking place during most of the stanza. This potato catalog, however, does not seek to render the Irish famine on equal footing with the Jewish Holocaust. As evidence for this distinction between the two events, Longley has cited Gerard Delanty's public rejection of "'grotesque attempts to promote the 150th anniversary of the Irish famine as an 'Irish Holocaust.' To equate the Famine with the Holocaust is to devalue both."[62]

Stanza 8 of "Ghetto," the final one, employs one last list, the series of drawings done by the children at Terezin, as a reminder of the lingering power of art to imagine a place free from oppression. These "drawings of kitchens, / And farms, farm animals, butterflies, mothers, fathers / Who survived in crayon . . ." fill up the blankness and horror of the school with dynamism and movement. Although there was no way

out of this particular school for these doomed Jewish children, their surviving drawings suggest that art offers an escape from the imprisonment
of the body, soul, and mind: "And the only windows were the windows
they drew" (*GF*, 43).

Longley's memorial to these Jewish Holocaust victims is finally
conflated with a memorial to victims of the Northern Irish Troubles
and inscribed in a western Irish landscape depicted in the poem following "Ghetto" in *Gorse Fires*, "The Cairn at Dooaghtry." The "Children
[who] lie under the cairn" are "unhallowed souls" (*GF*, 44). Presumably
these children are victims of sectarian killings in Northern Ireland, perhaps by the IRA, whose members have often buried bodies in remote
places. They are "unhallowed" because of their lack of a proper burial;
they have been unceremoniously dumped under the cairn. The emphasis
on stones in the poem as a symbol for rigid violence recalls the stony
hearts Yeats associates with the Easter rebels in "Easter, 1916" in their
obsession with founding an independent Ireland. The "playground" of
the children buried under the cairn "should be the duach and the dunes"
(44), soft shifting banks of sand, but instead their bodies lie immobile
under those rocks.

The connection between these children and the Jewish children
from Terezin is quickly drawn by the speaker's startling statement that
the height of the duach and dunes in this particular part of western Ireland is "No higher than little children walking on tiptoe / Past SS guards
at the selections in Terezin" (*GF*, 44). This link across continents and
time periods, effected by a mental movement on the part of the speaker,
inspires him to invest the static western Irish landscape with motion as a
memorial to both groups of children and their liveliness: "The cairn has
become a scree, the scree a landslide / And a raised beach the memorial
to all of them" (44). The elevated beach that results symbolizes the consciousness Longley hopes to have raised in specifically rendering the potential and promise in the individual lives of the Jewish and Irish children, including himself, in these poems. His own escape as an embryo
from death has encouraged him to portray the lives of others in his
generation who were killed.

"Buchenwald Museum," a brief poem from *The Ghost Orchid*, links
World War I and the Holocaust, as did the earlier "No Man's Land,"

and again the absence of bodies dominates. One of the exhibits seen by the speaker at the museum "Was an official apology for bias" (*GO*, 41). Immediately, the viewpoint moves outside the museum to a white blankness, "a snowfall [that] had covered everything" (41). In the snow, "A wreath of poppies was just about visible" (41). The splash of scarlet on white signifies the blood spilled not only in World War I—symbolized by the traditional flower of that war, the poppy, which is still worn on Remembrance Day in Britain—but also the lives taken during the Holocaust. The last couplet of this six-line poem urges remembrance despite the passage of time and its obscuring effects: "No matter how heavily the snow may come down / We have to allow the snow to wear a poppy" (41).[63] In a similar fashion to the sequence "Wreaths," which was offered as a garland to the victims of the Troubles, "Buchenwald Museum" memorializes the dead of World War I and the Jewish dead of the Holocaust through its floral imagery.

"A Linen Handkerchief" from *The Weather in Japan* continues Longley's floral imagery in his Holocaust poems and suggests its particular staying power. Dedicated to his friend Helen Lewis, the poem trades in the images and even the title of his earlier poem, "The Linen Industry":

Northern Bohemia's flax fields and the flax fields
Of Northern Ireland, the linen industry, brought Harry,
Trader in linen handkerchiefs, to Belfast, and then
After Terezin and widowhood and Auschwitz, you,

Odysseus as a girl, your sail a linen handkerchief
On which he embroidered and unpicked hundreds of names
All through the war, but in one corner the flowers
Encircling your initials never came undone.

(*WJ*, 19)

Those embroidered flowers on the bodice of the lover in "The Linen Industry" are resurrected once more but transfigured yet again. In the earlier poem, they were flowers of death; here they are flowers of life, surviving on the surface of a fragile linen handkerchief that symbolizes her husband's enduring love for her in the midst of the violence of World War II. An echo of "The Linen Workers" sounds in "A Linen Hand-kerchief" as well. Our recall of those scared linen workers who were massacred on the side of the road because of their religious persuasion emphasizes the fear of the Jews in Terezin and Auschwitz who were slaughtered because of their faith.

Helen Lewis's survival, echoed by the enduring flowers on her hus-band's handkerchief, sets a determined tone that lingers into the next Holocaust poem in *The Weather in Japan*, "A Bunch of Asparagus." The poem plays on the image of asparagus, which resembles the symbol of Roman authority, the *fasces*, or bundle of sticks. Roman and Nazi bru-tality are linked as the speaker describes how "the mouthwatering fasces" were prohibited from being sold to Jews (*WJ*, 19). The speaker brings his friend "a bunch held together with elastic bands," and they "prepare melted butter, shavings of parmesan," so that they can "make a meal out of the mouthwatering fasces" (19). Loosening the bundle of asparagus in preparation for eating it is equated to the dissolution of this imperial, cruel symbol, used by both the Romans and the Nazis. The anticipated enjoyment of this meal should be read in the context of the starving Jews boiling leather for their children to eat in the earlier poem "Ghetto." The gleeful devouring of a symbol of Roman but especially Nazi oppression brings Longley's Holocaust poems full circle, from absence, hunger, and death to presence, fullness, and life.

Asian Miniatures

Most recently, Longley's increasing fascination with Asian cultures affirms his interest in form and ceremony as bulwarks against violence. Longley spent three weeks in Japan in 1991, and his subsequent think-ing about its rich culture is manifested in poems in *The Ghost Orchid* such as "Massive Lovers," "A Gift of Boxes," "A Grain of Rice," "A Pair of Shoes," "Chinese Objects," "Chinese Whispers," and "Chinese Oc-casions"; in the title poem, "Birds and Flowers," and "Invocation" from *The Weather in Japan*; and in "Moon Cakes" and "Snow Water" from *Snow Water* (2004). Longley told McDonald in an interview that the miniature poems about Asia in *The Weather in Japan* demonstrate how poetry's power can be concentrated in a near-silent form, a direct link between the silence and relative brevity of many of his Holocaust poems:

> My next collection will take its title from a two-line poem, a new form I've invented and am trying to impose on the world in the belief that the haiku is garrulous and overweight. Should I call it [my new form] the low-ku? The title runs into the first line, and the couplet has to be as short as possible, and it has to rhyme: "The Weather in Japan" (that's the title) "Makes bead curtains of the rain, / Of the mist a paper screen." That's my near-silent way of suggesting what poetry might be. And in naming the book after such a brevity I might be making a point about scale and importance.[64]

The move toward a compressed form even as Longley's geographic range expands to encompass Asia seems paradoxical, but by formally concentrating his poems he is able to focus on the particular aspects drawn from the wealth of Asian culture, such as its delight in delicate objects and its penchant for ceremony, which appeal to him, and to incorporate these into his theory about the necessity for civilizing actions and discourse in quotidian life.

Longley's Asian poems bring the section of this study on his poetry full circle because they achieve the buoyancy he depicted in a number of poems from *No Continuing City* that were discussed in the second chapter, while also employing compressed stanza forms, including couplets, as a formally freeing exercise, in contrast to the recourse to couplets in that first volume, which finally signaled an onset of writer's block. Whereas in *No Continuing City* he desired buoyancy in the content of his poems, in these later poems he seeks and finds buoyancy at the level of both style and content, fulfilling his aim to "become simpler and more insouciant" and to achieve a "lighter utterance that can somehow accommodate everything."[65] Just as in those early poems, weightlessness signifies artistic creativity and receptivity to poetic stimuli.

Several of Longley's Asian poems capture his marriage of buoyant form and content in their microscopic examination of miniatures. For example, "A Gift of Boxes" from *The Ghost Orchid* encloses its carefully constructed quatrains around a series of tiny objects, such as the "Rice grains between my chopsticks" in line 1, the "makeshift ideograms of wet leaves, green tea," in line 8, and the "two boxes the size of tears" in line 12 (*GO*, 17). These objects hover or float: the rice grains are poised in midair, while the tea leaves float on the surface of the "single earthenware bowl" (17). The third stanza even shows how air itself can be captured and condensed in tiny containers:

> You make a gift of boxes by putting boxes inside
> Boxes, each one containing the Japanese air you breathe,
> More and more of it in diminishing boxes, smallness
> Condensing in the end to two boxes the size of tears.
>
> (17)

The recourse to water imagery to describe these last two boxes purposefully adds figurative buoyancy to objects that are already nearly weightless. Their very smallness, however, makes them more precious and more vivifying, since they condense the air breathed by the speaker's friend.

"Birds and Flowers" from *The Weather in Japan* similarly exalts in buoyancy, linking it again to friendship by recalling a moment in which Longley floated in volcanic pools with his Japanese friend Fuyuji Tanigawa. Upon receiving a letter from Tanigawa informing him that he has "been spending time with" his "little children" but vowing to return "'to the world of letters soon,'" Longley affirms his friend's pursuit of family and friendship, which are inherently fragile, just like the natural world, by concluding:

> . . . Fuyuji,
>
> The world of letters is a treacherous place. We are weak
> And unstable. Let us float naked again in volcanic
> Pools under the constellations and talk about babies.
> The picture you sent to Belfast is called "Birds & Flowers."
>
> (*WJ*, 64)

Briefly rendered like babies themselves, the poet and his friend float naked in volcanic pools—both literally in the past and now in the present of Longley's imagination—vulnerable, exposed, and talking of babies,

the most fragile of humans who need constant care. Putting ourselves
in the position of those in the most need has often been a theme of
Longley's poetry dealing with World War I, the Troubles, or the environment, and he seems to suggest here that art—represented by his friend's
painting—also needs such attention to preserve its delicacy, nuance,
and delight.

The ceremonial aspects of eating and gift giving in "A Gift of Boxes"
and of bathing in "Birds and Flowers" suggest that Longley continues to
artfully affirm ceremony as a distinguishing hallmark of culture whereby
reconciliation across cultures might occur. In "Snow Water," the title
poem from his most recent volume, the poet "scald[s] my teapot" and
"measure[s] out some Silver Needles Tea, / Enough for a second steep-
ing" (*SW,* 3). The ceremonial process of tea making is highlighted and
enhanced by Longley's continuing zest for the catalog as he lists "Other
favourites [which] include Clear / Distance and Eyebrows of Longevity /
Or, from precarious mountain peaks, / Cloud Mist Tea (quite delectable)"
(3). He waits for "competent monkeys [to] harvest" this last tea and
bring the leaves to him where he waits "With my crock of snow water"
(3). This fanciful meditation on tea confirms Longley's understanding of
civilization as inhering in the daily round of activity and the precision
with which we carry out seemingly mundane but deeply ceremonial tasks,
just as his lamented greengrocer and ice-cream man did in "Wreaths,"
"The Ice-cream Man," and "All of These People." Longley told his Japanese friend Mitsuko Ohno that his time in Japan had convinced him that
"even life's most humble moments are worthy of ceremony."[66] Thus he
writes himself into the community of these dead men and other, living
people who lose themselves in their particular, civilizing activities in such
a way as to reach a transcendent state of mind.

Ben Howard has shown the specific link in "Snow Water" between
brewing tea and making poetry, arguing that its fifth line, "Tea steam
and ink stains," sets up a number of felicitous associations between the
two: "Both require single-minded concentration. Both involve the harvesting of necessary ingredients: tea leaves for the brewer of tea and
life-experience for the poet. Both require patience. And both require a
transforming agent: water for the tea-connoisseur, imagination for the
poet. . . . What the poet requests for his sixtieth birthday is not only
pure water for his tea but poetic imagination for the making of his

poems."[67] As we have seen in the poems of *No Continuing City* such as "Freeze-up" and "Leaving Inishmore," water often signifies poetic inspiration, while frozen water suggests poetic writer's block. But the water that runs through Longley's Asian poems such as "Birds and Flowers" and "Snow Water" suggests that he is now more comfortable with images of water in its various forms, whether volcanic pools, snow, or water made from snow. The fact that he feels he can make purified water for his tea from snow heralds his enhanced ability to receive poetic inspiration and make poetry from some of the same figurative materials that might have prevented him from doing so earlier in his career.

Part of Longley's new confidence in his poetic powers may stem from his enhanced contemplative practices, such as his interest in the Buddhist meditative tradition, as Howard has argued. Howard holds that "the fastidious, methodical, and single-minded character of Longley's narrative [in "Snow Water"] calls to mind the tea ceremony and the Way of Tea, which have deep roots in Zen monastic practice."[68] Though a movement toward Asian culture and art may seem incongruous with the themes discussed already in this chapter, the Asian insistence on precise form and specific words coheres perfectly with Longley's view of the particular contribution of language, especially the precise language of poetry, to critiquing monolithic identities and abstractions.[69]

In an interview with Eileen Battersby, Longley affirmed that poets' primary responsibility is to the imagination but argued that they also must use the imagination in such a semantically specific way that the truthfulness of the words confronts and deflates falsehood: "Though the poet's first duty must be to his imagination, he has other obligations— and not just as a citizen. He would be inhuman if he did not respond to tragic events in his own community, and a poor artist if he did not seek to endorse that response imaginatively. . . . In the context of political violence the deployment of words at their most precise and suggestive remains one of the few antidotes to death-dealing dishonesty."[70] Longley's fidelity to his imagination has enabled him to remain above sectarianism and stay committed to his art, while also enabling him to effectively critique sectarianism in a unique body of work still not fully recognized either for its astonishing linguistic and stylistic variety or for its contribution to enhanced cultural understanding in Northern Ireland. The miniature gems that constitute the majority of the poems in *The Weather in Japan* exemplify Longley's continuing fascination with form that began with his interest in the poets of the Movement such as Larkin and are part of his singular formal contribution to imagining ways out of the deterministic mind-sets that still dominate thinking about identity in the province and elsewhere.

With *Snow Water,* Longley's mature gifts as a senior poet are on full display. These include his masterly control of tone, lyric precision, and diction, as well as form. The volume is framed with two poems, "Overhead" and "Leaves," about a beech tree, presumably outside the poet's window. Both compare the poet to this tree and portray him in the midst of current and projected inspiration, respectively (*SW,* 1, 62). The poet's clear recognition of his aging self in these two poems emerges elsewhere in the volume through a series of elegies for dead friends, such as "Marsh Marigolds," "An October Sun," "Snipe," "White Water," and "Heron." These elegies accord with Ruth Ling's description of Longley's elegies in *The Ghost Orchid* and his 1998 chapbook *Broken Dishes*: "Hallowed and kept sacrosanct, such mourning rites are gently but appreciably complicated by the attendant admissions of his failure to achieve through them any lasting transcendence."[71] The quotidian titles of these elegies suggest Longley's continuing interest in the everyday and his complementary ability to make the ordinary extraordinary, often by investing a seemingly static scene with surprising emotional movement. The intertwining of natural and human life in all their fragility in these elegies and other poems in the volume suggests Longley's conception of a holistic, interrelated world, the variety and singularity of which is diminished by the deaths of friends, such as Penny Cabot, the poet Michael Hartnett, Sheila Smyth, the poet James Simmons, and the poet Kenneth Hoch in the respective elegies listed above, and of familiar animals like the badger ("The Sett") and the skunk ("Two Skunks"). Many of these poems are, after all, love poems, in an expansive sense of the term, and they caressingly survey the natural landscape and its inhabitants, especially its avian inhabitants, around the poet's second home of Carrigskeewaun.

Longley has always been interested in the temporary and provisional, as his poems about the wildflowers of the Burren suggest; some of those flowers bloom only for a day. He has observed, for example, that

Carrigskeewaun in County Mayo itself is "precarious, isolated and vulnerable. . . . The bones of the landscape make me feel in my own bones how provisional dwelling and home are."[72] This fascination with the temporary is allied to his interest in the quotidian. As Michael Allen has pointed out, "Longley's keynote . . . is normality."[73] In his foreword to the late 1999-to-early 2000 retrospective of the Northern Irish artist David Crone's work at the Ulster Museum in Belfast, Longley makes a remark pertinent to our exploration of his own poetry in this regard: "His watchful, edgy, ambitious work suggests that everything—from wild flower to boulder, from graffito to stone cross—is provisional. David Crone's wonderful paintings commemorate the interim."[74] "Snow Water" itself, as a poem and as an attitude, celebrates the temporary, the fleeting, the ephemeral, as does the title poem of the earlier volume "Ghost Orchid." The snow melts; the boiled water for the tea will cool; the petals of the orchid will soon droop and wilt. But what persists, despite the coming melting, cooling, and drooping, is a lovingly rendered vision of delicacy and transcendence. Longley's poetry implies that we must cling to such moments with all our might—even as they slip away—as temporary anchors in the maelstrom that is our frenetic world.[75]

Over the past several decades, as an essayist, editor, poet, and director for literature and the arts at the Arts Council of Northern Ireland, Longley has offered an antidote for the poisonous political discourse in the province by arguing for a conception of Northern Ireland as a heterogeneous regional entity that has been enriched by cultural contributions from both Catholics and Protestants. While he undoubtedly continues to view his native province in this manner, *Snow Water* offers additional ample evidence to that seen in earlier poems that his worldview has become expansive enough to encompass continents and, in so doing, to verbally suture wounds, personal and political. For example, the speaker in "Two Skunks," whom I take to be the poet himself, offers Longley's friend Helen Lewis, the Holocaust survivor to whom "A Linen Handkerchief" is dedicated, "a skunk spun out of glass / And so small as to be almost unbreakable" (*SW,* 33), a sort of replacement for the dead skunk he has recently seen near the Delaware River in America and a near-permanent artistic stay against the shattered glass of Kristallnacht in Germany of the 1930s. The poem's focus on the artistic endurance of glass art in "Two Skunks" recalls the poet's desire in the earlier poem "Glass Flowers" to bring lasting glass flowers to broken marriages (*GF*, 24).

The conclusion of "Heron" from *Snow Water* ends with the poet imagining another Jewish friend, Kenneth Koch, transformed into a heron flying "above a townland / That encloses Carrigskeewaun and Central Park" (*SW*, 61). Longley has spoken about being drawn to Koch's own poetry for its "kind of controlled verbosity" and "abundance."[76] Undoubtedly, Koch's penchant for feeling "the urge to name everything in the universe" when he wrote poetry attracted Longley, who has his own penchant for naming and listing.[77] Longley's adopted townland of Carrigskeewaun has now become more elastic, open, part of a transnational area that enfolds sites from different countries as well as different cultures, just as the poet himself has achieved a buoyant aesthetic that borrows freely from different cultures and floats freely in compressed and longer forms. The rhythms, formal control, and above all, sheer imaginative variety of the poems in Michael Longley's *Snow Water* and earlier volumes promise to widen the regions of each reader's mind that discovers these lyrics. His long commitment to the life of the imagination has enabled him to develop a truly radical aesthetic that has modeled and helped contribute to the ongoing process of reconciliation across the province and that seeks to promulgate understanding across other cultures as well.

CHAPTER FIVE

"To Make Myself an Echo Chamber"

SEAMUS HEANEY'S AUDITORY IMAGINATION

I have always listened for poems, they come sometimes
like bodies come out of a bog, almost complete, seeming to have
been laid down a long time ago, surfacing with a touch of mystery.
—Seamus Heaney

The language of Heaney's poetry . . . has extraordinary definition,
a braille-like tangibility, and yet also has a numinous quality, a power
that indicates the existence of a deeper zone of the inarticulated
below that highly articulated surface.
—Seamus Deane

Heaney and Creativity: Consciousness, Catholicism, and Rural Craftsmen

Robert F. Garratt has argued convincingly that the attempt of Irish poetry to deal with what he terms the "central dilemma of modern literary history," which is "the subject of discontinuity, the inevitable result of the clash of cultures," has naturally "evolved into a treatment of the artist himself, a probing of the psychic posture of one estranged from society."[1] Partly because of his estranged, marginalized status as a minority Catholic in Northern Ireland and partly because of his reflective temperament, Seamus Heaney has consistently probed his "psychic posture" in a series of poems about the role of the artist. In fact, Heaney has probably publicly pondered the creative process more than any other poet writing in English over the last fifty years. A dominant strand running throughout his essays and poems is his meditation upon his vacillation between inner exploration or reflective cogitation, often at a preverbal level, and how the conscious, outer self then makes that poetry. This "metapoetic" strand has enabled him to negotiate not only the poetic process but also the struggle between the contemplative life and the outer world, often violent, of his native province. Unfortunately, this crucial emphasis on the play of his mind has been relatively neglected by some major critics, who have often tended to analyze his work to see whether he perpetuates the Irish/British divide in Northern Ireland as a whole or merely to praise him for his experiential poetry without celebrating his work for its intellectual value.[2]

Hobsbaum's encouragement of Heaney's experiential poems during his time in the Belfast Group undoubtedly inspired the young poet to represent this aspect of his life in his early poetry. In his discussion of Heaney's time in the group, Michael Parker assesses a series of experiential poems, some of which remain uncollected. He finally concludes that "gradually Heaney was developing the confidence to write directly from his childhood experience, and consequently fewer poems rely on personae and distancing effects" (*SHMP*, 56). These experiential poems include "Digging," "Blackberry-Picking," "Death of a Naturalist," "Fisher," and "Mid-Term Break," along with a host of other poems celebrating life in Heaney's corner of rural County Derry.[3]

While this early poetry is crucial in understanding the development of Heaney's thinking about the poetic process and how his imaginative integrity evolved, that work and the criticism that has accrued around it have tended to suggest it is nonreflective. The author of one of the earliest and still best monographs on Heaney, Blake Morrison, has argued that there is a growing contemplative quality to Heaney's verse; this claim, however, stems only from his reading of selected poetry starting with *Wintering Out,* but especially the poems of *North,* and thus fails to recognize the deep reflective aspect of the earlier poetry.[4] A significant exception to the critical view of Heaney's early work as largely nonreflective is Daniel Tobin's landmark study *Passage to the Center: Imagination and the Sacred in the Work of Seamus Heaney,* a rigorous, far-ranging, and sympathetic exploration of the influence of theology and philosophy on Heaney's work, the whole of which suggests that "Heaney's poetry does nothing if not engage its readers to take up ideas."[5] Another sympathetic reader of Heaney, John Desmond, has recently held that Heaney has been highly influenced by Simone Weil's concept of the *metaxu,* the position humans occupy between the transcendent and the quotidian, but strangely argues that this emphasis can be found only in Heaney's poetry since the *Haw Lantern* (1987)—a position that effectively reinforces the critical demarcation between early "experiential Heaney" and later "intellectual Heaney."[6]

As this chapter will demonstrate, Heaney has always, even in his earliest poetry and essays, been attempting to articulate the dialectic between what he soon came to call "technique," the inner reflective process out of which words and images can then be made, and "craft," or the actual making of the poetry. What has perhaps obscured this process, at least in the minds of many of his critics, is that the early poetry so often foregrounds experience in the form of manual labor. But close examination of these anthropological depictions of traditional rural Ulster crafts reveals a series of deep meditations on the role of the poet as discoverer/maker in an analogue to various rural craftsmen. Understanding Heaney's changing, yet remarkably consistent conception of the poet's role enables a better appreciation of the two themes of this study that his work exemplifies: his continuing commitment to and exploration of the poetic imagination, which in turn have enabled him to imagine enhanced cultural understanding in Northern Ireland.

In one of his earliest statements on poetry, Heaney suggests the importance to him of this dialectic between discovering and making:

A writer at work is involved in a dual process of discovering and making, a process that is necessarily intimated, unique and (at the best times) unselfconscious. . . . Every poem is ideally a new beginning, written by a new "writer at work." It happens as the secret fertilization of an unquestioned, blurred impulse by an act of will and intelligence. It may be carried for weeks or come in an hour. Some poems one hoards like a miser for weeks in what Patrick Kavanagh might call the "fog of unknowing," reluctant to force them into language in case the language does not measure up; others may only begin to grow under the pen, so to speak.[7]

Heaney's description of this process as gestational reflects the intense way in which he can "carry" and brood upon an embryonic poem in his mind before he actually articulates it. Elsewhere, he has similarly described how Osip Mandelstam "implied that it was the poet's responsibility to allow poems to form in language inside him, the way crystals formed in a chemical solution. He was the vessel of language."[8]

Although this meditative, receptive process is in dialectic with the important "making" function, Heaney favors it over the more active role of crafting verse. His ideal poetic stance is that of a listener, hearing inner voices and drawing upon inner forces that give him images he can then cast into words. His best poems display this posture and attempt to verbalize it through his careful poetic craftsmanship. He thus explores the country of himself in a nonsolipsistic fashion before crucially turning to the outside world. It is a dynamic manifested in significant poems from his early volumes but explicitly developed only in the poetry starting with *Field Work*.

In his seminal essay "Feeling into Words," Heaney articulates an extension of his discovering/making dichotomy in "Writer at Work" by delineating a distinction between "technique" and "craft" that he has repeatedly turned to in other essays and poems. Contrasting his university days as a period of "all craft—and not much of that—and no technique," Heaney argues that while "craft is the skill of making," technique is much more, actually including and providing the grounds for craft:

Technique, as I would define it, involves not only a poet's way with words, his management of metre, rhythm and verbal texture; it involves also a definition of his stance towards life, a definition of his own reality. It involves the discovery of ways to go out of his normal cognitive bounds and raid the inarticulate: a dynamic alertness that mediates between the origins of feeling in memory and experience and the formal ploys that express these in a work of art. Technique entails the watermarking of your essential patterns of perception, voice and thought into the touch and texture of your lines; it is that whole creative effort of the mind's and body's resources to bring the meaning of experience within the jurisdiction of form. ("FW," 47)

Heaney then makes a memorable comparison between the poet and the water diviner: "And if I were asked for a figure who represents pure technique, I would say a water diviner. You can't learn the craft of dowsing or divining—it is a gift for being in touch with what is there, hidden and real, a gift for mediating between the latent resource and the community that wants it current and released" (47–48). The analogy between diviner and poet is artesian and active: "The diviner resembles the poet in his function of making contact with what lies hidden, and in his ability to make palpable what was sensed or raised" (48). Divining the waters of his hidden depths has remained Heaney's central poetic concern, and these chapters on his work explore just how that process of discovery has remained at the heart of his work in various ways and also articulate his notable deviations from that concern as the conflict in Northern Ireland worsened.

Other essays on poetry that Heaney has written clarify further his distinction between technique and craft as he identifies the deep concern of earlier writers such as Wordsworth and Eliot with immersion in technique as Heaney defines it. For example, in his 1978 lecture "The Makings of a Music: Reflections on Wordsworth and Yeats," Heaney distinguishes between "two contributory elements" in poetry: the literary, articulated tradition in which the poet writes and the illiterate, subconscious well of his mind. The second element is "derived not from the literate parts of his mind but from its illiterate parts, dependent not upon what Jacques Maritain called his 'intellectual baggage' but upon what I might call his instinctual ballast. . . . This unconscious activity, at the preverbal level, is entirely relevant to the intonations and appeasements offered by a poet's music."[9] Heaney's recourse to a nautical metaphor recalls his emphasis on water and particularly divining in "Feeling into Words" as suggestive of imaginative insights. He then approvingly cites Wordsworth's *Prelude* as exemplifying the ideal poetic technique, one he returns to in his own poetry time and again: "What we are presented with is a version of composition as listening, as a wise passiveness, a surrender to energies that spring within the center of the mind, not composition as an active pursuit by the mind's circumference of something already at the centre. The more attentively Wordsworth listens in, the more cheerfully and abundantly he speaks out."[10] For Heaney, speaking out on an issue, such as the conflict in Northern Ireland, is usually preceded by a contemplative process that filters outer events through his imagination.

Over a decade after his lecture "The Makings of a Music," in a T. S. Eliot Centenary Lecture at Harvard entitled "Learning from Eliot," Heaney underscored the continuing importance of technique as he had defined it in these earlier essays by praising the elder poet for his definition of "the auditory imagination." For Eliot, Heaney says, this involved "the feeling for syllable and rhythm, penetrating far below the conscious levels of thought and feeling, invigorating every word; sinking to the most primitive and forgotten, returning to the origin and bringing something back . . . [fusing] the most ancient and the most civilized mentality."[11] Eliot's fidelity to the auditory imagination was inspirational for the younger poet in exploring his own subconscious feelings: "His example of a poet's intelligence exercising itself in the activity of listening, all of this seemed to excuse my own temperamental incapacity for paraphrase and my disinclination to engage a poem's argument and conceptual progress. Instead, it confirmed a natural inclination *to make myself an echo chamber for the poem's sounds.*"[12] Becoming an "echo chamber for the poem's sounds" accords well with Heaney's description of technique in "Feeling into Words" as an artesian process by which hidden sounds or energies are brought to the surface.

In a 1996 essay on Robert Frost entitled "Above the Brim," Heaney articulates, probably via a backward glance at his early poem "Personal Helicon" from *Death of a Naturalist,* the image of a well as a symbol for the depths of the mind from which sounds can be summoned. In so doing, he says, we can "recapitulate and refresh a latent resource of our nature: one might say to them what Frost says of the well at the end of his poem 'Directive': 'Here are your waters and your watering place. / Drink and be whole again beyond confusion.'"[13] As Heaney claims later in "Above the Brim" in discussing Frost's "Birches," "The headiness of Frost's poetry has much to do with this revel in artesian energies."[14] Reveling in artesian energies has repeatedly sustained and reinvigorated Heaney's own poetry and made it a refreshing alternative to the dry, often deathly facts of daily life in Northern Ireland.[15]

Throughout his career, Heaney has been criticized for listening too much and not speaking out enough. Indeed, on some occasions, such as the 1983 pamphlet he contributed to the Field Day Theatre Company, *An Open Letter*, he has even wrongly condemned himself for not speaking out enough.[16] But the rudder of his poetic ship holds most true when he passively listens to his inner self; only then can he make deliberate, nuanced poetry out of his inner concerns that often responds more penetratingly to exterior political or cultural conflicts than any immediate propaganda could. Henry Hart has argued convincingly about Heaney's silence that "in a century when major writers have espoused Nazism, fascism, monarchism, and other antidemocratic creeds, Heaney's hesitancy to speak out politically seems noble rather than culpable."[17] In 2001 Heaney himself explicitly noted, in approvingly describing the salutary effect of the sonic qualities of poetry apprehended through listening, that "these under-ear activities, as they might be termed, may well constitute the most important business which the poem is up to and are a matter more of the erotics of language than of the politics and polemics of the moment."[18]

Heaney's movement from the pressing world of fact and history in his native Northern Ireland, which reaches its height in the poems of *North* (1975), to the more abstract concerns of the operation of the poet's consciousness reverses the trajectory of Yeats, his exemplar from the 1970s onward, from pure Symbolism to the concrete world of fact via his use of myth. In Denis Donoghue's equation, "The legends which allowed Yeats's mind to move freely and suggestively along their margins allowed him also to find their analogies in his own life; they gave him a terminology which he was free to apply and, applying it, to move from legend into history, his own history but history nonetheless."[19] The chiastic movement of Heaney's own poetry in relation to that of Yeats proceeds from his own history and the ground of lived experience to a contemplation of consciousness through his own musing upon legend, specifically the legend of Sweeney, as we will see in chapter 7. Yet Heaney has long been concerned with the operation of consciousness, as this chapter will attempt to show, even though it does not fully emerge as theme and content of much of his later poetry until his 1991 volume, *Seeing Things*.

Although it has become a critical commonplace to cite a radical change in Heaney's poetry from the more earthly early work to the more ethereal later verse starting with *Field Work* (1979) and especially *Station Island* (1984), he has always evinced a fidelity to the spiritual and

imaginative inner realms of himself, as the earlier poems demonstrate—
a fidelity that enabled him to withstand the various pressures that events
in Northern Ireland would come to place upon his work. Undoubtedly
his childhood Catholicism attuned him to this ethereal level of reality.
As he stated in a recent interview, his Catholic milieu encouraged a
contemplative state of mind:

> From the time I was conscious, I was in a highly, not only Chris-
> tian, but a Catholic environment. The house was full of holy pic-
> tures, and the rhythm of the week was determined, not by anything
> secular, but by mass and devotions. . . . If you take a humanist point
> of view, much of the effect of ardent religious institutions is to stult
> and to hurt. But if you take a poetic point of view, a Catholic child-
> hood and adolescence puts you right at the center of a radiant uni-
> verse. From the moment you begin to be aware, you [realize you]
> are a cell of the whole shimmering fabric, you know, and nothing
> you do is without significance.[20]

Any poet raised in a Protestant milieu would have had a close and
meaningful relationship with words because of the emphasis put on the
Word in that tradition, but Heaney's Catholic milieu gave him not only
an abiding fascination with words and etymology but also an immersion
in devotional practices that would prove useful for him as a poet in that
it enabled him to place himself in meditative postures to receive poetic
inspiration. Yet Heaney has a complex understanding of his Catholicism
that he has continued to revise and revisit over his career. John Desmond convincingly argues that Heaney's relationship to the Catholic
Christian tradition is epitomized by his being "ready to challenge and
reassess—though not completely abandon—his cultural religious inheritance and ready to make it a subject of imaginative transformation
in his poetry."[21]

Additionally, the central role played by the transubstantiation of the
Eucharist into Christ's body and blood in the Catholic mass has shaped
Heaney's sacramental perception of the world, just as it has for many
other Irish raised in the Church. Robert Welch argues that "the basic
conception of Catholic sacramental thought, therefore, is that the things

of existence, even insentient things such as bread and wine, have in them the potential, the power, to become other through Divine grace, just as man became God in the womb of Mary, the Virgin mother." Thus, since "the entire inclination of Catholic thinking is sacramental, it reverences profoundly all the minute activities of life and the flesh."[22]

There is some evidence that being steeped in this meditative, sacramental milieu has led Heaney to perceive himself as a poet-priest of the aesthetic, who exhibits the same sort of reverence toward the Other — poetry and its attendant mysteries — as the priest does before the Eucharist. Welch even claims that the deep sacramentalism of the Catholic Irish "tends to make them artists, because a sacrament is all about setting aside, for special and deliberate attention, something which in the ordinary course of events does not signify, but which, under the proper ordinance, may change the whole world."[23] We can see an early manifestation of Heaney's sense of himself as poet-priest of art in many of the early poems from the 1960s featuring rural craftsmen who display a worshipful attitude toward their respective crafts; this chapter later explores that series of poems.

Henry Hart has held that Heaney's use of writing as an excavating tool is inherently mystical: "As poetry replaces religion, Heaney demystifies the divine Word by transforming it into the poetic word. If Platonic and Judeo-Christian tradition has tended to denigrate writing as a cumbersome, improper medium for communicating sacred mysteries, Heaney . . . contradicts that bias by deploying writing as a principal way to excavate the ground from which mysteries and prejudices have always burgeoned."[24] Of course, both the Talmud and Christian scriptures also emphasize written language as linked to the divine. To give just one example of such a practice, John 1:1 states, "In the beginning was the Word, and the Word was with God, and the Word was God," where Christ is the revealed Savior, long written about and predicted in the Old Testament. Heaney's early writerly exploration of what lies beyond our everyday ken is, then, continuous with the kataphatic strand of Christian tradition (and later, with the apophatic tradition of negative theology, which involves an emptying out of the self) of using writing and images to reveal mystery: his appreciation of this practice combined with his own great power as wordsmith leads him ever deeper into spiritual realms that reveal poetic treasures to him. Michael Cavanagh has argued in this regard that "from the 1990s onward, Heaney is inclined to celebrate his Catholic background, not exactly for the doctrinal element, or for the pagan element, but for the access it seems to give to large vistas of space and time and feeling."[25]

Another crucial legacy of Heaney's long immersion in Catholicism, one linked to his concept of the poet as listener, has been its emphasis on patience. In a 1967 interview, Heaney recalled his mother's religious influence on him, especially stressing the importance of patience: "The attitude to life that was inculcated into me—not by priests, but by the active, lived thing of prayers and so on, in my house, through my mother—was really patience. At the bottom I think that probably patience is the best virtue" (quoted in *SHMP,* 4). That long-standing absorption in patience would stand him in good stead as he was increasingly assailed with the concerns of the outside world when the conflict in Northern Ireland accelerated.

Additionally, while Heaney did draw upon his Catholic heritage, especially in some of his early poetry, culminating in *North,* in such a way as to occasionally posit himself as the voice of the aggrieved Catholic minority in Northern Ireland, a much more significant influence of his Catholic upbringing has been to affirm and strengthen his fidelity to poetry over his allegiance to his community, though this other allegiance has always been strong. As we will see, nowhere is this tension stronger than in his volume *Station Island,* when his literal pilgrimage intersects with his poetic pilgrimage, but he is finally able to focus on his inner life rather than on the conflict raging outside.

A final invaluable aspect of his Catholic heritage that will be explored in the section of this study devoted to Heaney is his concept of forgiveness, which has been largely neglected in Heaney criticism but which is crucial to understanding his contribution to cultural understanding and reconciliation in Northern Ireland. Chapter 7, for example, analyzes the ethical underpinnings of the well-known poem "Punishment," whose occluded Gospel narrative recalls Christ's interaction with the adulteress and Pharisees in John 8, a narrative also referenced in his important essay "The Government of the Tongue." Because his poetry's ethical system is derived from his adult transformations of his early

Catholic faith, Heaney has felt all the more obliged to incorporate the aspects of that faith, like forgiveness, that he feels are the most relevant to changing the (often literally) morbid political situation in Northern Ireland.

Although the drift of this discussion might seem to render Heaney's work increasingly abstract, because of his immersion in an incarnational faith he has been able to seamlessly resolve the long-standing Cartesian duality between inner and outer, body and spirit. Thus he has been able to perceive the continuities between the outer, public life and the inner, private world of the self. Hence his concreteness—not just his carefully deployed diction but also his depictions of physical activity—is often allied to abstract meditations on the nature of poetry itself. Terry Eagleton has similarly argued that Heaney rejects a Cartesian model of language and recognizes its materiality: "The recovery of the materiality of language—the growing refusal of Cartesian, metaphysical models which would relegate language to a pale reflection of another pale reflection (thought), and privilege the apparently immaterial 'voice' over the more obtrusively material 'script'—is a precious theoretical development which Heaney's poetry in some way parallels. . . . Heaney recognises that if language is indeed in some sense material, it has its own specific mode of materiality, complexly related to work, Nature and human relationships."[26] Although Eagleton's veiled attempt to make Heaney into a closet Marxist is ideologically suspect, his claim about Heaney's recovery of language's materiality has great validity, especially since Heaney writes so carefully and vividly about bodily work.[27]

As John Wilson Foster and later, Helen Vendler have pointed out, many of Heaney's early poems celebrate the declining rural crafts of his native Ulster as part of his poetic function as folklorist and anthropologist.[28] Many of his later poems do this as well, however. In a way that has not been understood yet in Heaney criticism, his poetic broodings upon the traditional crafts of Ulster in the strand of poetry that John Boly has termed his "mentor poems" mirror his descriptions of the ways in which his "technique" is accessed.[29] The rhythm of crafts he observes reflects the rhythm or becomes the rhythm under whose spell he places himself in order to reach the meditative state at which he can receive preverbal images that he can then make into poetry. Thus his careful observation of other crafts leads him to extended contemplation of the meditative process by which he employs his own craftsmanship. This process is essentially religious because of poetry's unpredictable arrival: in his interview with Karl Miller, Heaney notes, "I have some notion of poetry as a grace."[30] His poems that pair rural crafts and poetry include not just the famous apprentice poem "Digging" and the well-known elegy "Casualty" from *Field Work* but lesser-known ones such as the "Lough Neagh Sequence" from *Door into the Dark* (1969), "A Daylight Art" from *The Haw Lantern* (1987), and "'Poet's Chair'" from *The Spirit Level* (1996).

Although he juxtaposes a variety of crafts with poetry, Heaney returns repeatedly to the craft of fishing, finding in it deep analogies for poetic technique and rhythm. In the last stanza of one of his earliest poems, "Fisher," he explicitly links the two activities: "I cast a line baited with metre / And images ripple, words scatter. / I hook verse dead as an old stump" (*SHPM*, 3). As these lines indicate, Heaney feels that his poetry is somehow already preexisting and that he must undergo a process of retrieval to access it and render it verbally. He explained this method to Karl Miller: "I never want to get out of my phonetic depth, as it were. I like to feel that the line I am writing is being paid out from some old inner voice-reel, that it is coming up from the place I re-enter every time I go back to where I grew up."[31] Understanding this negotiation between technique and craft enables us to realize the fundamental continuity underlying much of his major poetry—the verbal manifestation (craft) of the meditative process (technique) undertaken to create the poem.

Lest this discussion seems completely removed from the atrocities that were occurring on the streets of the province and were much on Heaney's mind for most of this period, it should be said that only by understanding Heaney's textual representations of this poetic vacillation can we understand how his imagination resisted the pressure of the temptation of immediate poetic "reportage" and how it was able to offer new ways of seeing the conflict in the province, new ways of imagining alternatives to it when he chose to do so. Moreover, despite his Catholic heritage and use of Catholic meditative techniques, Heaney's poetry is often open to other cultural influences and thus all the more able to offer unifying images and language to the range of cultures coexisting in the province. In comparing Heaney's poetry with that of one of his exemplars, the fellow Catholic Patrick Kavanagh, Michael Parker has pointed out that because Heaney's early poetry was written "for a 'mixed' audience, at a time when Protestant and Catholic writers were coming into closer and more creative contact with each other than ever before, Heaney's first poetry does not display the intensive Catholic allusion one finds in Kavanagh, since it might exclude, if not alienate some readers" (*SHMP,* 32). For a poet professing allegiance to both the minority-Catholic community and, to a lesser but still powerful extent, Britain, it is crucial to understand his first and primary allegiance, as Seamus Deane has remarked in a seminal essay on his poetry: "He is indentured, finally, to the idea of poetry itself."[32] Eventually, Heaney's emphasis on the auditory imagination and his lesser but still important interest in rapprochement, even reconciliation, coalesce in his articulation of a position where mind rises above the pressures of reality to become its own "field of force" and binaries are engaged in a dialectical process by which their potency is recognized and their harm rejected.

The Early Poetry: *Death of a Naturalist* and *Door into the Dark*

As innumerable commentators have remarked, Heaney's first major poem, "Digging," from *Death of a Naturalist* (1966), is an apprentice poem in which the poet both aligns himself with the family tradition of digging and crucially breaks from that tradition, declaring himself by the poem's end to be a poet whose tool will be very different from the spades employed by his father and grandfather. The concrete pen with which the poem concludes, however, is reached only after Heaney digs into his memory, an abstract process that he undergoes by reflectively listening to and seeing his own father digging outside his windowsill. The primary linkage between Heaney and his ancestors in this poem comes not from the slightly strained analogy of digging and writing and the corresponding tools of shovel and pen but from the rhythm of the three Heaney generations as they practice their crafts: Heaney thus writes a rhythmic poem about his inheritance of rhythm from his father and grandfather. The pen is "squat" and "snug as a gun" in the first stanza because the poet sees it as a tool much like the shovels of his predecessors. Its snugness suggests how firmly the poet holds his implement, which will enable him to write more deeply, much as his father and grandfather held their shovels snugly to more deeply penetrate the earth and the bog, respectively. In this regard, his father's shovel is tellingly "levered firmly" (*DN*, 1).

In stanza 2, Heaney hears "a clean rasping sound / When the spade sinks into gravelly ground: / My father, digging" (*DN*, 1), which is not created by a unique motion; rather, Heaney is hearing the rhythm of his father repeatedly digging, a fact emphasized by the present participle of the verb. And just as Heaney is hearing repeated digging, we realize that he has repeatedly sat and listened to his father repeatedly digging. This listening represents Heaney's typical poetic posture that he displays time and again in his poems. He is listening, pen held in reserve, to his father digging in the present in stanza 2 and in the past in stanza 3. Patrick Heaney's particular potato-digging rhythm is mentioned explicitly in this third stanza as the son now *looks* out the window: "I look down // Till his straining rump comes up twenty years away / Stooping *in rhythm* through potato drills / Where he was digging" (1, emphasis mine).[33] These lines first recall Foster's description of Heaney as anthropologist in his recognition of the dying craft of digging potatoes by hand. Later in the volume, in "At a Potato Digging," a poem naturally paired with "Digging," the poet shudders in disdain at the cold chaos of the "mechanical digger [that] wrecks the drill, / Spins up a dark shower of roots and mould" (18). Second, the poet is remembering and holding in his mind his true heritage—his father's rhythm—continually accessed by memory.

Although no commentator has realized the resonance of rhythm in the poem as exemplary for Heaney's development as a poet, Michael Molino's misreading of this aspect of the poem is surprisingly obtuse: "The fact that the father has some kind of 'rhythm' implies the naturalness of his actions, although it could be the speaker's perception of the father being in harmony with nature, a trait the speaker feels he does not share."[34] The actual focus of the poem is on the *harmony* that Heaney feels his rhythmic verse shares with the digging rhythms of his father and grandfather. In this sense, he is able to also harmonize with nature, albeit vicariously.

Where the opening stanzas convey Heaney's listening to and viewing the repetitive motions of Patrick Heaney digging repeatedly in "the flowerbeds" (*DN*, 1) of the present and the potato drills of the past, the

sixth and seventh stanzas articulate a specific memory of the poet's encounter with his grandfather, a turf cutter. The childish boast—that
"My grandfather cut more turf in a day / Than any other man on Toner's
bog"—if true, is true because of the old man's extraordinary digging
rhythm and penchant for working steadily. On this particular occasion,
after the young Seamus gives his grandfather "milk in a bottle / Corked
sloppily with paper," and he "straightened up / To drink it," the older man
"then fell to right away / Nicking and slicing neatly, heaving sods / Over
his shoulder, going down and down / For the good turf. Digging" (2).
The neatness of his digging precisely contrasts the sloppily corked bottle
of milk given him by his grandson and personifies his personal rhythm.
He deftly and deeply makes his cut, does not overreach, and then dex-
terously tosses the turf "Over his shoulder." In this stanza, Heaney re-
members and accesses the repetitive rhythm of his grandfather's turf cutting as a guide to his own rhythmic art (2). Previously associated with the
paper that corks the bottle of milk as a child, the grown man will also use
paper but attempt to write precisely and rhythmically on it, unlike the
child who sloppily corked the bottle with paper.

Since he concludes, "But I've no spade to follow men like them"
(*DN,* 2), he crafts an extremely well-made poem, framed with the image
of the pen in equipoise "Between my finger and my thumb." This image
has now been transformed from the martial image in line 2—"snug as a
gun"—to the exploratory, peaceful image in the concluding line, decisive
in its affirmation of art—"I'll dig with it" (1, 2). This admittedly self-
conscious but confident decision has been mischaracterized by the usually
astute critic Terence Brown, who misunderstands the poet's workmanlike and rhythmic association of pen and gun and argues that the poem
"scarcely disguised its embarrassment at the inadequacy of a poetic career in comparison with Heaney's father's more obviously useful skills.
The association in that poem . . . of the pen with gun seems a rather
desperate stratagem to invest the poet's art with something of the male
authority of the father's spade and the ancestral achievement it consoli-
dates. 'Real men don't write poems' is the emotional undercurrent of the
piece."[35] Blake Morrison's argument about the gun simile in one of the
first books published on Heaney anticipates Brown's: "It is too macho,
melodramatically so, and not even the insertion of the adjectives 'squat'

and 'snug' can allay the feeling that the analogy is in any case not right—inaccurate visually and misleading in its implication that what follows in *Death of a Naturalist* is the work of a poetic hard man. The real interest of the image is that it seems to be over-compensating for the poet's shame at departing from lineage."[36] Morrison places too much emphasis on this particular simile, however, as *the* stance of the poet in the rest of the volume, when it is only a temporary stance in the poem itself.

Both Morrison and Brown seem not to realize that "Digging" is more exploratory and proud than embarrassed and fail to perceive that Heaney recognizes and receives his true inheritance of rhythm, enabling us to see how he too has now written himself into the male vocational tradition of his family. Just as Yeats, in the first stanza of "Adam's Curse," defends poetry as the most difficult of labors and argues that poetic labor must seem natural and easy to the public, Heaney holds in "Digging" that writing is arduous but must be achieved and characterized by seemingly effortless, rhythmic labor.[37] In discussing this poem in a 2001 interview with Jerome Weeks, Heaney suggests another reason why that poetic pen is held so firmly—because he saw his role in the poems of that period as being that of an apologist for poetry: "It's one of my notions, that a function of the poet is to stand up for poetry."[38]

His ancestors' gift of rhythm will enable him to access, not physical, underground depths, but those of his subconscious. As Molino correctly notes about the implications of the present participle form of the title, "The father and the grandfather are captured in a continually present moment as events from the past continue, or echo, in the present"; the poem thus exists in a "consistently present moment that, while inhabited with echoes of the past, truncates and reinscribes those echoes as they occur."[39] Typically then, and in a way that Molino has not articulated, this early poem obliquely suggests that Heaney's mind functions as a sort of sound chamber where the rhythms of various types of digging in the past and present trigger, then echo with the rhythms of his writing the poem in the present. In this sense, "Digging" accords with T. S. Eliot's theory that "a poem, or a passage of a poem, may tend to realize itself first as a particular rhythm before it reaches expression in words, and . . . this rhythm may bring to birth the idea and the image."[40] This early poem thus adumbrates part of Heaney's theory of "technique" as a necessary process of retrieving images of poetry that lie submerged in the inner depths of his psyche and that can be located through reveries often precipitated by liminal spaces such as the window in the opening lines.

The significance of this poem in the Heaney oeuvre has been much remarked, but its full impact for his artistic project has not yet been realized. For in "Digging," Heaney enacts in miniature the two poetic projects that have marked his entire career: he celebrates and affirms his allegiance to art and rejects the violence he might have resorted to as a disaffected minority Catholic in 1960s Northern Ireland, gesturing instead, even at this early point in his career, toward a shared cultural ground of understanding for the two dominant cultures in Northern Ireland. As Vendler points out, Heaney's dilemma was typical of the Irish Catholic child at the time: "[This child] grew up between the offers of two instruments: the spade and the gun. 'Choose,' said two opposing voices from his culture: 'Inherit the farm,' said agricultural tradition; 'Take up arms,' said Republican militarism. . . . It is significant in this—the first poem in his first book—Heaney rejects the concept of writing as aggression, and chooses the spade as the final analogue for his pen: the pen will serve as an instrument of exploration and excavation, yielding warmth (like his grandfather's turf for fires) and nourishment (like his father's potatoes)."[41] I accept Vendler's explanation that Heaney's choice of his poetic vocation represents a third way between farming and republican violence but agree with Adrian Frazier's rejection of the forced analogy of the poet's pen to turf and potatoes in Vendler's argument: "The potatoes and slabs of turf seem too definitively converted by Vendler's analysis into symbols of warmth and nourishment. The poem's language associates potatoes instead with 'cool hardness' and the turf with 'squelch and slap'; the sensuous properties of the things themselves, not the utilitarian functions of those things or their cultural symbolism."[42]

Frazier, however, makes far too much of the pen/gun analogy in the opening lines, seeing it as an example of Heaney's underground nationalism, which Frazier fleshes out by misreadings of other militaristic nouns scattered throughout *Death of a Naturalist*.[43] More disturbingly, John Wilson Foster, the first critic to question the "snug as a gun" line, has argued that "since the poem is about digging, the image of the gun introduces a piece of gratuitous menace. Often with equal gratuity, images of ballistics and detonation pepper the volume. . . . The menace of the book, however vindicated in the gun-law of Ulster society since, is unearned."[44] Heaney's righteous anger at the mistreatment of the Catholics in the province is usually manifested in other, more public genres of his work, such as his stirring essays for the *New Statesman* and the *Listener* in the late 1960s, and in fact, he introduces the gun image only to undercut it and violence generally as the poem and the volume develop.[45] Both Vendler and Frazier, however, miss the emphasis on rhythm associated with the three different (four if you count the two types of digging done by Patrick Heaney) activities in the poem, especially Heaney's metapoetic emphasis on the formal rhythm of the poem itself stemming from its meditations on rhythmic craftsmanship.[46]

Despite all of this poem's emphasis on the process of poetry, it also signals something critics have never recognized before: a willingness to engage in the creation of an inclusive society through writing. To wit, the gun and pen that Heaney so famously connects in his opening simile respectively hint at his fear in 1964 that a movement in 1960s Northern Ireland toward cultural inclusivity could be taken over by proponents of violence but should be led by intellectuals, even writers. In a passage from his little-known 1964 essay on the leaders of the 1798 Rising, "Our Own Dour Way," Heaney hopefully remarked, "I only hope that their descendants of the 1960s follow their example—with the pen which is so much mightier than the pike."[47] Heaney would later repeatedly draw parallels between the 1798 rebellion and the 1960s civil rights movement in Northern Ireland, often expressing his desire that the non-violent aspect of the marches would succeed in securing Catholic civil rights in ways that the 1798 fighting did not. Clearly, by employing his opening martial simile and then dropping any reference to the gun by the end of the poem while retaining his mention of his pen, Heaney suggests a version of the old saw, "The pen is mightier than the sword." The passage I have cited from "Our Own Dour Way," published in *Hibernia* in April 1963, precedes the original December 4, 1964, publication of "Digging" in *New Statesman*[48] and suggests that by the end of 1964 Heaney was still meditating on the failure of violence to secure Catholic emancipation in 1798 (among the Rising's other objectives) and on the possibility for a new, nonviolent society led by writers and thinkers in the 1960s. This most famous of Heaney's early poems, then, announces the arrival of a writer uncommonly devoted both to the labor of his craft and to the ethical responsibility of helping do the hard work of building a new, more inclusive Northern Ireland.

Heaney carefully framed the poems of *Death of a Naturalist* to highlight his emphasis on poetic technique as he would later define the term in "Feeling into Words." For example, in "Personal Helicon," the volume's concluding poem dedicated to fellow Belfast Group poet Michael Longley, he introduces an image he would explore more fully in "Feeling into Words"—that of the well. There he argues that repeated poetic craft can lead to an apprehension of technique: "Learning the craft is learning to turn the windlass at the well of poetry. Usually you begin by dropping the bucket halfway down the shaft and winding up a taking of air. You are miming the real thing until one day the chain draws unexpectedly tight and you have dipped into waters that will continue to entice you back. You'll have broken the skin on the pool of yourself. Your praties will be 'fit for digging.' At that point it becomes appropriate to speak of technique rather than craft" ("FW," 47).[49] The Wordsworthian child of the poem's first four stanzas who could not be kept from wells is transformed by the final stanza into the adult poet who seeks poetry as a legitimate vocational alternative to the previous avocational practice of playing in wells:

> Now, to pry into roots, to finger slime,
> To stare, big-eyed Narcissus, into some spring
> Is beneath all adult dignity. I rhyme
> To see myself, to set the darkness echoing.
>
> (*DN*, 44)

Characteristic of Heaney's careful craft, his evocation of his technique here is reinforced by his mixed use of para-rhyme and full rhyme in the first four stanzas, culminating in the full rhyme of the last, which suggests the intersection of craft and technique in a typically metapoetic way.[50]

Molino has pointed out that the double meanings of *helicon* here enable Heaney to meditate upon both artistic sources and the means of expressing art, thus linking the concerns of "Personal Helicon" with those of "Digging": "The poem's title refers to the Helicon, a Grecian mountain range that was the mythic home of the Muses. The word is used synonymously for artistic inspiration. A helicon is also a musical instrument, something that must be played, and whose musical qualities exist only in the present moment. Thus, a personal helicon is both the source of inspiration and the instrument for that inspiration—just as digging is the method and result of writing."[51] The adjective of the title "Personal Helicon" also suggests the necessity for the artist to remove himself somewhat from the company of others in order to fully explore and develop his art, while keeping an eye on the community. "Digging" both evokes the image of a writer isolated from his family, despite the enabling gift of rhythm from those ancestors, and hints at the need for a community of writers to usher in a new age of cultural understanding in Northern Ireland. "Personal Helicon," on the other hand, implies the essential solitude of the writer even if he maintains a connection to his community.

But if "Personal Helicon" foreshadows Heaney's technique/craft dialectic and emphasizes the relative importance of technique, it also enacts another dialectic—between the freedom of contemplation and the prison of self-absorption—as he pointed out in a BBC radio interview:

> In one way, it's about the self-entrancement of the writer which is reprehensible in social terms, if you like. That where that freedom starts is in the gaze inward—that where you begin transforming is by looking into yourself. "Look in thy heart and write," the Muse says to Sydney. But this poem also uses the image of Narcissus; we all know what happened to Narcissus—he drowned in himself. That is the danger of poetry carrying its own artfulness to an extreme. That it becomes cut off and it ends up admiring itself in its own pool. But, I think that there is a halfway house between drowning in the pool of the art and the obliteration of the pool by the onset and the accumulation just of the world around it.[52]

This "halfway house" is a typical liminal image for Heaney, who is drawn to such images as a way to express how living on the boundary is neces-

sary for achieving a dynamism that can mediate between competing attractions, usually variants of contemplation and action. The contemplative nature of art, then, must not become solipsism, for that posture leads
to complete isolation from community. Heaney has always resisted such
isolation: he has consistently sought to critique societal problems, especially the great social and religious divide between Catholics and Protestants in Northern Ireland, through his pensive work.[53]

Door into the Dark (1969) continues Heaney's emphasis on technique and craft, while also adumbrating concerns for reconciliation
in the province that will bulk larger in his later poetry beginning with
Wintering Out (1972). Blake Morrison has convincingly argued that
Heaney was raised in a culture that valued silence, and *Door into the Dark*
amply demonstrates this.[54] Although Morrison extrapolates from this
claim to argue that Heaney experienced "inhibitions" "about the writing of poetry" as a result of being a member of a persecuted minority
community that valued silence, this formative milieu of silence actually
proved fruitful for Heaney in realizing the ideal stance of the poet as
one of silent listening.[55] The reticent craftsmen he saw around him in
rural Ulster also lent a continuing currency to the conviction, audaciously
displayed in "Digging," that he was the poetic inheritor of the rhythm
they employed in practicing their crafts. Morrison points out that *Door
into the Dark* reflects Heaney's growing confidence in his poetic abilities:
"Composition is no longer self-conscious labour [as it was in *Death of a
Naturalist*] but a matter of trust and trance."[56] Although Morrison does
not proceed to explain how this process of "trust and trance" is explored
in the volume's poetry, the phrase perfectly captures the thrust of the volume in its patient, near-religious waiting on poetry to arrive in the subconscious mind of its maker.

There is a Yeatsian component to this waiting. Yeats's underappre-
ciated poem "Three Beggars," in which the seemingly indifferent crane
hopes for a fish and the beggars strive in vain to win a contest that will
make one of them rich, may well have confirmed Heaney's patience in
listening for the rhythms and images of his poetry. While none of the
beggars achieves riches through his efforts, the crane that opens and
closes the poem finally thinks that in the subsequent silence engendered
by the collapse of the exhausted beggars, "maybe I shall take a trout / If

but I do not seem to care."[57] Daniel Albright has suggested that these lines and the thrust of the poem as a whole display a parable-like quality, "recommending self-surrender and indifference," but notes, "There may also be an artistic corollary: the imagination is best rewarded by images when it sinks into a passive state of trance, instead of laboring fretfully."[58] Heaney's patience is Yeatsian in its indifferent though disciplined self-surrender, and when it achieves a state of trance, he too is rewarded with images that swim up from the depths of his mind. Heaney is speaking of his own process of disinterested introspection when he writes of Robert Frost that "any interference by the knowing intellect in the purely disinterested cognitions of the form-seeking imagination constitutes poetic sabotage, an affront to the legislative and executive powers of expression itself."[59]

The volume's title links Heaney's ongoing concern for outer realities in Northern Ireland with his inward interest in poetry's spiritual capacity. If the window in "Digging" was simultaneously a portal to the past and an opening to the future, the door of "The Forge" functions as a similar threshold that the poet traverses between the profane, outer world and the sacred, inner world, to use Mircea Eliade's terms. Eliade points out that the door of the modern, urban church "actually signifies a solution of continuity" between the church itself and the street, yet "also indicates the distance between two modes of being, the profane and the religious. The threshold is the limit, the boundary, the frontier that distinguishes and opposes two worlds—and at the same time the paradoxical place where those worlds communicate."[60] The blacksmith's forge is both a sort of church for Heaney where the craftsman practices the mysteries of his art and an analogy for the subconscious mind, "the dark." Placing himself literally or mentally in the doorway, the poet can keep a weather eye on the outer world while gazing at the exemplary figure of the blacksmith, lost in his work.

Throughout *Door into the Dark,* Heaney makes clear analogies between the Yeatsian patience of the fisherman or the blacksmith and that of the poet that all must exercise if they are to practice their craft well. For example, in "The Salmon Fisher to the Salmon" and "The Forge" Heaney implicitly links the craft of making poetry with the crafts of fishing and blacksmithing. In the former poem, the fisherman "stand[s]

in the centre, casting," waiting for the fish, an action and stance comparable to Heaney's waiting on poems to arrive from his subconscious even
as he casts for them, a subtle yoking of his technique/craft dialectic
(*DD*, 6).

In "The Forge," Heaney again invokes the center as a repository
of craft but makes more explicit craft's (and thus poetry's) oblique relationship to and replacement of religion. Here the anvil, which "must be
somewhere in the centre," is described as "an altar / Where he expends
himself in shape and music" (*DD*, 7). Again in this poem, technique,
the preverbal part of poetry that is accessed through the "door into the
dark" of the poem's first line, is subtly soldered with craft in the figure of
the taciturn blacksmith. Waiting and listening is thus obliquely portrayed as the ideal stance of the poet hoping to receive poems. Only after
doing this can the poet make a "music" similar to what he hears from
the blacksmith's forge in line 9. This is a reminiscent, bucolic poem like
"Digging" because the blacksmith looks back to a time of cows, not cars,
as "traffic" that "is flashing in rows" (7). He contrasts the relatively weak
metal of the modern cars to the "real iron" (7) he hammers on his forge,
suggesting that thoughtful, well-meditated art withstands the passage
of time. Additionally, "The Forge" implies, as does "Digging," that good
poetry requires rhythmic work for its achievement.

This poem also exemplifies Heaney's reverent attitude toward real
craftsmanship, whether shaping iron or making poetry. Glenn Arbery
holds that "this anvil-altar, virginal, an 'immoveable' omphalos, combines private memory with a mythology of *poeisis* that goes back to Way-
land and Hephaistos. It is the center that sacralizes the labor of any
making in which the maker expends himself 'in shape and music.'"[61]
Extending his argument about the artistic sacralizing of the poem, Arbery claims that its form enables a transcendence of "both the author's
'self' and its specific 'historical circumstance.' When the poem stirs, it is
because some otherwise inaccessible power increasingly passes through
the poem by means of the poet's work."[62] "The Forge" thus demonstrates how the formal structure of the poem, which is, after all, a sonnet, even if a hybrid example of the Petrarchan form, enables the poet
to undergo his process of technique — that of retrieval and recovery —
and to bring the content of the embryonic poem to the surface of his

mind and into harmony with the poem's outline. In the sonic manifestation of its form, the finished poem, like finished ironwork, sounds a particular way. Heaney finally implies that both poetry making and iron making are durable, partially oral arts.

Patrick Grant's description of the metapoetic strain of Heaney's work strengthens and fruitfully complicates Arbery's reading of the poet's reverent attitude toward his craft in "The Forge" and other poems that share its sacramental attitude toward art. Heaney, Grant claims, "retain[s] something of Dante's sacramental reverence . . . , even as he turns to Wordsworth to adapt the figural mode to a less explicitly Catholic view of the world than that imparted by his early upbringing. He then effects a resolution—by way of Modernism—offering up the poem itself as a quasi-sacramental act. We might describe the compound effect of these elements as 'post-Romantic figural.'"[63]

The most sustained analogy, however, in the volume between craft and poetry comes in "A Lough Neagh Sequence," where Heaney once again returns to his favorite analogy between fishing and poetry.[64] Each of the seven poems in the sequence focuses on eels, from the catching of them (in "Up the Shore," "Bait," "Setting," "Lifting") to their migratory experiences ("Beyond Sargasso," "The Return," and "Vision"). The central poem of the sequence, "Setting," is also centrally important in suggesting the deep analogy Heaney sees between fishing and poetry. Its opening stanza hints that finding and catching eels and finding poetic images are remarkably similar processes:

> A line goes out of sight and out of mind
> Down to the soft bottom of silt and sand
> Past the indifferent skills of the hunting hand.
>
> (*DD*, 29)

Just as the eelsmen's lines go down to the bottom of the lough, so too, the craft of poetry, Heaney implies, must cast for buried words and images that are lodged in the dark recesses of the mind.[65] Craft, then, both creates an access, a "door into the dark" of the subconscious by which those words and images are retrieved, and renders them into an articulate shape and form. This emphasis on craft in the early poetry does not mean, however, that Heaney favored it over technique; indeed, his inclination to burrow inwards in many of these poems suggests that he favored the contemplation associated with technique. His lifelong preoccupation with the analogy of fishing and poetry is dynamic in that periodically a different part of the technique/craft dialectic will be emphasized while a residual emphasis will nonetheless be placed on the remaining term.⁶⁶

Significantly, Heaney's craftsmen are always alone, never in a crowd, which suggests he was gradually learning that art must be conducted in solitude, though not solipsism. The various arts depicted in these early poems—digging, thatching, ironworking, fishing—all are concerned with producing finished works that will feed and warm, shelter, shoe, and feed again, respectively, the people for whom the labor is done. The poems offer a sheer joy in the work itself, a quality Heaney shares with his rural Ulster craftsmen. His observation of these solitary workers lent a practical weight to the theoretical advice about the necessity of practicing poetry in solitude that he was acquiring from reading T. S. Eliot's poetry in the early 1960s, as he has noted in a remark that employs the language of craftsmanship: "What one ultimately learns from Eliot is that the activity of poetry is solitary, and if one is to rejoice in it, one has to construct something upon which to rejoice."⁶⁷ Learning to rejoice through poetic solitude would prove a potent and fruitful endeavor for Heaney as the violence in the province quickly swelled shortly after the publication of *Door into the Dark.*

"Requiem for the Croppies," one of two major historical poems in the volume (the other is "Bogland"), suggests the ways Heaney's imagination was engaging with the outward problems occurring in the province as a natural outgrowth of his emphasis on poetic craft, which forced him to emerge from his inner depths. In this poem, Heaney affirms his true republicanism, embracing the spirit of the 1798 rebels' ecumenism. Instead of evoking images of buried mud or consciousness as he does elsewhere in the volume, this poem concludes with a different image, also buried, but in the ground of history: "They buried us without shroud or coffin / And in August the barley grew up out of the grave" (*DD*, 12). In these last two lines, the rebels who were on the run with pockets "full of barley—" in line 1 have been cut down, "shaking scythes at cannon"

(12). But the image of sprouting barley lends a hopeful air to the poem. As Heaney would later argue, this image had an ideological dimension as well: "The oblique implication was that the seeds of violent resistance sowed in the Year of Liberty had flowered in what Yeats called 'the right rose tree' of 1916. I did not realize at the time that the original heraldic murderous encounter between Protestant yeoman and Catholic rebel was to be initiated again in the summer of 1969, in Belfast, two months after the book *[Door into the Dark]* was published" ("FW," 56). While Heaney's tone certainly has a nationalist tinge to it, he realized the ecumenical nature of the 1798 rebellion and approved of the fact that it was led in part by radical Protestants, as demonstrated in his stirring 1970 radio play *Munro*.[68] At the same time, in his review of Thomas Pakenham's book about the 1798 rebellion, *The Year of Liberty*, in late November 1969, Heaney lamented how "each element of nightmare . . . succeeded the dream of hope," pointing out how Pakenham linked the self-government of Ulster that failed in 1798 with the Stormont experiment beginning in 1921, in which "Catholics have remained poor, politically powerless, and alienated from government" (quoted in *SHMP,* 87).

Thus the poem does attempt to infuse what Heaney termed "subcultural material" into an "official English-poetry form," the sonnet, in an attempt to register the presence of Catholics in the province.[69] Within a few years, however, he realized the poem could be used as IRA propaganda, noting, "By the mid-Seventies, to recite 'Requiem for the Croppies' in Ireland in public would have been taken as a gesture of solidarity with the Provisionals. From being a 'silence-breaker' it would have turned into a propaganda tool, something inflammatory."[70] The most important implication of the poem—and one that is not usually registered in criticism on Heaney—lies in its all-too-brief evocation of a period of ecumenical relations between Protestants and Catholics in the northern part of Ireland.[71] He would return to this hopeful period time and again in his poetry and prose, finally seeing the Belfast Agreement of 1998 as a worthy successor to the 1798 movement.

A poem that I view as the best of his many "bog poems" concludes *Door into the Dark*. "Bogland" successfully juxtaposes, in its opening lines, the "progressive" view of America as a horizontal, ever-expanding frontier (up until 1890, according to the famous thesis of Frederick Jackson Turner) with a conception of Ireland as a vertical, finally more expansive bog:

> We have no prairies
> to slice a big sun at evening —
> Everywhere the eye concedes to
> Encroaching horizon,
>
> Is wooed into the cyclops' eye
> Of a tarn. Our unfenced country
> Is bog that keeps crusting
> Between the sights of the sun.
>   (*DD*, 41)

While this view of the bog could be taken for mere environmental idealism, the poem refuses such a construction, offering up instead preserved treasures: "the skeleton / Of the Great Irish Elk" and butter that "Was recovered salty and white" (41). While these objects issue forth from the bog, tellingly, its "wet centre is bottomless" (42). This last line represents Heaney's perfect poetic incorporation of a symbol of the bottomless depths of the imagination that naturally developed from the subterranean musing of poems like "Digging" and "Setting" in "A Lough Neagh Sequence."

Those earlier poems, while crucial in establishing dark spaces as emblematic of technique or imagination, nonetheless are a bit limiting for him because their central images can be plumbed, while the wet center of "Bogland" cannot and thus stands for a constantly renewing sense of potential, in contrast to the finally limited American frontier. This seemingly inexhaustible natural source functions as a correlative of the poet's subconscious out of which poems emerge when he casts himself into a receptive mood, as he has noted: "I have always listened for poems, they come sometimes like bodies come out of a bog, almost complete, seeming to have been laid down a long time ago, surfacing with a touch of mystery."[72] The concluding focus on the bog, not its buried objects, is salutary, especially since this symbol for the imagination was asked to do too much at times in the poems of *North,* whose bodies that came forth from different bogs were perhaps too material and thus overwhelmed the theoretical possibilities of that original imagined bog for Heaney. An additional problem with those later bog poems, as the next chapter will show, concerns Heaney's viewing of those bodies through the medium of the still photograph. The portrayal of the abstract potential of memory and imagination—though they are none the less real or, for that matter, Irish, for their abstractness—renders "Bogland" one of his best poems.[73]

While this image of the imagination as bottomless extended Heaney's conception of technique and its importance in his developing poetic, he also realized that the charged political atmosphere in the province must necessarily press against his imagination and that the two could combine for powerful poetry. As the Catholic minority in the North struggled for recognition, Heaney realized that his vocation was inextricably intertwined with events occurring around him. In a 1978 lecture he gave at the University of Surrey, "Yeats As an Example?" Heaney explains how Yeats resolved the tension between his art and his life:

> What is finally admirable is the way his life and his work are *not* separate but make a continuum, the way the courage of his vision did not confine itself to rhetorics but issued in actions. . . . Yeats bore the implications of his romanticism into action: he propagandized, speechified, fund-raised, administered and politicked in the world of telegrams and anger, *all on behalf of the world of vision.* His poetry was not just a matter of printed books making their way in a world of literate readers and critics; it was rather the fine flower of his efforts to live as forthrightly as he could in the world of illiterates and politicians.[74]

Heaney's affirmation of the absolute validity of the artistic process in Yeats's work has functioned as his own compass in his poetry, as this passage clearly shows. Furthermore, his approving statement of Yeats's activity of behalf of his imagination—"All on the behalf of the world of vision"—sums up Heaney's lifelong continuum or marriage between his own life and work. A year after he gave this lecture on Yeats, Heaney would insist to James Randall that Yeats "shows that by dint of fierce commitment to the art you can pay into the public life."[75] For a young Irish poet already devoted to seeing things, perceiving different dimensions of reality or appreciating opposing political views, Yeats's supple yoking of contemplation and action held special warrant for Heaney and demonstrated that while poetry would hold his first allegiance, it could also, if properly practiced, imagine transformative action.

CHAPTER SIX

"The Road to Derry,"
Wintering Out, and *North*

NORTHERN HARMONY, NORTHERN VIOLENCE

Heaney's Move to the Republic of Ireland: "The Road to Derry" and the Aftermath of Bloody Sunday

Heaney resigned his post as a lecturer in English literature at Queen's University in Belfast in April and then moved to the Republic of Ireland at a crucial moment during the Troubles in August of 1972, the same year his third volume, *Wintering Out,* appeared. The murders of fourteen Catholic civil rights protesters had occurred on January 30 of that year in what would become known as "Bloody Sunday." IRA attacks on British soldiers skyrocketed, and the British Embassy in Dublin was burnt to the ground on February 2, the day the funerals for the Bloody Sunday victims were held. Heaney's wife, Marie, "had escaped by only a few minutes a bombing in Belfast," and he and Michael Longley "had been threatened for participating in a peace march following Bloody Sunday earlier in the year."[1] That spring thus constituted one of the all-time low points in the Troubles for Heaney personally and for the province generally.

Critics have generally neglected to discuss Heaney's near-immediate poetic response to Bloody Sunday, the nationalist ballad "The Road to Derry," and have preferred to focus on his later meditation on the event, "Casualty," which was collected in *Field Work* seven years later.[2] Their neglect of the ballad undoubtedly stems from its lack of publication until the twenty-fifth anniversary of Bloody Sunday, January 30, 1997, in the *Derry Journal* and its reprinting in the *Guardian* the next day, and Heaney's refusal, on aesthetic and ethical grounds, to publish it in any of his poetry collections.[3] Even after it was printed in the *Derry Journal,* Heaney refused to let the well-known Irish folk singer Christy Moore sing it so many years after the atrocity, as he recalled to Karl Miller: "I said, 'Christy, we can't do that now; that's now "good guy" stuff, and it would be irresponsible.' It's one thing to launch into the dangerous waters of the moment, but a very different thing to punt the currents later on."[4] And in *Stepping Stones,* echoing the language of his interview with Miller, Heaney told Dennis O'Driscoll, in response to a question about whether he was tempted to include it in one of his collections,

> It belonged to the moment that produced it. It was what Wordsworth called "a timely utterance" that gave relief. Like any song, it was made for the communal voice. If it had been sung by Luke Kelly, it would have functioned immediately and rightly as an expression of shared grief and outrage. If, on the other hand, I had reprinted it later in a book, I'd have felt I was currying favour with a certain constituency, writing propaganda and basically letting myself down. Doing the kind of thing Brodsky used to mock with the phrase, "Here come the good guys."[5]

On the basis of these comments, Heaney clearly feels that the ballad was written to the moment for the Northern Irish Catholic community. When Luke Kelly of *The Dubliners* did not sing it, he withheld it from his poetry collections, which generally feature poems that align the poet against the community's expectations, as we have seen already and will see in the next chapter in my discussion of "Casualty," which privileges the imaginative solitude of the poet over the limited groupthink of the community.

Moreover, Heaney himself was not convinced of the poem's quality and wrote Brendan Hamill on January 8, 1973, telling him that the poem "wasn't good enough, or durable enough to let out."[6] Heaney's withholding of the poem on purportedly aesthetic grounds—it "wasn't good enough"—is certainly understandable, given his desire for control over dissemination of his art. More interesting is his claim that it was not "durable enough to let out," which suggests his fear that this occasional poem was written too close to the moment and thus not sufficiently filtered through his powerful imagination. To be sure, the later, more meditative, calmer "Casualty," which finally concerns the role of the poet in a time of violence after briefly elegizing the Bloody Sunday victims, coupled with the poet's and critics' neglect of the angrier ballad, fits the narrative of Heaney as reconciler that I have been trying to establish. But "The Road to Derry" is worth examining as an example of Heaney's growing anger and fear at the time (although there is still hope for justice in the song). Those feelings may well have led him to leave the province within a couple of months, a decision he had already been mulling over for some time because of his desire to become an independent writer.

Heaney set "The Road to Derry" to the tune of a late eighteenth-century ballad, "The Boys of Mullaghbawn," written about men from Mullaghbawn, a townland in south County Armagh, who were transported to Van Diemen's Land around 1798 for either agrarian offenses, involvement in the 1798 Rising, or the attempted abduction of an heiress.[7] The original ballad and Heaney's "The Road to Derry" capture his equivocal attitude right after Bloody Sunday. On the one hand, he hopes for justice from the British government—"And in the dirt lay justice like an acorn in the winter / Till its oak would sprout in Derry where the thirteen men lay dead."[8] And not just any justice, but justice specific to the events in Derry, symbolized by his hope that an oak "would sprout in Derry," signifying its linguistic origins in the Irish word "*Doire,*" or oak grove. The end of the poem thus states the hopes of many Catholics in Northern Ireland who want and expect justice from the British government for this atrocity and further implies that they will applaud the British if justice is done. Such a springing hope echoes the language at the end of "Requiem for the Croppies," in which the barley grows up out of the mass grave of the Croppie Boys after they are killed in the 1798 Rising.

While such hope for justice was certainly felt by Northern Irish Catholics in early 1972, Heaney's debt to the original ballad on the question of justice is strong. In "The Boys of Mullaghbawn" the speaker praises the English squire Richard Jackson, who actually lived on his own estate and tilled his own land, unlike many so-called "absentee landlords" of the time. Jackson provided for his tenants in his will and is still remembered fondly in the district. According to the third stanza of the song, "Squire Jackson he's unequalled for honour and for reason / He never turned traitor nor betrayed the rights of man."[9] Heaney's closing invocation of justice that implicitly recalls Squire Jackson's fairness to his tenants thus suggests that Britain owes its citizens in Derry (and implicitly in the rest of Northern Ireland) fairness and impartiality under the law and indeed is obligated morally to care for them, much as Jackson did for his tenants. Because Britain had become so intimately involved with affairs in Northern Ireland by the time of Bloody Sunday, Heaney implies that they are obliged to stay involved with this particular issue and pursue justice.

Whether or not the popular view that the Boys of Mullaghbawn were participants in the 1798 Rising is true does not finally matter to our understanding of Heaney's poem's inspiration from the ballad; he seems to be using this belief to suggest both the promise and the peril inherent in this pivotal moment in early 1972 Northern Ireland by obliquely referencing the 1798 Rising. We have seen previously how early poems like "Digging" and "Requiem for the Croppies" finally are colored by Heaney's hope for enhanced cultural understanding and eventual full civil rights for Catholics in Northern Ireland in the early to mid-1960s and how he compares that pre-Troubles period to 1798 by emphasizing the earlier period's emphasis on equality and its unfortunate descent into violence. The original ballad's setting in South Armagh in the eighteenth century connotes danger, for this was an area known then as "bandit country" for the many attacks on passersby and later, during the contemporary Troubles, for its widespread IRA activity. Heaney uses as his source this particular ballad set in another county from where Bloody Sunday occurred to suggest that the hope among the nationalist population of Northern Ireland that the British government would investigate Bloody Sunday in then-contemporary Londonderry/Derry is analogous to the hope embodied in Squire Jackson in eighteenth-century County Armagh, who upheld "the rights of man," language redolent of the 1798 Rising. Even though in "The Road to Derry" Heaney drops the pejorative language of the original ballad—that the new landlord is "a vile deceiving stranger / Who has ordered transportation for the boys of Mullaghbawn"[10]— knowledge of the earlier ballad would linger for any contemporary reader or hearer of Heaney's poem, and that audience would thus realize there was a real possibility the British government would deceive the Catholic population of Northern Ireland about Bloody Sunday, as indeed the Widgery Inquiry, as it came to be known, would end up doing. The danger that would redound upon the "vile deceiving stranger" of the original ballad and the British in the present was real, signified by South Armagh's ancient and contemporary reputation for violence, and Heaney seems to have foreseen that danger in the form of increased republican activity in Derry and throughout Northern Ireland, even though the poem itself stresses his hope for justice.

Yet within this hope vibrates his anger; he admits, "My heart [is] besieged by anger, my mind a gap of danger."[11] I believe that such sentiments in "The Road to Derry" lie partly behind Heaney's move within a few months to County Wicklow. He has often explicitly rejected such suggestions, stating recently, for example, that the main motivation for the move was "writerly" and was urged on him and Marie by their artist friend Barrie Cooke and Sonja Landweer in County Kilkenny. "What clinched it finally," he told Dennis O'Driscoll, was "Ann Saddlemyer's offer of Glanmore Cottage early in 1972." He also noted that he needed a change from the "too settled and circumscribed aesthetic" he shared with other poets in Northern Ireland.[12] But he *was* threatened in a 1970 phone call that his mother-in-law took one night after a TV program, called "Heaney in Limboland," that expressed strong opposition to the B-Specials, Northern Ireland's main counterinsurgency force, and described them as having an animus against Catholics.[13] Five years later, Heaney would also famously say to Seamus Deane in an interview from 1977 that his own poetry "is a kind of slow, obstinate, papish burn, emanating from the ground I was brought up on."[14] Given that he had been threatened at least once, and given the anger he mentions in "The Road to Derry," which he expresses in his earlier columns about the civil rights movement published in the *Listener* (see chapter 5), as well as in the Deane interview, fear and anger undoubtedly contributed to his decision to leave the North even if the main motivation came from his decision to be an independent artist.

The first part of this line from "The Road to Derry, "My heart besieged by anger" (line 9 in the poem as it was printed in the *Derry Journal* in 1997), cleverly and audaciously reclaims a central and public narrative, the Siege of Derry, from the Protestant community of the city (which they call Londonderry). In that narrative, the Protestant Apprentice Boys locked the gates of the city against the besieging forces of the Catholic King James. Heaney, in admitting that his own heart is besieged by an invading anger that he desperately seeks to fend off, is inscribing a new, intensely Catholic and nationalist narrative about a private siege over the public, Protestant narrative of the Siege of Derry, which is reenacted by the Apprentice Boys each year at the walls of Derry.

Indeed, much of the poem functions as a contemporary *dinnseanchas,* or piece of place lore, about Bloody Sunday, as Heaney references areas he drove through on the way to Derry—"Glenshane and Foreglen and the cold winds of Hillhead"—and areas within Derry, such as the Bogside, where the shootings took place, Shipquay Gate, and Lone Moor.[15] In the penultimate stanza of "The Tollund Man," first published in *Threshold* in the summer of 1970, Heaney had already offered a *dinnseanchas* of prehistoric murders in Jutland—"Tollund, Grauballe, Nebelgard" (*WO,* 48); now he offers a litany of contemporary sites in Northern Ireland that he passes on the way in to Derry, where the victims were murdered in the Bogside neighborhood. As we will see, in the book of poetry, *Wintering Out,* which he would release later that year, he often uses place names and dialect words that are potentially unifying for Catholics and Protestants in Northern Ireland, but the anger and evocation of such place names in "The Road to Derry" make it not just a lament for the dead but both a personal grievance and a public one for the nationalist community in Northern Ireland, despite Heaney's hopes for justice.

Wintering Out and Unifying Ulster Dialects

In a 1975 interview, Heaney told Caroline Walsh he had decided to write full time because "I think if you commit a lot of your attention and your tension in another place, you close your receiving stations."[16]

The phrase "receiving stations" is a resonant one for the poet because he believes strongly in the creative process of receiving images from the depths of his unconscious that he can then consciously craft into poetry. The rich and varied dialectical words employed in many poems from *Wintering Out* offer a glimpse into his thinking about the problems of cultural identity and demonstrate how he poetically rendered them into his vision of a linguistically unified province. Throughout his career, Heaney has actively pursued linguistic plurality in his poetry and translations: Conor McCarthy notes that "his commitment to linguistic pluralism is a way of overcoming a binary view of English and Irish, in favor of what he refers to in the introduction to the *Beowulf* translation as an unpartitioned linguistic country, where language is not a badge of identity but an entry into further language."[17] *Wintering Out*, dedicated to David Hammond and Michael Longley, represents a turn from the metapoetic concerns of technique in *Death of a Naturalist* and *Door into the Dark* to an emphasis on the craft of poetry, particularly his skilful fusion of dialect words from Irish English and Ulster English in delineating the linguistic aspects of his unifying conception of Ulster regionalism.[18]

Heaney had long been interested in exploring the Ulster dialects he heard around him, and this interest, coupled with his literary discoveries of the dialects employed by the Scots and other regional writers such as the Northern Irish Protestant poet John Hewitt, led him deep into a poetic-linguistic exploration of the word-hoard of his native province. In a series of prose essays that are beyond the scope of this chapter to explore, Heaney engages with the work of Northern Irish and other regional writers to comprehensively articulate his pluralistic concept of Ulster regionalism.[19] Hewitt's work on Ulster dialect, finally published in *The Rhyming Weavers and Other Country Poets of Antrim and Down* in 1974, shares with Heaney's *Wintering Out* the conviction that representing the Ulster vernacular in print might produce a culturally unifying effect, as Tom Paulin has pointed out: "This recurrence to the vernacular in Hewitt and Heaney is one expression of the political crisis in the North—both poets are using local speech to define a distinctive Ulster identity."[20] Blake Morrison dates Heaney's interest in local dialects to his attending the "English-language lectures of John Braidwood and G. B. Adams" in the late 1950s at Queen's University. Later these two men helped publish

Ulster Dialects: An Introductory Symposium (1964). Their lectures and this book "may well have influenced Heaney, for it used technical terms like *spirant, plosive,* and *fricative* which he incorporated into his work." Morrison argues that "in its meticulous examination of the relationship between language and land, *Ulster Dialects* encouraged Heaney to become a 'fieldworker' in the archives of grammar and pronunciation."[21]

Heaney's traditional concern with the craft of poetry, specifically poetic diction, enabled him, in *Wintering Out,* to articulate concerns of cultural identity that are largely expressed through the confluence of dialects he draws upon in several of its poems. Richard Wall has illustrated the degree to which Heaney's twin linguistic heritages inform his poetry. He argues that Heaney uses both Hiberno-English and Ulster English in his poetry and that neither of these two dialects is pure, as demonstrated by Heaney's mingled use of them: "Hiberno-English is a contact vernacular which has its genesis in the interaction of two languages and cultures, Irish and English, over a very long period of history, while Ulster-English has its genesis in the relatively recent, seventeenth-century Plantation of Ulster. The principal difference between them is that Hiberno-English is heavily influenced by Irish in vocabulary and syntax, while Ulster-English is heavily influenced by the Scots of Lowland Scotland, from which the majority of the planters came. Neither vernacular is monolithic: they vary greatly, both geographically and socially, and interpenetrate considerably." Wall briefly elucidates how Heaney's recognition of the multiple meanings inherent in words such as *kesh* and *loaning* shows his full awareness of his dialectical heritage and his extensive use of it in his poetry.[22]

The implications for identity, both personally and provincewide, are significant: Heaney clearly draws upon his Scots, Irish, and English linguistic heritage in his poetic vocabulary, implicitly suggesting that so should the inhabitants of Northern Ireland in order to form an imagined community. Thomas Flanagan has been one of the few commentators to notice Heaney's attempts at building a sonic community through an evocation of shared dialects: after mentioning the Gaelic, Scottish, and English dialects present in Northern Ireland, Flanagan argues that "Heaney's art . . . touches community through language."[23] Throughout his career, Heaney has argued that the shared pluralistic languages and dialects of the province form a linguistic community, an anticipation of Benedict Anderson's conception of imagined communities that are formed through a common language.

Anderson claims that "much the most important thing about language is its capacity for generating imagined communities, building in effect *particular solidarities.*"[24] Heaney's imagined community of Northern Irish Catholics and Protestants living in relative harmony with one another is all the more striking given the nationalist sentiment in Northern Ireland, increasing in the late 1960s and reaching a fever pitch by the early 1970s, that the "Six Counties" had to be reunited with the Republic, and given the increased unionist sentiment there at the same time that the union with Great Britain had to be maintained. Heaney is a constitutional nationalist, but he saw a culturally united province as an essential first step toward a future united Ireland. Language was the medium he chose to effect this cultural unity, which is nowhere more fully explored than in the Ulster dialects that in *Wintering Out* he sees Northern Protestants and Catholics as sharing.

Harold Bloom has said of this volume that "few books of poems brood so hard upon names, or touch so overtly upon particular words as words."[25] Indeed, several of the poems are virtual meditations upon words, especially place names. For example, "Anahorish" and "Broagh" form a natural pair with their joint emphasis on the residual rural Gaelic culture of the two townlands between which Heaney's family farm, Mossbawn, was located. Water imagery abounds in "Anahorish," which literally means "place of clear water," as the poet tells us in the first line. In lines 5 and 6, the springs of the first stanza metaphorically wash into the second, lapping onto the "darkened cobbles / in the bed of the lane" (*WO*, 16). Immediately, the mellifluous place name "Anahorish" appears: "*Anahorish*, soft gradient / of consonant, vowel-meadow" (16). Uttering this place name in this miniature example of a *dinnseanchas,* or piece of Irish place lore, acts as an affirmation of residual Irish lore and language, though the poem also symbolizes a site of respectful Catholic and Protestant understanding and rapprochement, as we will see.

In "Broagh," however, the place name actually serves to mark off boundaries dividing an imagined linguistic community of Catholic and Protestant locals from presumably English or foreign "strangers," while the overall effect of the poem registers Heaney's effort to "do justice to all the elements of heritage in my natural speech."[26] Almost every line in this poem has an "o," and some lines have several. The aural effect of this vowel is soothing through the first three stanzas, which feature words such as "long," "broad," "ford," "mould," "*Broagh*," "low," and "boortrees" (*WO,* 27). However, the "low tattoo" of the uttered "*Broagh*" that sings in the "boortrees" in stanza 3 abruptly stops in stanza 4: it "ended almost / suddenly, like that last / *gh* the strangers found / difficult to manage" (27). As the echo of the place name stops abruptly, so does the effect of the "o" sounds, culminating in a last line containing the fricative "difficult" and the harsh "a" sounds of "manage." The effect on the reader is jarring, and he is forced to literally reshape the sounds issuing from his mouth, echoing the difficulty of the "strangers" (presumably English) in uttering "Broagh."[27] As Heaney would claim later, "Small as it is, this piece of verse represented a turn of the tide. I felt that I had made Broagh exclusive, made the English language work to tell my story."[28] Heaney's recognition of his various dialectical heritages in the poem paradoxically enabled him to claim his Irishness and convey that part of his identity through the English language, a perfect illustration of how he draws upon and unifies seemingly opposed spheres of influence.

More important, however, for our understanding of Heaney's developing linguistic theory of reconciliation, "Broagh" was one of Heaney's first attempts to bring Irish, Elizabethan English, and Ulster Scots "into some kind of creative intercourse and alignment and thereby to intimate the possibility of some new intercourse and alignment among the cultural and political heritages which these three languages represent in Northern Ireland."[29] As he recalls the intent of the poem in more detail, he further claims, "I very much wanted to affirm the rights of the Irish language to be recognized as part of that Ulster mix, to correct the official, east-of-Bann emphasis on the province's ur-languages as Ulster Scots and Elizabethan English."[30] This impulse stems naturally from Heaney's desire, confirmed by his readings of poetry by Patrick Kavanagh and John Montague, to incorporate the Northern Irish Catholic subculture into the life of the province.[31] But the ultimate trajectory of the poem is conciliatory, stemming from Heaney's ecumenical urge to unify the divided cultures of the province through a shared language. While "Whitehall ministers" could not have pronounced the name "Broagh" properly, "everyone native to Northern Ireland, Protestant or Catholic, Planter or Gael, whatever their separate myths of linguistic exile from Irish or Ulster Scots—every one of them could say 'Broagh,' every one of them was fitted to dwell in at least phonetic amity with the other. I wanted to suggest, therefore, that it was at this first level of utterance that the foundations of a common language were to be sought."[32] As David Kennedy has noted in his close linguistic analysis of the poem, it demonstrates that "language crosses sectarian divides."[33]

Kennedy wrongly argues, however, that this linguistic and cultural unity evoked in the first stanza of "Broagh" is undercut by the thrust of the second stanza, which "implies that this is all surface and overlay."[34] He claims, "Under the present-day speech community lies a Celtic point of origin: pre-modern and mystical. The means of accessing this—'The black O' of 'your heelmark'—is also pertinent. . . . The heel is literally 'put down' below the surface of 'the garden mould,' but this leads to a recovery of the Celtic *bruach* ['riverbank'] via the modern 'Broagh' so that a reconnection to an Irish Celtic identity becomes the other way of 'putting one's foot down,' asserting power and independence."[35] While interesting, this reading is tenuous and slightly forces the alleged link to Celtic culture by grouping "Broagh" with two other poems, as Kennedy himself admits in an endnote: "The poem does not refer to Celtic culture specifically, but the two poems with which 'Broagh' is usually grouped—'Anahorish' and 'Toome'—confirm this identification by referring to, respectively, 'mound-dwellers' and 'torcs.'"[36] "Anahorish" does, of course, make reference to "mound-dwellers," suggesting Heaney's mental exhumation of a Celtic culture, as does its evocation of the Gaelic words for "place of clear water," but it also was the site of his primary school in his formative years, a school that had a mixed population of Catholics and Protestants and undoubtedly laid the foundation for Heaney's interest in reclaiming the common culture and language between the two groups. "Anahorish" after all, suggests an Edenic, prelapsarian locale, free from conflict, and is described as "the first hill in the world" (*WO*, 16). Finally, Heaney's comments cited from "Burns's Art

Speech" above make clear that "Anahorish" constitutes a search for "the foundations of a common language" between Northern Irish Catholics and Protestants, further suggesting the thrust of the poem as an attempt to recover an originary yet unifying literal and also metaphorical language in the province—one of respect and mutual understanding.

Other poems in *Wintering Out* also focus on the unifying dialectical confluence in Northern Ireland, while simultaneously affirming the presence of the Irish language in the province, as do "Anahorish" and "Broagh." An exception would be "Fodder," which, as Michael Parker has pointed out, "shifts ground from the linguistic pluralism of the opening of 'Broagh'" and is "an assertion of autonomy, particularity, familial, local, cultural, and perhaps ethnic difference."[37] For example, in "Traditions," the speaker opens by noting that

> Our guttural muse
> was bulled long ago
> by the alliterative tradition,
> her uvula grows
>
> vestigial . . .
>
> > (*WO*, 31)

"Bulled" implies that John Bull or England effectively forced itself upon the Irish language, "Our guttural muse," then forgot it until the language grew "vestigial" from lack of use. While this stanza also negatively notes the rise of the "alliterative tradition," we must remember that Heaney approves the way in which Ted Hughes's alliterative verse is connected to that of *Sir Gawain and the Green Knight* and argues that Hughes is an important regional writer in "Englands of the Mind."[38] The point here seems to be that "the alliterative tradition" became *too* dominant in Ireland and suppressed the native Irish language, especially since in the next section Heaney somewhat mockingly embraces his "Elizabethan English" and the Ulster Scots dialect.

Section 2 contrasts the decline of the Irish language in stanza 1 with the approval given to vestiges of Elizabethan English and Ulster Scots, the dialects of the planters:

> We are to be proud
> of our Elizabethan English:
> "varsity," for example,
> is grass-roots stuff with us;
>
> .   .   .   .
>
> Not to speak of the furled
> consonants of lowlanders
> shuttling obstinately
> between bawn and mossland.
>   (*WO*, 31–32)

The phrase "We are to be proud" sounds ironically contemptuous of this English linguistic heritage (the difference is the "to be"; "We are proud" would be a straightforward affirmation of this heritage). The last quatrain of this section clearly refers to the speech of the transplanted, lowland Scots, as Heaney brilliantly has their speech mimic the action of the shuttle they use in making wool. Although these quatrains seemingly mock the other dominant "languages" of the province, they must be understood in the context of Heaney's project to unite the province through a common language while recognizing Irish and its dialect of Hiberno-Irish to be on the same level as the other two tongues. Elsewhere, as we have seen, Heaney approves of the use of older forms of English and of Ulster Scots employed by other writers. For example, the choice of "Furled" in this poem, although used in a different way, recalls Heaney's approving use of the way in which "the Scots and Latinate English *furl* together in a downpour of energy" in Hugh MacDiarmid's "Water Music," published in 1972, the same year *Wintering Out* appeared.[39] And although the "furled consonants" shuttle "obstinately / between bawn and mossland," suggesting the cultural resistance of the Ulster Scots to other traditions, these lines actually bespeak a grudging admiration for the Scots' steadfastness and an approval of their craft, concerns that link these qualities to those in "The Wool Trade," as we will see.

Section 3 injects a dramatic note into the poem as it juxtaposes the question that the character MacMorris from *Henry IV* asks with Leopold Bloom's answer in Joyce's *Ulysses* in an attempt to answer the question of nationalism and cultural heritage:

MacMorris, gallivanting
round the Globe, whinged
to courtier and groundling
who had heard tell of us

as going very bare of
learning, as wild hares,
as anatomies of death:
"What ish my nation?"

And sensibly, though so much
later, the wandering Bloom
replied, "Ireland," said Bloom,
"I was born here. Ireland."

(WO, 32)

MacMorris's question is the central question of the entire volume, while Bloom's soft and quiet answer to the overzealous nationalist Citizen in the so-called "Cyclops" episode of *Ulysses* indicates both Heaney's qualified nationalism in his own claim of being born on the island of Ireland and his recognition that Irishness includes elements of other nationalities and ethnicities (like the Jewish Bloom). The assimilative nature of Ireland is a historical commonplace; Heaney's recognition of this aspect of Irishness in this poem is buttressed by the mixture of dialects and cultures inherent in the poems I have already described. In this sense, Heaney might be seen as arguing that once its Gaelic traditions are appreciated, Northern Ireland may be the most Irish of all areas on the island in its assimilative urge.

While "Traditions" implies the unifying power of a shared language in the province, "The Wool Trade" celebrates the Protestant artisanry of weaving and its sturdy language. The first of these is prefaced by Stephen Dedalus's famous exclamation from Joyce's *A Portrait of the Artist as a Young Man* in his discussion with the Dean over the use of the word *tundish:* "'How different are the words "home," "Christ," "ale," "master," on his lips and on mine.' STEPHEN DEDALUS" (*WO*, 37). In this passage, Stephen has not yet realized that *tundish* is a perfectly good English word and feels locked out of the English language. Later, of course, his discovery that *tundish* is an English word will signal his own realization that he is fully at home in the English language, perhaps even more varied in his usage of it than the English. The linkage with the epigraph from Joyce here is with the monosyllabic, Anglo-Saxon words of line 4, "To shear, to bale and bleach and card" (37). Although culturally distant from this tradition, the speaker seems to approve of this sturdy, concrete language used to describe processes of wool making. He finishes by lamenting,

> O all the hamlets where
> Hills and flocks and streams conspired
>
> To a language of waterwheels,
> A lost syntax of looms and spindles,
>
> How they hang
> Fading, in the gallery of the tongue!
>
> And I must talk of tweed,
> A stiff cloth with flecks like blood.
>   (37)

The poet mourns the loss of the localized communities—mainly in Scotland and England—that evolved a particularized language to describe the process of making wool. Vendler argues correctly that these closing lines' approval of the cloth-making tradition bring "Protestant artisanry in the wool trade into the orbit of which the poet is the elegist."[40] At the same time, the narrator feels he "must talk of tweed, / A stiff cloth with flecks like blood," an ominous image that intrudes upon the soft "o" sounds that precede it and suggests the violence he also associates with this tradition (37).

As we have seen, Heaney was at pains in *Wintering Out* to affirm the other traditions of Northern Ireland from which he was culturally disconnected, such as weaving, and other dialects, such as Ulster Scots and Elizabethan English, that still live on his tongue. In "The Other Side," he makes a genuine effort to portray cultural and religious understanding between Protestants and Catholics in the North. In the first two stanzas, Heaney recalls his family's Protestant neighbor, particularly his recourse to phrases referencing Scripture, such as "'It's poor as Lazarus, that ground'" (*WO*, 34). The young child's ear was attuned to this different language and is portrayed "swallowing / his fabulous, biblical dismissal, / that tongue of chosen people" (34). Although the Catholic Heaney was both theologically and politically not one of the "chosen people" like his Presbyterian neighbor, he nonetheless celebrates his turns of phrase, his skills as farmer, and his affinity for the Bible, the ultimate written Word.

Section 2 concludes by comparing the neighbor's mind to a Presbyterian church in its sparse tidiness: "His brain was a whitewashed kitchen / hung with texts, swept tidy / as the body o' the kirk" (*WO*, 35). Although the usually perceptive critic George Watson claims that "the poet seems to strip the neighbour of any living tradition beyond his somewhat antiseptic (and basically Scottish) religion," Heaney's descriptive diction actually compares the man's mind to the ideal rural Ulster farmhouse kitchen, not only clean and neat but also literate, partaking in a long written tradition.[41] While this written tradition and the man's brisk, even brusque oral sayings contrast with the mournful "dragging" of the Heaneys' recitation of the rosary in the third stanza, the poem as a whole celebrates *both* traditions in the province and even offers a glimpse of cultural and religious understanding on the part of the Protestant neighbor as he patiently waits "until after the litany" to knock on the family's door and say hello. This purposeful pause is respectful and not uncommon: the neighbor's wait occurs "sometimes when the rosary was dragging" to indicate that his visit was usual enough to employ the habitual sense of the verb (35).[42]

The poem concludes by offering an imagined scene of cultural understanding between the now-grown Heaney and his former neighbor. Presumably, the man is long since dead, but the poet recalls him in his mind's eye:

He puts a hand in a pocket

or taps a little tune with the blackthorn
shyly, as if he were party to
lovemaking or a stranger's weeping.
(36)

His shyness has rubbed off on the poet, who concludes by musingly asking himself,

> Should I slip away, I wonder,
> or go up and touch his shoulder
> and talk about the weather
>
> or the price of grass-seed?
>   (36)

The reference to grass seed suggests that a tentative reconciliation has
been planted between the neighbors that will bear fruit through their
talk, even if this conversation is imagined. This image of potential fruit-
fulness suggests that despite the fertility of the neighbor's ground and
the fallowness of the Heaney family's — symbolic of Protestant domi-
nance of and Catholic exclusion from the political life of the province,
respectively — dialogue between members of the two traditions might
lead to full civil rights for Catholics in the province through Protestant
help. While these two scenes — the neighbor respectfully approaching
the Heaney household in the past and Heaney hesitantly approaching
the man's memory in the present — do not offer anything that remotely
achieves full understanding and communication between Northern Irish
Catholic and Protestants, the joint shyness of the neighbor and Heaney
does signify respectful cultural deference, a necessary and often neglected
starting point for more significant cultural and religious reconciliation,
and one largely absent in the Northern Ireland of the early 1970s — at
least in its official discourse.

Heaney has recalled writing "The Other Side," however, as an exercise in creative freedom, not primarily as a poem to promote reconciliation: "[It gave me] fundamentally a literary pleasure. . . . It was not fundamentally intended as a contribution to better community relations. It
had come out of creative freedom rather than social obligation, it was
about a moment of achieved grace between people with different allegiances rather than a representation of a state of constant goodwill in
the country as a whole, and as such it was not presuming to be anything
more than a momentary stay against confusion."[43] His claim encapsu-
lates the two major claims of this entire project: that only when poems,

especially those written under great pressure to evoke solidarity with the poet's particular cultural and political community, affirm as their first allegiance poetry itself and engage in the pleasures of poetic freedom can they then effectively—if only temporarily and often more indirectly than in "The Other Side"—and creatively address and critique problems embedded in that community, should they even choose to do so. Another way of articulating this point is that the poet must first build a verbal and imaginative community with the words and the form of the poem itself before he turns to issues of his quotidian community.[44]

Having said this, Heaney is too modest in his claim that the poem does not presume "to be anything more than a momentary stay against confusion." "The Other Side" suggests that cultural understanding is best conducted with deference, indecision, ambiguity, and humility, not through slogans and partisan politics.[45] Heaney's next volume would place the cultural and political conflict in the province in a widening geographic and linguistic compass that unfortunately was all too easily misunderstood by many critics who would equate his exploration of tribal atrocities there and across the northern Atlantic with a tacit approval of the increasingly violent nationalist movement. He would turn inward again in significant poems from that volume, listening, finding his true north in the excavation of his own poetry.

North: Looking Outward at Beauty and Violence, Looking Within for Buried Treasure

After his emphasis on the province's mixed and unifying cultural heritage in the obliquely political poems of *Wintering Out,* Heaney somewhat surprisingly took on the Northern Irish situation directly in *North,* his 1975 volume of poetry. John Wilson Foster has pointed out that Heaney's previous move to the Republic was widely misunderstood but that it enabled him to internalize events and reissue them in new, less immediately recognizable forms:

> There were those who disapprovingly saw his removal from Belfast to Dublin in 1972 as an Irish nationalist's gesture of delinquency, others who disapprovingly saw it as an Irish nationalist's gesture of

inherited commitment. Unlike John Montague and Thomas Kinsella, two other fine Irish poets, Heaney did not speak out directly against British policy in Northern Ireland, coming closest to political rhetoric in *Part II* of *North* (1975) and in *An Open Letter*. . . . But if he did not speak *out*, he spoke *in*, which is what a poet in his truest office does. Events are absorbed and internalized, re-issued, and sometimes recognizable in their translation only by our disciplined reading.[46]

"Speaking in" allows the poet to filter events through his imagination and reflect upon them in a more intimate manner, which in turn will allow him to connect with his audience better than if he were utterly direct and overly didactic.

Critics have not accorded *North* the recognition that it deserves in Heaney's developing concepts of artistic fidelity and cultural reconciliation, instead focusing mostly on its at times divisive politics. Whereas in *Wintering Out* he drew on the range of dialects in Northern Ireland, in *North* he employs a variety of Anglo-Saxon words and compounds. But while he had articulated a unifying Northern Irish regionalism based on a shared dialectical vocabulary in the earlier volume, he uses specifically Anglo-Saxon words in *North* to ascribe a negative unity of violence endemic to cultures in Northern Ireland and throughout the northern Atlantic. *North* vacillates between evoking and critiquing that common geographically northern culture of violence through carefully crafted diction and articulating Heaney's true north—his role as a poet—through reflections upon technique, the varying ways in which the poetic imagination accesses the subconscious.

Ciaran Carson claims that in these poems "Heaney seems to have moved—unwillingly perhaps—from being a writer with the gift of precision, to become the laureate of violence—a mythmaker, an anthropologist of ritual killing, an apologist for 'the situation,'"[47] and his charge may continue to have its proponents—despite, I think, Heaney's best intentions—when we view these poems. Yet despite serious problems that I document below with the bog poems particularly, the critique of violence in *North* is radical, condemning its various manifestations across a range of cultures and historical periods. While several poems unfortunately reify stereotypes of England and Ireland, the three best poems of the volume, "North," "Punishment," and "Exposure," affirm a salutary ethical stance in their personal metapoetic reflections upon the task of poetry and the poet in a violent society, confuting Maurice Harmon's assertion that the *North* poems sublimate Heaney's personal feelings about the atrocities into impersonal, "large, ceremonial gestures."[48] Together, these three poems form a complex argument about the intersection of the poet's aesthetic and ethical tasks that is elucidated by reference to his later essay "The Government of the Tongue" and is expanded upon in later volumes of poetry.

Written shortly after Heaney moved to County Wicklow in 1972, these poems are reflections about the troubled state of the province at a literally safe distance from the Northern Irish conflict, which had exploded with the Bloody Sunday murders in January, the subsequent burning of the British Embassy in Dublin, and the introduction of direct rule from London shortly afterward. Heaney has discussed this volume at some length, noting that it emerged as the nationalist community rapidly lost the "moral high ground" they had previously held before themselves becoming complicit in the violence:

> It was a time when victim status had become complicated. The Northern minority for about a year and a half, I suppose two years, had enjoyed a certain heady victim status. And there was a moral high ground in having been fifty years at the mercy of a gerrymandered system and so on, and all this was coming to the fore and being noticed by the liberal press in Britain; so this was all hunkydory. Well then of course, once the killing starts and once the Provisional IRA starts to establish their rights by arms, as it were, the moral high ground was taken away from the nationalist community. And instead of protesting their victim status, they also had to endure and internalize and take on their oppressor status or their violence-dealing status. So of course, the poems are complicated by that.[49]

Despite the well-documented protests by Carson, Conor Cruise O'Brien, Edna Longley, and Blake Morrison that Heaney ritualizes violence in *North* and in so doing at least tacitly approves of it, he often resists tribalism in this volume, as the above statement makes clear, critiquing violence in a multitemporal context across a variety of cultures.[50] As Denis Donoghue has remarked about the archeological aspect of the *North* poems, Heaney's "sense of time circumvents the immediacies of historical event by recourse to several different levels of experience, the accretion of cultures."[51]

Michael Parker argues that in *North*, Heaney refrains from merely reacting to the current events in the province by "present[ing] in Part One a universalist image of the suffering that attended/attends the struggle for territory, while in Part Two he maps out the contours of a personal mythology, identifying formative moments from his Catholic past. The *North* poems certainly embody a legitimate anger, but they also display the poet's determination to seek out images, rich in energy, which might serve as a 'binding force' for his community, and provide him with the solace of a shape" (*SHMP,* 126). Part One certainly does universalize territorial suffering, as images of bones, skeletons, and funerals in the North, Viking Dublin, and Scandinavia abound. While virtually every commentator writing on Heaney's interest in "bog bodies" dates his interest in these exhumed bodies to his discovery of the archeologist P. V. Glob's *The Bog People* in 1969, he had already shown a sustained interest in skeletons and cadavers in two little-known poems from *Death of a Naturalist,* "At a Potato Digging" and "For the Commander of the *Eliza.*" In the former poem, watching the laborers picking potatoes evokes images of the starving Irish in the Potato Famine of 1845: "Live skulls, blind-eyed, balanced on / wild higgledy skeletons, / scoured the land in 'forty-five, / wolfed the blighted root and died" (*DN,* 19). If the ground is "faithless" in "At a Potato Digging" (20), the British sailors who meet the six starving Irishmen "off West Mayo" are faithless to humanity in the latter poem (21). Because he had no "mandate to relieve distress / Since relief was then available in Westport—," the captain refuses food to the starving men, "Six wrecks of bone and pallid, tautened skin" (21). While the linkage between inhumanity past and present in *North* enabled Heaney to critique violence associated with bodies generally in a multitemporal, multinationalist context, in *Death of a Naturalist* he could render those bodies only as Irish, in a unitemporal, nationalist context.[52]

This multitemporality is forced at times in *North*. For example, in "Funeral Rites" Heaney imagines a Northern Irish Catholic funeral in the present having megalithic trappings: "the procession drags its tail / out of the Gap of the North / as its head already enters / the megalithic doorway" (*N*, 8). The modernity of the "purring family cars" (8) competes with this ancient imagery to such a degree that the image finally falters. In the third part of the poem, the context is extended to encompass Scandinavian funerals as the mourners "drive north again / past Strang and Carling fjords" (8). These northern fjords undoubtedly and rightly remind Heaney of the more famous ones in Norway, but the concluding image of Gunnar who is "unavenged" (9) jars with the vast majority of revenge and punishment murders that Heaney describes in the bog poems of Part One and that parallel the contemporary situation in Northern Ireland.

In their visceral images and other evocations of violence, the bog poems worked together to shock readers who had been following Heaney's earlier poetry (including his first real bog poem, "Bogland"), which largely cast spells on readers by introducing them to the secret places and memories of his childhood—a body of work whose effect on readers is consistent with what Rita Felski calls "the blissful enfolding and voluptuous pleasure that we associate with enchantment."[53] Recall the wondrous preservative properties of the bog evoked in "Bogland," the seemingly miraculous appearances of the Great Irish Elk and the intact butter; that is a poem, like so many in Heaney's first three volumes, of enchantment. For Felski, shock is enchantment's antithesis, "invad[ing] consciousness and broach[ing] the reader's or viewer's defenses. Smashing into the psyche like a blunt instrument, it can wreak havoc on our usual ways of ordering and understanding the world."[54] Readers approaching, or rather, viewing Heaney watching and trying to describe in alternating direct and indirect language the bog body featured in "Punishment" now must grapple with his transformation of the bog's preservative, miraculous qualities in "Bogland" into a sort of medieval morgue with bodies splayed out, wounds gaping. If we flinch, are shocked, Heaney's poetry reveals our humanity and implies a universal revulsion against violence even as its reveals the opposite of that tendency—our propensity to treat others cruelly, savagely, even murderously.

Unfortunately, Heaney's decision to write a series of poems based on photographs of these victims and his swerving between realistic and metaphoric language through much of the first half of "Punishment" somewhat vitiates his project because of the tendency of photography toward rendering its subjects inanimate, as Susan Sontag has argued consistently, and because of his inclination to aestheticize them. There is an additional problem with Heaney's gaze in "Punishment": it verges on pornography in evoking beauty and pain and making us feel help-less, but that drawback is finally obviated and redeemed by a full under-standing of beauty's effect of the perceiver, not just the subject, in acts of perception and by his striking allusion to the biblical narrative of Christ's forgiveness of the adulteress caught in sin, which convicts us of our own breathless fascination with atrocity and of our own sinfulness, finally giving us hope for forgiveness.

Criticism of the bog poems in *North* has generally not dwelt on the problem of the medium itself: that Heaney was inspired to write them by gazing at photographs of these long-forgotten victims.[55] While Susan Sontag's early work on photography in *On Photography* has been justly lauded, her more recent work *Regarding the Pain of Others* (2003) is more applicable to the aesthetic problem of Heaney's use of pictures from P. V. Glob's famous book *The Bog People*.

Sontag convincingly shows the authority of photography over the constant stream of information in our twenty-four-hour news cycle, over written accounts of atrocities, and over the imagination itself. With re-gard to this first instance of its authority, she argues that although "non-stop imagery (television, streaming video, movies) is our surround . . . when it comes to remembering, the photograph has the deeper bite. Memory freeze-frames; its basic unit is the single image. In an era of in-formation overload, the photograph provides a quick way of apprehend-ing something and a compact form for memorizing it. The photograph is like a quotation, or a maxim or proverb."[56] Just as iconic images of particular atrocities in the Northern Irish Troubles, such as the picture of Father Edward Daly waving a white handkerchief as others drag a wounded man away during the events of Bloody Sunday, have become part of our storehouse of images, unlike the fuller narrative that is still emerging from that horror today, Glob's photographs of the bog bodies in Jutland have become privileged over the rich nuances of their narrative that he provides in his landmark book. By focusing his bog poems in *North* so sharply on pictures of the bodies themselves, Heaney risks producing "snapshot poetry"—recall those famously short quatrains, that procession of monosyllabic words—that achieves a lasting visual impression in its relative verbal terseness. "Punishment" seemingly offers an impoverished narrative of the atrocity inflicted on the girl whose body was found in the bog as well as the more current atrocities, mentioned later in the poem, that the IRA has inflicted on "betraying sisters" for having sexual relations with the enemy. The controlling narrative of the poem, however, the reference to the passage from the eighth chapter of John's Gospel about the adulteress Christ encounters, finally instantiates a narrative richness that, until its introduction, the poem shuns.

Another problem with Heaney's use of Glob's images concerns the nature of atrocities in general and the way photography "freezes" or kills them, in effect killing the subject all over again. Left with only an image of these bodies in death, we are largely unable to revivify them in our minds, such is the authority of the image over our imagination.

Finally, photographs, although purportedly objective, are never fully so, and as it turns out, Glob's photograph of "the Windeby Girl" that Heaney writes so movingly about in "Punishment" also finally lies. In 2007, an anthropologist named Heather Gill-Robinson discovered that "the Windeby Girl" was actually a fourteen-year-old boy, not a girl, who died, not from stoning for adultery, but from starvation.[57] This discovery, of course, has major repercussions for Heaney's poem because his gendered focus on this so-called adulteress is now severed from his evocations of the New Testament adulteress and the then-contemporary Catholic women tarred and feathered by the Irish Republican Army. Perhaps now, with our surer knowledge of the sex of the poem's subject, we can begin conceiving a larger context for understanding suffering in the poem by realizing that, almost despite itself, the poem does justice to suffering past and present experienced by both men and women.

The language of "Punishment" is potent, suggesting how this bog body is part of a larger narrative of suffering transcending time. Heaney begins by identifying with "her" in the opening lines, feeling "the tug / of the halter at the nape / of her neck, the wind / on her naked front"

(*N*, 30). Her physical description is multicultural and multitemporal, suggesting the persistence of violence among communities throughout the northern Atlantic: her nipples are "amber beads," perhaps echoing the Catholic rosary beads of "Funeral Rites," while her ribs are comparable to the "frail rigging" of an ancient vessel, perhaps a Viking ship. The compound words used to describe her partially decomposed body, "oak-bone" and "brain-firkin," underscore the archaic nature of the violence by linking it implicitly with Anglo-Saxon language and society (30).

Yet at least until the incorporation of the biblical narrative of the adulteress about halfway through it, part of the charge Heaney levels at himself in the poem—that he is "the artful voyeur" of this body—is reinforced by his struggle to find words to properly describe her, to tenderly humanize her. Stanza 1, for example, uses direct language to describe her and a first-person point of view, as does stanza 3, but stanzas 2 and 4 resort to metaphor and a third-person point of view, and stanza 5 to simile and a third-person point of view: "her shaved head / like a stubble of black corn." The direct language could be viewed as literally unbelievable: Can he really "feel the tug / of the halter / at the nape of her neck"? More believably, he says in stanza 3 that "I can see her drowned / body in the bog" (*N*, 31). But in switching to metaphorical language in stanzas 2 and 4, he does risk aestheticizing her.

More particularly, Heaney's perception of the bog bodies as beautiful troubles our sense of the relationship between aesthetics and ethics. In the essay "Feeling into Words," he directly asks about the relationship of the bog bodies to the Northern Irish conflict, "'How with this rage shall beauty hold a plea?'" and answers with a quotation from Yeats, "by offering 'befitting emblems of adversity'" ("FW," 57). Few critics, however, have paid very much attention to the question of beauty in the bog poems of *North*, although Michael Cavanagh has recently pointed out "several references to beauty and attraction associated with violence and death, from the 'beauty and atrocity' of the Grauballe Man, to the 'leathery beauty' of the exhumed girl's head in 'Strange Fruit,' to the 'odd beauty' of the drawings of skeletons on anatomic plates in 'The Digging Skeleton: After Baudelaire.'"[58] In an interview Heaney has admitted about "The Grauballe Man," that not only he himself but also others tend to aestheticize these bodies when viewing them: "I think that that's what's happened to us when we look at the bog bodies—that you are aware that you are looking at a thing of atrocity which has been turned into a thing of beauty almost."[59] He wrote Brian Donnelly a letter in which he noted that the bog bodies were "made strangely beautiful by the process of lying in bogs."[60] It is difficult not to think of Yeats's haunting refrain from "Easter, 1916," another poem about sacrifices made to the Irish republican cause: "A terrible beauty is born."[61] Just as Yeats did not condone the Easter Rising, Heaney surely is entitled to admit that the bog bodies are "thing[s] of beauty almost" while rejecting the cult of violence that led to their destruction.

In this sense, "Punishment" and the other bog poems from *North* accord even further with "Easter, 1916," where Yeats ascribes the terrible beauty to the stoniness of the rebels' hearts in the third stanza: "Hearts with one purpose alone / Through summer and winter seem / Enchanted to a stone."[62] But where Yeats's rebels' hearts become stony in their obsessive pursuit of an independent Ireland, Heaney's "rebels," the scapegoats such as the "adulteress" in "Punishment," are petrified by their murder and entombment in the dark, preserving bog on behalf of the "protectors" of community, whose hearts are clearly stony and who even cast stones in the poem. In a telling remark, Heaney himself has said about the bog bodies that "I think I was holding them like a Perseus shield almost against what was happening."[63] Here, Heaney casts himself as Perseus indirectly looking at Medusa, whose direct gaze would petrify anyone, in his shiny shield shortly before he cuts her head off. He thus implies his fear of becoming stonelike himself by gazing too deeply and directly at contemporary atrocities in Northern Ireland; his solution was to approach the violence in the North more obliquely by staring at Glob's pictures of the northern European bog bodies. Patrick Grant has articulated the long tradition in Ireland and Northern Ireland of how violence is thought to harden human beings but notes further, drawing on Simone Weil's reading of the *Iliad,* that "the notion of violence as a petrifying agency" is "deeply rooted in Western literary tradition."[64]

While Rita Felski seems to believe that beauty cannot be part of the realm of the shocking because shock "names a reaction to what is startling, painful, even horrifying," Heaney's "Punishment" and other bog poems from *North* heighten their sense of shock precisely through their suggestion of the bog bodies' beauty that works to make us as potentially fascinated by them as he is.[65] This is a particular kind of beauty not often discussed (when beauty itself is discussed, which is not often in much of today's "literary" criticism). To her credit, Sontag considers the issue at some length in *Regarding the Pain of Others,* arguing for the potential beauty of photographs of atrocity just as we consider the terrible beauty of war in many paintings. She even argues that "photographs tend to transform, whatever their subject; and as an image something may be beautiful—or terrifying, or unbearable, or quite bearable—as it is not in real life."[66] This analysis reverberates with Heaney's quotation above about the Grauballe Man, on how "a thing of atrocity . . . has been turned into a thing of beauty almost." In one of the major recent discussions of beauty, Denis Donoghue has briefly explored a passage from *The Things They Carried,* the Vietnam novel by the American author Tim O'Brien, in which the narrator points out the beauty and allure of watching combat. Donoghue recoils from this linkage, terming it an instance of Adorno's "cruelty of imagination . . . unless you decide that the speaker's personality is woefully split or his moral sense inert." He then harrumphs, "No wonder Frederic Jameson argues that 'the visible is *essentially* pornographic, which is to say that it has its end in rapt, mindless fascination.'"[67] Without agreeing with Jameson's totalizing theory of the visible in general, I believe Heaney's bog poems do seriously verge on pornography in Jameson's sense of it because of their rapt fascination (not mindless, never mindless with Heaney) with their subjects that are nearly rendered objects.

Additionally, the depiction of the so-called "Windeby Girl" as both naked and in pain dangerously conflates age-old desires to behold two kinds of images: as Sontag argues, "The appetite for pictures showing bodies in pain is as keen, almost, as the desire for ones that show bodies naked,"[68] an observation that should indict us as much as Heaney indicts himself in the poem. The conflation of our desire to see naked bodies with our desire to see bodies in pain colludes with how "the gruesome invites us to be either spectators or cowards, unable to look. . . . Torment, a canonical subject in art, is often represented in painting as a spectacle, something being watched (or ignored) by other people. The implication is: no, it cannot be stopped."[69] Sontag's claim here echoes Ciaran Carson's specific objection, noted earlier, to Heaney's poems as essentially endorsing the ineluctable nature of sectarian violence or any violence driven by myth.

But we should realize that our modern conceptions of staring that we often like to call "objectifying" run counter to the long tradition, at least in the West, of equating the gaze with creation. As Elaine Scarry points out, staring "is a version of the wish to create; it is directly connected to acts of drawing, describing, composing, lovemaking."[70] Heaney's poem clearly recognizes this tradition when he calls himself "the artful voyeur," a phrase that links art and gazing.

The discomfort and unease that he clearly feels in this and other bog poems also recall the belief, long-standing in Western tradition, that gazing at beauty imperils the perceiver, a fear that we seem to have largely forgotten in our contemporary critical distaste for "objectification." Scarry cites the man's beholding of the beautiful young boy in Plato's *Phaedrus* and his subsequent disorientation and eventual growing of feathers, along with Dante's trembling at encountering Beatrice in the *Vita Nuova,* as examples of how perceiving beauty endangers us.[71] So merely noting Heaney's perception of the bog body in "Punishment" attends to only one side of the equation of gazing by neglecting his own discomfort that he rightly records.

Moreover, beholding beauty, even the terrible beauty of the "Windeby Girl" (or actually young man) becomes an ethical act, according to Scarry: "Beauty is pacific: its reciprocal salute to continued existence, its pact, is indistinguishable from the word for peace."[72] Lest this sense of beauty sound merely theoretical, Scarry further argues that beauty calls us to pursue the ethical through a process that begins with "a radical decentring" that occurs "at the moment we see something beautiful."[73] That is, our apprehension of beauty leads us out of ourselves and our imaginary position at the center of the universe. As we move into a position adjacent to the beautiful object, we experience a condition of lateralness that models equality generally. As Scarry puts it, "It is clear that an *ethical fairness* which requires 'a symmetry of everyone's relation' will be greatly assisted by an *aesthetic fairness* that creates in all participants a state of delight in their own lateralness."[74] Finally, once we perceive beauty, we are led actively to be stewards of it, to act "to protect or perpetuate a fragment of beauty already in the world or instead to supplement it by bringing into being a new object."[75] Heaney's gaze at the terrible beauty of the bog body in "Punishment" therefore attempts to engender our protective care of fragile people and things by helping us realize our lateralness to them.

Finally that fascination, that concentration of gaze on the part of Heaney in the poem, and implicitly, on our part, is broken by Heaney's allusion to a redemptive biblical narrative that offers a different, redressive focus to readers and causes us to recognize our similarity to these "adulteresses" in our own sinfulness. That is, if we attend to Heaney's allusion in all its power, our gaze is redirected inward: our previous voyeurism shifts toward ourselves and becomes an interrogative, moral vision.

Heaney specifically calls the bog "woman" "Little adulteress," linking her not only to the "adultery" perceived in the contemporary Northern Irish Catholic women by the IRA but also to the real adultery committed by the woman in John's Gospel who is saved from stoning by Jesus: "I almost love you / but would have cast, I know, / the stones of silence" (31). This hidden adulteress is the pivot upon which this very visual poem swings because she is a figure who was fully guilty and not punished, unlike the drowned bog woman and those contemporary women in Northern Ireland, all of whom have been punished, not necessarily for committing any actual crimes, only perceived ones, either with death or tarring and feathering. Her importance has been obscured in criticism of the poem because her body is not imaged as are those of the other women, which are linked by the mention of the "tar-black face" of the bog body and the description of the Catholic women as "cauled in tar" (31). But as a symbol of forgiveness, in contrast to the other women associated with revenge punishments, she is like a shaft of light that cuts through the darkness of the violent bog poems.

The biblical narrative that Heaney references in relation to this hidden adulteress suggests the forgiveness needed to break the ritualized cycles of violence here and in the other bog poems. The episode occurs in the eighth chapter of John's Gospel when the scribes and Pharisees present Jesus with a woman who had been caught in adultery. Noting that Moses called for such women to be stoned to death, they attempt to get Jesus to flout the law so they can in turn condemn him. His response, however, turns the table on his accusers:

> But Jesus stooped down and began to write with his finger in the dust on the ground. But as they persisted in their questioning, he straightened himself up and said to them, "Let the one among you who has never sinned throw the first stone at her." Then he stooped down again and continued writing with his finger on the ground. And when they heard what he said, they were convinced by their own consciences and went out, one by one, beginning with the eldest until they had all gone. Jesus was left alone, with the woman still standing where they had put her. So he stood up and said to her, "Where are they all—did no one condemn you?" And she said, "No one, sir." "Neither do I condemn you," said Jesus to her. "Go home and do not sin again." (John 8:6b-11)[76]

Christ's response to the woman recognizes her sin of adultery, offers forgiveness for it, and urges her to not sin anymore, a powerful trio of actions that culminates in the shaming of the assembled crowd, all of whom had assembled to stone her and all of whom are convicted of their own sin. David Parker calls this story "the *locus classicus* of judgmentalism," further noting that "Jesus' reply forces the woman's accusers to look into their consciences and to admit that they are not simply 'different' from her; they look within themselves and find an element of *similarity* to her, which convinces them that they do not belong to another moral universe at all."[77] Even if Heaney, too strongly, states he would have stoned her, whether he means it literally or, more likely, figuratively, by withholding his protest at her threatened stoning, those sentiments are addressed by the lingering force of the forgiveness that is enacted by Christ in John's narrative and is still available to anyone who chooses to adopt it in situations of hurt.

In the conclusion of his important essay "The Government of the Tongue," undoubtedly inspired by his treatment of this biblical allusion in "Punishment," Heaney references the scriptural episode, substituting poetry for Jesus' writing in the sand and remarking upon its power. He argues that poetry's oxymoronic status makes it seem unhelpful for achieving a civil society but that it actually has a limitless sense of potential for righting wrongs:

> Here is the great paradox of poetry and of the imaginative arts in general. Faced with the brutality of the historical onslaught, they are practically useless. Yet they verify our singularity, they strike and stake out the ore of self which lies at the base of every individuated life. In one sense the efficacy of poetry is nil—no lyric has ever stopped a tank. In another sense, it is unlimited. It is like the writing in the sand in the face of which accusers and accused are left speechless and renewed. I am thinking of Jesus' writing as it is recorded in Chapter Eight of John's Gospel.[78]

After he recites the passage, Heaney argues that Jesus' writing in the dust and poetry generally set up an interim space that functions as a mirror for the crowd: "In the rift between what is going to happen and whatever we wish to happen, poetry holds attention for a space, functions not as distraction but as pure concentration, a focus where our power to concentrate is concentrated back on ourselves."[79]

Reading "Punishment" through the lens of poetry's potential outlined in "The Government of the Tongue" makes clear in retrospect that the poem had this concentrating effect on Heaney himself: this is why he inserts himself into the poem at its beginning and end, placing himself at the scene of punishments past and present. While he calls himself an "artful voyeur" for gazing too intently at this ancient body and making poetry out of his observation, he is too hard on himself because the poem itself "holds attention for a space" and makes us all reflect on our implication in violence and sin generally. In a 1998 interview on BBC Radio 4, Heaney affirmed this reading of the poem, indeed of all the bog body poems: "They were a form of pause, I think."[80] Only when this realization that we are all complicit in violence becomes more widespread among a given populace, the poem suggests, can tribal violence be critiqued, then condemned and stopped. Jesus' objection "to an ethic of difference that obliterates any sense of common humanity" should effect a realization of our unifying human condition.[81]

Donoghue partially misperceives Heaney's intent in *North* regarding violence. Arguing that Heaney is turning away from the historical concept of time, he rightly suggests that "precisely because he does not present history in linear terms, Heaney offers the reader not a teleology implicit in historical interpretation but a present moment still in touch with its depth," but he then wrongly draws the conclusion that "the procedure has the effect of releasing the reader—for the moment, God knows, and only for that—from the fatality which otherwise seems inscribed in the spirit of the age."[82] The actual sense of the present invoked in a poem like "Punishment," however, lies in the moment of its reading. That act of reflection, undertaken upon every reading of the poem, should make us realize our own universal involvement in hatred and prompt us to reject it and seek reconciliation.

The "stones of silence" that recall the story of forgiveness from John are supplanted later in the poem by the "numbered bones" (*N,* 31) of the dead adulteress, clearly a reference to the psalm Christ recited on the cross. His urging of forgiveness—"Father, forgive them; they do not know what they are doing" (Luke 23:34a)—is the last act of mercy by the crucified Savior before his death and coheres with his general philosophy of forgiveness expressed in the adulteress story.[83] In both cases, Christ's forgiveness undercuts the efficacy of mob violence. The vocalization of this forgiveness is crucial in the passages from scripture and is incorporated into Heaney's poem: even if Heaney himself has "stood dumb / when your betraying sisters, / cauled in tar, / wept by the railings" (*N,* 31) the poem speaks loudly about the need for personal and community-wide forgiveness. Only that process, repeated over the decades among people who originally hated each other, will eventually break the cycle of "the exact / and tribal, intimate revenge" (31) that the poet understands even as he recoils from it. The poem performs this function even if the poet himself cannot.[84]

Despite several outstanding poems such as "Punishment," there are lingering problems with the volume. One significant problem concerns the detail with which Heaney describes the bodies preserved in the bog in the "bog poems." As I have noted earlier, the bog had proved a powerful symbol of the poetic imagination in "Bogland," from *Door into the Dark,* precisely because of its bottomless, murky depths and the poem's concluding emphasis on this feature. Although all of the bog bodies are very skillfully visualized in *North,* the relative neglect in describing the bogs themselves results in a sharp diminution of the potency of this image.

Another shortcoming is the volume's occasional trading in stereotypes such as Ireland as feminine and England as masculine, as in
"Ocean's Love to Ireland," in which Walter Ralegh, representing England, rapes a maid, symbolizing Ireland:

> Speaking broad Devonshire,
> Ralegh has backed the maid to a tree
> As Ireland is backed to England
>
> And drives inland
> Till all her strands are breathless:
> "Sweesir, Swatter! Sweesir, Swatter!'"
> (*N*, 40)

This poem's stereotypical representations, coupled with those of "Bog
Queen," in which the Danish princess functions as an archetype of Kathleen Ni Houlihan, "Kinship," with its "mother ground" and "goddess" as
symbols of Ireland (38, 39), and "Act of Union," which refers to Ireland's
"stretchmarked body" (44) work against Heaney's avowed attempt after
1969 to expose the constructed cults of femininity associated with Ireland
and masculinity associated with England and delineate their struggle:

> To some extent the enmity can be viewed as a struggle between the
> cults and devotees of a god and a goddess. There is an indigenous
> territorial numen, a tutelary of the whole island, call her Mother
> Ireland, Kathleen Ni Houlihan, the poor old woman, the Shan Van
> Vocht, whatever; and her sovereignty has been temporarily usurped
> or infringed by a new male cult whose founding fathers were Crom-
> well, William of Orange and Edward Carson, and whose godhead
> is incarnate in a rex or caesar resident in a palace in London. . . .
> [This idiom] is not remote from the bankrupt psychology and my-
> thologies implicit in the terms Irish Catholic and Ulster Protestant.
> ("FW," 57)

The poems cited above do not seem to critique these "bankrupt" representations of Ireland so much as reify them, and unfortunately weaken
the volume in the process. One senses that Edna Longley is right when

she argues that too many of the bog poems are there to round off the volume and impose an unwarranted homogeneity on it: "In contrast with the fecund variety of *Wintering Out* there is system, homogenisation. Certain poems seem dictated by the scheme (rather than vice versa), commissioned to fill in the myth or complete the ritual. Conspicuous among these are three first-person quatrain sequences, all in six parts: 'Viking Dublin: Trial Pieces,' 'Bone Dreams,' and 'Kinship.'"[85] Longley's claim also implies that Heaney formally relies too much on the quatrain, an argument that has been made by Philip Hobsbaum about some of the poems of *Wintering Out*: "In Seamus Heaney the loose quatrain all too often circumscribes itself into a four-line stanza, and the effect is that of a good poet on his best behavior."[86] It is a testament to the potentially freeing power of "Punishment," "North," and "Exposure" that they overcome the relative stanzaic rigidity of their quatrains.

Edna Longley's most damning and convincing criticism of the *North* poems holds that some of them render Heaney too involved with metapoetic representations of his imagination: "Every poet worth his salt imprints his poetry with a subtext about poetry itself—as Heaney does, profoundly and skillfully, in 'The Forge' or 'Bogland.' . . . The protagonist's high profile in the *North* sequences, however, reveals him almost incestuously involved with the contents of his own imagination."[87] As evidence of this claim, Longley cites the concluding quatrain about the poet's words licking "around / cobbled quays" from "Viking Dublin" (*N*, 16) and the stanza in which the poet compares himself to a weeping willow from "Kinship" (37). Although she exempts "Mossbawn: Two Poems in Dedication" and "Exposure" from this charge (and rightly so), I would also exempt "Punishment," already examined, and "North."

"North" features Heaney in the poetic stance he has always given the most credence to—listening, not speaking. He carefully hears the advice given him by the "fabulous raiders" of Iceland and Greenland (*N*, 10) to avoid violence and by a Viking longship to look inward to his own "word-hoard" and to "Compose in darkness" (11). In this regard, the poem's elevation of wordplay over the swordplay of the Vikings is laudatory. As the poem opens, the narrator has "returned to a long strand, / the hammered shod of a bay" (10). Heaney's fondness for rural crafts seemingly emerges in this second line with his use of "hammered," but hammering, especially metalworking, in the poem represents violence and destruction, whereas in "The Forge," from *Door into the Dark*, black-smithing was linked positively with poetry as a constructive art. The "ocean-deafened voices" warning the poet in the first half of the poem all belong to a series of fighters who collectively tell the poet to steer clear of violence: "those fabulous raiders, / those lying in Orkney and Dublin" whose "long swords rusting" are joined in the chorus by "those in the solid / belly of stone ships," and "those hacked and glinting / in the gravel of thawed streams" (10).

These voices fade in the fifth stanza and are replaced with that of "The longship's swimming tongue," which "was buoyant with hindsight—" (*N*, 10). It first tells the poet that "Thor's hammer swung / to geography and trade, / thick-witted couplings and revenges, // the hatreds and behindbacks / of the althing" (10–11). Having seen the warriors' violence spurs the longship to warn Heaney to avoid the same fate since this kind of tit-for-tat violence, reminiscent of the atrocities being carried out in Northern Ireland at the time, is endless, cyclical, and vacuous. Instead, the tongue of the longship urges him to look inward:

> . . . "Lie down
> in the word-hoard, burrow
> the coil and gleam
> of your furrowed brain.
>
> Compose in darkness.
> Expect aurora borealis
> in the long foray
> but no cascade of light.
>
> Keep your eye clear
> as the bleb of the icicle,
> trust the feel of what nubbed treasure
> your hands have known."
>
> (11)

The compound *word-hoard* was a kenning for the poet's vocabulary in Anglo-Saxon times. Its appearance signals Heaney's recognition of his rich, archipelagic, truly northern geographical linguistic heritage and his desire to burrow into it for poetic inspiration. His desire to delve into his "furrowed brain" suggests that inward gazing into his own mind is the poem's focus, which is unlike the emphasis on his outward, somewhat voyeuristic viewing of the "brain-firkin" and other body parts of the dead girl's body in "Punishment." Thus the withdrawal of the poet into himself in "North" balances his immersion in violence in "Punishment." The entreaty of the longship's tongue to "Lie down" leads the poet into a metaphorical posture of prostration similar to the literal prostration of the bodies of "those fabulous raiders, / those lying in Orkney and Dublin" (10). Yet his prostration is voluntary, mental, and properly alive in its submission to the imaginative power of language, while theirs is involuntary, bodily, and literally dead in their embrace of violence. Furthermore, his desire to engage in the deliberate, peaceful acquisition of linguistic treasure stands in stark contrast to the Vikings' greedy, martial pursuit of earthly treasure.

The full significance of that "tongue" of the longship, however, has eluded commentators of the poem. Just as "Punishment" adumbrates the concluding emphasis on forgiveness in the later essay "The Government of the Tongue," "North" foreshadows the opening concern—poetry's autonomy—of that essay. There Heaney explains that poetry is "its own vindicating force. In this dispensation, the tongue (representing both a poet's personal gift of utterance and the common resources of language itself) has been granted the right to govern. The poetic art is credited with an authority of its own."[88] In this equation, the longship's tongue represents not just "the common resources of language itself" available to Heaney but his "personal gift of utterance" as well. In typical metapoetic fashion for Heaney, the poem itself illustrates how poetry "is credited with an authority of its own."

As Heaney argues further, submission to "the jurisdiction of achieved form" is effected "by the self-validating operations of what we call inspiration."[89] He cites the Polish poet Anna Swir, who writes of the creative process as a "psychosomatic phenomenon,"[90] a statement that accords with Heaney's argument in "Feeling into Words" that technique "is that whole creative effort of the mind's and body's resources to bring the meaning of experience within the jurisdiction of form" ("FW," 47). Swir argues that through this holistic creation the poet becomes a sort of receiving station for different voices that enable him to access his subconscious in certain moments: "This seems to me the only biologically natural way for a poem to be born and gives the poem something like a biological right to exist. A poet becomes then an antenna capturing the voices of the world, a medium expressing his own subconscious and the collective subconscious. For one moment he possesses wealth usually inaccessible to him, and he loses it when that moment is over."[91] Reading the first part of the poem again with his approval of Swir's description of poetry as reception, we realize that Heaney's submission to his conception of technique when writing *North* enabled him to become "an antenna," capable of hearing all the "ocean-deafened voices" of violence in history, which warned him away from celebrating belligerence in his poetry, and to listen to the "tongue" of the longship, which advised him to trust his "nubbed treasure" or the "wealth usually inaccessible to him" made available in this liminal moment of openness.

He realizes that his immersion in words will be long and lonely, characterized mostly by darkness with occasional epiphanies (the "aurora borealis"). But if he remains true to words, to his art, trusting "the feel of what nubbed treasure" he has known, his fidelity to poetry will stay strong. In its evocation of treasure as a symbol for his core identity, the poem also previews Heaney's characterization of poems in "The Government of the Tongue" as affirmative of individual identity: "They strike and stake out the *ore* of self which lies at the base of every individuated life."[92] That "North" is the title poem of the volume makes clear its importance for Heaney in confirming his contemplative vocation as poet—his true north—in the midst of the external violence in the streets of Northern Ireland that he registers in a multitemporal context in many of the volume's other poems.[93] The volume's concluding poem, "Exposure," is in a similar vein, as we will see.

This taciturn stance is perfectly in keeping with the poet's outlook in "Whatever You Say Say Nothing," the long second poem of Part Two, but unfortunately this poem is marred by an incorporation of phrases that gives it a reportorial air. The speaker arrives back in Northern Ireland in stanza 1 to a din of voices all asking clichéd questions about "'the Irish thing'" (*N*, 51). The vocabulary of war has become engrained in the language of politicians and reporters who sanitize the conflict through catchphrases—"'the provisional wing,'" "'long-standing hate'"—that cannot do justice to the complexities of the situation (51). The poet sings that he is "Expertly civil-tongued with civil neighbours" (51), joining in with their chorus of restrained disdain for the violence, but adds that "The 'voice of sanity' is getting hoarse" (52).

Tongued here has only a literal meaning, unlike the tongue of the longship in "North," which also metaphorically stands for the autonomy of the poem. It is a measure of the paucity of the imagination exercised in "Whatever You Say Say Nothing" that "tongued" stays on the surface in this section, although the famous lines from section 2, "Long sucking the hind tit / Cold as a witch's and as hard to swallow / Still leaves us fork-tongued on the border bit" (*N*, 52), clearly have a multiplicity of cultural and political meanings, as Joe Cleary has pointed out: "It may suggest that the border has grown deeply into the groove of nationalist consciousness; that it is a bit that chafes because, complex sentiments about it having had to be curbed for so long, a language adequate to their expression does not exist; that various modes of censorship, including self-censorship, have generated elaborate circumlocutions of forms of doublespeak that express positions on the partition question even when they appear to sidestep that uncomfortable topic altogether."[94] These compelling meanings overwhelm the power of poetry itself in the poem, however, and suggest Heaney's frustration with the potentially transformative power of poetry in this fairly hopeless time of violence in the province.

Heaney critiques knee-jerk tribalism in the second section, citing both the Celtic football supporter who says, "'The Pope of Rome/'s a happy man this night,'" and "the eructation of Orange drums / Allergic equally to Pearse and Pope" (*N*, 52). In the midst of all this bigotry, the poet searches in vain for his Muse:

> . . . I sit here with a pestering
> Drouth for words at once both gaff and bait
>
> To lure the tribal shoals to epigram
> And order. I believe any of us
> Could draw the line through bigotry and sham
> Given the right line, *aere perennius.*
>
> (53)

This last assertion is perfectly in keeping with Heaney's belief that language at its most precise can have a powerful unifying effect.[95] Unfortunately, the poem recapitulates so many clichés that it sinks under their weight, rendered incapable of the kind of specific, memorable diction that characterizes the typical Heaney poem. The poem ends with utter silence — "We hug our little destiny again" — in a deflated reversal of the noisy pandemonium of its opening lines (54). Its defeatist silence in the face of external voices of despair contrasts with the kind of contemplative silence Heaney rightly embraces in "North" to access his subconscious and hear its hopeful inner voices.

However, in "Exposure," the final poem of the sequence "Singing School," Heaney has turned into a pensive walker in County Wicklow, apparently fully removed from the violence in the North and prepared to listen again for poetry. He asks, "How did I end up like this?" and wonders whether he moved south for the sake of his poetry or "For the people?" (*N*, 66), a possible reference to his audience or even his family. Regardless of his intentions in emigrating to the Republic, he now claims the identity, not of a participant in the Catholic civil rights struggle in the North, but of an internal voyager in the landscapes of the mind: "I am neither internee nor informer; / An inner émigré, grown longhaired / And thoughtful . . ." (67). He is camouflaged, "Taking protective colouring / From bole and bark, feeling / Every wind that blows. . . ." (67) He feels that he has missed out on something essential — maybe the very force of life — in his previous attempts to write poetry out of the troubled violence of his land:

> Who, blowing up these sparks
> For their meagre heat, have missed
> The once-in-a-lifetime portent,
> The comet's pulsing rose.
>   (67)

The difference in the heat between poetry produced by the "sparks" and "The comet's pulsing rose" suggests that the real force of Heaney's poems lies in their attempts to naturally bear witness to the wonder of life and to the imaginative power of his mind above even the powerful violence in the province.

"Exposure" also demonstrates Heaney's "similar[ly] pluralistic attitude to identity" that he shares with Yeats, as Eugene O'Brien has argued in his comparison of the poem to Yeats's poem "A Coat": "The
vulnerability that unites Yeats's nakedness and Heaney's similar openness to the elements is caused by their mutual forsaking of the simplici-
ties of tribal enunciation; instead they have both chosen a far more difficult road, that of centrifugal and dialogic examination of identity."[96] As
I have tried to argue in this analysis of the poems in *North,* Heaney can
critique monolithic, tribal identities only through his fidelity to his art
in the midst of conflict. "Exposure" nicely counterbalances the exposed
images of bog people featured in the first part of this volume in its stress
upon the exposed nature of Heaney the poet, indicating his growing
sense of attunement to the inner life of the imagination, an act of artistic, even spiritual faith.[97]

In a manner similar to that of Michael Longley, Heaney's interest
in his dual inheritance—his Britishness and Irishness—emerges explicitly in the poems of *Wintering Out* and *North.* Especially in the poems of
Wintering Out, he explores his joint linguistic heritage through skilful
meditations on words and phrases from Ulster Irish, Elizabethan English, and Hiberno-Irish. His celebration of his mixed cultural heritage
is tempered, however, by his stark exploration in *North* of the disturbing
political legacies of these cultures. As Tom Paulin has argued, Heaney
has managed to oppose the Northern Irish state's oppression of Catholics while simultaneously rejecting nationalism's allure: "To oppose the
historic legitimacy of that state and at the same time refuse the simplici-
ties of traditional nationalism is to initiate certain imaginative postures
and offer a gracious and civil trust."[98] Heaney fully acknowledges the repression of the Northern Irish Catholic Church in "Freedman," the cruel
violence of the IRA in "Punishment," and the presence of the triumphal
Northern Irish Protestant culture in "A Constable Calls," "Whatever You
Say Say Nothing," and "Orange Drums, Tyrone, 1966." The restrictive-
ness of these traditions causes Heaney the poet to retreat into himself
and start exploring the realm of his imagination. In becoming the "inner
émigré" of "Exposure," he took the measure of his varied cultural inheritance, winnowed out and celebrated its etymological and topographical significance, and finally discarded its pernicious aspects. His next
volume, *Field Work* (1979), would be his transitional one, for ostensibly

political poems such as "Casualty" actually prove to be, upon closer examination, extended meditations upon the craft of poetry and the spiritual dimensions of reality springing from his immersion in Catholic meditative techniques rather than meditations on his status as Catholic civil rights victim and spokesman, like some of the poems from *North*. Yet he continued to believe that his allegiance to poetry accorded with an emergent reality of a pluralist Northern Ireland previously only found in his imagination and that of a few others.

Field Work through *The Haw Lantern*

BURROWING INWARD, LOOKING OUTWARD

Ghosts of the Troubles in *Field Work*

Almost every critic writing on Heaney has argued that a major shift in his poetry occurred with the publication of *Field Work* as he moved from poems grounded in the soil of his native Derry to verse more contemplative and abstract. Chapter 5 of this study, however, shows the poet's early and abiding interest in contemplation of the abstract through his exploration of his auditory imagination. And the near-unanimous critical characterization must be further qualified, for certain practices, such as the poet's penchant for employing agricultural metaphors about his poetry, continue in these later volumes, as demonstrated in the sonnet section "Clearances" from *Field Work* and poems such as "'Poet's Chair'" from *The Spirit Level* (1996), and his interest in viewing rural craftsman and their "art" as analogues for the poet and his art, as exemplified by the figure of Louis O'Neill in "Casualty" from *Field Work* and by Heaney's friend Norman MacCaig in "A Daylight Art" from *The Haw Lantern*. Finally, while in his poetry appearing after *North* Heaney does not often employ the twinned dialects of Ulster Scots and Irish English as he did in *Wintering Out*, his interest in uniting the province through its shared dialects continues in his translation of the Irish language epic *Sweeney Astray*.

In his early career the poet suggests in his metapoetic "Antaeus," which begins *North* proper and was written in 1966, that he would be very uncomfortable if he were to move away from writing about his native ground. Antaeus, like the poet, fears heroes who could "throw me," lifting him "off the earth," which is the source of his power, and thereby leading to "My elevation, my fall" (*N*, 3). Starting with *Field Work*, Heaney seeks out a symbolic but still real elevation, trusting that his poetic powers have matured fully enough so that he can, at least in crucial moments, leave his native ground and imagine a new realm of airy opportunities. In his 1979 interview with James Randall, Heaney recalled writing a letter to the Irish playwright Brian Friel after *North* was published that claimed, "I no longer wanted a door into the dark—I want a door into the light."[1] Yet the process of approaching higher, airier elevations, he realized, must be conducted through a continued gazing at the ground, at particular places, even dark ones.

Heaney's emphasis on physical places often has led him into mental reveries within the region of himself. We see this process taking place in "Digging," "The Forge," "Bogland," "North," "Punishment," and "Exposure" and in many of his essays. The recognition that contemplation of physical spaces can result in psychic exploration has grown in fascination for Heaney almost inexorably, and while he has continued to ponder the problems of his province, he has turned more and more inward, exploring the regions of his own mind. This movement is not solipsistic but a radical process that affirms the limitless sense of potential within the poet's core while enabling him, when he so chooses, to pluralistically effect more pointed critiques of received cultural and political identities. This interiority has increasingly been featured in important poems beginning with "Casualty" from *Field Work*. Thus in these later volumes he extends his conception of "technique," the preverbal, meditative process necessary for writing poetry first adumbrated in "Feeling into Words," and significantly employs it to gain access to a rich mental frontier. This contemplative outlook, always present in the meditative poems that dwell on traditional crafts, especially fishing, has continued to help him make poetic analogies between these crafts and his poetry in these later volumes, notably in one of his best poems, "Casualty."

While several of the poems of *North* feature the exhumed bodies from bogs in Denmark that Heaney meditates upon in order to critique violence across cultures and throughout history, starting with the poems of *Field Work* he moves definitively back to his home ground of Northern Ireland and writes a series of revenant poems featuring ghosts of the Northern Irish Troubles who flickeringly appear before him and urge him to meditate upon poetry in the midst of the violence. Despite these haunting presences, the poems achieve an immediacy that the more mythological poems of *North* do not, as Seamus Deane has noted: "In *Field Work,* all trace of a consoling or explanatory myth has gone. The victims of violence are no longer distanced; their mythological beauty has gone, the contemplative distance has vanished. Now they are friends, relatives, acquaintances."[2] One of the major poems in which the ghostly becomes intertwined with questions of culture — politically and vocationally — is "Casualty," an elegy to a fisherman friend of Heaney's (Louis O'Neill) who was killed after disobeying a curfew in the Catholic community in the province not long after the events of Bloody Sunday on January 30, 1972.

Heaney has pointed out in his essay-review of Thomas Kinsella's translation of *An Duanaire: Poems of the Dispossessed* that "the unrepentant note which he appended to 'Butcher's Dozen' in his recent collection, *Fifteen Dead,* is continuous with the swell of political energy in the poems of the middle section of this anthology."[3] Kinsella's poem was written in response to the Widgery Tribunal's exoneration of 1 Para, the company of British soldiers who killed fourteen unarmed Catholic protesters on Bloody Sunday, and suffers as a result of being written too close to the moment. Heaney's poem is continuous with the swell of his own political energy in his poetry, especially in *North* and *Field Work,* but is more distanced from the violence than Kinsella's and thus more effective.

In "Casualty" the narrator clearly is Heaney himself, who admires the fisherman for many of his qualities. The fisherman, in turn, becomes the ideal audience for the poet. Each is a craftsman and a loner. The fisherman is largely silent when on his own, just as earlier craftsmen like the blacksmith featured in "Door into the Dark" were, yet Heaney imagines him "a natural for work" (*FW,* 21), repeating the poet's question about culpability in such a way as to confirm Heaney in his own natural vocation.[4]

"Casualty" enacts a conversation with earlier poems about violence from *Wintering Out* and *North*. In "Casualty," Heaney moves from the uneasy position of tribal solidarity among Northern Irish Catholics that he somewhat reluctantly confessed in "Punishment" to a solidarity/ communion with the fisherman O'Neill, the transgressor of the tribe's solidarity, and thus into a position of solidarity with his own art. In so doing, he also renovates the opening image of "The Tollund Man" from *Wintering Out*. The last line of the first quatrain in that poem figures the Tollund Man's preserved head as a "pointed skin cap" (*WO*, 47). The poet confesses in the conclusion of "The Tollund Man" that "I will feel lost, / Unhappy and at home" (48) in Jutland where the man's body was found, linking that body to those produced by the similarly vengeful violence practiced then in contemporary Northern Ireland. In "Casualty," O'Neill wears a "peaked cap" (*FW*, 22), recalling the Tollund Man's "pointed skin cap." But while the Tollund Man reminded Heaney of the entrapping violence of Northern Ireland and his uncomfortable recognition of its familiar intricacies, O'Neill releases him from this milieu and enables him to find his poetic voice again in silence and fluidity. The release is signified by the poem's refusal to gaze upon the body of O'Neill after his death, unlike "The Tollund Man"'s dwelling on that preserved body. Instead, O'Neill is rendered present in a spectral, questioning sense, as he becomes Heaney's artistic conscience: "my tentative art / His turned back watches too" (22). "Casualty," then, reverses the poet's voyeuristic vision of the girl's body in "Punishment" by having O'Neill watch the poet. Moreover, the ghostly plural voices of the "fabulous raiders" in "North" are replaced by the solitary, monitory voice of O'Neill's ghost.

After the fisherman is out "drinking in a curfew / Others obeyed" (*FW*, 22), he is killed in a bomb blast. The ghastly rendering of the "score" between 1 Para and the Catholic civil rights protesters—"PARAS THIRTEEN . . . BOGSIDE NIL"—hovers in the background as a grotesque graffito here. The fisherman's presence haunts the rest of the poem, as do the funerals of the Bloody Sunday victims, where "Coffin after coffin / Seemed to float from the door / Of the packed cathedral / Like blossoms on slow water" (22). Later in this second section, Heaney asks the question that is also raised in "Punishment": "How culpable was he / That last night when he broke / Our tribe's complicity?" (23) The "complicity" of the tribe has already been shown at the end of the first stanza in this second section:

The common funeral
Unrolled its swaddling band,
Lapping, tightening
Till we were braced and bound
Like brothers in a ring.

(22)[5]

Heaney's poignant question also illustrates his own growing awareness of the Catholic community's complicity in the overall carnage in the province through its early support of the IRA.

In the third section, the imagery of O'Neil's funeral, which Heaney missed, quickly becomes conflated with a memory of a trip the poet took with him on his boat, just as the water imagery of the first part of section II gives way to a description of the man's drinking "like a fish" (*FW*, 23). In this last section, the mourners are portrayed rhythmically "Shoaling out of his lane / To the respectable / Purring of the hearse . . ." (23). The rhythm of their walking and of the "Purring of the hearse" recalls part of the second section of "Funeral Rites," from *North*, in which the speaker describes another funeral as having "customary rhythms" and gives as examples "the temperate footsteps / of a cortège, winding past each blinded home" (*N*, 7), and "purring family cars [that] / nose into line" (8). While "Funeral Rites" continues its long visual image of the funeral procession and ends up in a megalithic burial mound, "Casualty" ends more hopefully, with a memory of the dead man's habitual activity of fishing. The visual present participle *shoaling* and aural present participle *purring* transport the speaker into an eternally present memory of fishing with the murdered man. This ongoing moment, signified by the use of the present and present participle forms, accords with Mircea Eliade's conception of sacred time, which is "indefinitely recoverable, indefinitely repeatable" and constitutes "an ontological, Parmenidean time; it always remains equal to itself, it neither changes nor is exhausted."[6] Heaney reads his fishing trip with O'Neill through the sacred ceremony of the dead man's imagined funeral, allowing him to inscribe their fishing as similarly sacred, an inexhaustible model for poetry.

There is a subtle but clear connection in the last passages of "Casualty" to the linked concerns of fishing and poetry in "A Lough Neagh

Sequence," especially in the fifth section of that earlier sequence, "Lifting." In "Lifting," the description of the Lough Neagh eel fishermen's technique, "The line's a filament of smut // Drawn hand over fist" (*DD*, 29), uncannily anticipates the description of O'Neill's technique: "The line lifted, hand / Over fist" (*FW*, 23). In each case, fishing in this deliberate, relatively dispassionate fashion functions as an analogy for writing poetry, specifically the retrieval of images from the depths of the subconscious, signified in "Casualty" by the speaker's description: "haul / Steadily off the bottom," and

> . . . find a rhythm
> Working you, slow mile by mile,
> Into your proper haunt
> Somewhere, well out, beyond . . .
>   (24)

Both fishing and making poetry have led the dead man and the speaker into this sacred space.

Heaney's having "tasted freedom with him" (*FW*, 24) in this way enables the poet to forgive the fisherman and himself for breaking their tribe's complicity, which gives him a real position of artistic freedom from which he can evince full fidelity to poetry. There is thus an implicit rejection in the poem of the politics of Sinn Fein, the political wing of the IRA, which translated into English means "Ourselves alone." Heaney finally affirms a different, aesthetic version of this motto as he concludes the poem by recalling himself alone with Louis O'Neill, an enabling solitude contrasting what he suggests is the disabling solidarity of Sinn Fein and perhaps the Catholic community's solidarity after Bloody Sunday, a critique signaled by the swaddling band imagery in section I of the poem. The poet realizes the man's instinctual habits of drinking and fishing are no different than his own habit of making poetry—each simply cannot help it. In these lines, Heaney's meditative recall of the rhythm of that fishing trip casts him into a reverie out of which he is able to form poetry contemplating the act of making poetry.

But crucially, this poem ends by going beyond craft—into technique, in the terms of "Feeling into Words"—with the poet "somewhere well out beyond" listening to the voice of O'Neill, which confirms his own instructive inner voice. Neil Corcoran has placed this poem in context with the other significant vocational poems of Heaney that we have seen: "The apparently confident analogies between poetry and rural crafts in the earlier work, which 'bound' the poet to the community, have been replaced, in the analogy of 'Casualty,' by something much edgier, more uncertain, more 'tentative': one of the community's skills, as it is practiced by the strong-willed O'Neill, offers a lesson in questioning the community's own values and presumptions."[7] The craftsmen of Heaney's poetry always stand at a remove to the community, of it but not in it fully. Their silence and hard work prefigure the same qualities in his fisherman friend and suggest that listening and laboring are the true ground of the poet. Even though the poet does crucially learn to question "the community's own values and presumptions" from his friend, this political questioning is importantly subsumed to a continuing artistic exploration that continues to view writing poetry as a process in which buried images in the subconscious, symbolized by fishing off the bottom of Lough Neagh, are retrieved by a wandering mind lost in reflection. O'Neill's example gave Heaney a better stance, a more helpful posture, by which this poetic retrieval process might take place and affirmed solitude as the crucial state for the making of poetry, in the process secondarily enabling him to reject disabling political, cultural, and religious solidarities.

Despite the poem's affirmation of fidelity to the poet's art, however, it still reveals a political element through drawing in part on the Irish *aisling*, which means "dream" or "vision." The last three lines of the poem are a charge from Heaney to the ghost: "Dawn-sniffing revenant, / Plodder through midnight rain, / Question me again" (*FW,* 24). This ghost prefigures the ghosts of Heaney's later "Station Island," some of whom are also victims of sectarian murders who question his complicity in their deaths. Thus this masculinized variation on the *aisling* is the first in a series of *aislings* written by Heaney, including "Station Island" and his 1993 volume, *The Midnight Verdict,* a verse translation of extracts from Brian Merriman's famous *aisling The Midnight Court,* bracketed by translations from Ovid's *Metamorphoses.* Heaney's use of the genre fully incorporates it into contemporary Irish poetry and extends its use as a vehicle for an evenhanded political commentary that obliquely rejects both the British Army's murder of the fourteen unarmed protesters on Bloody Sunday and, flourishing in the wake of these shootings, the vengeful nationalism that led to O'Neill's death.[8]

Heaney's emphasis on the ghostly in "Casualty" fittingly shows a dual heritage—from the Irish *aisling* and from an Anglo-Irish tradition of Gothic literature. As W. J. McCormack has observed, "The gothic novel endlessly exposed the violence and corruption that lay behind authority, ancient authority for the most part; in this sense it was a subversive force in the eighteenth century and the period following the French Revolution."[9] Ghosts have been a staple of Irish Gothic since the novels of Le Fanu and Stoker in the nineteenth century, and Irish Gothic survives into the twentieth century in the plays of Synge and Yeats. McCormack further points out in his discussion of Yeats's attraction to Irish Gothic that "the ghost. . . formed part of a chain linking the past and the present, through lines of attachment to place or guilty conscience."[10] The ghost of Louis O'Neill in "Casualty" serves essentially this same function: it suggests the continuity of violence in Ireland generally and marks a specific site of violence.

This poem is further haunted—by the spirit of Yeats. "Casualty" is even in trimeter, the same meter as Yeats's "The Fisherman." Heaney and Yeats share an affinity for the lone fisherman as a necessary counterbalance to their selves. Michael Parker argues that "for each poet, the fisherman is 'The most unlike,' a kind of 'anti-self,' who embodies independence, wisdom, integrity—a refusal to submit to the will of the crowd" (*SHMP*, 164). However, Heaney has actually always valued these qualities in his poetry and clearly associates his craft with O'Neill's, suggesting the strong affinity he feels with him. The salient point is that Heaney's actual friend O'Neill functions as the ideal audience for him, just as Yeats's invented fisherman did. O'Neill's watchfulness, solitude, "turned observant back" (*FW*, 21), slyness, questioning of the values of the community, and love of hard work were exemplary qualities for Heaney as he continued to refine his own poetic vocation.

In his Nobel Prize address, Heaney invokes Yeats repeatedly, citing, among other poems, his "Meditations in Time of Civil War," in which the speaker muses upon a starling's nest in a crevice of the wall of his

tower. Heaney notes that this poem is a favorite of the Irish people because of its combination of tender-mindedness and tough-mindedness:
"It is as tender-minded towards life itself as St Kevin was and as tough-
minded about what happens in and to life as Homer. It knows that the
massacre will happen again on the roadside, that the workers in the mini-
bus are going to be lined up and shot down just after quitting time but
it also credits as a reality the squeeze of the hand, the actuality of sympathy and protectiveness between living creatures" (*CP,* 26). Heaney's
"Casualty" fulfills the dual function that he lays out here: it tells the truth
in all its stark reality and admits the possibility of further atrocities, but
it also displays a certain softness, a resiliency that enables it to open a
space for dialogue and understanding between opposing factions in its
emphasis on listening through its sonic characteristics.[11]

The elegies of *Field Work* differ in their open quality from the more
closed, agonizing ones of *North,* as Jahan Ramazani has shown in his definitive discussion of Heaney's elegies. Whereas in *North* the poet "ago-
nizes over the proper relation between 'murder' and 'ceremony,' worrying
that his elegiac poems may aestheticize death," in the more personal elegies of *Field Work* "his self-interrogations become less violent, his language more open to traditional poetic graces."[12] At the same time, other
elegies in *Field Work,* especially his political ones, pay homage to other
of Heaney's friends killed in the provincewide violence of the 1970s and,
through the tripartite function of the traditional elegy to lament, praise,
and offer consolation for the dead, suggest how these dead, like the ghost
of Louis O'Neill in "Casualty," continue to lead exemplary ghostly after-
lives for the poet.[13]

For example, in "A Postcard from North Antrim," the poem immediately preceding "Casualty" in the volume, Heaney recalls how his
friend Sean Armstrong had a voice that adumbrates the apolitical stance
of Louis O'Neill: "It was independent, rattling, non-transcendent /
Ulster—old decency" (*FW,* 20). The poem concludes with a joyous picture of this friend, also characterized like O'Neill by a snapshot of his
life-affirming qualities in the present participle: "Chorus-leading, splash-
ing out the wine" (20).

"In Memoriam Sean O'Riada" again resorts to aquatic imagery
and specifically fishing in a poem that simultaneously remembers the

246 Poetry & Peace

famous man and suggests how he too stands as an exemplary, largely silent figure for the poet in a time of violence. In the poem, when O'Riada is asked how he works, Heaney has him reply, "'Sometimes I just lie out / like ballast in the bottom of the boat / listening to the cuckoo'" (*FW*, 29). The poet quickly recalls an afternoon spent fishing with the conductor and praises his fishing abilities as an example of "*sprezzatura, //* more falconer than fisherman, I'd say" (29). O'Riada's ability to work hard and make it look easy carried over to his own playing and conducting, as shown in the poem's conclusion where he is described as "Minnow of light. / Wader of assonance" (30). O'Riada's labor recalls that of Heaney's friend Louis O'Neill, who wore literal waders and loved to work and finally demonstrates to the poet how his own music might be achieved and presented artfully after time spent listening for its rhythms.

Finally, the much-discussed elegy "The Strand at Lough Beg," in memory of the poet's cousin Colum McCartney, also is set near water and concludes with the poet's imagining himself wiping his cousin's wounds with moss and using "green" rushes to "plait / Green scapulars to wear over your shroud" (*FW*, 18). The emphasis on the greenness of the rushes ostensibly embraces Irish nationalism but actually signals the volume's concern with new life — in poetry, if not yet in politics — springing from the dead.

Certain moments in "Triptych," such as the concluding quatrain of the first part, "After a Killing," also offer the hopeful signs of plant life as emblems of the optimism that remains in the poet's mind in the midst of sporadic outbreaks of violence:

> And to-day a girl walks in home to us
> Carrying a basket full of new potatoes,
> Three tight green cabbages, and carrots
> With the tops and mould still fresh on them.
>   (*FW*, 12)

The sibyl who answers the poet's question "'What will become of us?'" in "Sibyl," the next section of "Triptych," invokes hope through budding plant life:

"I think our very form is bound to change.
Dogs in a siege. Saurian relapses. Pismires.

Unless forgiveness finds its nerve and voice,
Unless the helmeted and bleeding tree
Can green and open buds like infants' fists."
                                    (13)

In a remarkable maneuver, Heaney colors as green not Irish nationalism but political forgiveness and reconciliation. Taken in this context,
Colum McCartney's death, then, while terrible, is marked not only by
the Catholic scapulars of green but also by a springlike hope that such
an atrocity will lead to forgiveness, not more vengeance.

By the middle of the volume, the poet's hopes seem to lie in poetry
itself, which is now characterized by the agricultural metaphor of till-
ing the earth. In the first of the well-known "Glanmore Sonnets," the
speaker opens by forcing the metaphor on the reader immediately, perhaps too quickly, after the careful aquatic analogies offered with poetry
in earlier poems in the volume: "Vowels ploughed into other: opened
ground" (*FW*, 33). The speaker then terms "art a paradigm of earth new
from the lathe / Of ploughs," and states, "My lea is deeply tilled" (33).
The ghosts that now enter his mind are not ghosts of the Troubles but
harbingers of poetry: "Breasting the mist, in sowers' aprons, / My ghosts
come striding into their spring stations. / The dream grain whirls like
freakish Easter snows" (33). These lines suggest the fertile images and
symbols of poems, sowing themselves, as it were, into the soil of his
subconscious. Cultivations follow in the rest of the sequence.

In the second sonnet, the poet stands in his favored posture, receiving the hints and beginnings of poems that present themselves to him:
"Sensings, mountings from the hiding places, / Words entering almost
the sense of touch / Ferreting themselves out of their dark hutch—"
(*FW*, 34). After briefly recalling another rural craftsman, Oisin Kelly the
stonemason, the poet

    . . . landed in the hedge-school of Glanmore
    And from the backs of ditches hoped to raise

A voice caught back off slug-horn and slow chanter
That might continue, hold, dispel, appease:
Vowels ploughed into other, opened ground,
Each verse returning like the plough turned round.
(34)

A student again, he listens for the voice of his poems and finds them in a repetitive, incantatory dreamlike state he inhabits for the rest of these sonnets.

The third sonnet teasingly introduces the notion of the poet and his wife as William Wordsworth and his sister Dorothy, and indeed the remembrances of childhood epiphanies in the subsequent poems sketch out a *Prelude*-like search for poetic inspiration, much as book I of that long sequence does. Sonnets 4 and 5 portray the poet as a child, crouching and listening for a train and waiting in a tree, respectively. The tree in sonnet 5 is the culmination of the various positive green images of plants featured in earlier poems in the volume, such as "Triptych." He describes this tree as having "green young shoots" and as being "our bower as children, a greenish, dank / And snapping memory as I get older" (*FW*, 37). Although the child called it a "boortree," the adult has learned to call it "elderberry" but soon reverts to calling it "boortree" again (37). Recalling the game of "'touching tongues'" he played with others in the tree as a child, the adult realizes he is now fully engaged in a search for poetic inspiration and growth and concludes by crouching in the silence of that ever-green tree of memory: "etymologist of roots and graftings, / I fall back to my tree-house and would crouch / Where small buds shoot and flourish in the hush" (37). Significantly, his reclamation of this tree as a site where poetry might flourish is symbolized by his use of the Ulster-Scots term *boortree,* another example of the poet's egalitarian willingness to remain attuned to his culturally mixed dialectical inheritance.

This fifth sonnet signifies another way in which Heaney steadies his poetic self after the shocks of yet more violence in his native province, figured as ghosts who beckon him to listen to them. His resolve in this poem to become childlike, to renew his mind and his poetic vocabulary, enables him to find his feet again poetically. The rhythm and form of this sonnet sequence free up a space for new content, new subjects for his poetry. His advice in his 1996 commencement address at the University of North Carolina at Chapel Hill is apposite in this regard: "Unless that underground level of the self is preserved as a verified and verifying element in your make-up, you will be in danger of settling into whatever role or profile that the world, or your position in the world, prescribes for you—in danger of molding yourselves in accordance with the laws of growth other than the laws of your own intuitive being."[14] That "underground level of the self" is precisely what Heaney was trying to preserve in the beautifully wrought and textured sonnets of this sequence because he desperately needed an anchoring device at that time. In these same commencement remarks, Heaney concludes by invoking Wordsworth's *Prelude* in a way that uncannily recalls his poetic endeavors in these poems: Wordsworth "was implying that history, and our life within it, constantly involves the same effort at starting again and again."[15]

The last, tenth sonnet of the sequence recalls both "Exposure" from *North* and "The Strand at Lough Beg" at the beginning of *Field Work*. In a drizzle that evokes the one featured in "Exposure," the speaker and his lover sleep "in a moss in Donegal / On turf banks under blankets, with our faces / Exposed all night in a wetting drizzle" (*FW*, 42). The image of wiping his cousin's face with "moss / Fine as the drizzle out of a low cloud" in "The Strand at Lough Beg" (18) is thus replaced with an image of lovers at rest on moss, their faces wiped clean by the "wetting drizzle," which leads the speaker to recall the time after the lovemaking of the first night of his married life, "The respite in our dewy dreaming faces" (42). This dream of their long-ago faces as "dewy" is a marital, domestic image the poet uses as a stay against the martial atrocity of his cousin's death in "The Strand at Lough Beg, "where he "gather[s] up cold handfuls of the dew / To wash you, cousin" (18). Washed metaphorically in a different, more calming memory, the poet rests at the end of the poem, connected to his wife through memory and the flesh, even though earlier in the poem he had felt hunted, saying they were like the mythological Irish lovers Diarmuid and Grainne (42).

The restored poet is able to offer an answer to his question posed in the ninth Glanmore sonnet, "What is my apology for poetry?" (*FW*, 41) in the loveliest poem in *Field Work*, "The Harvest Bow," which is a repository of earlier images in the volume. Written from the point of view of the poet as young boy, the poem opens by remembering the way in which his father "plaited the harvest bow" (58), a naturally mature, peaceful image in contrast to the immature green scapulars, only embryonically suggestive of the peace that the poet imagines himself plaiting in "The Strand at Lough Beg." His father here is the ultimate silent craftsman, surpassing all the other silent craftsmen in Heaney's poetry:[16]

> You implicated the mellowed silence in you
> In wheat that does not rust
> But brightens as it tightens twist by twist
> Into a knowable corona,
> A throwaway love-knot of straw.
>
>   (58)

The green shoots and buds imaged in earlier poems in the volume, such as "Triptych," are elided and replaced here with the golden color of the harvest bow, a symbol of the fully ripened, mature poetic gifts to which Heaney aspires. Just as he had described Sean O'Riada as conducting "the Ulster Orchestra / like a drover with an ashplant" in "In Memoriam Sean O'Riada" (29), Heaney associates his father's hands with "ashplants and cane sticks" (58) in the later poem.

The harvest bow becomes for the poet the ultimate symbol of art, as it enables him to "spy into its golden loops" (*FW,* 58) and figuratively see into his past life with his father but also to reflect that its motto could be "*The end of art is peace*" (58). There is no end to the harvest bow; its circularity bespeaks an eternal past rendered present to the poet when he gazes upon it, yet he somehow sees through it metaphorically as well, perhaps perceiving a time in the future when the conflict in the province might end. This peace will be prepared for by a carefully and subtly crafted art that celebrates life in all its frailty, a life that is represented by the fragile, twisted harvest bow.

The Transformation of *Sweeney Astray*: A Unifying Regionalism

"The Strand at Lough Beg" from *Field Work* contains an image that had been reverberating in Heaney's mind for some time—that of Sweeney, the mythological Irish figure who "fled before the bloodied heads, / Goatbeards and dogs' eyes in a demon pack / Blazing out of the ground . . ." (*FW,* 17). Writing about Colum McCartney's murder in the same area of Northern Ireland, the Fews, where Sweeney was pursued may have suggested to the poet how to celebrate the leaping Irish hero in a way that would pay further homage to his cousin and model cultural unity in the province.

The history of composition of Heaney's first Sweeney translation reveals its early version as too antagonistic toward the dominant union-ist ethos in the province, in stark contrast to his attempts to linguisti-cally unite the two major cultural and religious traditions in many of the poems of *Wintering Out.* Neil Corcoran has pointed out, for example, that according to Heaney his first translation of the legend, completed by April 1973, was "done with 'a strong sense of bending the text to my purposes' (St Ronan, for instance, was referred to as 'the bully boy,' when the Unionists were accused of using 'bully boy tactics' in the North, and Sweeney was given such lines as 'My relief was a pivot of history')."[17] The poet finally decided "that this version was too 'infected with the idiom of the moment'" and did not return to it for seven years.[18]

In his introduction to *Sweeney Astray,* Heaney observes how the por-trayal of Sweeney implies the quarrel between the imagination and soci-etal constraints; at the same time, more optimistically, he offers this hero as an example of a bicultural, unifying figure for contemporary North-ern Ireland by arguing that "Sweeney's easy sense of cultural affinity with both western Scotland and southern Ireland" should be taken "as exem-plary for all men and women in contemporary Ulster."[19] As Heaney goes on to point out, "My fundamental relation with Sweeney, however, is topographical. His kingdom lay in what is now south County Antrim and north County Down, and for over thirty years I lived on the verges of that territory, in sight of some of Sweeney's places and in earshot of others—Slemish, Rasharkin, Benevenagh, Dunseverick, the Bann, the Roe, the Mournes."[20] Heaney is recounting his formative years spent in a geographically liminal state, "on the verges" of the linguistic and geo-graphic terrain about which he would later write. In such a position, he grew up influenced by the presence of this older, Gaelic tradition and drew upon it for imaginative respite and sustenance. In the final transla-tion, Heaney marries a tradition of *dinnsheanchas,* or Irish place lore, to Anglicized place names in an effort both to remain true to the spirit of the original landscape and the reality of its current state and to offer a "united Ulster mythology."[21]

The later, published translation also signifies the poet's renewed attempts to be faithful to poetry, consistent with the important poems from *North* and *Field Work* already discussed that preceded the completion of the translation. In his essay "Earning a Rhyme," Heaney recalls returning to the *Sweeney* translation in 1979 and becoming "more obedient to the metrical containments and battened-down verbal procedures of the Irish itself" than he had previously been.[22] Recalling his more formal attempts at this translation that led to his breakthrough ability to finish it, Heaney points out that in comparison to the political and cultural context out of which he was writing as a Northern Irish exile in the Republic, "the true anxiety and the true motivations of writing are much more inward, much more to do with freshets that start unexpectedly in moments of intent concentration and hope." By the time he finished the translation, he thankfully recalls, "I had got fed up with my own mournful bondings to the 'matter of Ulster' and valued more the otherness of *Buile Suibhne* as a poem from beyond." He then was able to quickly write "the speedy poems included in *Station Island* under the general title 'Sweeney Redivivus.'"[23] As we will see, those poems offer the clearest picture yet of the poet's artistic freedom and integrity.

Expanding the Depths of Consciousness in *Station Island* and *The Haw Lantern*

Field Work prefigures many of the concerns of the more mature Heaney, especially his increasing inward mental exploration that naturally evolved from his promotion of a geographic and cultural regionalism in Northern Ireland.[24] While continuing to promote this latter concept of regionalism, Heaney burrowed even further inside himself, listening to voices from deep within his consciousness. He was aided in this transition from a physically imagined region, which he still retains, to a mentally imagined one, which he has emphasized beginning in the late 1970s, by a return to the poetry of Patrick Kavanagh and to that of Edwin Muir, both of whom, among other regional writers, had led him to closely focus upon his home ground in the 1960s. Heaney's reading of the elder poet's late work, as expressed in "The Placeless Heaven: Another Look at Kavanagh" (1988), suggests that his exploration of luminous imagined places within and without himself was inspired, at least in part, by Kavanagh's later poetry.

As Heaney argues in this essay, "a definite change" occurs in Kavanagh's poetry starting with "Epic"—a poem that was salutary for both Heaney and Longley, along with other contemporary Irish poets, in developing their affirmation of their geographic region—and continuing with his "Canal Bank sonnets" from the late 1950s. In these later poems, Kavanagh's places "are luminous spaces within his mind. They have been evacuated of their status as background, as documentary geography, and exist instead as transfigured images, sites where the mind projects its own force."[25] This argument develops from Heaney's assertion, in his 1975 essay "From Monaghan to the Grand Canal: The Poetry of Patrick Kavanagh," that the elder poet's early poems contain "matter-of-fact landscapes, literally presented, but contemplated from such a point of view and with such intensity that they become 'a prospect of the mind.'"[26] Heaney's overall argument about Kavanagh's places suggests that long contemplation of the actual finally leads to imagining the possible.

Citing Kavanagh's poem "Innocence," Heaney finally holds in "The Placeless Heaven" that "the country he visits is inside himself."[27] We might say that Heaney's imagined region of Northern Ireland is increasingly inside himself from the late 1970s onward, as he reverses his tendency, in the earlier volumes, to project the region outward. The Scottish Muir's poetry, Heaney implies in an essay from 1989, also has been salutary for him; as he notes, "It is dream states that underlie and are induced by his most characteristic poems. Muir's level best involves access to a far-off, slightly somnambulist plane of consciousness."[28] This new "mental regionalism," or "plane of consciousness," however, should not be thought of as a solipsistic retreat from the still-pressing concerns of the province; rather, its interiority paradoxically enlarges its scope until this new, imagined country of the poet's mind offers a potential site of deep rapprochement and reconciliation and functions as a region of the mind that offers itself as a proleptic correlative to a realistic region where the province's inhabitants might live in harmony.[29]

"The Placeless Heaven" suggests that in a poem like Kavanagh's "Innocence" poetry itself offers a radical encounter with "the white light of meditation" found "at the edge of consciousness."[30] Heaney's increased focus on consciousness through mentally dwelling upon physical locales has enabled him to gain access to "luminous spaces" in his mind. He has made it clear that consciousness negotiates between at least two different realities—the seen and the unseen, or reality and desire. In this regard, the work of philosopher Michael Polanyi sheds a great deal of light on his theory of consciousness. In *The Tacit Dimension*, Polanyi takes as his *point d'appui* the claim that "we can know more than we can tell."[31] After demonstrating this claim, he goes on to articulate a theory that he calls "tacit knowing." Tacit knowing comprises several aspects—the functional, the phenomenal, the semantic, and the ontological. Polanyi finally argues that tacit knowing "brings home to us that it is not by looking at things, but by dwelling in them, that we understand their joint meaning." By scrutinizing too closely "the particulars of a comprehensive entity . . . their meaning is effaced, our conception of the entity is destroyed."[32] Heaney's conception of poetry as a mediator between levels of consciousness has allowed him variously to see reality, knowledge, or identity as holistic and integrated—as they really are, not as "the particulars of a comprehensive entity." Furthermore, "by dwelling in" poetry, Heaney has achieved a deep knowledge that transcends superficial insights or categories.

In pursuing this subterranean knowledge, Heaney has increasingly cast his vocation in religious terms. As he says in his 1978 essay "The Poet as a Christian," "The poetic vocation involves a pursuit of psychic health, a self-possession, an adjustment between outer and inner realities, a religious commitment to the ever-evolving disciplines of the art which the poet has to credit as his form of sanctity."[33] Despite leaving the Catholic Church, being raised in such a milieu has enabled him to grasp the transcendent qualities necessary for his own work and the discipline necessary to enter states of mind in which he might be more receptive to the promptings of his unconscious.[34]

Nowhere is this disciplined pursuit of his art more evident than in *Station Island* (1984). This volume demonstrates Heaney's increasing penchant for placing himself in a geographically and psychographically liminal position in order to hear his inner muse. This emphasis on listening—which I have already argued pervades other volumes of Heaney's poetry such as the concluding sequence in *North*—prepares the poet for the advice of the various pilgrims he will encounter in the central section of the volume. Heaney had undertaken the pilgrimage to St. Patrick's Purgatory four times as a boy and thus knew the literal and spiritual terrain well.[35] This middle section is shot through with elements of liminality, and the central and titular poem occurs as a purgatorial dream sequence, purposely placed in the middle of the entire volume. This section dramatizes a series of dramatic meetings with various personages, including Heaney's second cousin Colum McCartney, who first appeared in "The Strand at Lough Beg," and James Joyce. *Station Island* would also prove to be a transitional work for Heaney: previously his poetry had been grounded in the soil or bogs of his native Derry or his adopted Wicklow, but with *Station Island* Heaney shows he is attuned to a more ethereal kind of poetry, increasingly Yeatsian in its interchange with the other world and in its preoccupation with the nature of his poetic mission.

There is a loose correspondence to Dante's *Divine Comedy* in the three sections of the volume. The first poem of Part One is entitled "Underground"; in it the poet enacts a literal descent, not to the underworld, but to the London Underground. In Part Two, "Station Island," the poet enters the middle passage that signifies the process he must follow to receive poetic insight. Finally, in Part Three, "Sweeney Redivivus," the poet ascends into an airy realm of the imagination in which he affirms a new poetic role for himself. In its tripartite structure, *Station Island* accords with Jonathan Hufstader's sequential delineation of Heaney's "ritual procedure" in many of his poems: "[There is an] entrance rite, [a] central action, and [then] the subject's emergence from the ritual in a new state of mind."[36]

The theme of liminality is most fully explored in the second, purgatorial section of the volume, but echoes of it abound throughout the work. For instance, in the first section this choice of a liminal route, poetically and personally, is emphasized in the poem "Making Strange," in which the speaker stands between a man with "tawny containment" and "speech like the twang of a bowstring" and "another, unshorn and bewildered" (*SI*, 32). The former may be a British soldier and the latter an Irishman, between whom Heaney negotiates a sort of passage for himself. He does so by heeding "a cunning middle voice" that urges him to "'Be adept and be dialect'" (32). The pun here is on the dual meanings of *dialect:* first connoting how he must switch between an Ulster dialect that he uses with fellow speakers from Northern Ireland and an official, more standard speech that he might employ with someone from the British mainland, and second emphasizing the dialectical nature of Heaney himself, as someone who has always oscillated between the poles of Irishness and Britishness as a Catholic growing up in officially British Northern Ireland.

As Heaney the poet progressively tunes himself to hear this middle voice throughout the volume, he draws strength and insight from it. In "The Loaning," he finds himself "in the limbo of lost words," which eerily presage the status of the ghostly pilgrims he will encounter in "Station Island" (*SI*, 51). These soft, quiet voices are contraposed with the "Big voices in the womanless kitchen" (51) in the second stanza, but then in the third and final stanza the speaker again finds a middle way, telling himself and the reader to "Stand still. You can hear / everything going on" (52). This emphasis on listening, which pervades earlier poems such as "Digging" and "North," prepares the reader and the poet for the advice of the various pilgrims they will encounter together in the central section of the volume.

"Station Island" is itself set in a liminal place, on the island of the same name in Lough Derg, County Donegal; this physically marginal position must have been especially attractive to Heaney as he went through the Catholic pilgrimage rite of doing penitential stations on the island as both a penance for his sin and a way of plumbing his poetic depths. To appreciate Heaney's ambiguous receptive state of mind in this middle section we must properly understand the concept of pilgrimage, which is itself liminal, according to the anthropologists Victor and Edith Turner. In their *Image and Pilgrimage in Christian Culture,* the Turners point out the similarities between Christian pilgrimages and passage rites: "Pilgrimage, then, has some of the attributes of liminality in passage rites: release from mundane structure; homogenization of status; simplicity of dress and behavior; communitas; ordeal; reflection on the meaning of basic religious and cultural values; ritualized enactment of correspondences between religious paradigms and shared human experiences; emergence of the integral person from multiple personae; movement from a mundane center to a sacred periphery which suddenly, transiently, becomes central for the individual, an *axis mundi* of his faith."[37] Heaney's pilgrimage shares a surprising number of these attributes; perhaps most important, he emerges as a more "integral person from multiple personae" by the end of the sequence, the various aspects of his personality integrated and functioning supremely well and his poetic mission clear.

Although I have been using the term *liminality* as a description of an in-between position in which Heaney often places himself to receive poetic images, in *Station Island* this usual sense of his liminality coalesces with his position as a social liminar undergoing the rite of religious passage that all pilgrims to the island must undergo. Liminars are especially open to receiving sacred or poetic knowledge in their condition of powerlessness and ambiguity, as the Turners note:

> Liminars are betwixt and between. Liminars are stripped of status and authority, removed from a social structure maintained and sanctioned by power and force, and leveled to a homogeneous social state through discipline and ordeal. Their secular powerlessness may be compensated for by a sacred power, however — the power of the weak, derived on the one hand from the resurgence of nature when structural power is removed, and on the other from the reception of sacred knowledge. Much of what has been bound by social structure is liberated, notably the sense of comradeship and communion, or communitas; while much of what has been dispersed over the many domains of culture and social structure is now bound, or cathected, in the complex semantic systems of pivotal, multivocal symbols and myths, numinous systems which achieve great conjunctive power.[38]

Heaney enters a twilight world between the living and the dead that empowers him to receive ghostly urges and advice for his poetry. The "multivocal symbols" common to the religious and sociological processes of liminality just described suggest the voices of the various figures from Ireland's and Heaney's own past that he hears in the first eleven sections of this middle section.[39] Their advice is subsumed, however, by the multivocal arrival of James Joyce, a figure of artistic importance whom Heaney meets in a car park after the end of the pilgrimage. His entrance, though silent, triggers verbal echoes in the poet's head: "His voice eddying with the vowels of all rivers / came back to me, though he did not speak yet" (*SI*, 92).

This twelfth section of the sequence famously culminates with Joyce's advice to Heaney

> ". . . to write
> for the joy of it. Cultivate a work-lust
> that imagines its haven like your hands at night
>
> dreaming the sun in the sunspot of a breast
> . . . .
> Let go, let fly, forget.
> You've listened long enough. Now strike your note."
> (*SI*, 93)

Heaney then steps into a liminal space luminous with potential: "It was as if I had stepped free into space / alone with nothing that I had not known / already" (93). Polanyi's discussion of "tacit foreknowledge" is apposite here, since Heaney seems intensely familiar with this situation yet surprised at finding himself in it. In developing this theory, Polanyi draws on Plato's discussion of arguments and solutions in the *Meno*: "He says that to search for the solution of a problem is an absurdity; for either you know what you are looking for, and then there is no problem; or you do not know what you are looking for, and then you cannot expect to find anything. The solution which Plato offered for this paradox was that all discovery is a remembering of past lives. . . . The kind of tacit knowledge that solves the paradox of the *Meno* consists in the intimation of something hidden, which we may yet discover."[40] Polanyi's conception of tacit foreknowledge is vital to understanding Heaney's discovery at the end of this sequence. Having replayed his past life in recalling the various personages that speak to him in the first eleven sections—and perhaps his earlier vocational possibilities that these ghosts signify, as Helen Vendler claims—he has unconsciously enacted Plato's solution to the *Meno* and created a freed-up space in which he can now be receptive to discovering new direction about his true vocation of poetry.[41] That space has been there all along, but he has been too preoccupied with his own past and his fidelity to other attractions besides his poetry, to fully enter it, although he returns to it in his best poems of *North* and *Field Work*. By reenacting the familiar ritual of the penitential stations with his body, a discipline that even then was still second nature to him, Heaney's mind was allowed to wander in a limitless space of potential, reliving and finally purging his past and imagining his poetic future.

After meeting Joyce, Heaney tells him of the inspiration he has gained from Stephen's diary entry "'for April the thirteenth'"—the passage in which Stephen Dedalus in *Portrait of an Artist* realizes that *tundish* is a perfectly acceptable English word, despite the Dean's professed ignorance of it (*SI*, 93). Joyce's response is swift and derisive:

. . . "Who cares,"
he jeered, "any more? The English language
belongs to us. You are raking at dead fires,

a waste of time for somebody your age.
That subject people stuff is a cod's game,
infantile like your peasant pilgrimage."
(93)

This advice explicitly rejects the victim mentality sometimes deployed by the IRA as a response to the ongoing Northern Irish Catholic immersion in a neocolonial state. Joyce's own mastery of the English language, the tongue of the colonizer, enables Heaney too to fully claim this language as his own and to revel in it, to reconfigure it for his own uses. Joyce, in the role of aesthetic priest, thus absolves Heaney from his enslavement to the past and from an absorption with "postcolonial" musings.[42]

This meeting signifies Heaney's setting out for the frontier of writing, as he takes Joyce's advice to

. . . "swim

out on your own and fill the element
with signatures on your own frequency,
echo soundings, searches, probes, allurements,

elver-gleams in the dark of the whole sea."
                                      (*SI*, 94)

In keeping with the poet's theory of himself as a receiving station for poetry, the term *frequency* casts him as a listener for voices throughout the bandwidth of his mind. This position is congruous with his receptive state at the end of "Casualty," as signaled by the "elver-gleams" that recall the eel fisherman Louis O'Neill from that poem. Joyce and O'Neill both thus figure as revenant reminders for Heaney that his essential poetic posture is listening in isolation away from the alluring voice of the tribe.

The aquatic imagery of this poetic advice is heightened by the burst of rain around Joyce as he strides off, signaling a moment of insight for the poet. Heaney has followed the procession of pilgrims until he has reached his ultimate destination, not so much a position of spiritual exaltation as an artistically enabling space in which he can receive the advice given him by his aesthetic priest, Joyce. This advice is his road map to writing, as he will increasingly negotiate between the world of the living and other realms by the brightness of the "elver-gleams"—the flashes of poetic inspiration that occur from his encounters with spirits as he bestrides the division between two dimensions of reality.

Heaney's mediating and meditative pilgrimage to Station Island suggests not only that he is a pilgrim in the liminally enabling geographic, religious, social, and poetic senses that I have identified but also that he is a "traveler" in the historical and etymological senses that Paul Fussell has delineated. Fussell argues that the real traveler occupies a mediating position between the old-fashioned explorer and the modern tourist: "The genuine traveler, is, or used to be, in the middle between the two extremes [of exploration and tourism]. If the explorer moves toward the risks of the formless and the unknown, the tourist moves toward the security of pure cliché. It is between these two poles that the traveler mediates, retaining all he can of the excitement of the unpredictable attaching to exploration, and fusing that with the pleasure of 'knowing where one is' belonging to tourism."[43] In these terms, Heaney's travel has enabled him to liminally explore the excitement of an unknown place—the island itself—while knowing exactly where he is as he repeats the familiar penitential stations. The interaction of his physical, geographic exploration and psychic, religious "tourism" (he is after all revisiting, as it were, his formerly deep faith) in this sense has resulted in a process of travel-as-suffering, in keeping with the etymological sense of *travel*. *Travel* is derived from *travail*, as Fussell relates: "A traveler is one who suffers *travail*, a word deriving in its turn from Latin *tripalium*, a torture instrument consisting of three stakes designed to rack the body."[44] The physical pain of kneeling and walking around the island, combined with the mental torments by which the ghosts assail him, collectively casts Heaney in the role of student. And travel-as-suffering is meant to instruct: "Before the development of tourism, travel was conceived to be like study, and its fruits were considered to be the adornment of the mind and the formation of the judgment."[45] Heaney's artistic travelogue serves a crucial instructive process in helping him evince fidelity to his art above all other allegiances—even cousin and country.

The third and final section of *Station Island,* "Sweeney Redivivus," functions as an extended metaphor for Heaney's poetic attempts to adhere to the *via media* between his poetry of the past and his poetry of the future, the latter of which beckons him to fly even higher from the treetops of his lines. He offers us a glimpse of the increasingly spiritual bent of his poetry throughout this volume. In its last poem, "On the Road," the road upon which Heaney drives throws him into a "trance" and "ma[k]e[s] all roads one" (*SI*, 119). In this liminal state, he hears Christ's words to the rich man to "*Sell all you have / and give to the poor*" (119–20). Heaney's reaction has been to take Christ's command metaphorically, harvest his poetic gifts, and offer them as an enhancement to those imaginatively poor. As Sammye Crawford Greer has pointed out, this section of the volume links Heaney with Dante in its affirmation of his poetic mission and in his discharge of his artistic obligation to his audience: "[It] confirm[s] the centrality of the pilgrim-poet's realizations in Heaney's continuing exploration of the consciousness of the artist and leave[s] us with a poet who has, as Heaney says of *The Divine Comedy,* 'an overall sense of having come through . . . of faring forth into the ordeal, going to the nadir and returning to a world that is renewed by the boon won in that other place.'"[46]

Already poetically liberated by Joyce, Heaney reflects on this aesthetic/spiritual ascent:

> I was up and away
>
> like a human soul
> that plumes from the mouth
> in undulant, tenor
> black-letter latin.
>
> > (*SI,* 120)

For the remainder of the poem, he is "Noah's dove," signifying hope and maintaining a life of exile, meditation, and exaltation (120). Just as Joyce's Stephen Dedalus would try to fly by the nets that his country had laid for him, Heaney here is increasingly trying out his wings, slipping by constraining nets such as an Irish overabsorption with the past or victim status. In his otherwise convincing essay on what he terms Heaney's "station poems," those ritualized poems including *Station Island,* Jonathan Bolton argues that this third and last stage of the station poem, the "epode or 'aftersong,' typically involves some form of return, as if from a trance, a resurfacing or unearthing motion that completes the ritual and brings the excavated find or renewed sense of racial consciousness to light."[47] While "Sweeney Redivivus" clearly marks the poet's return from a trancelike state in which he was interrogated by the ghosts of his past, it significantly does not offer a recovered physical artifact and certainly not "a renewed sense of racial consciousness," suggesting instead that Heaney's new poetic project will be more abstract and cosmopolitan.

Station Island signals the end of Heaney's long search for a stable self in his poetry, a process marked by extended contemplation and soul-searching. It seems that his concern in his 1968 essay "Writer at Work" has finally been answered: "Until he has more or less fully realized his vision, has discarded his provisional identities for a final self, it is dangerous for him to enquire into this process too closely or too publicly."[48] By the time of his very public Nobel Prize Address in 1995, eleven years after the appearance of *Station Island*, Heaney could look back and with no small satisfaction note, "I began a few years ago to try to make space in my reckoning and imagining for the marvelous as well as for the murderous" (*CP*, 20). This remark captures perfectly his spirited exploration of a new poetic space liminal in position between his rooted past and imaginative, airy future in *Station Island*. Significantly, the importance of listening that shaped so many of his earlier volumes, while still crucial, would gradually be subsumed by an emphasis on *visual* imaginings of the marvelous in volumes such as *Seeing Things* (1991), *The Spirit Level* (1996), *Electric Light* (2001), and *District and Circle* (2006).

The Haw Lantern (1987), while a slighter volume than earlier ones, nevertheless contains the lovely sonnet sequence "Clearances" in honor of the poet's mother, along with two poems helpful in understanding Heaney's continuing articulation of the poet's role in society in the context of his increasingly deep exploration of his own consciousness. The first of these, "A Daylight Art," returns to the concerns of some of his earliest poetry in its metapoetic exploration of his craft. Dedicated to Norman MacCaig, a Scottish poet influential for Heaney in formulating his earlier, more geographically inclined regionalism, the poem revisits his favorite analogy between fishing and poetry. In the poem, Socrates, "On the day he was to take the poison" (*HL*, 9), finally tells his friends of his lifelong dream in which he has been repeatedly told, "*Practise the art*," which he had previously taken to mean philosophy (9). Now, however, he realizes the admonition is meant literally, and he spends his last day on earth "putting Aesop's fables into verse" (9).

MacCaig, the silent and effaced true subject of the poem, is a kind of anti-Socrates in the sense that he has always been called to practice his poetry and has done so well and naturally. So the speaker tells us, "Happy the man, therefore, with a natural gift // for practicing the right one from the start — / poetry, say, or fishing . . ." (*HL*, 9). MacCaig and other born practitioners of their craft, along with, presumably, Heaney himself, have "nights [that] are dreamless; / whose deep-sunk panoramas rise and pass // like daylight through the rod's eye or the nib's eye" (9). These craftsmen, like Heaney's fisherman friend Louis O'Neill in "Casualty," are all naturally hard workers who completely dedicate themselves to their art, and their broad, panoramic visions somehow slip out from their minds through the fine, narrow tips of rods and pens, directed skillfully at their audiences, whether these are fish or readers. Significantly, their art is shot through with light as it radiates from them, prefiguring the sort of radiant spaces found at the end of the eighth and last sonnet from "Clearances" and throughout *Seeing Things.*

This space at the end of "Clearances" signifies the absence of a long-dead chestnut tree that becomes the space Heaney's mother's soul inhabits metaphorically: "Its heft and hush become a bright nowhere, / A soul ramifying and forever / Silent, beyond silence listened for" (*HL*, 32). I suspect that one of the first instances of Heaney's apprehension of these luminous spaces occurred during his visit to the remarkably preserved Gallarus Oratory on the Dingle Peninsula in 1967. Recalling his state of mind engendered by his immersion in the darkness of that unmortared but watertight stone structure, he felt that he was "bowing under like the generations of monks who must have bowed down in meditation and reparation on that floor. I felt the weight of Christianity in all its rebuking aspects."[49] But "coming out of the cold heart of the stone, into the sunlight and the dazzle of grass and sea, I felt a light in my heart, a surge towards happiness . . . [a] sudden apprehension of the world as light."[50] There are even earlier examples of this literal entrance into light in his poetry. For example, the pregnant mother in his uncollected poem "Expectant" rests easily, knowing that the baby inside her "works away beyond the heat and cold, / Prospecting light, making me his tunnel" (*SHPM*, 9). These early glimpses of literal light give way in the later poems to visions of imagined, light-filled spaces in the mind.

Heaney's later poetry clears luminous spaces for his increasingly epiphanic discoveries. Epiphanic revelation for Heaney implicitly involves the constant pressure of reality and is not a process of pure fantasy or mental wandering: "Poetically, it is an aspect of the place to which the quester in Robert Frost's poem 'Directive' is guided, and of the place in which the speaker of Thomas Hardy's poem 'Afterwards' arrives—an elsewhere beyond the frontier of writing where the 'imagination presses back against the pressure of reality.'"[51] In describing the "characterization of imaginary space" in poems such as "From the Frontier of Writing" and others in *The Haw Lantern,* Dillon Johnston has argued that Helen Vendler's description of the volume as "Heaney's first book of the virtual" is useful, since "*virtual* avoids the conventional Otherworld of Irish narratives and substitutes a universal concept familiar to children and other cyber-space cadets while remaining mysterious to adult readers."[52] Heaney has increasingly been exploring this frontier of writing in his recent poetry.

"From the Frontier of Writing" ostensibly is political, much as the surface and situation of "Casualty" seems to be, yet like that poem it acquires its lightness and buoyancy from an advancement into a region in which the speaker is fully himself, free from menacing aspects of his culture. The narrator of the poem tells of being stopped and interrogated by British troops at a roadblock, then driving on to "the frontier of writing / where it happens again." After the speaker safely passes through this obstruction, he observes with relief,

> And suddenly you're through, arraigned yet freed,
> as if you'd passed from behind a waterfall
> on the black current of a tarmac road
>
> past armour-plated vehicles, out between
> the posted soldiers flowing and receding
> like tree shadows into the polished windscreen.
>
> (*HL,* 6)

There is some beautiful imagery operating in this passage: the speaker compares his "escape" from the soldiers to edging behind a waterfall, which then metamorphoses into the flowing "black current" of the road, down which he flees, with the soldiers receding like tree shadows reflected in the burnished windshield. Water constantly signals the possibility of an imaginative elsewhere through its linguistic and geographic duality in Heaney's mind. The concluding emphasis on water imagery illustrates the narrow pathway the speaker must tread to successfully get by the soldiers, and both the waterfall and the road function as the

via media down which he must travel to get to the frontier of writing—
a place that is curiously free of obstacles. The residual fear and pressure
created by the soldiers hover in the back of the speaker's mind but are
finally subsumed by the poet's imaginative trip inward. This poem illustrates the characteristics of Heaney's particular type of liminality—a
transformative space that springs from his divided sense of place and
geography.

In his 1988 lecture "The Place of Writing: W. B. Yeats and Thoor
Ballylee," Heaney expands upon his sense of the place of writing, calling it "a destination in art arrived at by way of art."[53] As he further explains, "The poetic imagination in its strongest manifestation imposes
its vision upon a place rather than accepts a vision from it."[54] Although
he is speaking of the poetic imagination of the later Yeats, after age
fifty, the approval implicit in noting that Yeats's late "poems have created a country of the mind rather than the other way round" suggests
Heaney's own desire to invert the terms of his earlier relationship to region, to no longer be, as Yeats in his earlier career was, "a voice of the
spirit of the region."[55] Unsurprisingly, Heaney himself would turn fifty
the year after this lecture and had been contemplating how he might
arrive at the frontier of writing for several years, a country of the mind
that would serve as a fitter subject for his later poetry than the merely
physical region of Northern Ireland. This new mental landscape would
be marked by an increasing immersion in the marvelous imagination of
the poet himself.[56]

CHAPTER EIGHT

Redressing Reality

Seeing Things and *The Spirit Level*: Gazing at the Marvelous, Returning to Foreknowledge

In his introduction to his Oxford lectures of 1995, *The Redress of Poetry*, Heaney briefly discusses George Herbert's poem "The Pulley" and the eighth poem from his own sequence in *Seeing Things*, called "Lightenings." Heaney's poem relates the story of a ghost ship that appeared to the monastic community of Clonmacnoise during the Middle Ages. The narrator notes that the ship's anchor caught in the altar rails and one of its crewmen climbed down to release it; however, he could not release the anchor by himself, so the monks helped him and he disappeared along with the ship, climbing "back / Out of the marvellous as he had known it" (*ST,* 62). "The Pulley," of course, concerns God's plan of withholding rest as a blessing so that the hearts of men will be turned heavenwards, despite their mortal preoccupations. Heaney claims that "both poems are about the way that consciousness can be alive to two different and contradictory dimensions of reality and still find a way of negotiating between them."[1]

In a 1996 interview with Christopher Lydon, Heaney discussed the implications of the interaction between the human and mortal worlds in his own poem:

I think it's about knowing that there are two levels of understanding and being able to move between them. The little crewman who comes down out of the dreamship will drown in actual historical conditions; on the other hand, for a full enhancement of their historical life, the people on the floor of the church have an immense enlargement when the dreamship appears there. It's a story. I mean it's got the absoluteness of story, and once you hear the story, something awakens in you. But for me it has become an allegory about the two dimensions or the two poles or the two calls to poetry, to art of all sorts. To witness to what's on the floor of history and at the same time to portray what's in the heaven of the imagination.[2]

Heaney is undoubtedly thinking of Yeats in this last sentence: "on the floor of history" is an allusion to Yeats's recognition of the dawning of a new epoch through the birth of "The uncontrollable mystery on the bestial floor" in "The Magi," which finally is identified as the "rough beast" of the Apocalypse in "The Second Coming."[3] The phrase "in the heaven of the imagination" refers to Yeats's "The Cold Heaven."[4] This passage from the Lydon interview restates a central concern of these chapters on Heaney: how to integrate the imaginative life with the world of external experience by affirming an allegiance to art, yet letting it subtly and secondarily witness history and perhaps reimagine reality.

Heaney's solution, as I hope to make clear in this chapter, has been reached through manipulating consciousness for himself and attempting to put the reader through this experience as well. As he goes on to say in the Lydon interview about his poem from the "Lightenings" sequence, "The crewman is the poet but the crewman is, as it were, the poet in the reader also. The crewman is that part of each person, is that little elevator that goes up and down in consciousness between your realism and your desire if you like."[5] Heaney's employment of poetry as a means of transforming our thinking about what is known and what is perceived—what hovers on the edge of consciousness—indicates a pervasive personal concern with psychological and mental processes and a realization that knowledge of any entity or ideology must involve more than merely what can be quantified.

Heaney speaks about this capacity of poetry by noting in his Nobel Prize lecture that he sees poetry as a negotiator between the core of the mind and its periphery: "I credit poetry, in other words, both for being itself and for being a help, for making possible a fluid and restorative relationship between the mind's centre and its circumference" (*CP*, 12). This conception of the fluid nature of the mind ostensibly resembles Yeats's concept of the shifting borders of the mind he espoused in his 1901 essay "Magic."[6] However, Heaney's statement is much clearer than Yeats's and suggests, not that all minds flow into one, but that individual minds, to be properly balanced, must have two-way traffic, as it were, between their cores and their peripheries. Terence Brown has described Heaney's imagination as "synthetic and osmotic (in the sense that ideas and intuitions seep across thin membranes to blend with each other)."[7] This osmotic quality of Heaney's imagination enables us to understand how his mind works and opens itself to several dimensions of reality or identity in his most recent volumes of poetry.

In his theory of consciousness and its bearing on poetic insight, Heaney has become an epiphanic heir to Wordsworth and his famous emphasis on "spots of time" as engendering moments of insight. Nicholas Roe has traced this epiphanic urge in Heaney all the way back to "Death of a Naturalist," which Roe sees as an unsuccessful attempt at a redemptive moment: "'Death of a Naturalist' suggests that Heaney is drawn to the Wordsworthian spot of time but unable to admit its redemptive adequacy. Wordsworth's 'spot' discovers its shape from within, but Heaney significantly imposes a mythic framework upon his experience in which 'Miss Walls' appears as an external author of guilt — perhaps a sexual awakening — which infects the child's subsequent visit to the flax-dam."[8] Heaney most explicitly states his commitment to dwelling on these spots of time and then drawing on them for poetic inspiration in the introduction to his scarce 1975 volume of prose poems, *Stations.* He discusses a delay between writing the first poems in the volume and the rest of them, which was partly because of the influence of the recent publication of Geoffrey Hill's *Mercian Hymns* upon him and partly because of the utter intrusion of the violence in the North, from which he was able to become free only after moving to Wicklow in 1972.

In an extension of his conception of himself as a receiving station for poetic signals, he writes,

> Those first pieces had been attempts to touch what Wordsworth called "spots of time," moments at the very edge of consciousness which had lain for years in the unconscious as active lodes or nodes, yet on my return a month after the introduction of internment my introspection was not confident enough to pursue its direction. The sirens in the air, perhaps quite rightly, jammed those other tentative if insistent signals. So it was again at a remove, in the "hedge-school" of Glanmore, in Wicklow, that the sequence was returned to, and then the sectarian dimension of that pre-reflective experience presented itself as something asking to be uttered also. I think of the pieces now as points on a psychic *turas,* stations that I have often made unthinkingly in my head.[9]

If Heaney had trouble admitting the "redemptive adequacy" of Wordsworthian spots of time in his first volume, he has surmounted this hurdle in his later work.

Seeing Things radiates light and the poetic hope won by Heaney's forays into the newly discovered regions of his mind, a boundless space stemming from his long obedience to the demands of form in his poetry. He has recalled that while he wrote an essay on Yeats for the *Field Day Anthology of Irish Literature* and annotated his poems, he received the first poem of what would become the "Squarings" sequence as he sat in the National Library: "I now realize it came probably from that poem by Yeats that begins, 'Suddenly I saw the cold and rook-delighting heaven' ["The Cold Heaven"]. It is about being visited, about the capacity for illumination, splendour and elation. Anyhow, the words came into my head."[10] The first twelve-line poem in the sequence was answered by other twelve-liners, and that formal structure enabled a freedom in content: "What inspired me was the twelve-line form, and a sense that a weight had been lifted and that some light had entered in. Words like 'soul' and 'spirit' were beginning to be plied, and I relate that to the fact that my father and mother had recently died."[11] Just as the formal qualities of these twelve-line poems enabled a freeing up of poetic content, the foundation for this new poetic territory was laid by Heaney's long use of formal structures such as the quatrain in much of his early poetry and the sonnets from some of the middle volumes, such as the "Glanmore Sonnets" from *Field Work* and the sonnet sequence "Clearances" from *The Haw Lantern*. His long immersion in form finally led, then, to an openness in subject matter.[12]

Yeats's "The Cold Heaven" is worth exploring briefly for the insight it sheds into Heaney's own process of poetic inspiration that led to the luminous spaces pervading *Seeing Things*. Yeats's speaker experiences an ecstatic vision that leads him into a state "out of all sense and reason."[13] Although this moment anticipates Yeats's argument in *A Vision* that the soul lives over again the events of its life, experiencing first its most intense and painful moments, the visionary state itself articulated in the poem, one in which the speaker is "Riddled with light," constitutes the important influence upon Heaney.[14] "Out of all sense" is an ambiguous Irish expression meaning "to an extent far beyond what common sense could justify" and "beyond the reach of sensation."[15] The latter meaning suggests a visionary ecstatic state beyond normal sensory perception, somewhat analogous to part of Heaney's own formulation of "technique" in "Feeling into Words." While "technique" and "craft" as Heaney defines them in that essay have existed in a dynamic relationship for many years in his work, *Seeing Things* fully signals his return to reclaiming a central feature of technique: "the discovery of ways [for the poet] to go out of his normal cognitive bounds and raid the inarticulate" ("FW," 47).

The perceptive vision that so dominates *Seeing Things* has a different quality from the more literal vision in many but certainly not all of Heaney's earlier poems. As I have tried to make clear, many of his metapoetic poems from his first four volumes capture fleetingly his moments of visionary transcendence as the poet receives his poetic material from his subconscious. We might say, however, that Heaney's poetry beginning with *Seeing Things* has moved fully into receptive gazing in a Yeatsian sense. In an evocative essay on Yeats, Denis Donoghue argues that while the glance skims the surface of the known world, the gaze looks finally inward to the ineffable and secretive, leading to reverie, then trance: "Yeats distinguishes between the gaze and the glance; the glance is objective, administrative, as when the eyes of a civil servant look upon a world to be controlled, a world in which subject and object are sharply distinguished and names are attached, with undue confidence, to things: the gaze is internal and secret. . . . To gaze is to set one's mind dancing in its own circle, until reverie passes into trance."[16] Never guilty of merely glancing in this sense, Heaney has gazed intently at the work of rural craftsmen in many of the early poems, as we have seen, with exemplary effects on his poetry. Now he gazes even more intently at objects themselves, effecting a dissolution between object and subject such that the boundaries between them collapse and the subject partakes in the secret life of the object. As we have seen, a striking earlier instance of the gaze in this sense is found in "The Harvest Bow," from *Field Work,* in which the poet's deep gazing upon the harvest bow made by his father enables him to envision peace in the province.[17]

The opening poem from the "Lightenings" sequence in *Seeing Things* even employs the term *gazing,* as the speaker describes "A gazing out from far away, alone," a moment that takes place "after the commanded journey" (*ST,* 55). In an earlier poem in the volume, the suggestively titled "Field of Vision," the speaker describes the long vision of a woman who refuses to glance, in Yeats's terms, and instead gazes

> Straight out past the TV in the corner,
> The stunted, agitated hawthorn bush,
> The same small calves with their backs to wind and rain,
> The same acre of ragwort, the same mountain.
>
> (24)

Her refusal to see these physical things by dwelling on them and her enforced isolation in her wheelchair enable her to achieve a state of mind that is transcendent: "Her brow was clear as the chrome bits of the chair" (24). Daniel Tobin suggests that Heaney's likening of the "woman's steadfastness to the window she has looked out of for years" enables him to emphasize "the positive liminality of her seemingly disabled existence."[18]

Gazing deeply at the woman reminds the poet of another vision: staring at "a well-braced gate" (*ST,* 24), another liminal image, through which

>   . . . you could see

> Deeper into the country than you expected
> And discovered that the field behind the hedge
> Grew more distinctly strange as you kept standing
> Focused and drawn in by what barred the way.
>   (24)

Tobin's reading of this stanza is revelatory: "Stasis is transformed into ecstasy through the recognition of the primary relationship between self and other—consciousness is 'focused and drawn in by what bars the way.'"[19] Just as important, the "field behind the hedge" may symbolize Heaney's long immersion in the concerns of Northern Ireland, a vision that grows "more distinctly strange" as he gazes at the gate itself, a correlative to the border of his own mind, his new country of exploration. Read in this manner, the closing lines of "Field of Vision" suggest the continuity between Heaney's early and later poetry and imply that despite his own attraction to the marvelous that has superseded the pressing actual concerns of his province, those immediate concerns nevertheless remain, although they too, have grown stranger, perhaps more marvelous.

As Peter McDonald has adroitly pointed out about Heaney's later poetry, "It might well be argued that a central ambition for Heaney is to write beyond the possible restrictions of his work's historical context."[20] "Field of Vision" achieves this ambition in its arrival in a state similar to that explored in the poem "From the Frontier of Writing," a place of liberation and potential, a place, paradoxically, that implicitly anticipates the hoped-for condition of another state in the future—that of the political province of Northern Ireland. "Field of Vision" reveals Heaney to be in the position that, drawing on John Keats's notion of negative capability, he has described the contemporary Northern Irish poet as occupying in 1984: "Stretched between politics and transcendence, . . . [he] is often displaced from a confidence in a single position by his disposition to be affected by all positions, negatively rather than positively capable."[21] Heaney's imagination, then, is strengthened by his refusal to dwell within the past "restrictions of his work's historical context," in McDonald's phrase, even as it transcends those bounds through its focused vision in the foreground of an actual gate leading to an imagined strange new country that may anticipate a new province of Northern Ireland in the background of the poet's mind.[22]

Limits and restrictions were, after all, much on Heaney's mind at this time. A significant poem from *Seeing Things*, "Markings," demonstrates his interest in reaching a state of mind that overcomes physical and other demarcations. The public life of this poem has been incredible: Rand Brandes notes that "in Dublin in September 1993, 70,000 screaming Gaelic football fans from Cork and Derry had the chance to read Seamus Heaney's poem, 'Markings,' on page 17 of the All-Ireland Final program."[23] The speaker recalls marking off a football pitch with "four jackets for four goalposts" (*ST,* 10). But this literal field, much like that featured in "Field of Vision," is made strange by the boys' immersion in their game until they reach a state of athletic transcendence: "Some limit had been passed, / There was fleetness, furtherance, untiredness / In time that was extra, unforeseen and free" (10). It is as if the boys play in a limitless field of possibility during an infinite, unmarked penalty time.

Although Heaney terms this particular moment "unforeseen," many of the visions in *Seeing Things* involve a return to that which was once known or that which was foreknown. In his 1995 lecture "Further Language," Heaney speaks of one of his first recognitions of a moment of foreknowledge, an epiphany created by John Braidwood in one of his lectures that Heaney attended in the late 1950s. Braidwood's revelation that *whiskey* is essentially the same word "as the Irish and Gaelic word uisce, meaning water," and further suggestion that "the River Usk in England is therefore to some extent the River Uisce (or Whiskey), a stream still issuing forth from some Celto-British Land of Cockaigne," had a profound effect on the poet: "the Irish/English antithesis, the Celtic-Saxon duality were momentarily collapsed, and in the resulting etymological eddy a gleam of recognition flashed through the synapses and I experienced an elsewhere of potential which felt at the same time like a somewhere being remembered."[24] More important for our purposes, Heaney actively began writing about foreknowledge in 1975, when he recalled in the preface to his prose poem collection *Stations,* using language similar to that concerning his epiphanic revelation at the Braidwood lecture, "I wrote each of them down with the excitement of coming for the first time to a place I had always known completely."[25]

Michael Polanyi's discussion of "tacit foreknowledge" in Plato's *Meno,* which I discussed in chapter 7 in my analysis of *Station Island,* remains relevant for our understanding of the central concern of *Seeing Things.* Polanyi's insistence that for Plato "all discovery is a remembering of past lives" helps us understand that the many poems in *Seeing Things* that reclaim past moments of the poet's life enable him to discover new dimensions within himself, as gazings upon the ordinary become extraordinary moments in which he achieves a spiritual state of déjà vu.[26] Moreover, Polanyi's further explanation of tacit foreknowledge in the context of scientific discovery seems especially applicable to Heaney's continuing poetic journey toward solitary but nonsolipsistic knowing in *Seeing Things*:

To hold such knowledge is an act deeply committed to the conviction that there is something there to be discovered. It is personal, in the sense of involving the personality of him who holds it, and also in the sense of being, as a rule, solitary; but there is no trace in it of self-indulgence. The discoverer is filled with a compelling sense of responsibility for the pursuit of a hidden truth, which demands his services for revealing it. His act of knowing exercises a personal judgment in relating evidence to an external reality, an aspect of which he is seeking to apprehend.[27]

Heaney's moments of insight throughout the volume are marked by precisely the sort of conviction Polanyi articulates in this passage. Polanyi's articulation of tacit knowing here attends to both personal and public dimensions of this process, a dialectic, as we have seen, that Heaney has taken some pains to maintain throughout his career. Even though the emphasis in *Seeing Things* is on the personal, the visions revealed to us are "filled with a compelling sense of responsibility for the pursuit of a hidden truth." This sense of public responsibility to reveal personally won poetic insights was modeled for him by a similar compulsion in W. B. Yeats.

In the early 1980s, Weldon Thornton concluded a seminal apologia for Yeats's mysticism by claiming that "whatever degree of enlightenment Yeats may have achieved (and no one can know that precisely), he never permitted it to lure him away from his commitment to this mortal

life; rather, it enhanced that commitment. No one can say what glories
Yeats glimpsed or what allurements he resisted. We can only be thankful
that he was, in Joseph Campbell's terms, the true hero, who, not content
simply to achieve a boon, felt that he must bring it back for the benefit
of his fellow men."[28] We can be similarly grateful that Heaney has returned time and again from his own reveries to offer us the insights he
has acquired in these states. His return to us, bearing gifts of the spirit,
indicates his rejection of sheer solipsism and his recognition of the redemptive power of poetry for all humanity.

The last poem in the sequence entitled "Squarings" offers a reclamation of the previously known as a new region of the poet's mind. As
the speaker notes in its opening lines,

> Strange how things in the offing, once they're sensed,
> Convert to things foreknown;
> And how what's come upon is manifest
>
> Only in light of what has been gone through.
>
> > (*ST,* 102)

The speaker finally imagines a moment "when light breaks over me /
The way it did on the road beyond Coleraine," where "silver lamé shiv-
ered on the Bann / Out in mid-channel between the painted poles"
(102). "That day," he says, "I'll be in step with what escaped me" (102).
Heaney's description of recovering the foreknown in this poem recalls
his analysis of the effect of the Irish playwright Brian Friel's effect on
his audience: "Their elation comes from the perception of an order beyond themselves which nevertheless seems foreknown, as if something
forgotten surfaced for a clear moment."[29] In a volume full of journeys,
crossings, and surfacings of the foreknown from the familiar, the ordinary, actual, and projected journey "on the road to Coleraine" serves as
a fitting summary of Heaney's new stage on his poetic journey to assay
the depths of his mind, that strange new country he had traversed
many times before but never so deeply.

This new space, what I have been terming Heaney's new country
of the mind, has been developed from his long attention to the poetic

process in the context of geographic place. He consistently has used agricultural terms drawn from his own early immersion in farming and interest in geographic regionalism to describe this state of mind, as he does in his description of the work of his friend the artist Henry Pearson: "There is a finely balanced equilibrium in his work, an equilibrium held between his attraction to a formal repose and his equal attraction to a postmodern subversiveness. To be carried completely towards one or the other of these poles is to be displaced from the field of force where genuine artistic action occurs: it is to end up in either an aesthete's limbo or a self-mocker's hall of mirrors. Pearson's work is the stronger for dwelling in the middle of the field."[30] As Heaney has stated, in a passage fully relevant to the poems of foreknowledge sprinkled throughout *Seeing Things*, poetry induces the mind to create a new country, "a new plane of regard for itself": "We go to poetry, we go to literature in general, to be forwarded within ourselves. The best it can do is to give us an experience that is like foreknowledge of certain things which we already seem to be remembering. What is at work in this most original and illuminating poetry is the mind's capacity to construct a new plane of regard for itself, a new scope for its own activity."[31] "Field of force" and a "new plane of regard" together imply a state of creative tension in which the mind is properly self-conscious of its own operation even as it is lost in thought, a condition that precludes solipsism even as it rejects a sheer dwelling upon reality.

Yeats's usual invocations of a trancelike state imply that this condition has been there all along—that it is there waiting for those of us bold enough to enter it.[32] While poems such as "Digging" and "North" accord with Yeats's theory of poetic perception, they represent a significant but incomplete part of Heaney's liminal theory of poetry. He is finally arguing, implicitly in *Station Island* and in later volumes such as *Seeing Things* and explicitly in his later prose, that the most original poetry will redress a given vision of reality and artistically transform it into another equally plausible representation of reality. Moreover, it is only through the discovery of this other liminal zone, "the frontier of writing, the line that divides the actual conditions of our daily lives from the imaginative representation of those conditions in literature," that the poet can create, not merely occupy, this new position.[33]

"'Poet's Chair'" from *The Spirit Level* (1996) foregrounds Heaney's
occupation of such a position and significantly suggests that foreknowledge is at the heart of any endeavor thoughtfully undertaken, but especially the poetic endeavor. The poet's chair of the poem is variously occupied by a stunning array of personages, suggesting poetry's transnational
and transcultural appeal to the human condition. The chair even seemingly has agency:

> Angling shadows of itself are what
> Your "Poet's Chair" stands to and rises out of
> In its sun-stalked inner-city courtyard.
> On the *qui vive* all the time, its four legs land
> On their feet— . . .
>
> (*SL*, 46)

In stanza 2, Socrates sits in the chair on the day of his suicide, recalling
the concern of "A Daylight Art" from *The Haw Lantern*, which also
imagines his death. Whereas "A Daylight Art" casts Socrates as a late
artist, only that day realizing his gifts in contrast to Heaney's friend
and fellow poet Norman MacCaig, who has always practiced his art,
here Socrates functions as a sort of *summa* figure of all Heaney's silent
craftsmen and artisans who have appeared in the earlier poetry. He sto-
ically takes his poison amid silence, having long known he would be
in this position. And "for the moment everything's an ache / Deferred,
foreknown, imagined and most real" (47, emphasis mine). The moment
of death itself, fully real, is temporarily stayed by the philosopher's
brave resolve in facing it, even as death presses in upon him. This situation uncannily recalls Heaney's definition of the frontier of writing
given above, a situation he describes as "an elsewhere beyond the frontier of writing where the 'imagination presses back against the pressure
of reality.'"[34]

The last stanza of the poem returns to the agricultural metaphor
for poetry put to such good use in "The Glanmore Sonnets" from *Field
Work*, but this time the poet watches his dead father work the land:

> My father's ploughing one, two, three, four sides
> Of the lea ground where I sit all-seeing

At centre field, my back to the thorn tree
They never cut. . . .

(*SL*, 47)

His father squares the field as the poet sits "at centre field"—a suggestive image, given the traditional equation of four fields with the traditional four provinces of Ireland, so that Heaney would figuratively be occupying the mythical fifth province of Ireland, the *Mide*, or the middle.
This conjecture is supported by his long association with the Field Day
Theatre Company, for whom the "Fifth Province," an imagined space, is
a central image.[35] Heaney's occupation of a middle "province" suggests
that he believes that his long poetic project to occupy such a position has
been successful to some degree.

Significantly, while "The horses are all hoof / And burnished flank,
I am all *foreknowledge*" (*ST*, 47, emphasis mine), the poet's foreknowledge does not mean he has forecast the various problems in the province and somehow provided answers to fairly intractable political and
cultural issues; rather, it means that he trusts poetry or "the poem" to be
"a ploughshare that turns time / Up and over" (47). Paul Muldoon notes
that poems like Heaney's "Keeping Going" "clear their own space, bringing us 'all together in a foretime,' if I may borrow that phrase from section 3 of 'Keeping Going.' This 'foretime' is the 'kingdom' to which we
are to be *re*stored, of course, a sense of 'foreknowledge' Heaney associates
with a work of art in 'Poet's Chair,' also collected in *The Spirit Level*."[36]
Heaney's sense of poetry's proleptic power, then, has a unifying, restorative function.

Finally, the image of poetry as a digging implement is, after all,
where we began with the concerns of "Digging": Heaney's earliest successful poem sees the poet's pen as an implement that can unearth the
past successfully and equip the poet for the concerns of the future. A significant amount of his published poetry (from *Death of a Naturalist*
through *The Spirit Level*) thus is framed with an image of the pen and
the poet's chair; having long ago resolved to use the pen to dig, the poet
affirms this resolution in "'Poet's Chair,'" sitting in the figurative, comfortable solidity of the foundations of his art, airy yet grounded, engaged
yet detached, a sort of Tiresias who knows the future is bright given the
field of force in which his poetic imagination operates.

Heaney's creation of a position of poetic reception seen in "'Poet's Chair'" finally differs from Yeats's theory of liminal poetic reception in yet another way—through his role as a mediator between harshness and hope. Yeats's poetry is hopeful in certain ways but does not often transcend determinism in the same way that Heaney's does. Even "The Cold Heaven" is a brilliantly imagined vision of the soul's forced dreaming back over its most intense moments of life. And throughout Yeats's poetry, humans and demigods such as Cuchulain seem trapped by their particular fates as moods descend on them. Heaney had instead to look to Eliot for inspiration in this last aspect of poetic reception. He finishes his lecture on Eliot's poetry by affirming that "in the realm of poetry, as in the realm of consciousness, there is no end to the possible learnings that can take place."[37] Heaney's poetry, by creating a different dimension of reality, enables his poetic characters, narrators, and audience to at least temporarily escape their present realities: he creates hope by virtue of his creation of a new reality, shimmering with not just new aesthetic possibilities but fresh cultural and political possibilities as well. Seamus Deane's suggestion about this capacity of Heaney's poetry seems particularly apposite to this argument: "In Heaney's work, peace needs a space that is not emptiness: it needs to be a rich space, brimming with light."[38] In this created, imagined reality, Heaney has achieved something analogous to what he has approvingly termed Yeats's "attempt to launch upon the world a vision of reality that possessed no surer basis than the ground of his own imagining."[39] One of the driving propositions behind this entire study, Denis Donoghue's contention that "literature makes counterstatements" to reality, which I have cited in the introduction, suggests the appropriateness of Heaney's effort in this regard.[40]

In its employment of light imagery, its longer lines, and its rhyme scheme, "Tollund," from *The Spirit Level,* compellingly suggests just how far Heaney believed Northern Ireland had come by the time of the IRA Ceasefire in 1994. In his essay "Further Language," Heaney recalls visiting the bog at Tollund in Jutland "the Sunday morning after the [IRA] announcement." He speaks of the announcement as "not only inspir[ing] a new and better public language" but also "provid[ing] that unforeseen tremor of joy which can get a new poem going; it seemed as if brightness had been admitted into a dark room."[41] That language of brightness pervades the poem: the poet even remarks the "Light traffic sound" and likens the landscape to one featured in a well-known John Hewitt poem, "a still out of the bright / 'Townland of Peace,' that poem of dream farms / Outside all contention." And he notes in the poem's last stanza that he and his companion are "Unfazed by light" even though he compares them to "ghosts" (*SL,* 69).

Rejecting the lingering gaze at the Tollund Man's body and the static atmosphere of "The Tollund Man" from his 1972 volume, *Wintering Out,* the poet writes of traveling to "Tollund Moss," where "The low ground, the swart water, the thick grass / [are] Hallucinatory and familiar" (*SL,* 69). The foreknowledge that we have come to expect with recent Heaney volumes, including this one, is promised in this fourth line but does not result in the expected familiarity. Instead, emblems of modernity abound and surround the area of "Willow bushes; rushes; bog-fir grags": There is a "satellite // Dish in the paddock" and "tourist signs in *futhark* runic script / In Danish and English" (69). Together, the satellite dish and new tourist signs signify the welcome encroachment of modernity to this archaic area and suggest that heightened communication marks both this part of Jutland now and by extension, Northern Ireland, where the "two sides" are beginning to speak to each other more and realize their commonalities.

The poem's quatrains mark a return to Heaney's heavy use of that four-line stanza so characteristic of his bog poems, but with a crucial lengthening of lineation that signifies the changes and openness that have occurred in the province by late 1994. No line in the quatrains of "The Tollund Man" is longer than seven words and many lines are shorter, formally suggesting the tenseness and anxiety during the Troubles. But "Tollund," which significantly focuses on the expansive qualities of the place itself, not the restrictive nature of the man's body, revels in more open language and longer lineation. Line 1, for example, is seven words long, while line 2 is composed of nine words. The third line and the twenty-first line are the longest of all, composed of nine and eight words, and dangle indolently, just as the speaker and his companion loiter around the site and take their time perceiving how the changes in the current landscape differ from the pictures in P. V. Glob's book *The Bog People*; this landscape, Heaney tells us, "could have been Mulhollandstown or Scribe"

(*SL,* 69), where in "Further Language" he recalls having spent "summer days . . . in the Tollund-like mosses in County Derry, deep in the heart of townlands with names like Mulhollandstown and Scribe."[42]

Rhyme often bespeaks constraint, as it did for Milton, say, in signifying the monarchy that he rejected ideologically and formally in his great epic *Paradise Lost,* but Heaney's use of rhyme and near-rhyme throughout "Tollund" suggests instead a formal harmony and order that are analogous to the political harmony, or at least lack of complete dissonance, and order beginning to emerge in Northern Ireland by the mid-1990s. Each quatrain features an envelope rhyme of roughly *abba,* as, for example, in the first quatrain, where the end-words of lines 1 and 4— "far" and "familiar"—frame the end-words of lines 2 and 3—"Moss" and "grass." The next two stanzas have a full *abba* rhyme, as does the fifth stanza (*SL,* 69).

The other two stanzas, besides stanza 1, that are not fully *abba* rhymed are stanzas 4 and 6, their alterations in rhyme complementing their significant statements about the changes that have taken place in both this area of Jutland and Northern Ireland. Stanza 4, for example, concludes with the half, end-stopped line, "Things had moved on," which does not fully rhyme with "stone" in the first line of that stanza, suggesting in its departure from the full rhyme of the preceding two stanzas that change is afoot politically. The word *moved* too, connotes the dynamic rhyme scheme in this stanza, which imparts a sense of motion in its marriage of form and content. Stanza 6, the poem's last, features in its first and fourth lines the least sonically aligned pairing of words in the poem: "abroad" and "bad," which together frame the fully rhymed lines "beginning" and "sinning" (*SL,* 69). Why would this be? The poet portrays himself and his companion in the first line of this stanza as "More scouts than strangers, ghosts who'd walked abroad," implying that the ground they are reconnoitering in Tollund is new to them, just as the figurative landscape of peace is new to Northern Ireland. Because they are harmoniously making "a new beginning" and making "a go of it, alive and sinning," they are "Ourselves again, free-willed again, not bad" (69). Their free will and that beginning in the province as it emerged from the Troubles is thus signified by the only slight chime between "abroad" and "bad"; the near-full break in the expected rhyme implies a break with the bad old days of the past. John Desmond argues that the poem's conclusion thematically rejects an abstract notion of transcendence "in favor of the *metaxu* [Simone Weil's term for the space between the transcendent and the mundane] and the down-to-earth work of making 'a new beginning,'"[43] and indeed, the poem's literal groundedness in the bogs of Jutland and Derry, along with its occasional breaks in rhyme scheme, acknowledges that achieving peace will be laborious.

But by the mid-2000s, "The Tollund Man in Springtime," from *District and Circle* (2006), suggests great hope about the peace process by returning to the subject of the Tollund Man and this time animating him, imagining him passing "Into your virtual city" in the first of six fourteen-line lyrics (*DC,* 53). The sequence imagines him being dug up and reinterred, as it were, in a museum case, where "I gathered / From the display-case my staying powers" (53). In this fourth lyric, images of an airy resurrection abound, from the "meadow hay / Still buttercupped and daisied," to the "sky [which] was new," and culminate in the lovely image of potential expressed by the "transatlantic flights stacked in the blue" (56). The Tollund Man finally escapes both his history and the museum, portrayed in the last three lines of the sixth lyric as reenacting stages of Heaney's own career, from the poems of ground-gazing to the moment that he recalls in *Crediting Poetry* when he "straightened up" and began "to try to make space in my reckoning and imagining for the marvelous as well as for the murderous" (*CP,* 20): "As a man would, cutting turf, / I straightened, spat on my hands, felt benefit, / And spirited myself into the street" (*DC,* 58).

Heaney's Work after the September 11 Attacks

Despite the great hope and potential of "The Tollund Man in Springtime," Heaney's developing theory of foreknowledge was severely jolted by the events of September 11, 2001. In its aftermath, he has revealed that he is wise enough to realize that even poetry cannot imagine the worst events that can occur in reality, an attitude displayed in a 9/11 poem, "Anything Can Happen," from *District and Circle.* This poem, originally published in the *Irish Times* on November 17, 2001, as

"Horace and the Thunder," an adaptation from Horace (*Odes* 1.34), suggests that sometimes reality's surprises can outstrip poetry's counter-reality. The flat tone of the end-stopped first half line offers no inkling of what comes next: "Anything can happen." The poem then immediately asks,

> . . . You know how Jupiter
> Will mostly wait for clouds to gather head
> Before he hurls the lightning? Well, just now
> He galloped his thunder cart and his horses
>
> Across a clear blue sky.
> (*DC*, 13)

This is the only almost fully enjambed stanza in the poem, and its continuity and diction ("mostly") suggest the habitual reality of Jupiter's usual actions of allowing clouds to offer a sort of warning before "he hurls the lightning." At the same time, its enjambment into the next stanza implies that this unusual action of Jupiter is also consistent with his nature. The musing tone of the poem's second sentence seems to bespeak no real shock—not yet—on the part of the speaker at this unforeseen action. Instead, he seems resigned to Jupiter's action as a whim of this chief Roman god.

The diction and tone here should not obscure the sea-change in Heaney's poetry that this poem signals, however. For a poet long drawn to the dialectic between the earth and the sky, first expressed in the 1966 poem "Antaeus," and signified in "Crediting Poetry" as the "murderous" and the "marvelous," respectively (*CP*, 20), "Anything Can Happen" signals the poet's surprise that something ominous, even murderous, can come out of "a clear blue sky." There is the early fear of immersion in skyward things in "Antaeus," signaled by passages spoken by the title character such as "I cannot be weaned / Off the earth's long contour, her river-veins" and the corresponding fear of being lifted "off the earth" and experiencing "My elevation, my fall."[44] But as we have seen, certainly by the time *Seeing Things* was published in 1991, Heaney's gaze was largely fixed on the sky and its manifestations of wonder. John Wilson Foster has articulated the frequency of such words in Heaney's poetry after *The*

Haw Lantern as "*air, light, water, space, sunlight, stream, waver, lift, soul, sky, spirit, river*—the language of the elemental, the transformative, the unconstrained."[45] "Anything Can Happen" brilliantly deploys these formerly positive words from Heaney's recent lexicon—*sky, river, streams, air,* and *lifts* all feature in the poem, as do the four major elements of earth, wind, fire, and water—and in so doing troubles and complicates the assumption in his poetry from *Seeing Things* through *Electric Light* that the heavens contain largely images of delight.

As we have seen, Heaney often approached meditations on the contemporary Northern Irish Troubles through indirection and obliqueness: here, his choice to cast the events of September 11 in the context of not only Roman mythology (Jupiter's actions that implicitly usher in a period of war, whose god, Mars, was Jupiter's son) but also of Greek mythology (the River Styx, Atlas) risks ignoring the particularity of the attacks on the World Trade Center. But lending the events of that day a mythological aspect also universalizes them and suggests the continuing persistence of violence in our world, just as the bog poems did.

Again similarly to the bog poems, "Anything Can Happen" largely refuses to focus on the perpetrators of violence; but unlike the bog poems, it does not dwell on the victims either, instead meditating on the event itself and its aftershocks. This neglect of the victims of the attacks is another risky maneuver that threatens to render the murdered abstract and faceless. The fundamentalist Muslim hijackers are also ignored, save for the half line that begins line 10, "Those overlooked regarded" (*DC*, 13). Instead, "Stropped-beak Fortune / Swoops," a brilliant image of Fortune as a rapacious bird of prey, recalling the mechanical "birds"—the airliners employed by the hijackers (13). But invoking Fortune in this way makes the attacks sound inevitable and runs another risk—that of seeming to absolve the hijackers of responsibility and of conceding to the inevitability of violence, a charge that Heaney had already experienced with the poems of *North.*

One more similarity to the bog poems concerns the choice of quatrains for the poem's form. Early Heaney often uses quatrains in poems with subterranean urges: he has notably said that "with *North* and *Wintering Out* I was burrowing inwards, and those thin small quatrain poems, they're kind of drills or augers for turning in and they are narrow and long and deep."[46] For such a public poem as "Anything Can Happen," with its sense of horrible potential and acknowledgment that the world order has permanently changed, the choice of quatrains seems odd at first glance. Their formal compression almost does not seem able to contain the undeniable rippling effect from the September 11 attacks, and their previous connotation of privacy in Heaney's third and fourth volumes that he mentions above seems at odds with the public tone of the poem. Their appearance here is odd too because this poem, again, focuses on manifestations of the murderous figured in the sky, not on the ground, as the burrowing quatrains of the bog poems signified.

Perhaps the choice of quatrains, however, continues to signify narrowness, only now in an ideological sense — to suggest both the terrorists' sectarian agenda and, in Heaney's mind, the U.S. military's unnecessary response in attacking Afghanistan and Iraq. In his essay on the poem from 2004, published three years after the attacks, he reflects that "the irruption of death into the Manhattan morning produced not only world-darkening grief for the multitudes of victims' families and friends, but it also had the effect of darkening the future with the prospect of deadly retaliations. Stealth bombers pummeling the fastnesses of Afghanistan, shock and awe loosed from the night skies over Iraq, they all seem part of the deadly fallout from the thunder cart in Horace's clear blue afternoon."[47] The blocky denseness of the poem's four quatrains, then, may well suggest not only the darkened sky over Manhattan after the attacks and the "darkening grief" for those who knew the victims but also those skies darkened by U.S. bombing runs over Afghanistan and the night sky of Iraq during the American air assaults there.

Other formal aspects of the poem, including other instances of enjambment and a striking medial caesura, underscore its particular content. I have already remarked upon the nearly full enjambment of the first four and a half lines, which is employed by Heaney to show how Jupiter habitually gives warning before unleashing his thunderbolts. Nowhere in the rest of the poem is there such lengthy enjambment, although lines 5 and 6 are enjambed, as are lines 8 and 9, lines 9 and 10, and lines 13 and 14. All of these lesser enjambments are significant, respectively showing how the attacks shook "the earth / And the clogged underearth"; how "the tallest towers [can] // Be overturned"; how "Stropped-beak Fortune / Swoops"; and how "The heaven's weight / Lifts up off Atlas like a kettle-lid" (*DC*, 13). In each of these examples, the enjambment echoes the continuity of each particular event, perhaps most disturbingly with the overturning of the towers, one of which was first collapsed into the other. In one instance, the almost dead center of the poem, a caesura is used to indicate the terrible continuities of that day on which the towers toppled. In line 8 — "Anything can happen, the tallest towers" — explicitly changes the opening line — "Anything can happen. You know how Jupiter" (13) — and imparts a sense of strain through the use of the comma much as Yeats's semicolon does in his famous third line from "The Second Coming" — "Things fall apart; the center cannot hold."[48] The opening line's medial end-stopped satisfaction thus shows how the usual contained narrative of Jupiter's thrown thunderbolts is presaged by clouds, while the caesura of line 8 implies that this usual narrative has been overturned just as the towers have been. The change in punctuation immediately following the repetition of the opening half line in line 8 therefore signifies a change in world history. Yet there is a formal way or, really, set of ways in which "Anything Can Happen" strains against its content, indeed shows through this conflict how "nothing resettles right," as the fifteenth line has it (13).

These continuities just elucidated run up against a series of lines and half lines with partial and full stops like waves crashing against granite, in the process showing how the finally unsettled last stanza of the poem bespeaks the newly unsettled nature of Heaney's poetry and of the world after September 11, 2001. For example, line 9 has a full medial stop like the opening line — "Those overlooked regarded" (*DC*, 13) — which makes us linger and gaze briefly at the "overlooked" — the terrorists or perhaps even Muslims worldwide? Beginning with the last line of this third stanza, which is the last in the original ode by Horace, four of the last five lines of the poem are end-stopped. Heaney's original stanzaic contribution to this adaptation from Horace is the fourth stanza, which has an opening medial stoppage, a caesura in its third line, and three concluding end stops for its last three lines:

Ground gives. The heaven's weight
Lifts up off Atlas like a kettle-lid.
Capstones shift, nothing resettles right.
Telluric ash and fire-spores boil away.
(13)

The original last line, as originally published in the *Irish Times* and in the booklet *Anything Can Happen* for Amnesty International, was "Smoke furl and boiling ashes darken day."[49] Heaney may have changed this last line to indicate a brief opening of literal and figurative daylight after the attacks that the United States then obscured (in his mind) by squandering the international goodwill engendered by the attacks with its own attacks on Afghanistan and Iraq. More important, the constant punctuation stops in this last stanza attempt to contain the event even as it boils over and carries the weight of heaven off Atlas's broad shoulders. Such punctuation thus strains against the content of the lines here, showing the poem finally to be in conflict with itself, suggesting not only that the ground around the former World Trade Center towers has shifted but also that Heaney's poetry and worldview have undergone a lasting upheaval. "Anything Can Happen" proves the truth of James Longenbach's claim that poetry's power depends not only on its own ephemerality but also on its resistance to itself, on "turning against itself again and again" as a "composition unraveling."[50]

"Anything Can Happen" is a strangely empty poem, devoid of any human victims or terrorists but "peopled" with gods who seem to toy with mortals who are completely offstage. Its emphasis on the way in which something beyond our ken transfigures and transforms recalls Yeats's "Easter, 1916," a poem in which Yeats speculated at length on the evolution of the Easter rebels, though Heaney's poem, unlike Yeats's, refuses to even identify the terrorists. But "Anything Can Happen" may in time come to be seen as Heaney's "Easter, 1916" because it not only registers Heaney's utter surprise—and indeed that of the world—at the events and aftermath of September 11, 2001, but also shows how everything has "changed, changed utterly," to borrow Yeats's words from his very public poem.[51] Like "Easter, 1916," Heaney's poem is forever linked to a specific date, employs a haunting refrain—"Anything can happen"—and was withheld for a time, reworked, and not published in its final form for some five years after September 11. Heaney's poem uncannily recalls Yeats's even as it departs from it in warning us, not of the emergence of a new Ireland, but of contemporary terrorism and the subsequent and misnamed "War on Terror," a war that never really ends.

This poem may also signal a new turn in Heaney's thinking about the sacred, for if anything can happen, does reality's capriciousness,

figured as religious/mythological whim, foreclose on poetry's attempts
to preserve life, to set up conversations and communities between the
living and the dead? At the very least, "Anything Can Happen," like the
following poem about the 9/11 attacks in *District and Circle*, "Helmet,"
admits that human devices and constructions are flimsy things in the
face of sustained fire. Here is the conclusion of "Helmet":

>   . . . shattering glass
>
> And rubble-bolts out of a burning roof
> Hailed down on every hatchet man and hose man there
> Till the hard-reared shield-wall broke.
>
> (*DC*, 14)

"The hard-reared shield wall" recalls the language of Heaney's translation of "Beowulf" and injects a mythological tone into the poem as
the firefighters are implicitly likened to heroic dragon fighters. Poetry
too is flimsy, and its consolations, as discussed in the introduction and
throughout this study, are comforting in their very ephemerality. But
the fleeting power of poetry does not preclude the poet's continual attempts to form verbal worlds where we may linger, in either wonder or
disgust, at man's generosity or capacity for violence.

Heaney's creation of a space, or series of spaces, in which poetry
imagines potential while attending to and redressing reality finally stands
as his most lasting poetic achievement and contribution to the ongoing
process of reconciliation in Northern Ireland and other war-torn areas of
the world. As even Peter McDonald has argued recently in the context
of his discussion of Heaney's literary criticism, particularly that collected
in *The Redress of Poetry*, "Literary significance is not an abstract affair:
poems *do* things, and good poems do more than anything the critical
summaries of their effects can hope to account for."[52] Heaney's poems
"do things" because of the ambiguous position he occupies at his best.
For example, as Alan Peacock has observed in an essay chiefly concerned
with Heaney's role as a poet in his verse drama *The Cure at Troy*, "The
role of the chorus in fact echoes the position of the poet in its liminal,
mediating function. . . . Just as the chorus acts as a bridge between audience and action, so poetry occupies a liminal role, poised between hope

and what ineluctably is."[53] Heaney has become a veritable poetic ambassador of hope on the world stage because his work demonstrates that literature can make things happen, especially by reconfiguring the imagination and creating new communities of readers and citizens. Heaney's poetry that is true to itself has thus instilled liberating, life-giving attributes in the formerly static political and cultural milieu of Northern Ireland. As he claimed in the late 1990s about poetry, "I totally believe in its political effects. I believe that it does have a strong intravenous effect within a society—maybe not immediately. . . . So while I would defend the integrity of poetry, I have absolutely no doubt about its political effect and its political valency and its place in the polis."[54]

The question Hugh Underhill has asked in his exploration of the assets and liabilities of modern poetry's "exploration of subjective consciousness" highlights the importance of Heaney's concern to create community through exploring the limitless possibilities of his own consciousness: "What kind of worthwhile 'community' can there be, or for that matter, what kind of social action or 'revolutionary' course can be worth contemplating, that does not accord a place and value to inwardness, 'feeling-awareness,' the facts of 'subjective' life?"[55] In its harnessing of the energies of the poetic imagination to create community, Heaney's work has abundantly answered Tim Hancock's musing in 1999 that "it remains to be seen whether his future poetry will convincingly channel these [visionary] forces or just be about them."[56]

Seamus Heaney's best poems and criticism, through their specific language and imaginative integrity, promulgate a model of hope and transformation for cultural, political, and religious reconciliation in Northern Ireland. What he offers in his best poetry, like Yeats, is a "vision of reality . . . [that] is transformative, more than just a print-out of the given circumstances of its time and place. The poet who would be most the poet has to attempt an act of writing that outstrips the conditions even as it observes them."[57] Increasingly, this Janus-faced poet is straddling the threshold between what is, "a print-out of the given circumstances," and what can be, a transforming vision of reality. His poetic invitation to us is to join him in a new country of the mind, at the frontier of writing, where hope, tempered by reality, awaits us.

Coda

This project has been concerned with articulating how two of the most prominent members of the Belfast Group of writers have emerged from Northern Ireland in the last several decades to formulate a body of work with considerable integrity and power and, secondarily, to make literary and cultural critiques of identity in the province. Michael Longley's poetry has been concerned with representing the commonality of human experience across the province's two major cultural groups through an intense focus on the fragility of human, animal, and plant life amid urban and pastoral landscapes and through an ecumenical Christian concern for human rights and forgiveness. His reclamation of a typically Catholic and Irish landscape — the western part of Ireland — signifies the heritage Northern Irish Protestants share with their Catholic neighbors. At the same time, his emphasis on the Scottish aspects of Northern Ireland and the Protestant contributions in World War I makes industrial Northern Ireland part of a much broader Irish cultural heritage than the rural, Catholic de Valerian ideal. Longley's poetic penchant for listing specific objects, names, or places acts as an important semantic stay against globalizing, more abstract notions of culture and identity. Finally, the increasingly wide geographic scale of his later poetry, with significant explorations of the Holocaust and Japanese culture, for example, suggests Longley's interconnected, ceremonial vision of civilized human, animal, and even plant communities held together by their particular emphases on dignity and freedom.

Seamus Heaney's early forays into his consciousness enabled him to begin establishing an imaginative country of the mind in his early poetry even as he strove to promote a shared literary and geographic community in Northern Ireland. After briefly being seen and only very occasionally seeing himself as part of the nationalist "tribe" in the province, Heaney wrote significant poetry in *Wintering Out* that partakes linguistically of both the Irish language and Ulster dialects still common in the province. He moved on from his unifying work on these potentially divisive linguistic issues to critique calcified political identities and the violence attendant upon these identities in the province in *North* and *Field Work*. His later work, in a more readily apparent way than his early poetry, tends toward the ethereal and spiritual, though his immersion in this realm is never divorced from reality. Instead, through his fully realized concept of consciousness, he is constantly searching for ways in which the imagination can redress static notions of reality, such as the polarized thinking about political and cultural identity that has dominated Northern Ireland for many years.

As this entire study has sought to demonstrate, Longley and Heaney share a commitment to the imagination above all else, a position that makes them faithful artists and thus able to largely resist the siren call of pressure to make their poems propaganda that could then be employed by ideologues to advance sectarian agendas. Even when they have entered the fray in Northern Ireland by writing more directly political poems denouncing violence, these have not always been as successful as their less political, more indirect ones. For example, Dennis O'Driscoll argues that "Heaney's finest work, because it is so securely rooted in time and place, can be effortlessly and indeed unconsciously political. . . . Conversely, the poems ('Whatever You Say Say Nothing,' for instance) which are explicitly political or topical in theme are less frequently successful, and several such poems remain uncollected."[1] Similarly, Longley's belief in poetry's power has generally enabled him to write with an exceptional imaginative integrity that has protected him from any attempts to conscript him to a particular political or poetic party line. Thus Peter McDonald holds that "poetry's substance, for Longley, always sets the agenda, and this means that notions of what poetry should be doing (or meaning) are always liable to be disappointed or undermined" (*MI*, 143).

Differences between Longley and Heaney abound, of course, and can be determined only through a series of close readings of their work, which this study has attempted. My argument about Longley's twin penchants for ceremony and the visual catalog could be summed up by the phrase "ceremonial particularity." That quality is not shared with Heaney's early poems, which often emphasize singularity of sounds, as in the dialect poems of *Wintering Out*. And Heaney's later poems that focus on visual marvels are similarly individual, not aggregate, in their focus.

Another difference between the two poets' work involves the level of emotion generated. Longley's environmental poetic recalls Angus Fletcher's description of this poetic as one "where emotion is subordinate to the presentation of the aggregate relations of all participants."[2] This is not to say that Longley's poems are cold, stoic affairs; indeed, they often evoke great emotion, especially the noncatalog poems such as "Wounds" and "Ceasefire." But I do believe that Fletcher's assessment of this type of poetic is revealing for Longley's catalog works such as "The Linen Workers" and "The Ice-cream Man," which privilege "the aggregate relations of all participants" over eliciting an emotional reaction from the reader or listener. Longley's poetic is simultaneously particular yet panoramic, while Heaney's poetic is relatively focused in its epiphanic singularity.

Heaney's intense epiphanies revealed in poems such as "Digging," "Punishment," part 12 of "Station Island," and "Anything Can Happen" are, by virtue of their ecstatic energy, more intense than many Longley poems. A natural heir of Wordsworth, Heaney's attempts to render "spots of time" and convey the emotion associated with such moments is epitomized by his *Stations* pamphlet from 1975 and by the central section of *Station Island,* especially in the latter volume, where he links particular stations of the cross to memorable moments of his past, but also, supremely, by *Seeing Things.* Such poems combine joy and melancholy because they recognize, like many of Wordsworth's major poems, that "such spots — memories that collapse space and time into a condensed, obdurate place in consciousness — are, as Wordsworth writes, 'hiding places' of a 'power' that is simultaneously one's own and elusive of full possession or (to use Wordsworth's term) of 'restoration.'"[3] Heaney's visions are singularly luminous, quivering with energy and emotion,

whereas Longley's are holistic, radiant with an awareness of the interconnectedness of all things.

It is also worth considering the difference between Longley's environmental poems and Heaney's rural poems. As I have already argued,
Longley's environmental poetry presumes something like a total relationship between all of humanity, all flora and fauna, which he encapsu-
lates in a particular microcosmic yet broad vision. Heaney's rural poetry,
however, feels intensely contained, even time bound, in its presentation
of a particular locale, whereas Longley's ecological poetry is grounded in
an awareness of place as mutable and fragile. Heaney's pastoral poetry
can be at times antipastoral, as in the second half of "Death of a Naturalist," but is more often traditionally pastoral in its efforts to preserve a
seemingly Edenic moment in amber even as it realizes the impossibility
of recovering such a time and place.

The two-mindedness of both poets binds them together perhaps
more than any other quality that they share besides their commitment to the imagination. Longley loves to wallow in uneasiness and in-
betweenness, and so does Heaney, although the latter would not characterize liminality as a position of uneasiness. In his search for dwelling in
such a position, Longley repeatedly strikes a tone of playful spontaneity
that is not often found in Heaney's typically more earnest poetry. Longley's recourse to jazz in such early work as "Words for Jazz, Perhaps" and
later poems such as "Jug Band" signals a respect for the improvisational
in general throughout his poetry that contrasts markedly with the search
for stability and tradition in Heaney's poetry. Longley's willingness to sus-
pend himself between cultures and traditions—as a Northern Irish cultural Protestant who loves Irish western landscapes and English World
War I poetry, for example—leads him into such a position of improvisation, perhaps best characterized by his image of the "man lying on the
wall" (discussed at the end of chapter 2), or his evocation of no-man's-
land in a number of poems.

The similar impulse in Heaney to recognize his cultural two-mindedness, for example, in his embrace of the great tradition of English poetry and his recovery of Irish-language poetry from the traditional province of Ulster, has led him into what seems a position of unease similar
to Longley's but instead is one of rootedness, as he has anchored himself

in multiple languages—Irish, English, Old English—that are redolent of the various landscapes of geography and mind he has inhabited. Both finally see two- or even three-mindedness as an enabling, creative artistic position oscillating between cultures and identities, one that secondarily has helped them develop their theories of imagined community.

This sort of oscillation has become a sign of the intellectual and cultural flexibility needed in new conceptions of Northern Ireland, although it is crucial to point out that much of Longley's and Heaney's poetry does not explicitly seek rapprochement or reconciliation and simply evokes such a mutability as an affirmation of the nimble imagination. Yet in so doing, as Longley told Dillon Johnston in a 1986 interview, "I think the artists of Belfast have imagined an ideal Belfast. Art does cross all the barriers and the frontiers, and it doesn't admit of borders."[4] Citing Paul Muldoon's 2004 comment that Longley's poetry emblematizes "an imaginative domain in which we can all move forward," Fran Brearton agrees with Muldoon: she argues that despite Longley's marked verbal precision, his tentativeness—"the realization that words cannot grasp the world"—affirms Muldoon's audacious claim, and she notes that "Longley's 1990s poems are suggestive of the capacity to transform, partly because they don't presume to possess any final answers; the process is what matters." Brearton holds that in the context of the peace process in Northern Ireland in the 1990s, "while there might be an instinctive desire for closure, as if a society's problems can be finally resolved, the point rather is that the 'process' should never cease."[5]

Process, not closure, has long been part of Heaney's poetry as well, within individual poems, across poetic sequences, and throughout the many transformations of his career. Heaney's revisiting of P. V. Glob's Tollund Man in a series of poems exemplifies his belief in progression, suggesting how over time deadly, static certainties can be reimagined as living fluidities. While "The Tollund Man" focused on the preserved body of this man, frozen in time, locked into deep-seated patterns of sectarian hatred, the last glimpse of this figure we get, in "The Tollund Man in Springtime," shows him animated, shot through with resurrection energy as he escapes his glass display case "and spirited myself into the street" (*DC,* 58). The man's freedom is further signified by his own narration of this lyric sequence in first person. But like Longley, Heaney has been cautious about positing an end or ultimate solution to the divisions in Northern Ireland or indeed, other conflicts, instead suggesting through such recent poems as "Anything Can Happen" that overt terrorism, while largely gone from the streets of Northern Ireland (the major paramilitaries have decommissioned their weapons or are in the process of doing so, though some problems with paramilitaries continue), flourishes in many places around the world. But there is also latent hope in the title of that September 11th poem: if anything can happen, such as the violent toppling of the World Trade Towers and the murder of thousands, surely there is also the possibility that Western-Islamic relations will undergo a similarly seismic shift in a positive direction.

A final point of seeming difference but actual similarity between Longley and Heaney concerns their conceptions of the private and public role of the poet. For many years, Longley, through his position of combined arts director at the Arts Council of Northern Ireland, was able to publicly proclaim the value of cultural dialogue and understanding in ways that his quieter poetry did not have to, although a significant strand of this earlier poetry, examined in chapters 2 and 3, does seek to explore the grounds of such cultural understanding. But after leaving the Arts Council in 1991, Longley has explicitly made his poetry more public, supremely so in the case of "Ceasefire" (discussed in chapter 3). "Ceasefire," however, blurs Longley's commitment to the life of the imagination above all else in his attempt to influence such a cease-fire by its newspaper publication in the *Irish Times* around the time of the IRA ceasefire in 1994. The poem also runs the risk of itself offering a sort of violent closure to the conflict by urging reconciliation for many who were not ready for it yet, although I do think, as I noted earlier, that its emphasis on the temporary nature of the cease-fire and its broken sonnet form create a potentially transformative space of both formal and imagined political fluidity.

Heaney, on the other hand, has since 1990 tried even more than Longley to separate his poetry—usually much more private and personal—from his prose—often public and explicitly political, although, as we shall see, he has also "gone public" with two of his major works from this period, *The Cure at Troy* and "Anything Can Happen." As we have seen earlier in this study, Heaney made sure that his angry

essays published in the *Listener* about the persecution of Catholics during the beginning of the civil rights movements, then the Troubles, and
such angry plays as *Everyman,* his poem "The Road to Derry," and
even *An Open Letter,* were kept carefully apart from his collected prose
and individual and collected volumes of poetry, as was, for example, his
signing of a 1974 statement calling for the "immediate release of all in-
ternees in Northern Ireland," which could be construed as a nationalist
position.[6] Heaney's purposeful publication of these cultural and political commentaries in the more ephemeral media of newspapers, journals, and pamphlets enabled him to exercise public responsibility even
as he sometimes seemed to eschew that responsibility in his poetry and
even as he condemned himself for doing so in poems such as "Punishment." Significantly, a poem that was retained early in his career, the
biting "Docker," about a bigoted Protestant whose "fist would drop a
hammer on a Catholic" (*DN*, 28), collected in *Death of a Naturalist* and
in Heaney's first collected volume of poetry, *Poems, 1965–1975,* was
excluded from *Opened Ground: Selected Poems, 1966–1996.*

The singular language of Heaney's poems, often so different from
the directness he adopted in his more public pronouncements (think of
An Open Letter again), has been described by Dennis O'Driscoll as "so
personal, so individual, so inimitable, so far removed from any official
idiolect used by politicians or businessmen that it can never be confused
with a media-speak of borrowed opinions, received assumptions or stock
responses." O'Driscoll goes on to state that in Heaney's poems "Every
idea is examined afresh, as every word is coined anew; he is a subscriber
to no one's manifesto, political or literary."[7]

Yet there are the very public examples of Heaney's play *The Cure at
Troy* and his poem "Anything Can Happen," both written in response to
current events and both given extraordinarily public airings—the play
in an acclaimed production by the Field Day Theatre Company in 1990
and the poem in the *Irish Times* and the *Times Literary Supplement,* as I
will discuss later in this coda. Heaney has also increasingly issued statements on the peace process through the Irish press, as in his signing of
a December 2, 1993, petition in the *Irish Times* about the prospects for
a peace deal in Northern Ireland.[8] After the worst years of the Troubles,
both poets, beginning in the early 1990s, have increasingly written

poetry and, more often, prose that has urged the peace process along and resonated with public audiences worldwide.

Edna Longley's contention that literature, and poetry especially, can help create a cultural corridor in which intransigent elements of the province can meet and articulate their issues is worth assessing given the aims of this study. From the public and critical acclaim that has attended the work of Michael Longley and Heaney, this role of their poetry has certainly been effective, despite some well-publicized misunderstandings about the ideologies behind their greatest works. The reason is that these two poets finally serve only the imagination, not some political cause or party. Only through their imaginations could such a dizzying array of viable critiques of identity and politics in the province have been articulated; the normal politicized discourse would not have worked. The imaginative power of poetry from Northern Ireland has been a powerful example for politics, as Edna Longley has suggested: "Like poetry, peace must also be imagined."[9]

I have also asserted, following Edna Longley, that poetry's specificity could help erode the power of compact majorities—that it can subvert monolithic, abstract thinking about identity in Northern Ireland. Poetry's singularity as defined in the introduction carries an implicit ethical charge. The cultural and creative work of Michael Longley and Heaney affirms these assertions. For example, both Longley's use of the literary list in his catalog of plant and place names and Heaney's careful choice of words from a word-hoard common to all the inhabitants of Northern Ireland specifically deny the power of abstraction and depict precise notions of identity that are much more relevant to the everyday lives of Northern Irish people than received political categories. The body of work by these imaginative writers offers a compelling reexamination of identity in the province and in a nondidactic manner urges human beings there to find their common heritage—geographically, imaginatively, spiritually. This regional unity is urgently needed, as Edna Longley has argued in the context of her discussion of the 1998 Good Friday Agreement: "A shared regional locus of allegiance must evolve, whatever other horizons beckon."[10]

One of the unstated assumptions of this study that is mooted in the introduction and implicitly hovers in the background of subsequent chapters concerns the care with which Longley and Heaney reverently gaze upon their poetic subjects, perceiving their beauty. Beauty is often thought to be a merely aesthetic conception, but as Elaine Scarry has shown, the apprehension of the beautiful can lead to heightened ethical concerns. This reading of beauty carries significant implications for the peace process in Northern Ireland or anywhere by establishing the mental conditions of equality, as I established in my reading of Heaney's "Punishment" in chapter 6. Longley and Heaney's doubly creative example of protecting the beauty in the world through their well-wrought poems is salutary for all of us: reading their work with the care that it deserves ineluctably leads us into a similar desire to protect the living beauties of this world—flora, fauna, and people. Such a position of stewardship, of valuing life generally, is a precondition for a peace process that moves away from celebrations of death to commemorations of life.

This project has often invoked the aesthetic and the spiritual as the venues where Longley's and Heaney's poetry has made its greatest contributions. But there is ample evidence that their poetry has also made some significant contributions to helping begin and continue the process of reconciliation in Northern Ireland. For example, the civil authorities in Northern Ireland and leading press outlets have given them extensive recognition. Some lines from Michael Longley serve as a foreword to the Opsahl Report, which was formed in May of 1992 by the independent citizens' group Initiative '92 to inquire into ways to move Northern Ireland toward peace. The Opsahl Committee held six weeks of hearings in Northern Ireland and received 554 submissions from citizens. Some of Longley's lines were cited in the July 13, 1993, report by the Tanaiste and Minister for Foreign Affairs to the Irish Senate (Seanad Eirrean): "for me / And you to stay alive / by sharing thought and word." He concludes by asking, "Are you within hearing? / Am I being heard?"[11]

One of Longley's most striking recent prose contributions to the reconciliation process in Northern Ireland is his lecture "Memory and Acknowledgement," which was given as part of a symposium entitled "Reconciliation and Community: The Future of Peace in Northern Ireland," organized by the Foundation for a Civil Society and the University of Ulster, that took place on June 6–8, 1995, in Belfast. I have quoted from this essay, which concludes with Longley's commentary on and reading of "Ceasefire," in chapter 3's discussion of Longley's contribution to thinking about suffering and memory in the context of the Troubles. Here I would just add that the public presence of Longley at such symposia signals a continuing recognition on the part of poets in Ireland that careful attention to language, poetic and otherwise, enables better, clearer communication and potentially aids the long and vexed process of reconciliation.

Longley's semantically precise poems continue to influence the discussion of the Troubles and the peace process. For example, the Northern Ireland victims commissioner Sir Kenneth Bloomfield, KCB, added one of Longley's poems, "The Civil Servant," from his sequence "Wreaths," as a formal postscript to his April 1998 report on the victims of the Troubles, "We Will Remember Them."[12] "The Civil Servant" was also featured on the BBC Northern Ireland "Study Ireland Poetry" television series and is featured on the series' Web site under the topic of "War" for eleven- to sixteen-year-olds.[13] This series was requested of the BBC by the Education Broadcasting Council for Northern Ireland and was a five-part thematic series on contemporary poetry designed for pupils following the Northern Ireland Curriculum for English Language and Literature to GCSE (General Certificate of Secondary Education), key stage 3–4.

A few months after the Good Friday Agreement, the Irish speaker Pol O Muiri wrote a fascinating column in the *Irish Times* about how artists such as Longley have the best chance to subvert the binary thinking promoted by political parties in Northern Ireland such as Sinn Fein and some unionist parties. O Muiri noted that "it would be a mistake . . . to let any political party or pressure group in the North set the cultural agenda. Writers and artists are the ones who should be doing that. It is through their work that the willfully constructed stereotypes of 'our' culture and 'their' culture are most effectively challenged."[14] He goes on to cite the work of Donegal novelist Seamus O'Grianna and Donegal poet Cathal O'Searcaigh (both from the Donegal Gaeltacht), and Longley (he gives as an example Longley's Ulster-Scots vernacular in his rendition of the Greek poem "Phemios and Medon") as indebted to the Scots language as recreated in the poetry of Robert Burns. All three writers, notes O Muiri, were influenced by Burns in differing, intimate encounters with his poetry that stand in stark contrast to the current unionist emphasis on the Scots vernacular as "a counterbalance to a republican cultural agenda."[15] O Muiri is suggesting that cultural dialogue occurs most effectively in spontaneous, often intimate ways that cannot be co-erced or enforced by official government policies, however well-meaning.

Part of the cultural importance of poetry about atrocity that this study has tried to document is its function as a record of individual lives that are rendered more fully and completely from their imaginary life cre-ated on the page. Longley has warmly recalled receiving letters from rela-tives or friends of those killed in the Troubles, making sure to point out that neither he nor they view poetry as a consolation for lives lost: "from two or three people who have been bereaved as a result of the Troubles, letters which thanked me for poems. But they are not thanking me for consolation; they are thanking me for something which I hope is much more vigorous and dynamic, more practical than that. The letter I got from the ice-cream man's mother matters to me, but she is not con-soled. She is accompanied in her sorrow by a poem or by the person who wrote the poem. . . . You go side by side with the person to the grave."[16] As he goes on to say in this same interview, "All talks of ceasefire and peace involve political movement and gyrations and, in the case of the peace process, manipulation. Because of all these abstract chess moves it is very easy to forget the victims, to forget the people who have had their legs blown off or who have lost a father. One of the things that poetry can do is bear witness."[17] Despite the welcome appearance of the volu-minous recent attempt to chart the loss of every person in the Troubles, *Lost Lives: The Stories of the Men, Women and Children Who Died as a Re-sult of the Northern Ireland Troubles,* imaginative literature such as Long-ley's poetry vivifies its elegiac subjects in a way that no statistical record can.[18] Distinguished BBC foreign affairs correspondent Fergal Keane has recently said as much in his forty-minute television documentary on Longley, broadcast on January 22, 2008, on BBC One Northern Ire-land: "For me, Longley's poetry rescued the dead from the land of sta-tistics. It was his voice that caught me first—generous and tolerant."[19] Such recognition testifies to Michael Longley's continuing relevance as a humane poetic voice asking calmly to be heard amid violence and mis-understanding.

While Heaney's Nobel Peace Prize recognizes his contribution to reconciliation and peace in Northern Ireland, the February 22, 2007, award of a special Ewart-Biggs Memorial Prize to Longley does as well. This prize annually recognizes those who have promoted reconciliation in Ireland. Longley was given a special Ewart-Biggs Prize to recognize his lifetime achievement in promoting reconciliation in Northern Ireland just a few months after his *Collected Poems* was published. The respected historian and Yeats biographer Roy Foster noted at the time that Longley is "a tremendously accomplished poet who has never flinched from recording the Northern experience."[20]

Longley's and Heaney's continuing influence on the cultural life of Northern Ireland is also indicated by their many broadcasts on BBC Northern Ireland Radio over the last several decades, including their broadcasting as part of BBC NI Radio's schools program. This project has made use of some of these broadcasts, which often reached a wide audience. The widespread recognition both poets have been given for their role in being faithful to poetry's integrity and daring to imagine a different future for the province is shown by the frequent use of their poetry in school curricula north and south of the border.

Probably Longley's two most anthologized poems, the earlier "Wounds" and the later "Ceasefire," are both on the school curriculum in Ireland, and Heaney's *Death of a Naturalist* is cited as a resource in a thematic unit on citizenship for key stage 3 of "Language and Literacy" on the official Northern Irish school curriculum.[21] Heaney's poetry has often been featured on the GCSE exams in English literature for Northern Ireland, the exams that determine students' university eligibility and placement. Like Longley's "The Civil Servant," Heaney's "The Grauballe Man" was featured on the BBC Northern Ireland "Study Ireland Poetry" television series and is featured on the series' Web site under the topic of "War" for eleven- to sixteen-year-olds.[22]

Heaney's work toward reconciliation is, of course, most amply evidenced by his Nobel Peace Prize for Literature in 1995, but he has also been recognized by the civil authorities in Northern Ireland for such work. For example, shortly after Heaney won the Nobel Prize, British Secretary of State for Northern Ireland Sir Patrick Mayhew presented him with a new spade in a reception in the poet's honor in front of a cross-sectarian audience at Hillsborough House, affirming both the poet's explicitly articulated efforts to dig into his imagination and his more indirect aim of promulgating cultural understanding in what is still one of his most famous poems, "Digging" (discussed in chapter 5).

Heaney's poetry, like Longley's, has seized the popular imagination both in the North and beyond. If his most-cited line during the Troubles was "Whatever you say, say nothing," from the poem of that same name in *North*, that line has now been replaced with some of the chorus's closing lines from his 1990 play, *The Cure at Troy*, a translation of Sophocles' *Philoctetes* that Heaney retrospectively dedicated to the victims of the Real IRA bombing at Omagh on August 15, 1998, that killed twenty-nine people and injured hundreds more. The Field Day Theatre Company originally produced *The Cure at Troy* at the Guildhall in Derry on October 1, 1990. Directed by Stephen Rea, like Heaney one of the original founders of Field Day, the play shares Field Day's concern to create a "fifth province" of the mind where cultural dialogue can occur.

To properly understand the chorus's role at the beginning and end of the play is to realize that Heaney uses it here to chart the entire trajectory of the Northern Irish Troubles, beginning with its indictment of "both sides" who have been disconnected and obsessed with their own narratives of suffering, and concluding with its hope in hope, that the impossible miracle of the end of violence might be at hand, with the start of reconciliation not far behind.

Taking their lead from Heaney, a series of politicians, literary critics, artists, journalists, at least one actor, and many ordinary people have cited two stanzas spoken by the chorus a few pages from the play's conclusion:

History says, *Don't hope*
On this side of the grave.
But then, once in a lifetime
The longed-for tidal wave
Of justice can rise up,
And hope and history rhyme.

So hope for a great sea-change
On the far side of revenge.
Believe that a further shore

Is reachable from here.
Believe in miracles
And cures and healing wells.
        (*TCAT,* 77,
        emphasis in original)

It is impossible to trace all the uses of these lines or parts of them subsequently in print and in public ceremonies, but several examples should suffice to show how they have become part of the province's cultural discourse about how it and its citizens might both emerge from the Troubles and begin to understand their lingering impact.

Just as Longley believes that one of poetry's proper functions is to bear witness in general and especially to atrocity, so does Heaney, and others have read the first stanza just quoted from near the conclusion of *The Cure at Troy* to be about both the perils and the promise of Northern Ireland and other societies worldwide. Heaney himself has pointed out about the lines starting with "once in a lifetime" and running through "And hope and history rhyme" that then-president of Ireland Mary Robinson "quoted these lines—in response to the distresses of famine in Africa, for example, as well as in other contexts" in the early 1990s.[23] He goes on to note, "I was delighted and surprised when, at the opening of the post-cease-fire Forum for Peace and Reconciliation in Dublin last autumn the lines were quoted again, directly, by Dick Spring, the Irish Minister for Foreign Affairs, and when my allusion to hope (in another context, still tied to *The Cure at Troy* chorus) was invoked on that same occasion in the speech that followed—by Gerry Adams, the leader of Sinn Fein."[24]

Moreover, a book entitled *Hope and History: Eyewitness Accounts of Life in Twentieth-Century Ulster* appeared in 1996, subsidized by the Arts Council for Northern Ireland. That main title, *Hope and History,* echoes Heaney's line "And hope and history rhyme," and indeed the editors give the whole stanza that concludes with the line as an epigraph to the collection. The book's eyewitness accounts start in the Edwardian period and are innocent enough, but as the Troubles begin, the last four decades of accounts are largely concerned with them. The penultimate statement in the collection is Heaney's own essay, "Light Finally Enters the Black

Hole," written after the IRA and Combined Loyalist Command cease-fires in 1994. Despite its bleak final entry on the IRA bombing of the London Docklands on February 9, 1996, which broke the IRA cease-fire, *Hope and History* seems to tentatively suggest, with the imprimatur of the Arts Council of Northern Ireland, that the political climate was changing by 1996, as indeed it was, and that art might at least lead to hope of peace and serve as a source of reflection about the past.

More interestingly, when Heaney dedicated the second stanza quoted above from the chorus that begins "So hope for a great sea-change" to the victims of the Omagh bombing in 1998, those lines became a text that accompanied the exhibition "Petals of Hope," created by the artist Carol Kane to incorporate the donated flowers and wreaths sent to Omagh.[25] Each group of two lines from this six-line stanza became the title for three different textured paper pieces that incorporated the donated flower petals. On March 10, 1999, a private viewing of the paper pieces was held for the families of the twenty-nine killed, and each family was given one of the paper pieces. The use of Heaney's poetry in such a public venue seems to affirm that like Longley he realizes poetry may not console but may bear witness to acts of violence and elegize the dead in personal ways not possible in bland political calls for peace and understanding. Yet there seems to be a palpable hope of consolation in this stanza—if not in this life, in the next—with the chorus's repeated entreaty to "Believe." Moreover, there is a definite wish for reconciliation in the imminent future if we "Believe that a further shore / Is reachable from here." Such a "sea-change" would truly be miraculous, as the conclusion of the stanza indicates.

The impossible optimism of the stanza is tempered, however, by its not being cast in rhyming couplets, which would have lent a definite sonic sense of something accomplished, something completed. And indeed, the seldom-quoted last lines of the chorus are much more measured than the more commonly quoted stanza just analyzed, which occurs several pages from the conclusion:

Suspect too much sweet talk
But never close your mind.
It was a fortunate wind

That blew me here. I leave
Half-ready to believe
That a crippled trust might walk

And the half-true rhyme is love.
(*TCAT,* 81)

Notice that "mind" and "wind" are eye-rhymes but not true rhymes,
while the only couplet, which rhymes "leave" with "believe," is then undercut by the nonrhyming of the last two lines that tentatively advance
a hope "That a crippled trust might walk," which is itself then mitigated
by the statement that "the half-true rhyme is love." Overall, these lines
advocate a cautious open-mindedness about the possibility of an emerging end to violence in the maimed province. Like Longley's "Ceasefire,"
this stanza from Heaney's *The Cure at Troy* suggests that hope is a fragile
thing and that peace will come dropping slow (to severely twist the context of a line from Yeats's "The Lake Isle of Innisfree").

The best popular representation of this blend of hope and trepidation
expressed by Heaney's chorus may be in the Northern Irish actor Liam
Neeson's reading of a portion of the chorus's lines on the widely publi-
cized compact disc *Across the Bridge of Hope,* released on November 11,
1998, in aid of the Omagh Fund. I suspect that Heaney himself may be
responsible for the balanced, contextualized, and accurate sense of his
own position on art's role in the peace process as given by Neeson. Neeson
begins by reading a stanza that comes two stanzas before the often-cited
stanza about hope and history. This stanza is sobering in its honesty:

Human beings suffer,
They torture one another,
They get hurt and get hard.
No poem or play or song
Can fully right a wrong
Inflicted and endured.
(*TCAT,* 77)

Neeson then skips the next stanza, which mentions both "A hunger-
striker's father" and "The police widow in veil," both clear and disturb-

ing references to the Troubles, and reads all of the stanza on hope and history and all but the last two lines from the stanza about the hoped-for "sea-change," crucially leaving out the last two lines of that stanza about "miracles" (77). Neeson's reading thus properly inscribes the cruel realities of the conflict in the public mind and makes clear that Heaney realizes art cannot effect a full redress of a suffered wrong, while putting these concepts into a dialectic with the more hopeful stanzas, whose hope is somewhat diminished by the omission of "miracles."

But more often, the public's imagination has seized solely on the two stanzas about hope and history and sea-change and miracles, often neglecting their context in a play that begins by criticizing dead-end, self-defeating narratives and concludes by only tentatively hoping for love and peace. The unionist Ian Young from Derry articulated the feeling of many ordinary people when he told journalist Susan McKay in 1998 that he was hopeful for the future of the province and that he had recently quoted in a speech the lines "Hope for a great sea change / on the far side of revenge / Believe that a further shore is reachable from here."[26] And in the UK *Independent* on January 1, 2008, a lead editorial about Northern Ireland that borrowed as its title part of Heaney's line from one of the two often-cited stanzas in *The Cure at Troy* opined that "in the course of the year" the province "successfully underwent, in the words of its poet Seamus Heaney, its 'great sea-change on the far side of revenge.'"[27] Comparing the murders attributable to paramilitaries in 2007 with those from 1998, "the year of the Omagh bombing," the editors noted that "there were almost 60 people killed" in 1998 but "only three or four in 2007." They concluded by noting that "once again Heaney put it best in prophesying that the near-impossible was actually achievable: "'Believe that a further shore / is reachable from here. / Believe in miracles / And cures and healing wells.'"[28] One does not want to be churlish, especially in the face of the continuing largely encouraging news from Northern Ireland, but it is worth repeating that in both the citations given here these lines from Heaney's chorus are not their last words in the play and are taken out of context, and further, that reconciliation is a process that usually happens at only a glacial pace. Nevertheless, the hope embodied in these two stanzas clearly must have served to inspire people from across the province that were interested in its future in the late 1990s to imagine that Omagh was the last major atrocity of the Troubles, which indeed it has been, and to believe that their society was on the brink of a "great sea-change."[29]

Increasingly, Michael Longley and Seamus Heaney seem to believe in the emerging reality of an imagined province as first articulated by writers through their use of the ambiguous, subtle language that can secondarily exemplify often politically unanticipated solidarities. Indeed, the 1998 Good Friday Agreement, supported by 71 percent of the citizenry of the province, uses such imaginative, even literary language, a crucial point Declan Kiberd was probably the first to recognize in print. Kiberd, invoking the work and life of Oscar Wilde in his discussion of the agreement, argued in 1999 that "a lot of the language in the Belfast Agreement is vague or even 'poetic.' That is because it offers a version of multiple identities of a kind for which no legal language yet exists."[30] More recently, Edna Longley has suggested that because of the "especially self-conscious" nature of language in Northern Irish poetry, this quality "makes the poetic conversations a model of a genuine peace process, as well as of cultural complexity."[31]

Both Michael Longley and Seamus Heaney have also gleefully remarked upon this fact. Longley told Peter McDonald in an interview that "in its language the Good Friday Agreement depended on an almost poetic precision and suggestiveness to get its complicated message across. The good poetry that has emanated from here is like that too, and for exactly the same reasons."[32]

One day after the signing of the Good Friday Agreement, on April 11, 1998, Heaney offered his views on the peace settlement in an *Irish Times* column that takes as its theme music and the transformation of the island from a place "full of comfortless noises" to one of redemptive melody characterized by the dynamism of its cross-cultural language:

> "Heard melodies are sweet, but those unheard are sweeter." It may seem flippant to greet history with a play upon John Keats's lines, but language itself seems to have gained a new friskiness through the signing of the inter-party agreement yesterday. Even the term "party rules" loses a bit of sectarian weight and begins to suggest something more innocent and celebratory. By devising a set of structures and a form of words which have the potential to release all

sides from their political and historical entrapment, Senator Mitchell, the Taoiseach, Prime Minister Blair and all the talks participants have done something evolutionary. If revolution is the kicking down of a rotten door, evolution is more like pushing the stone from the mouth of the tomb. There is an Easter energy about it, a sense of arrival rather than wreckage, and what is nonpareil about the new conditions is the promise they offer of a new covenant between people living in this country. For once, and at long last, the language of the Bible can be appropriated by those with a vision of the future rather than those who sing the battle hymns of the past.[33]

Heaney's language here reflects the inclusivist language of the Good Friday Agreement, which promises to recognize the varied cultural and religious traditions in Northern Ireland. His metaphor comparing the new state of relations to a game of football "on the same pitch" signals further the "new friskiness" of language with which he began his column and reimagines the conflict in a more acceptable form, presumably with referees and new rules.[34]

Heaney recognizes that many unionists will not welcome the new agreement, especially since "Sinn Fein's inclusion in the democratic fold" will test them severely, for "in the unionist mind Sinn Fein is to blame for the devastation which the IRA wrought on the economic and social life of the province—'their' province—over the past 30 years."[35] But he suggests that unionists too should focus on the future, with all its promise and potential that Northern Irish poetry has helped generate:

Everybody has to contend with what Thomas Davis called "felt history." Revisionists have created new perspectives (and contentions) and generations of gifted Northern poets have let the linguistic cat out of the sectarian bag, setting it free in the great street carnival of "protholics and catestants," but in Drumcree and on the Lower Ormeau Road, neither the victories of creative spirit nor the dodges of post-modernism are going to have much immediate effect. And yet it is at the level of creative spirit, in the realm of glimpsed potential rather than intransigent solidarity, that the future takes shape.[36]

The creative spirit—whether in literature or some other branch of the arts—at this moment in history offers another glimpse at flexible possibility, not stubborn intransigence.[37] Poetry, as Heaney has written in the context of the events of September 11, 2001, in America, seems especially suited to envisioning such potential through its element of oracular surprise: "The indispensable poem always has an element of surprise about it. Even perhaps a touch of the irrational. For both the reader and the writer, it will possess a soothsaying force, as if it were an oracle delivered unexpectedly and irresistibly."[38]

This soothsaying quality of poetry has lent itself to incorporation into Nobel Prize speeches by the far-seeing former leaders of the two more moderate major political parties in Northern Ireland, the Ulster Unionist Party (UUP) and the Social Democratic Labor Party (SDLP), though unfortunately the influence of those parties is currently on the wane with the ascendancy of the hard-line Democratic Ulster Party and Sinn Fein. As Anthony Roche has pointed out, both the UUP's former leader David Trimble and the SDLP's former leader John Hume quoted poetry in their acceptance speeches for their jointly awarded Nobel Peace Prize in December of 1998. Trimble quoted from one of Yeats's Irish Senate speeches dealing with the proposed influence of Catholicism on the new Irish constitution, a measure Yeats felt would discriminate against the Protestant minority in the Republic: "We against whom you have done this thing are no petty people."[39] As Roche notes, "The significance was not so much that a politician was quoting a poet (though the phenomenon is rare enough) as that an Ulster Unionist committed to the Union of Northern Ireland with Great Britain was admitting to a dimension of Irish identity." Hume, on the other hand, was also culturally magnanimous in citing some lines from the Northern Irish Protestant poet Louis MacNeice. Roche sagely concludes: "Both the quotations proved the adage that, in Ireland in particular, poetry is the news that remains news."[40]

Notes

INTRODUCTION. **Northern Irish Poetry, Imagination, and Ethics**

The chapter's three epigraphs are from Donoghue, *Speaking of Beauty*, 114; Mc-
Donald, *Serious Poetry*, 5; and Dawe, "Sound of the Shuttle," 68, respectively.

    1. Heaney, "Interview" [Randall], 7.
    2. Northern Ireland Executive, "McGuinness Announces Honour."
    3. M. Longley, *Jovial Hullabaloo*, 21, 22.
    4. Cavanagh, *Professing Poetry*, 220.
    5. *CPL*, 157, and see M. Longley, introduction to *Secret Marriages*, 3,
for an articulation of Longley's evocation of a Northern Irish cultural identity
as an enabling position between two or more cultures; see also my discussion
of his essay "Man Lying on a Wall" at the end of chapter 2.
    6. McDonald, "Faith and Fidelities," 63, 64.
    7. Clark, *Ulster Renaissance*, 10.
    8. Foley made this comment in an attempt to privilege James Simmons's
poetry over that of Heaney, Longley, and Mahon, as Clark, *Ulster Renaissance*,
177, has pointed out. See 177 n. 18 for the Foley citation.
    9. Quoted in Brearton, *Reading Michael Longley*, 77.
    10. Moriarty, "Writers Pay Tribute." Note the errors here, though, prob-
ably attributable to Moriarty, not Heaney: Mahon only attended one Group
meeting in Belfast by his own account; Boland was good friends with Longley
in the 1960s but was then based in Dublin, not Belfast, although Mahon did
bring her to Belfast in 1964 to meet the Longleys (see M. Longley, "Interview"
[Randolph], 298); Edna Longley is a critic, not a poet. And while they may
have met in Longley's flat occasionally, the Belfast Group met mainly in Philip
Hobsbaum's flat.

11. Brown, "Mahon and Longley," 133.

12. Heaney, "Interview with Seamus Heaney" [Randall], 9.

13. See, for example, Muldoon's comment to me that up until the poems of *Moy Sand and Gravel* (2002) he preferred to "step around" the looming presence of Yeats (Russell, "Yeatsian Refrain," 52). McGuckian feels linked strongly to Yeats through Heaney, having noted once that "if he hadn't been there, Heaney wouldn't be, and if Heaney hadn't been there, I wouldn't be. I feel that there is a continuum between Yeats and me through Heaney" (quoted in Gray, "Medbh McGuckian," 167).

14. Buckley, *Poetry and the Sacred*, 17.

15. Donoghue, *Sovereign Ghost*, 32.

16. Steiner, *Real Presences*, 203–4.

17. Ibid., 225.

18. Heaney, "Between North and South," 107.

19. Steiner, *Real Presences*, 227.

20. M. Longley, "Interview with Michael Longley" [Broom], 22.

21. M. Longley, "Playing Football," 10.

22. M. Longley, "Longley Tapes," 24.

23. Heaney, "Faith, Hope and Poetry," 217. See, too, Heaney's terming Mandelstam and other poets who stood up to totalitarianism artistic saints in his 1999 newspaper essay for the *Sunday Times*: "The twentieth century does indeed present us with a period during which the whole question of poetry's relationship to human values was worked out at extreme cost in the lives of the poets themselves, a period when the secular equivalent of sainthood was often attained by their devotion to vocation and when there has even been something like a martyrology of writers" (Heaney, "Peace of the Word," 10).

24. Deane, "Seamus Heaney," 174.

25. Heaney, "Government of the Tongue," 101.

26. Eliade, *Sacred and the Profane*, 21.

27. Girard, *Violence and the Sacred*, 14–15.

28. Heaney, "Interesting Case of Nero," xxi.

29. Kertzer, "Course of a Particular," 209.

30. Attridge, *Singularity of Literature*, 71.

31. Kertzer, "Course of a Particular," 220.

32. Rushdie, "Is Nothing Sacred?" 420.

33. Ibid., 421.

34. Ibid., 427.

35. Ibid., 428, 429.

36. M. Longley, "Playing Football," 10.

37. Heaney, "Interesting Case of Nero," xix.
38. Felski, *Uses of Literature*, 5.
39. Scott, *Poetics of Belief*, 1.
40. Levinson, "What Is New Formalism?" In her essay, Levinson distinguishes "two strains of new formalism," between "those who want to restore to today's reductive reinscription of historical reading its original focus on form" and those "who campaign to bring back a sharp demarcation between history and art, discourse and literature, with form (regarded as the condition of aesthetic experience as traced to Kant—i.e., disinterested, autotelic, playful, pleasurable, consensus-generating, and therefore both individually liberating and conducive to affective social cohesion) the prerogative of art. In short, we have a new formalism that makes a continuum with new historicism and a backlash new formalism" (559). The present study often sets literature in the context of historical events in Northern Ireland and beyond and, perhaps more important, sees literature, and poetry in particular, as capable of affecting politics and culture by the imaginative power of its subtle and oblique language, but as not seeking such change as its primary aim.
41. Felski, *Uses of Literature*, 7.
42. Brearton, "Poetry of the 1960s," 109.
43. M. Longley, "Playing Football," 10.
44. Mark 9:24 (King James version).
45. See Brearton, *Reading Michael Longley*, 155–63, for a nuanced discussion of Longley's writer's block and a clear refutation of the critical ascription of a ten-year or even an impossible "twelve-year silence" to him in the 1980s. Even during the relatively fallow periods of 1979–85 he wrote the fourteen *New Poems*, and in 1987–88 he wrote six more poems for what would become his 1991 collection, *Gorse Fires* (162).
46. Buckley, *Poetry and the Sacred*, 20.
47. Quoted in Brearton, *Reading Michael Longley*, 11.
48. Scott, *Wild Prayer of Longing*, 74.
49. Donoghue, *Speaking of Beauty*, 71.
50. Heaney, *Place and Displacement*, 4.
51. Longley, "Reading Notes" [folder 31].
52. Heaney, "Frontiers of Writing," 202.
53. Quoted in Hart and Parker, introduction to *Contemporary Irish Fiction*, 5.
54. Kavanagh, "Parish and the Universe," 282.
55. Longenbach, *Resistance to Poetry*, 108.
56. Yeats, *Collected Poems*, 295.

57. McDonald, "Faiths and Fidelities," 64.

58. Examples of the pernicious effect upon imaginative literature written immediately after an atrocity in the Troubles include Thomas Kinsella's "Butcher's Dozen," (1972) and Brian Friel's *The Freedom of the City* (1973). See Russell, "Liberating Fictional Truth," for a discussion of how Friel's imagined community of fictional characters enabled him to finally overcome his incorporation of too many factual details from the Widgery Inquiry into that atrocity. Kinsella's poem was written very soon after the reprehensible whitewash of the events of Bloody Sunday by the Widgery Tribunal in 1972 and suffers aesthetically as a result. The clunky rhyme scheme of this poem and its tone make it more propaganda than poetry. I briefly contrast Kinsella's poem with another, more effective poem about the same event, Seamus Heaney's "Casualty," in chapter 7 of this study. I argue there that by waiting several years Heaney was able to better delineate the personal and political fallout from Bloody Sunday and its effect upon the life of the individual then living in the province than Kinsella, who subverted poetry into pamphleteering by writing immediately after the inquiry into the event. A contrasting, aesthetically efficacious example of literature written in this "super-journalist" mode is Longley's own "Ceasefire," written in the hopes of influencing the first IRA cease-fire in 1994. I will discuss the ethical implications of the writing of this poem in chapter 3.

59. Longley, "Interview" [Randolph], 303.

60. Ibid.

61. Deane, "Artist and the Troubles," 45.

62. We may even have reached something of a canonization of this literature with Michael Parker's magisterial two-volume work on its crucial intersections with province history, *Northern Irish Literature*.

63. Weeks, "Nobel Winner," 6C.

64. Heaney, *Place and Displacement*, 6–7.

65. Ibid., 7.

66. Donoghue, *Speaking of Beauty*, 114.

67. Heaney, *Place and Displacement*, 7.

68. Kennedy-Andrews, *Fiction*, 7.

69. Heaney, "Government of the Tongue," 93–94.

70. Brearton, *Reading Michael Longley*, 60.

71. Heaney, "Staying Power of Poetry," 14.

72. Brooks, "Uses of Literature," 5.

73. Ibid., 5.

74. Quoted in Morrison, *Seamus Heaney*, 69. An implicit argument of this study is that the particularity of the poetic genre practiced by Longley and

Heaney itself paradoxically deflates abstract, monolithic notions of identity in the province.

75. Lederach, *Moral Imagination*, 159–60.

76. Ibid., 160.

77. Heaney, "Further Language," 15.

78. Dawson, *Making Peace*, 5.

79. Porter, *Elusive Quest*, 26.

80. Ibid., 255.

81. Ibid., 164.

82. Felski, *Uses of Literature*, 8–9.

83. Heaney, "*Cure at Troy*," 178.

84. Grant, *Breaking Enmities*, x.

85. Ibid., x.

86. The quotation is from the middle stanza of MacNeice's delightful poem "Snow": "World is crazier and more of it than we think, / Incorrigibly plural. I peel and portion / A tangerine and spit the pips and feel / The drunkenness of things being various" (MacNeice, *Collected Poems*, 30).

87. See E. Longley, "Opening Up," 24–25.

88. Dawe, "Just Images," 86–87.

89. E. Longley, "From Cathleen to Anorexia," 195.

90. M. Longley, "Playing Football," 10.

91. Buckley, *Poetry and the Sacred*, 21.

92. Ashley, "Writing on the Brink," 61.

93. Bottum, "Death and Politics." Steiner, writing in *Grammars of Creation*, argues that there are "two contrasting yet congruent tendencies . . . at work" in our current age's treatments of death: "Where massacre and social-economic misery prevail, death withers to naked routine. No especial significance honors the victim, so often skeletal in his or her trashed existence. Where superfluity obtains, death is sanitized and gentrified. Medical care and technology—those tubes, those softly lit rooms—privilege the moribund party" (324).

94. Lewis, *Experiment in Criticism*, 140–41.

95. E. Longley, "Introduction," 9.

96. Grant, *Breaking Enmities*, 71.

97. Donoghue, *Practice of Reading*, 73.

98. Ibid., 78.

99. Ibid., 79.

100. Livingston, "Literary Aesthetics," 660–61.

101. Ibid., 662, 667. The passage from McGinn occurs in his "Meaning and Morality," 41. For a helpful account of the need for an ethical criticism to balance political criticism, see D. Parker, *Ethics, Theory and the Novel*.

102. Bakhtin, "Discourse in the Novel," 259.

103. Ibid.

104. Corcoran, *After Yeats and Joyce*, 139.

105. Grant, *Breaking Enmities*, 71.

106. The metaphor of the cat's cradle is Michael Longley's. See his "Sketches of Britain."

107. *MI*, 17.

108. Mahon, "Poetry in Northern Ireland," 93.

109. Heaney, *Stepping Stones*, 383. "To hold in a single thought reality and justice" is from Yeats's 1937 version of *A Vision*, 25. Heaney also quotes this phrase in *CP*, 17.

110. Heaney, "Pathos of Things," 20.

111. Miller, *On Literature*, 33.

112. Kertzer, "Course of a Particular," 225.

113. For Kertzer on ethics, see ibid., 227–34.

114. Desmond, *Gravity and Grace*, 13.

115. See Russell, review of *Reading Michael Longley*, 226–28.

116. Attridge, *Singularity of Literature*, 124.

117. Ibid., 124, 125.

118. Ibid., 125.

119. Despite my general approval of Attridge's formulation of particularity, I share Felski's concern about a significant strand of ethical criticism that focuses on alterity as separating us from each other. In *Uses of Literature*, Felski holds, "In contrast to much recent ethical criticism . . . I do not see ethics as purely a matter of particularity and otherness. In our engagement with others, we surely seek not only a recognition of our differences but also an openness to potential commonalities and affinities" (138).

120. Nobel Foundation, "Nobel Prize in Literature."

121. Scarry, *On Beauty*, 9.

122. Ibid., 23, 23, 24–28, 28 ff.

123. M. Roche, *Why Literature Matters*, 28–29. See, too, Miller, *On Literature*: "It is, I claim, an essential feature of literature to hide secrets that may not ever be revealed" (40). But note that Miller earlier explicitly disagrees with Heidegger's position on language as referencing a universal truth: "To affirm that each work has its own truth, a truth different from the truth of any other work, sets what I am saying not only against mimetic or referential definitions of literature, but also against Heideggerian notions of literature or of 'poetry' as what he calls the 'setting-forth-of-truth-in-the-work.' For Heidegger the truth set forth in the work is universal. It is the truth of Being. That truth is not something unique to the work, with a singular truth for each work" (34).

124. Longley, "Brendan Corcoran and Michael Longley," 116.

125. The inside title pages of *Causeway* are a geometric representation of the hexagonal basalt stones that make up the Giant's Causeway in Northern Ireland, easily the most distinctive physical feature in the province. This pictorial emphasis on literal stepping stones underscores Longley's view of the arts as establishing figurative stepping stones toward cultural reconciliation.

126. MacNeice, *Poetry of W. B. Yeats,* ix.

127. Muldoon, "'Welsh Incident,'" 395.

ONE. Laying the Foundations

1. Kiberd, "Irish Literature," 329.

2. Hobsbaum, "Creative Writing."

3. Strickland, "F. R. Leavis," 183.

4. Hobsbaum, *Theory of Criticism,* 14. This book was published as *A Theory of Communication* in Britain.

5. See, for example, Kirkland's discussion of the Belfast Group and his marked disdain for Hobsbaum's absorption of F. R. Leavis's close reading method and extension of this method into the group as a counter to the growing structuralist movement in literary criticism (*LCNI,* 80–81).

6. Hobsbaum, "Belfast Group," 173–74.

7. "Belfast Group: Overview," 1.

8. "Belfast Group: A Symposium," 58.

9. "Belfast Group: Overview," 2.

10. "Belfast Group: A Symposium," 60.

11. For a survey of group members' attitudes toward the enterprise, see "Belfast Group: A Symposium."

12. Brearton, "Poetry of the 1960s," 109.

13. E. Longley, "Introduction," 19.

14. "Belfast Group: A Symposium," 54.

15. Heaney, "Belfast," 29. Despite the very real efficacy of Hobsbaum's efforts in promoting Ulster poetry as regional, he later tried to co-opt Heaney's wedding sequence in *Wintering Out* (1972) by describing it as being within "the central line of English poetry" (quoted in Foster, "Post-war Ulster Poetry," 71).

16. Clark, *Ulster Renaissance,* 142.

17. Other poets have felt that members of the Belfast Group have generally preserved an imaginative life of their own despite the continuing crisis in the province. For example, the Irish poet Eavan Boland, who knew Derek Mahon and Michael Longley at Trinity College, Dublin, and met Heaney as

well in the 1960s, has said, "Once the Troubles began they were conscripted poets. What's surprising is how independent they stayed. They kept their own lyric identities and they progressed. . . . I think that's a very important witness for Irish poetry" ("Backward Look," 293–94).

18. Brearton, "Poetry of the 1960s," 104.

19. Heaney, "Conversation," 38.

20. Hobsbaum, *Theory of Criticism*, 11.

21. M. Longley, *Jovial Hullabaloo*, 7.

22. Johnstone, "Climate Control," 72–74.

23. Actually, 1966 might serve as a more appropriate date for this new phase, since Heaney, Northern Ireland's most famous writer, published his first complete volume of poetry then. Rand Brandes points out that while Heaney's pamphlet garnered a mention in the *Belfast Telegraph* in 1965 and was glowingly reviewed by John Carey in the *New Statesman* on December 31 of that year, *Eleven Poems* was "immediately overshadowed" by *Death of a Naturalist*, which appeared in 1966 ("Secondary Sources," 65).

24. Heaney, "Interesting Case," xxi.

25. Richtarik, *Acting between the Lines*, 102.

26. Ibid., 103.

27. Heaney, "Light Finally Enters," A9.

28. M. Longley, "Review of Arts Funding." Though I do not have room here to fully explore his contribution to reconciliation in the province through his various positions on the Arts Council of Northern Ireland, see Longley's own recollections of his time spent on the council in *Tuppenny Stung*, especially the chapter entitled "Blackthorn and Bonsai, or A Little Brief Authority," 43–76. See also Tannahill, "More Than Just a Day Job," 115–17, for an apologia for Longley's commitment to Belfast's Blackstaff Press through Arts Council funding beginning in 1971.

T W O. **Lighting Out for the Unknown Territory**

1. M. Longley, "Interview" [Randolph], 296.

2. Brearton, "'Privilege / Of vertigo,'" 210, 209–11.

3. Hobsbaum, "Belfast Group," 176.

4. Ibid., 176–77.

5. See Heaney, *DN*, 1. For the best discussion of Heaney's early rhyming, particularly his tendency to rhyme masculine or monosyllabic words with polysyllabic or feminine words, see Hall, "Rhyme," which also briefly explores similar rhymes in Longley's early poetry.

6. In his unpublished essay on Yeats, Longley reflects on Yeats's positive example of rhyming in his early poems: "For myself, of the 38 poems in my first collection, all but two are rhymed. I know that I would certainly feel self-conscious about such 'traditionalism' were it not for the endorsement of Yeats's example. . . . Just as he did with pararhyme, Yeats, by insisting on a norm and then treating it so freely, gave back to English a metric which might have seemed played-out" (M. Longley, ["Yeats"]).

7. M. Longley, introduction to *Secret Marriages*, 2.

8. Besides Michael Allen, only Fran Brearton and Renee Fox have discussed Longley's early formal experiments in any depth. In reference to Longley's introduction to *Secret Marriages*, Allen notes that "he was then testing the possibility that the diminution of rhythm might be symptomatic of the drying-up of poetic inspiration" ("Options," 130). Allen believes that the accelerated and more expansive rhythm found in significant poems such as "Alibis" from Longley's next full volume, *An Exploded View*, suggest that he has now discarded the diminished rhythm he explored in the poems of *Secret Marriages* and that "this opening from Longley's more restricted rhythms provides the central, forward impetus of *An Exploded View*" (133). Brearton argues that *No Continuing City* strains against itself productively, with "the enclosed, tightened, almost repressive short poems that, however successful they may be in and of themselves, ultimately prove to be a closed circuit, trapped inside their own forms like a voice trapped inside its own head. . . . On the other [hand], the circling of subject, the location betwixt and between, in such poems as 'The Freemartin,' and 'Leaving Inishmore' proves revelatory rather than restrictive" (*Reading Michael Longley*, 40). Finally, Fox argues that "*No Continuing City* oscillates between elegy and epitaph, using the latter as a way to experiment formally with, and push to its limits, the poetics of absence that had become almost a commonplace criticism of nineteenth- and twentieth-century Irish poetry." She contrasts the ultimately consoling power of the traditional elegy with that of the epitaph, suggesting, "Rather than recalling to life and connecting with a no-longer-silenced voice, the epitaph stands in for, and thus reinforces the silence of the dead" ("Michael Longley's Early Epitaphs," 127, 128).

9. Brearton, "'Privilege / Of vertigo,'" 205.

10. M. Longley, "Tongue at Play," 119.

11. M. Longley, introduction to *Secret Marriages*, 2–3.

12. Brearton, *Reading Michael Longley*, 40.

13. M. Longley, "Tongue at Play," 120.

14. In "Tongue at Play," 112, Longley notes that he was largely unable to write poems in 1967 and 1968: "Through 1967 and 1968 I slowed to a stop. . . .

'Journey out of Essex,' subtitled 'John Clare's Escape from the Madhouse,' [was] the only poem from 1968 to survive. . . ." Elsewhere in this recollection he notes, "My poems were getting shorter and shorter" (112), a sign to him that he was beginning to experience writer's block right when the Troubles were flaring up and thus preventing him from commenting directly on them had he even wished to.

15. M. Longley, introduction to *Secret Marriages*, 2.

16. Brearton, *Reading Michael Longley*, 44.

17. In "Interview" [Randolph], 294, Longley explicitly terms writer's block a "freeze-up." Describing the way he believes his poetic subjects are intertwined, he notes, "I hope there are overlappings, the nature poetry fertilizing the war poetry, and so on. Advancing on a number of fronts at the same time looks like a good idea: if there's a freeze-up at points along the line, you can trickle forward somewhere else."

18. Douglas Dunn's sustained argument about Longley's poetic idiom in *No Continuing City* mentions its mixture of "colloquial and more formal poetic registers" and suggests the influence of Louis MacNeice's colloquial *terza rima* in *Autumn Sequel* on Longley's "A Questionnaire for Walter Mitty" ("Longley's Metric," 18–19). Dunn's general point about the evolution of Longley's or any poet's idiom is important for understanding how Longley's deep reading in Larkin led him to incorporate aspects of the elder poet's colloquialism: "A poet doesn't really choose his or her idiom. . . . It feels truer to recognize that it is brought about by personality, by 'moral attitude,' as well as through a near-religious exercise of devotion to those poets of the past for whose work the contemporary poet feels a profound affinity" (19).

19. See Lipsitz, "Jazz."

20. M. Longley, "Perpetual One-Night Stand," 91.

21. Ibid., 92.

22. M. Longley, "Tongue at Play," 113.

23. M. Longley, "Perpetual One-Night Stand," 92.

24. M. Longley, "Michael Longley: An Interview" [Harper], 69.

25. M. Longley, "Tongue at Play," 113.

26. M. Longley, "Michael Longley: An Interview" [Harper], 68.

27. M. Longley, "Perpetual One-Night Stand," 95.

28. Leggett, *Larkin's Blues*, 98.

29. Lipsitz, "Jazz," 137, cites this single couplet and laments its exclusion from the sequence: "Death like all your habits came to stay / Dared face your music, took your breath away."

30. M. Longley, "Perpetual One-Night Stand," 97.

31. M. Longley, "Michael Longley: An Interview" [Harper], 58.

32. M. Longley, "Perpetual One-Night Stand," 97.

33. M. Longley, "Reading Notes" [folder 30].

34. M. Longley, "Sketches of Britain." Longley cites these lines from Auden in his introduction to *Causeway* as well ("I," ix).

35. Ibid.

36. Ibid.

37. Longley's conception of the interconnection between the dominant Northern Irish cultures coalesces with his conception of the artist's duty in conflicted societies—to provide stepping stones of understanding—in the muted green and orange hexagons representing the Giant's Causeway on the inside title pages of *Causeway*. The intermingling of these politically significant colors on these pages pictorially affirms Longley's rejection of "the concept of a purely green Ireland and an orange Ulster" in his statement quoted above on p. 80.

38. M. Longley, "Neolithic Night," 99.

39. Ibid.

40. Brearton notes that the *abacbc* rhyme scheme of "The Hebrides" is borrowed from George Herbert's "Peace" ("'Privilege / Of vertigo,'" 206).

41. Brown, "Mahon and Longley," 141.

42. Ibid.

43. There is a connection between Longley's early fascination with the Hebrides and his later interest in the Burren area of western Ireland, which I explore in chapter 4. W. H. Murray notes that the Hebrides are treeless and have "richly fertile but narrow lazybeds between ribs of rock," and a similar abundance of "ancient monuments: chambered cairns, duns, brochs, standing stones, sun-circles, beehives, earth-houses and wheel-houses, and churches" (*Hebrides* 5, 179). With their rockiness and rich variety of flora, the Hebrides share environmental similarities with Longley's Burren. The fragility of these areas has prompted his exploration into the interconnectedness of humans and the natural world, especially their common vulnerability.

44. Pocock, "British History," 606.

45. Ibid., 606–7.

46. Ibid., 609.

47. Ibid., 609–10.

48. Ibid., 616.

49. Ibid., 620. For an expanded version of his original proposal, see Pocock, "Limits and Divisions."

50. M. Longley, "Man Lying on a Wall." The importance of this image for Longley is further signified by the title poem of his third volume, *Man Lying on a Wall*.

THREE. Longley's Poetry of War and Peace

1. McDonald convincingly argues that "the issue of the poet's function, powers, or responsibilities is never a central concern" in Longley's work, since he "allows his poetry to take more direct, spontaneous, and apparently improvisatory routes" than does Heaney ("Faiths and Fidelities," 70).
2. M. Longley, "Inner Adventure," 55.
3. M. Longley, "Interview with Michael Longley" [McDonald].
4. M. Longley, "A Tongue at Play," 119.
5. M. Longley, "Interview with Michael Longley" [Broom], 25. He reiterates this opinion in his 2004 interview with Margaret Mills Harper: "Really I like to think I'm receptive, waiting. Like an ovum waiting for fertilization, that's as far as I can prepare" (M. Longley, "Michael Longley: An Interview" [Harper], 71).
6. M. Longley, "Michael Longley," in *Reading the Future*, 12.
7. M. Longley, "Strife," 765.
8. In his essay on Propertius, Longley states explicitly, "A poet's first duty is to words. This fact cannot be stressed enough, especially in these days of commitment when we are inundated with politics and sociology and philosophy masquerading as poetry. A poets [*sic*] first duty is to words. He must look after words" ("Propertius").
9. Quoted in Brearton, *Reading Michael Longley*, 17.
10. A significant exception is *LCNI*. Kirkland's book is the most detailed and sophisticated analysis to date of Michael and Edna Longley's work in promoting Northern Irish literature and reconciliation. His book certainly merits reading, but its dense and elliptical prose style can be daunting. See too Kennedy-Andrews's excellent essay "Conflict, Violence," which recognizes Longley's lifelong engagement with the conflict by attaining a middle ground in his poetry. Although I have long been arguing that Longley's aesthetic is predicated upon essentially ethical terms, I was pleased to see this argument articulated so concisely by Kennedy-Andrews in this outstanding essay: "Longley's idea of interconnectedness includes the inseparability of the aesthetic and the ethical" (76).
11. Hufstader, *Tongue of Water*, 87, 88.
12. Ibid., 98, 99.
13. Kennedy-Andrews rightly critiques Smith's 1980 criticism of Longley as detached from the violence in the province, arguing that Longley's position in his poetry toward the violence is balanced and that he "insists that we all recognize our propensity to savagery" ("Conflict, Violence," 74). Patrick Grant also takes some pains to critique Hufstader's assertion of Longley's alleged bi-

furcation, noting that he, Grant, has instead "stressed the continuities enabling us to recognize a characteristic voice in Longley's work as a whole. Consequently, I have suggested that when Longley depicts violence, he does so, typically, by restraint, and the voice we respond to most fully is his own—the lyrical voice of a persona whose tact, clarity and compassion stand as an antidote to the thing he deplores" (*Literature, Rhetoric*, 37).

14. M. Parker, "Imprint of History," 153, explains this first targeted murder of British soldiers by the IRA: "On the night of Tuesday, 9 March [1971], in a bar in Belfast city centre, three Provisional IRA men fell into conversation with three young, off-duty soldiers from the Royal Highland Fusiliers, seventeen-year-old John McCaig, his brother Joseph, aged 18, and twenty-three-year-old Dougald McCaughey. The Provisionals are said to have invited the three Scots to a party. Instead they drove them to a quiet spot on a hillside near Ligoniel, where they shot them in the back of the head as they were relieving themselves by a roadside. The bodies were left there, and later discovered by local children."

15. M. Parker, *Northern Irish Literature*, 210. Agnew was shot by two sixteen-year-olds after "he pushed his young son and 10-year-old daughter into the living-room to protect them" (210).

16. McDonald offers a much more sophisticated and subtle reading of the concluding scene in the poem than Hufstader, pointing out that "the poem itself [like the bus conductor's wife] is open to the force of bewilderment, its abrupt ending catching appropriately another kind of unexpected termination: the persistence of detail, in the slippers, the television, and the supper dishes, is determinedly irrelevant to any larger designs for meaning which might be applied to the narrative itself" (*MI*, 65).

17. Brearton, *Great War*, 258.

18. Kennelly, "Letter to Michael Longley."

19. Hufstader, *Tongue of Water*, 95–96.

20. Ibid., 96.

21. Dunn, "Letter to Michael Longley."

22. Drummond, "The Difficulty of We," 38.

23. Ibid.

24. Mahon, "Letter to the Editor."

25. Mahon, "Personal Letter."

26. But see Clark, *Ulster Renaissance*, for an intriguing suggestion based on her reading of another portion of the letter by Mahon that I have just cited: "Mahon had attempted, at some level, to 'break' with Longley in order to pursue a more independent poetic path, and . . . the formerly sustaining relationship was evolving into something different. Indeed, at this time Mahon was

becoming more critical of the idea of a Northern renaissance, and more resistant to the claim that the best poetry in Ireland was being written north of the border" (187).

27. Moreover, as Drummond suggests in "Difficulty of We," the use of "we" in Longley's poem becomes "not simply a marker of friendship; it is also a political statement. For Mahon, that simple little word, 'we,' had pulled him into an unwanted public allegiance in which he, cast as Protestant writer, seemed to represent a particular community. The notion of how, and in what ways, a writer is supposed to represent a community is difficult when applied to any writer, but particularly so with Derek Mahon, whose poetic persona seems to avoid any kind of communal fidelity" (40).

28. Clark, *Ulster Renaissance,* notes that the original line 6 of the poem read, "The Catholics *we* scarcely loved" (185) and that Longley changed it to the version I have cited above, "The Catholics *we'd* scarcely loved" (my emphases), but as she observes, "This was hardly a concession" (188). Longley would later embrace a rural landscape populated by Catholics as he spent more and more time in western Ireland, especially Mayo. At this point in his life, however, he was obviously baffled by and alienated from not only some urban Catholics in Belfast but also the traditional Irish culture he discusses encountering on Inisheer later in "Letter to Derek Mahon": "We were tongue-tied / Companions of the island's dead / In the graveyard among the dunes, / Eavesdroppers on conversations / With a Jesus who spoke Irish— / We were strangers in that parish . . ." (*CPL,* 59). In "Michael Longley," an interview by Mike Murphy from Ni Anluain's *Reading the Future,* however, Longley claims that knowing the Fermanagh Catholic woman Lena Hardy, who helped his mother raise Longley and his brother after his father joined the British Army for a second time at the outset of World War II, enabled him to perceive Catholics ecumenically: "I loved her so much; in a sense all that sectarian superstitious nonsense was cancelled out in my heart and mind by her gentleness" (121). But immediately before this comment, he notes that Hardy was "my introduction to the strange world of the Sacred Heart and rosaries," suggesting he still viewed Catholicism as other.

29. Paulin, "Northern Protestant Oratory," 314.

30. M. Longley, "Letter to the Editor."

31. Gerald Dawe has briefly discussed some of the problems with this collection, singling out its "tasteless front cover—a heart split in two, green and orange, and bound by a black band" ("History Class," 79). But Dawe also argues that "the symphonic structure of the anthology deserved more critical attention" than did its cover (79).

32. M. Longley, "Tongue at Play," 120.

33. Heaney also alludes to this atrocity in his Nobel Prize address, *Crediting Poetry*, as I discuss in chapter 7.

34. Luke 22:19; 1 Cor. 11:24 (King James translation).

35. Certainly, the existence of interfaith communities such as the Corrymeela Community in Ballycastle and Belfast, the Christian Renewal Centre outside of Rostrevor, and the Columbanus Community of Reconciliation in north Belfast demonstrates the unique ability of Christ to heal the divisions between the two traditionally opposed communities. See Wells's *People behind the Peace*, 57–120.

36. Heaney insightfully notes about this conclusion that "the banal marvel of bodily wholeness restored through the fitting of a set of dentures is a sacramental rite to signify the desired world-miracle of wrongs redressed and wholeness restored through the intervention of the act of poetry itself" ("Pre-natal Mountain," 51).

37. The poem derives part of its power from his admiration of the unblinking, workmanlike cameraman who filmed the aftermath of this atrocity. Longley recalls that man's honesty in a recollection of a chance meeting between the two: "Some years ago in the South of Ulster ten working men were taken out of their van and shot dead because of their religion. A few days later I happened to be drinking in a Belfast pub beside the English cameraman whose pictures of the pathetic detritus of that scene had gone round the world. I asked him how he reacted in such nightmarish circumstances. He replied, 'I take out my light meter, and I focus the lens.' His honest words and the memory of my father's false teeth interacted to make this elegy" (M. Longley, "Reading Notes" [folder 22]).

38. Longley has long felt that love poetry is worth writing in the midst of death. See, for example, M. Longley, "Interview" [Randolph], 308, for his statement about how Apollinaire "finds connections in a bombardment of distractions and manages to be all embracing in a world that is being blown apart. He attempts love poetry in the shadow of death."

39. McDonald, "Lapsed Classics," 43.

40. Brown, "Michael Longley," 3. See Allen, "Longley's Long Line," for a detailed exploration of Longley's growing penchant for the long line, "a loose iambic pentameter often verging on hexameter," in his poetry beginning in *Gorse Fires* (121, 121–41, passim). Longley has remarked to McDonald in an interview that his formal immersion in the shorter, more compressed lyrics of his first four volumes probably enabled his control over the more recent lengthy poems like "The Butchers": "Perhaps I wouldn't have been able to control the

later big splotchy pieces like "The Butchers' if I hadn't set myself those formal challenges in my young days" (M. Longley, "Interview with Michael Longley" [McDonald]). In Longley's most recent volumes, *The Weather in Japan* (2000) and *Snow Water* (2004), however, he vacillates between poems composed of long lines and those written in short, terse lines.

41. Lewis, *Preface to "Paradise Lost,"* 41, 45.

42. M. Longley, "Interview" [Randolph], 306.

43. McDonald, "Lapsed Classics," 42.

44. Robert Fitzgerald translates this passage in this way: the ghosts of the suitors are led "in swift flight to where the Dead inhabit / wastes of asphodels at the world's end" (Homer, *Odyssey,* 445).

45. Taylor, *Loyalists,* 153–55.

46. M. Longley, "Interview with Michael Longley" [Broom], 18.

47. Longley does use this term in "Baucis and Philemon" when he writes of Hermes' Roman equivalent, Mercury, "Jupiter brought Mercury without his wand or wings" (*GO,* 22). Fitzgerald translates the opening stanza of book 24 as "Meanwhile the suitors' ghosts were called away / by Hermes of Kyllene, bearing the golden wand with which he charms the eyes of men or wakens whom he will" (Homer, *Odyssey,* 445). Significantly, Fitzgerald's translation does not compare Hermes to anyone, while Longley's simile in "The Butchers" is oblique but clear, likening Hermes to both Paisley and RUC officers.

48. M. Longley, "Memory and Acknowledgement," 157.

49. In a public reading of "The Butchers," Longley noted that it is "about the emptiness of vengeance" ("Michael Longley" [BBC broadcast]). He also has related to McDonald, in terms recalling the purges occurring within its text, that the poem "was a cleansing, a catharsis. I was purging feelings of distaste — distaste for Northern Ireland and its filthy sectarianism, for the professional career I'd pursued for twenty years, for Public Life and its toxins" (M. Longley, "Interview with Michael Longley" [McDonald]).

50. M. Longley, "Interview with Michael Longley" [Broom], 21.

51. Yeats, *Collected Poems,* 190.

52. M. Longley, "Michael Longley: An Interview" [Harper], 61.

53. Broom, "Learning about Dying," 110, 111.

54. McKay, *Northern Protestants,* 292.

55. Kennedy, "Northern Ireland."

56. Peters, "Interfaith."

57. Heritage Lottery Fund, "Digging Deeper Speaker Summary."

58. Quoted in ibid., 15.

59. E. Longley, "Opening Up," 24–25.

60. Quoted in Wells, *People behind the Peace*, 40.

61. Quoted in ibid., 41–42.

62. Ibid., 45.

63. Quoted in Gebler, *Glass Curtain*, 108.

64. As Duncan B. Forrester has argued, Christianity can make a singularly important contribution to political reconciliation, despite public misapprehension of the applicability of the Gospel to the political sphere: "There remains the widespread assumption that reconciliation and forgiveness belong in some religious sphere and are relevant in face-to-face relationships, but do not belong in politics. Traditionally, this position has sometimes been grounded in theories of the two kingdoms: reconciliation, grace and forgiveness belong in the spiritual sphere, while the temporal sphere operates on quite other principles. In modern days similar conclusions flow from the assumption that theological language is simply the in-house converse of the Church and can have no validity in the public realm. It is not too hard to show that this leads to a massive impoverishment of public political discourse, as well as a drastic narrowing and domestication of theological language. . . . So the Church and theology in their responsibility to God for the political sphere have to offer an account of reality, a language which is adequate to the intractable problems of politics, and a call to respond creatively to the reconciliation which has been achieved in Christ" ("Politics and Reconciliation," 112–13).

65. M. Longley, "Memory and Acknowledgement," 156.

66. Ibid., 157–58.

67. Dawson, *Making Peace*, 77.

68. Ibid., 79.

69. M. Longley, "Interview with Michael Longley" [Broom], 24.

70. Post and Turner, *Feast*, 115–16.

71. Ibid., 116.

FOUR. **Fragility and Ceremony**

1. M. Longley, "Interview with Michael Longley" [Healy], 557.

2. M. Longley, "Interview: Michael Longley" [Randolph], 295.

3. M. Longley, "Tongue at Play," 121.

4. Quoted in Buell, *Future of Environmental Criticism*, 50.

5. M. Longley, "Brendan Corcoran and Michael Longley," 116.

6. There are other Longley poems, however, that require us to slow our reading. Lyon, in "Michael Longley's Lists," 242, has pointed out that in "The

Ice-cream Man" "the lack of verbs, the rich unfamiliarity of so many of the flowers' names, the coming together of such a profusion of consonants and vowel sounds, the crafted balancing of polysyllables and monosyllables all make for attentively slow reading."

7. Cabot, "Big Man," 23.

8. Viney, "Michael in Mayo," 122.

9. M. Longley, "Playing Football," 9.

10. M. Longley, "Reading Notes" [folder 22]. Cabot, "Big Man," 24, reckons that "about one third of his poetry has been inspired here."

11. Lyon, "Michael Longley's Lists," 228–34.

12. Tim Robinson, in *Setting Foot,* delineates the great variety of these flowers. He points out that the limestone provides strikingly different habitats for flowers ranging from those normally associated with mild climes to those associated with alpine climes: "The limestone offers plants some very specialized habitats, of which two form a strikingly complementary pair. Down in the grykes, as the enlarged fissures are called, all is shadowy, still and dank; ferns such as the hart's-tongue and maidenhair thrive in this atmosphere from a Victorian bottle-garden. But the horizontal surfaces (the clints) between the grykes are dry and brilliantly sunlit, exposed to strong winds and searchingly grazed by cattle, goats and rabbits. Wherever a thimbleful of humus has accumulated some plant will root, of a sort adapted to these spartan conditions rather than to, say, the hurly-burly of a buttercup-meadow. Thus, close to the maidenhair fern, which is a plant of the mild, Atlantic side of southern Europe, one finds here species associated with severe sub-arctic or alpine climates, such as those two starts of the late May Burren show, the vivid blue spring gentian and the delicate, ivory-silk-petalled mountain avens" (47).

13. M. Longley, "Tongue at Play," 115.

14. This very long list also feels like something tangible Longley retreats into as an anodyne.

15. As Neil Corcoran has pointed out in his thoughtful reading of this poem, the linkage of the rhyming of the ice cream man's flavors suggests that "the activity of the ice-cream shop [is] a kind of poetry too and, in doing so, indicates something entirely characteristic of Longley: an aesthetic unpresumptuousness in which other—it may seem more mundane—activities are accorded a properly generous appreciation" (Corcoran, "My Botanical Studies," 105). For a less consoling reading of the poem, see Brearton, "Cenotaphs of Snow," which argues, citing Longley's remark that "a list like this one is meant to go on forever," that "the poem destabilizes its own achievement," since "the listing . . . is rhythmically slightly unsettled, particularly in the penultimate line: it looks in-

cantatory, but it sounds far more hesitant than that. That the list reaches further than the opening list of flavours marks its failure at consolation: one might list for ever, but the death still occurred" (185).

16. Belknap, "Literary List," 35–36.

17. Ibid., 47.

18. McDonald insightfully notes the intimacy of this poem and the way the poem draws on similar scenes in *The Winter's Tale* and in "Lycidas," arguing that its elegiac impulse depends upon its immediate environment and concluding by noting, "Such consolation as 'The Ice-cream Man' offers is fragile, and will dissolve altogether when taken out of the intimacy of its surroundings; any elegiac impulse is undercut by the pressure of actuality, so that Milton's closing reflection on the list of flowers in 'Lycidas' has relevance also to Longley's poem: 'For so, to interpose a little ease, / Let our frail thoughts dally with false surmise' (152–3)" (*MI*, 72).

19. Lyon, "Michael Longley's Lists," 236. In *CPL*, presumably to preserve their original order, Longley returns to the concluding order of *Gorse Fires*, with "The Ice-cream Man" as the third-to-last poem in the volume, followed by "Trade Winds," and "The Butchers."

20. M. Longley, "Interview: Michael Longley" [Randolph], 305.

21. However, a case can certainly be made for Longley's unease in urban Belfast as well. See, for example, Kennedy-Andrews's compelling discussion of the connection between Longley's provisional sense of home in Belfast in poems such as "Wounds," where the domestic space is violated in the poem's conclusion, and his home away from home in Carrigskeewaun, where disturbances—naturally occurring ones and more unnatural ones such as the news of violence from Belfast—have often intruded in poems such as "The West" (*Writing Home*, 139–40).

22. McGuckian, "Michael Longley," 216.

23. M. Longley, "Sketches from Britain."

24. Edna Longley has described the "implicitly Protestant poetic entry into western Catholic communities" in the poetry of Louis MacNeice and of Michael Longley as one that "tends to walk on tiptoe" ("Pastoral Theologies," 126).

25. McDonald, "Faiths and Fidelities," 71.

26. M. Longley, "Playthings for the Soul." Thus I disagree with Gerald Dawe's contention that Longley's "very indirection masks, through the sheer force of 'ordinary' detail and its concentration as 'artfulness,' the uncertainty and ambivalence that influences his self-awareness as a poet" ("'Icons and Lares,'" 227).

27. Peacock, "Michael Longley," 272.

28. M. Longley, "Interview," [Randolph], 305.

29. M. Longley, "Book Review," emphasis mine.

30. In the process, he implies both the presence of abundant stone monuments in this area and the association in his mind of these earlier "buildings" with the modern concrete dwellings and office buildings of Belfast. Robinson has pointed out the presence of some three hundred to four hundred ringforts, "scores of cashels and hundreds of lesser ringforts," the "webs of ancient field-walls," and the roughly sixty unexplored wedge tombs in the Burren—all in addition to its natural karst stonescape (*Setting Foot*, 48–49).

31. Craig, "Michael Longley's Belfast," 33.

32. M. Longley, "Longley Tapes," 14.

33. M. Longley, "Poet at Work."

34. M. Longley, "Book Review."

35. M. Longley, "Provocation of Orchids."

36. M. Longley, "Michael Longley: An Interview" [Harper], 61–62.

37. The tone and attitude of this poem are of a piece with what Robert Welch has identified as a strain in Longley that is "from the moralist aesthetic of English Protestant poetic tradition" ("Michael Longley and the West," 54). One of these characteristics of this strain, which according to Welch all Irish poets who write in English share, is a sense "that it is best to face the hard road of effort and duty rather than submit to the allure of emotion or sentiment" (54).

38. M. Longley, "Interview" [Randolph], 297.

39. Owen, *The Poems of Wilfred Owen*, 76.

40. Joe O'Toole was memorialized in "Between Hovers" (*GF*, 5).

41. Peacock, "How Do You Sew," 167.

42. Dawe, "'Icons and Lares,'" 222.

43. Montague, "Letter to Michael Longley."

44. There, Longley suggests "that, like much of the best art in Ulster, the Folk Museum is the product of such courage [to be parochial in Kavanagh's approving sense of the term]. Its founders recognized, with Kavanagh, that 'parochialism is universal; it deals with fundamentals'" ("I," 8). See Longley, "Patrick Kavanagh" for further insight into his understanding of Kavanagh and his work.

45. M. Longley, "Medbh McGuckian's Poetry."

46. M. Longley, "Thought for the Day."

47. M. Longley, "Walking Forwards," 39. See also M. Longley, "Brendan Corcoran and Michael Longley," 115, where Longley muses, "Adorno's statement that after Auschwitz there can be no poetry—I feel that unless poetry addresses such subjects—such as Auschwitz or the things happening now—there's no future for it really. What's the point of poetry then?"

48. M. Longley, "Interview with Michael Longley" [Healy], 561.

49. Writing in 1967, the poet and critic Stephen Spender captures this difficulty well when he suggests that "it is almost impossible . . . to those of us for whom the truths are things we read about, even to imagine the realities of tormentors and victims. A result of this is that it has become a problem for the writer to relate the small circle of his private experience to the immense circumference of contemporary human violence and suffering" (quoted in Langer, *Holocaust*, 23).

50. Brewster, "Rites of Defilement," 307. Brewster's citation of Lyotard is from that writer's *Heidegger and the Jews*, 8.

51. Schwarz, *Imagining the Holocaust*, 37.

52. Warman, "Precision and Suggestion," 52.

53. M. Longley, "Q. and A.," 22.

54. Tannahill, "More Than Just a Day Job," 116–17.

55. M. Longley, "Interview with Michael Longley" [Healy], 558.

56. M. Longley, "Memory and Acknowledgement," 156.

57. Ibid., 156.

58. M. Longley, *Poems, 1963–1983*, 206. David Wheatley notes that "Captain Robert Nairac was one of the most notorious British undercover agents in Northern Ireland. . . . According to legend Nairac's body was disposed of in a meat processing plant" ("That Blank Mouth," 7).

59. Brearton, "Snow Poet."

60. He must feel that he is a double miracle because the top of his father's penis was severed during an engagement in World War I; if it had been left untreated, he surely would have become impotent. As Longley notes in *Tuppenny Stung*, "His children owe their existence to skilled medical orderlies" (19). I suspect that Longley's many elegies about the war poets from that conflict stem in part from his vicarious sense of survivor's guilt, inherited from his father.

61. Concerning "Terezin" and its marriage of form and content, Longley told McDonald in an interview that its compression was purposeful since "I wanted my poem to approach the condition of silence" (M. Longley, "Interview with Michael Longley" [McDonald]).

62. M. Longley, "Memory and Acknowledgement," 157.

63. Several years later, Longley would redeploy snow as a symbol of remembrance in his World War I poem "The Cenotaph": "They couldn't wait to remember and improvised / A cenotaph of snow and a snowman soldier, / Inscribing 'Lest We Forget' with handfuls of stones" (*WJ*, 26).

64. M. Longley, "Interview with Michael Longley" [McDonald].

65. M. Longley, "Interview" [Randolph], 308.

66. Quoted in Howard, "Why Did the Buddhadharma," 71.

67. Ibid., 73.

68. Ibid. See 73–74 for an explanation of how traditional Japanese poetry, painting, and the tea ceremony are linked through Zen Buddhism.

69. Longley's interest in Asian art may have been sparked by his long-standing interest in the paintings of Felim Egan. He has praised Egan for his faithfulness to the Japanese penchant for compression: "Felim Egan has never been more true to the Japanese concept of karumi: not a brush-stroke or syllable too many. His habitual understatement grows more assured, his spare lyricism more eloquent. Purged of rhetoric, Beckettian almost, earthy and yet ethereal, his is a pianissimo world where whimsy swells into vision" ("Playthings for the Soul").

70. Longley, "Observing the Sons," 113. His conviction of this truth has remained remarkably consistent over the years: see, for example, his 1985 interview with Johnstone (M. Longley, "Longley Tapes," 24), where he emphatically argues that "the poet does have important responsibilities: to be as efficient and vigilant a custodian of the language as he can be, to be as true as possible to his own emotions and thoughts, and not to tell lies of any kind."

71. Ling, "Double Design," 40.

72. M. Longley, "Interview" [Randolph], 307.

73. Allen, "Normal Love."

74. M. Longley, "Fire in the Window," 8.

75. See McDonald's review of *Snow Water,* however, for what he sees as some startling ways in which the poems in this volume are open "to increased levels of strangeness and unpredictability," a characteristic McDonald finds new in the poet's work ("Cold Comfort").

76. M. Longley, "Brendan Corcoran and Michael Longley," 112.

77. Buell, *Future of Environmental Criticism,* 56.

FIVE. "To Make Myself an Echo Chamber"

The quote in the title is from Heaney's "Learning from Eliot," 37. The two epigraphs are from Heaney's "Belfast," 34, and Deane's "Seamus Heaney," 178–79.

1. Garratt, *Modern Irish Poetry,* 261.

2. Edna Longley, for example, in "Poetics of Celt and Saxon" (80–89), devotes several pages to arguing that Heaney's work adheres to this binary. Terry Eagleton replicates many early critics' praise of Heaney's verse as "expe-

riential" and dismisses him as an intellectual writer in an otherwise sensitive review of *Field Work* (1979): "But it is perhaps not surprising that he has been praised by a criticism which invests deeply in 'experience' and little in 'ideas.' On the latter score, Heaney does not show up particularly well in a comparison with much less technically accomplished writers, even if there is little to fault him on the former" ("Review of *Field Work*," 105).

3. A complete list of Heaney's Belfast Group poems is available online at http://chaucer.library.emory.edu/irishpoet/workshop/index.html.

4. In discussing Heaney's well-known move, beginning in *Wintering Out*, to "compressed, mostly two-stress lines, unrhymed, arranged in slender quatrains" as the enabling formal reason for his increased psychic burrowing, Morrison holds that "the rhyming quatrains and pentameters of his early work [*Death of a Naturalist* and *Door into the Dark*] had forced him into a superficial rationalist mode: the wide lines and blockish stanzas lie like planks boarding up the well of his imagination" (*Seamus Heaney*, 45). As this chapter will show, however, Heaney had been writing contemplative, inward poetry from the start of his career.

5. Tobin, *Passage to the Center*, 295.

6. Desmond, *Gravity and Grace*, 6, 3.

7. Heaney, "Writer at Work," 13.

8. Heaney, "Interesting Case," xix.

9. Heaney, "Makings of a Music," 62.

10. Ibid., 63.

11. Heaney, "Learning from Eliot," 36. Elmer Andrews has previously cited this passage and applied it to Heaney's poetry in much the same way I am doing (*Poetry of Seamus Heaney*, 6). I would add, though, that Andrews misunderstands Heaney's Wordsworthian composition process by contrasting it explicitly with that of Yeats's seemingly sole emphasis on poetry as a laborious making, citing an interview Heaney conducted with Patrick Garland in 1973 as evidence: "When he talked about poetry, Yeats never talked about the 'ooze' or 'nurture.' He always talked about the 'labour' and the 'making' and the 'fascination of what's difficult'" (quoted in *Poetry of Seamus Heaney*, 7). As this chapter and subsequent ones show, Heaney has learned to draw on another aspect of Yeats's theory of poetic reception, one closely akin to his own theory of "technique"— that of the trancelike surrender to the rhythm of buried words and phrases in the subconscious mind—as inspiration for his own growing fascination with poetic reception and mental exploration.

12. Heaney, "Learning from Eliot," 37, emphasis mine.

13. Heaney, "Above the Brim," 72.

14. Ibid., 75.

334   Notes to pages 172–175

15. John Keats's privileging of unheard over "heard melodies" in his "Ode on a Grecian Urn" has also been instructive for Heaney in this conception of himself as an echo chamber for the melody of the embryonic poem, as he has recently told Mike Murphy: "What you hear in the sanctum of yourself, that which strikes you as true, convinces you, steadies you—to provide that kind of heard melody is the function of poetry. To get into the true place by the truth in the language and the life of it" (Heaney, "Seamus Heaney," in *Reading the Future*, 92).

16. See stanza 7 of "An Open Letter": "And what price then, self-preservation? / Your silence is an abdication" (*Open Letter*, 8).

17. Hart, *Seamus Heaney*, 8. See, too, Grant, who argues in defense of Heaney's relative political fence-sitting that "poets are concerned to bring to the surface complex feeling structures that force us to reshape or reassess conventional categories of naming and labeling, and this is what Heaney means when he says that poetry always 'implies a politics' [in *Place and Displacement*, 8] even when it is not explicitly political" (*Literature, Rhetoric*, 48).

18. Heaney, "Through-Other Places," 405–6.

19. Donoghue, "Yeats," 46.

20. Heaney, "Interview with Seamus Heaney" [Wylie and Kerrigan], 132–33. Heaney uses similar language in linking his childhood Catholicism to his development as a poet when speaking to Karl Miller: "For a poet, the one invaluable thing about a Catholic upbringing is the sense of the universe you're given, the sense of a light-filled, Dantesque, shimmering order of being. You conceive of yourself at the beginning as a sort of dewdrop, in the big web of things, and I think that this is the very stuff of lyric poetry" (Heaney, "Conversation," 36).

21. Desmond, *Gravity and Grace*, 12.

22. Welch, "Sacrament and Significance," 108. In his interview with Karl Miller, Heaney implicitly endorses this sacramental understanding of the profound significance of every living thing and suggests it is a response to being taught that God knows and cares about our every thought: "I'm coming to believe that there may have been something far more important in my mental formation than cultural nationalism or the British presence or any of that stuff: namely, my early religious education. From a very early age, my consciousness was always expanding in response to the expanding universe of Catholic teaching about eternity and the soul and the sacraments and the mystical body and the infinite attentiveness of the Creator to the minutiae of your inmost thoughts" (Heaney, "Conversation," 32).

23. Welch, "Sacrament and Significance," 113.

24. Hart, *Seamus Heaney*, 4.

25. Cavanagh, *Professing Poetry*, 201.

26. Eagleton, "Review of *Field Work*," 103.

27. Heaney himself has flatly rejected Marxist theories of literature, stating in his review of the editors' efforts in *The Penguin Book of English Pastoral Verse* that "The Marxist broom sweeps the poetic enterprise clean of those somewhat hedonistic impulses towards the satisfactions of aural and formal play out of which poems arise" ("In the Country," 174).

28. Foster was the first critic to note that "not only are Heaney's poems about manual work on the farm—ploughing, planting, harvesting, horseshoeing, etc.—but they are themselves manuals on how the work is actually done. It is amusing, for instance, to set 'Churning Day' beside E. Estyn Evans's account of churning in *Irish Heritage* (1942) and *Irish Folk Ways* (1957). Heaney in such a poem is folklorist, recalling old customs that survived into his native Londonderry of the 1940s" ("Poetry of Seamus Heaney," 82–83). Writing much later, Vendler essentially repeats Foster's earlier argument about Heaney as folklorist, asserting that "he makes himself into an anthropologist of his own culture, and testifies, in each poem, to his profound attachment to the practice described while not concealing his present detachment from rural life" (*Seamus Heaney*, 18).

29. Boly, "Beloved Mentors," 146.

30. Heaney, "Conversation," 32.

31. Ibid., 29.

32. Deane, *Celtic Revivals*, 175.

33. Windows are always liminal objects that often catapult the mind into reverie, as the farmhouse window in Derry does here for Heaney's mind.

34. Molino, *Questioning Tradition*, 8.

35. Brown, "Witnessing Eye," 182.

36. Morrison, *Seamus Heaney*, 26.

37. Yeats, *Collected Poems*, 80.

38. Weeks, "Nobel Winner," 1C.

39. Molino, *Questioning Tradition*, 10–11.

40. Eliot, "Music of Poetry," 38.

41. Vendler, *Seamus Heaney*, 29.

42. Frazier, "Anger and Nostalgia," 18.

43. Frazier feels the opening simile comparing pen and gun is "awkward, rammed into the poem," and notes that "in this collection weapons are buried all over the farm: *grenades, safety-catch, armoury, gun-barrel, cache, bombs* all turn up in *Death of a Naturalist*" (ibid., 17). Frazier persuasively cites a small scattering of poems later in his essay that seem to support his claim (24–32). But Heaney clearly takes pains to dissociate himself from such implements of violence.

44. Foster, "Poetry of Seamus Heaney," 89.

45. See for example, Heaney's essays "Out of London's Troubles" and "Old Derry's Walls." See Corcoran (*Seamus Heaney,* 26–28) for other angry examples, however, such as Heaney's ironic contribution of a song—"Craig's Dragoons," set "to the Loyalist tune, 'Dolly's Brae'"—to Sean O'Riada's program on Radio Eireann in the aftermath of the Derry civil rights march on October 5, 1968 (26); his song lamenting the dead civil rights marchers of Bloody Sunday, which I discuss in chapter 6 (27); and his poem "Intimidation" criticizing the July 12 loyalist bonfires, published in the *Malahat Review* in 1970 (28).

46. The best prosodic reading of "Digging" can be found in Burris's *Poetry of Resistance,* which argues that "the poem in fact embodies a brief history of the English stanza—in succession appear a couplet, a tercet, a quatrain, and a quintet," and claims, "The burgeoning confidence of the lines derives from the poet's gradual discovery of his subject matter, and this confidence is reflected by the stanzaic patterns" (34).

47. Heaney, "Our Own Dour Way," 15.

48. Brandes, *Seamus Heaney,* 288, 290.

49. Heaney follows with the definition of *technique* given above when I first cited this essay.

50. Stanzas 1 and 4 each feature a full rhyme and a para-rhyme: "wells" and "smells" alternate with "windlasses" and "moss" in the first stanza, while "call" and "tall" alternate with "one" and "reflection" in the fourth stanza (*DN,* 44).

51. Molino, *Questioning Tradition,* 12.

52. "Radio Two Arts Programme."

53. For an early example of Heaney's critique of artistic solipsism, see his November 21, 1969, essay for *Hibernia* about the documentary film *John Hume's Derry,* in which he argues, "Writers may lose their public when they disappear too deeply into the burrow of their own private worlds" ("John Hume's Derry," 766).

54. Morrison argues that "the community Heaney came from, and with which he wanted his poetry to express solidarity, was one on which the pressure of silence weighed heavily. It was not only rural, renowned like all rural communities for its inwardness and reserve, but also Northern Irish and Catholic, with additional reasons for clamming up" (*Seamus Heaney,* 23).

55. Ibid., 24.

56. Ibid., 32.

57. Yeats, *Collected Poems,* 113.

58. Yeats, *W. B. Yeats,* 534.

59. Heaney, "Government of the Tongue," 93.

60. Eliade, *Sacred and the Profane*, 25. Although Eliade's work clearly illuminates Heaney's poem here, John Wilson Foster has told me that Heaney was unfamiliar with Eliade until Foster introduced his work to Heaney in the 1970s or early 1980s and subsequently sent him one of Eliade's books.

61. Arbery, *Why Literature Matters*, 35.

62. Ibid., 35.

63. Grant, *Breaking Enmities*, 60–61. Along with Michael Longley, Heaney is relatively exceptional among contemporary poets in his sacramental or quasi-sacramental approach to his poetry. In this regard, see Michael Schmidt's compelling brief lament about and discussion of the "secularization of imagination" in Schmidt's own generation among poets such as Jeffrey Wainwright, Tom Paulin, Carol Rumens, Jeremy Hooker, and John Ash and its consequent effect on poetry (*Reading Modern Poetry*, 19–29).

64. For the definitive discussion of this sequence, see Foster's "'Lough Neagh Sequence.'"

65. I disagree then, with Edna Longley, who in one of the earliest reviews of these poems argues that "the eel is only one of several portraits of the artist as trail-blazer and torch-bearer" ("*Door into the Dark*," 146). The eelsman, not the eel, is clearly the analogue of the artist in the sequence.

66. As Heaney argues in "Feeling into Words," in discussing the poems of his first two volumes, the dialectic should be properly tipped in favor of technique: "Technique is what allows that first stirring of the mind round a word or an image or a memory to grow towards articulation: articulation not necessarily in terms of argument or explication but in terms of its own potential for harmonious self-reproduction. . . . The crucial action is pre-verbal, to be able to allow the first alertness or come-hither, sensed in a blurred or incomplete way to dilate and approach as a thought or a theme or a phrase" ("FW," 48, 49). As we will see in *Wintering Out*, Heaney chooses craft instead of technique in his deployment of a variety of dialects from Northern Ireland and relative lack of meditative poems.

67. Heaney, "Learning from Eliot," 40. For an excellent analysis of Eliot's influence on Heaney's early poetry through *North*, see Cuda, "Use of Memory." For the definitive discussion of Eliot's influence on Heaney, see Cavanagh, *Professing Poetry*, 74–108.

68. See Heaney, *Munro*, 58–65. Heaney had been commissioned by BBC Northern Ireland in 1970 to write a verse play for its radio series "Books, Plays, and Poems" about Henry Munro, one of several County Down Protestant leaders of the United Irishmen sympathetic to Catholics during the 1798 rebellion. The play clearly admires Munro's regard for Catholics and his courage. See Russell, "Imagining a New Province," 149–51, for an analysis of this play.

69. Heaney, "Conversation," 20.

70. Ibid., 20. As indeed it has been. See plate 10b in Elliott, *Catholics of Ulster*, which depicts a mural of the Great Famine on a wall in the nationalist Ardoyne Avenue in Belfast. Its text reads: "*An Gorta Mor* [the Great Famine]: 'They buried us without shroud nor *[sic]* coffin'—S. Heaney."

71. Surprisingly, the sensitive and thoughtful critic Michael Parker, who has done more than anyone else to contextualize Heaney's poetry in its historical milieu, argues that "Heaney's words remind readers how the Nation's very survival as an imaginative possibility has been underwritten by acts of collective endeavour and sacrifice, and thus, like Yeats's play *[Cathleen ni Houlihan]*, perpetuates the comforting myth that bloody slaughter can reinvigorate and quicken the political will" (*Northern Irish Literature*, 1:66). The poem seems more of a warning about impending violence, however, and the statement from Heaney above makes clear that he laments the misreading of the poem as celebrating such violence.

72. Heaney, "Belfast," 34. Heaney has recently told Mike Murphy how "Bogland" sonically arrived, noting that the first line had come to him when he was in his sister-in-law's flat in Great Russell Street in London and was putting on his pants: "I was . . . putting my leg into the leg of my trousers, and the line came to me. Now that experience of putting your leg deep into the trouser leg is a kind of 'going through' experience, a pleasing, open-ended experience. I felt a buoyancy, an openness, as if things were going to open and tumble out like hay, and I heard this phrase, 'We have no prairies'" (Heaney, "Seamus Heaney," in *Reading the Future*, 85).

73. Heaney notes that memory was the inspiration for his early poetry and thus could be linked with its potent and specifically Irish correlative of the bog: "Since memory was the faculty that supplied me with the first quickening of my own poetry, I had a tentative unrealized need to make a congruence between memory and bogland and, for the want of a better word, our national consciousness" ("FW," 54–55).

74. Heaney, "Yeats As an Example?" 99–100, emphases mine.

75. Heaney, "Interview with Seamus Heaney" [Randall], 13.

six. **"The Road to Derry,"** *Wintering Out,* **and** *North*

1. Lensing, *Poetry, Senator McCarthy*, 16.

2. "The Road to Derry" and "Casualty" are printed together in Campbell and Heron, *Harrowing of the Heart*. See "Casualty" for a transformation of the original line in "The Road to Derry"—"flags like black frost mourning"—into "Whatever black flags waved" ("The Road to Derry," *FW*, 22).

3. M. Parker, *Northern Irish Literature*, 1:296 n. 26.

4. Heaney, "Conversation," 24.

5. Heaney, *Stepping Stones*, 214.

6. Quoted in M. Parker, *Northern Irish Literature*, 1:296 n. 26.

7. The notes to "Boys of Mullaghbawn" [Henry's Songbook] mention the possibility of agrarian offenses or involvement in the 1798 Rising. The notes to the lyrics at the Cantaria Web site for traditional folksongs ("Boys of Mullaghbawn" [Cantaria]) cite Thomas Wall's untitled article in the journal *Ceol* 3 (April 1968) that the boys were transported to Van Diemen's Land for the attempted abduction of an heiress.

8. Heaney, "The Road to Derry."

9. "Boys of Mullaghbawn" [Henry's Songbook].

10. Ibid.

11. Heaney, "Road to Derry."

12. Heaney, *Stepping Stones*, 149 (for his "writerly" motivation); 148, 149 (for Cooke and Landweer's influence); 149 (for the quotation about Saddlemyer); and 150 (for the necessity of his break from other Northern Irish poets).

13. Ibid., 149.

14. Heaney, "Unhappy and at Home," 67.

15. Heaney, "Road to Derry."

16. Heaney, "Saturday Interview," 5, quoted in *SHMP,* 246–47.

17. McCarthy, *Seamus Heaney,* 10.

18. Brown, citing Heaney's brief review of Hewitt's *Collected Poems: 1932–67,* holds that "Seamus Heaney's third volume, *Wintering Out,* employs his province as he tells us Hewitt, by example, enabled Northern Irish writers to do (and this is an aspect of Hewitt's achievement that deserves recognition): 'as a hinterland of reference, should they require a tradition more intimate than the broad perspectives of the English literary achievement'" ("W. R. Rodgers and John Hewitt," 94–95).

19. See Russell, "Seamus Heaney's Regionalism," for a full treatment of Heaney's ethical regionalism in these essays.

20. Paulin, foreword to *Rhyming Weavers,* vii.

21. Morrison, *Seamus Heaney,* 40.

22. For Wall, "Heaney's brief poem 'Nerthus,' the meaning of which hinges on two dialect words, underscores this linguistic complexity: 'For beauty, say an ash-fork staked in peat, / Its long grains gathered to the gouged split; // A seasoned, unsleeved taker of the weather, / Where kesh and loaning finger out to heather.'" Wall argues that "Kesh (<Ir. *Cis*) is a Northern Hiberno-English word for a causeway across a bog (its Southern equivalent is togher, <Ir. *Tochar*). 'Loaning,' of Scots and Northern English origin, is an Ulster-English word for a country

lane. Heaney could, if he wished, have substituted the Ulster-English word 'causey' for the Hiberno-English word 'kesh,' and substituted the Hiberno-English word 'boreen' (<Ir. *Botharin*) for the Ulster-English word 'loaning.' In addition, he could have substituted the Hiberno-English word 'turf,' or the Ulster-English word 'moss,' for the standard-English word 'peat.' Evidence, if such were needed, that Heaney was conscious of these options appears in lyric xxxii of his "Crossings" sequence: "A kesh could mean the track some called a *causey* / Raised above the wetness of the bog, / Or the causey where it bridged old drains and streams" (*ST,* 90). 'Causey' is of English origin, but now obsolete in standard English" (Wall, "Dialect Glossary," 69).

23. Flanagan, "Poetry of Seamus Heaney," xi.

24. Anderson, *Imagined Communities,* 133.

25. Bloom, introduction to *Seamus Heaney,* 2.

26. Heaney, *Among Schoolchildren,* 10. David Wheatley has pointed out about the poem's linguistic evocation of an imagined Northern Irish community that "The unifying vocable presages in microcosm a culture unified enough for the term 'strangers' no longer to carry overtones of sectarian division" ("That Blank Mouth," 6).

27. In the third part of his essay "Belfast," Heaney briefly discusses the Irish origins of these place names and the entrance of two famous strangers who brought with them the advent of the linguistic displacement of Gaelic: "Mossbawn [Heaney's family farm] was bordered by the townlands of Broagh and Anahorish, townlands that are forgotten Gaelic music in the throat, *bruach* and *anach fhior uisce,* the riverbank and the place of clear water. The names lead past the literary mists of a Celtic twilight into that civilization whose demise was effected by soldiers and administrators like [Edmund] Spenser and [Sir John] Davies, whose lifeline was bitten through when the squared-off walls of bawn and demesne dropped on the country like the jaws of a man-trap" (36). As he points out earlier in this essay, *bawn* is a Scots word that signifies "the name the English colonists gave to their fortified farmhouses," while the local "demesne" was "Moyola Park, an estate now occupied by Lord Moyola, formerly Major James Chichester-Clark, ex-Unionist Prime Minister of Northern Ireland" (35).

28. Heaney, *Among Schoolchildren,* 11.

29. Heaney, "Burns's Art Speech," 382. He is being especially inclusive by terming the dialects of Elizabethan English and Ulster Scots "languages," presumably on an equal footing with the Irish language.

30. Ibid., 382.

31. See, for example, Heaney's "From Monaghan," "Placeless Heaven," and "Sense of Place," where he discusses both Kavanagh's and Montague's poetry.

32. Heaney, "Burns's Art Speech," 383.

33. Kennedy, "Mound-Dwellers and Mummers," 304. Kennedy's research draws in part on the research of linguist James Milroy, whose work in turn builds on the research of linguist William Labov, who has argued that class and gender are much more influential in determining dialectical speech than is religion. Milroy's book, *Regional Accents of English: Belfast,* is a pioneering study in the field. His sixth chapter, "Social Variation in Belfast Speech," analyzes the social variations in the speech of male and female speakers in two different age groups, living in three separate religiously homogeneous areas of the city. Overall, Milroy's research in this chapter shows linguistic similarity among older male, originally rural speakers in West Belfast and a different, though still similar vernacular dialect among young males in various parts of the city, demonstrating how class and gender are more important factors than religion in determining dialects and giving credence to Heaney's own efforts to portray speech patterns common to both Northern Irish Catholics and Protestants (Milroy, "Social Variation").

34. Kennedy, "Mound Dwellers and Mummers," 305.

35. Ibid.

36. Ibid., 312.

37. M. Parker, "From *Winter Seeds,*" 136.

38. Heaney, "Englands of the Mind," 156, 150–59.

39. Heaney, "Tradition and an Individual Talent," 196, emphasis mine.

40. Vendler, *Seamus Heaney,* 84.

41. Watson, "Narrow Ground," 211.

42. Hobsbaum's reading of this poem credits Heaney for insight into the relations between Protestants and Catholics, while arguing that Heaney nevertheless implies that his tradition is the native one: "The Catholic way is defined with rueful irony: Heaney is by no means uncritical of his side of the house. But, in his quiet manner, he indicates that it is indigenous. The Protestant is like a stranger in the dark outside, embarrassed by the lovemaking and the weeping within. One can approach him only on the prosaic level of inquiries about the weather or the price of grass-seed. To that extent Heaney's vision is angled, and it would be extraordinary if it were not. Yet what insight into the relationship between two distinct cultures is shown here!" ("Craft and Technique in *Wintering Out,*" 38). Hobsbaum's assertion that Heaney sees his tradition as indigenous falters, however, when the last section of the poem is fully comprehended: Heaney reverses the situation and places himself as the outsider.

43. Heaney, "Frontiers of Writing," 194.

44. Looking back to this poem in a film script broadcast by BBC Northern Ireland in March of 1998, Heaney recalled that "there were times during

the last thirty years when I thought 'The Other Side' might be too consoling. Given the actual conditions on the roads and the streets, I thought it might be too benign, too tender in the face of assassination and explosion, too hopeful. And yet the subject had called words from my inner mind. They had dandered in and reminded me of the possible boundlessness of our sympathies" ("Something to Write Home About," 632).

45. Vendler views this poem as arising from "Heaney's enlarged adult capacity for empathy," and thus as more inclusive than the early dour portrait of a Protestant dockworker in "Docker" from *Death of a Naturalist* or the drummer in "Orange Drums, Tyrone, 1966" in *North* (*Seamus Heaney*, 83). Even Edna Longley, who would attack what she saw as Heaney's tacit endorsement of violent nationalism in *North*, writes approvingly of Heaney's attempt at cultural understanding in "The Other Side," noting that it "brings the two Ulster traditions into relationship and a strange wistful contact" ("Heaney's Hidden Ireland," 88).

46. Foster, *Achievement of Seamus Heaney*, 3.

47. Carson, "'Escaped from the Massacre'?" 183.

48. Harmon, "'We Pine for Ceremony,'" 76.

49. Heaney was speaking here as a participant in the roundtable discussion "Whatever You Say Say Nothing" [BBC].

50. See C. O'Brien's "Slow North-East Wind," E. Longley's "*North*," and Morrison's *Seamus Heaney*, 66–69.

51. Donoghue, "Literature of Trouble," 189.

52. Edna Longley is one of the few commentators to link these bodies from *Death of a Naturalist* with those in *North*, but she argues that they result in "his first embryonic fusion of Catholic experience in the North with the longer national history," which culminates in the poems of *North* ("*North*," 67). She refuses to recognize the multitemporal context of the *North* bog poems, arguing that they do not "offer a universal, Wilfred Owen style image of human suffering" (79).

53. Felski, *Uses of Literature*, 113.

54. Ibid.

55. The only exception to Heaney's bog poems that was not based on a photograph was "Bog Queen," as he has noted in *Stepping Stones*, 158.

56. Sontag, *Regarding the Pain of Others*, 22.

57. See Lange, "Tales from the Bog," who also reports, "The Windeby 'girl' may have lost his hair when archaeologists digging out the body were careless with their trowels. And growth interruptions in the bones indicated that the young man was malnourished and sickly and might have simply died of

natural causes. University of Hamburg archaeologist Michael Gebühr speculates that the body was blindfolded before burial to protect the living from the
gaze of the dead" (87).

58. Cavanagh, *Professing Poetry*, 82. Cavanagh's discussion of beauty in
the bog poems, however, is linked closely to Heaney's recuperation of a particular aspect of T. S. Eliot's criticism as representing the forbidden, and thus Cavanagh does not attend to the ethical implications of Heaney's representation
of the bog bodies as beautiful.

59. Heaney, "Interview with Seamus Heaney" [Mooney].

60. Quoted in Cavanagh, *Professing Poetry*, 82. This phrase from Heaney's
letter was first quoted in Corcoran, *Student's Guide*, 96.

61. Yeats, *Collected Poems*, 180, 181, 182.

62. Ibid., 181.

63. Heaney, "Interview with Seamus Heaney" [Mooney].

64. Grant, *Literature, Rhetoric*, 4.

65. Felski, *Uses of Literature*, 105; on *The Bacchae* and shock, see 110–12.

66. Sontag, *Regarding the Pain of Others*, 76.

67. Donoghue, *Speaking of Beauty*, 85.

68. Sontag, *Regarding the Pain of Others*, 41.

69. Ibid., 42.

70. Scarry, *On Beauty and Being Just*, 72.

71. Ibid., 73–74.

72. Ibid., 107.

73. Ibid., 111.

74. Ibid., 114.

75. Ibid.

76. The translation here is from *New Testament in Modern English*.

77. D. Parker, *Ethics, Theory*, 45.

78. Heaney, "Government of the Tongue," 107.

79. Ibid., 108.

80. Heaney, "Interview with Seamus Heaney," [Mooney].

81. D. Parker, *Ethics, Theory*, 46.

82. Donoghue, "Literature of Trouble," 193.

83. The translation here is from *New Testament in Modern English*.

84. C. O'Brien reads "Punishment" very differently, and his attitude typi-
fies the disgust evinced toward *North* by several critics at the time, including
Ciaran Carson and Edna Longley: "The poet here appears as part of his people's
assumption that, since the girl has been punished by the IRA, she must indeed
be guilty: a double assumption—that she did in fact, inform on the IRA and

that informing on the IRA is a crime. The IRA—nowhere directly referred to—are Furies with an 'understood' role and place in the tribe. . . . The word 'exact' fits the situation as it is felt to be: and it is because it fits, and because other situations, among the rival population, turn on similarly oiled pivots, that hope succumbs" ("Slow North-East Wind," 404). O'Brien's reading is difficult to sustain from a close reading of the poem, and in the light of Heaney's life-long approval of reconciliation.

85. E. Longley, "*North*," 86.

86. Hobsbaum, "Craft and Technique," 40.

87. E. Longley, "*North*," 87.

88. Heaney, "Government of the Tongue," 92.

89. Ibid., 92.

90. Ibid., 93.

91. Quoted in ibid., 93.

92. Ibid., 107, emphasis mine.

93. See Frazier, "Anger and Nostalgia," for an interesting reading of how "North" follows the example of Yeats in affirming Heaney's poetic vocation by "the theatrical way it stages the self in a moment of vision" (13). Frazier further argues, wrongly, I might add, that "the poem is written in the first person; it is meditative, world-historical, self-dramatizing, and declarative in ways characteristic of Yeats, but up until that point not characteristic of Heaney, who had been accustomed to representing himself as a child or not representing himself at all" (13). In "North," Heaney may be, as Frazier claims, "the mage under the spotlight in a symbolist theatre of Yeats's design" (14), but while Heaney may have been channeling Yeats here, the poem is continuous with many of the earlier poems such as "Digging," "The Forge," and others in its metapoetic exploration of the poet's role, often by analogy with rural craftsmen, giving the lie to Frazier's claim that the earlier poems about such craftsmen leave "the poet largely off stage" (14). The shift to first-person narrative in "North" instead suggests that Heaney's concerns about poetry and its autonomy in the face of violent pressures are now fully worked out and confidently represented, whereas in the earlier poems they were somewhat obscured by the seemingly detached third-person narration and the tentative, explorative quality of that work.

94. Cleary, "Fork-Tongued," 227.

95. A number of years later, after winning an award from the Ireland Fund in recognition of "his work promoting Ireland and England," Heaney was interviewed by Seamus McKee. McKee asks Heaney, "The citation refers to a book of essays of yours 'as a symbol of the desire for a nonviolent solution to our problems,' this on the whole theme of the use of words. . . . How comfortable are

you with that notion of the poet's role?" Heaney's response affirms the exact use of language in promoting sympathy among human beings: "The citation was written by Josephine Hart . . . [who] meant that what every person, I suppose, has to believe, the honest correct and exact use of language leads towards an exact and truthful relationship. And I am very happy with that notion—that a kind of honesty, a kind of accuracy, and of course, a kind of sympathy is promoted by the activity of the imagination. If people had more exact imagining and more sympathetic sense of the other and the diversity of life, it would promote a better society really" ("Good Morning Ulster").

96. E. O'Brien, *"North,"* 16, 17.

97. In *Crediting Poetry,* Heaney reflects on this stage in his life and his torturing of himself by taking on the burden of the world's woes in language that echoes the closing lines of "Exposure": "For years I was bowed to the desk like some monk bowed over his prie-dieu, some dutiful contemplative pivoting his understanding in an attempt to bear his portion of the weight of the world, knowing himself incapable of heroic virtue or redemptive effect, but constrained by his obedience to his rule to repeat the effort and the posture. *Blowing up sparks for a meagre heat.* Forgetting faith, straining toward good works. Attending insufficiently to the diamond absolutes, among which must be counted the sufficiency of that which is absolutely imagined. Then finally and happily, and not in obedience to the dolorous circumstances of my native place but in despite of them, I straightened up" (*CP,* 19–20, emphasis mine).

98. Paulin, "Political Verse," 129.

SEVEN. *Field Work* through *The Haw Lantern*

1. Heaney, "Interview with Seamus Heaney" [Randall], 20.

2. Deane, "Seamus Heaney," 182.

3. Heaney, "Poems of the Dispossessed Repossessed," 32.

4. In the James Randall interview, Heaney also uses the word *natural* about his relationship with O'Neill: "We had a natural, sympathetic understanding of each other" (Heaney, "Interview with Seamus Heaney" [Randall], 21).

5. Morrison has pointed out how this sartorial imagery "suggests the oppressiveness of the *Lumpenproletariat* ('swad' used to mean 'mass' or 'clump' and 'swaddish' means 'loutish'); and 'braced' and 'bound' are similarly destructive of the perfect commonalty that might have been suggested by the image of the ring. The tribe here begins to seem a threat to independence" (*Seamus Heaney,* 80). For the first use of a form of "swaddling" in Heaney's poetry, see "Strange Fruit"

from *North*, which more directly rejects tribal violence than "Casualty" seems to on a first reading. In that poem, line 3 describes archeologists working to preserve the head of an ancient woman found in a bog as having "unswaddled the wet fern of her hair"; *unswaddled* has a positive connotation here of revealing a victim of violence who has been trapped and hidden (*N*, 32).

6. Eliade, *Sacred and the Profane*, 69.

7. Corcoran, *Poetry of Seamus Heaney*, 138.

8. *Aislings* often portrayed a narrator who would fall asleep and meet a fairy woman. The *aisling* form still appeared in amatory verse as late as the eighteenth century, but it was largely a propaganda tool for the Jacobite cause, used to promote political deliverance after the Williamite war and the enactment of penal laws against Catholics. It was thus a natural form for Thomas Kinsella to turn to in "Butcher's Dozen" in protest of the Widgery Tribunal's ruling, which attempted to discredit the Catholic civil rights cause in Northern Ireland.

9. McCormack, "Irish Gothic and After," 831.

10. Ibid., 850.

11. I discuss the massacre alluded to by Heaney here in my discussion of Longley's "The Linen Workers" in chapter 3. While Longley movingly wrote of the men's material remains, Heaney was struck by a tender gesture immediately before the attack: the lone Catholic in the group, whose hand was squeezed by one of his Protestant workmates to prevent him from moving forward to what the workmate thought was certain death, but who stepped forward anyway, determined to spare the lives of his Protestant workmates in what he thought was a loyalist attack (it turned out to be an IRA attack and this sole man was spared). Reflecting on this atrocity in an interview with Karl Miller, Heaney told him musingly, "The frailty of that gesture is all we have to go on" (Heaney, "Conversation," 25).

12. See Ramazani, *Poetry of Mourning*, 335. See 334–60 for Ramazani's full and surefooted discussion of Heaney's elegies.

13. All of these functions of the elegy, as the editors of the *New Princeton Encyclopedia of Poetry and Poetics* note, respond to the experience of loss: "lament, by expressing grief and deprivation; praise by idealizing the deceased and preserving . . . his memory among the living; and consolation, by finding solace in meditation on natural continuances or on moral, metaphysical, and religious values" (Brogan, Sacks, and Fogle, "Elegy," 324).

14. Heaney, *Commencement Address*, 9–10.

15. Ibid., 15–16.

16. This poem is continuous with earlier poems such as "Digging" and "The Forge" in carrying out the preserving work of cultural anthropology in its evocation of a traditional Ulster harvest ritual, the harvest bow or knot. See

Paterson's *Harvest Home* for a detailed appreciation of other rural Northern Irish harvest customs, including the cutting of the Calliagh (the last sheaf of the grain), the Churn (the special meal that followed the cutting ceremony), and Harvest Home (the name for the entire ceremony of the last day of the harvest).

17. Corcoran, *Poetry of Seamus Heaney,* 32–33.

18. Ibid., 33.

19. Heaney, introduction to *Sweeney Astray,* n. pag.

20. Ibid.

21. This phrase occurs in a 1985 interview with Mitchell Harris in *An Gael.* In the interview, Heaney explains why the unionist population of the North should feel included by this particular translation: "Part of my intention of doing *Sweeney* was in the deepest (and least, I hope, offensive) sense political. I wanted the Unionist population to feel that they could adhere to it, that something could be shared. For example, names and landscapes. And that's why I changed all of the place names into their modern equivalents. This is hopefully very subtle. . . . Glens of Antrim, Dunseverick, Bushmills, Strangford, County Down, . . . these are all places which are kind of sacral Unionist sites in some ways. So [there is] a little subversive intent saying beneath this layer, there's Sweeney. . . . I wanted the *Sweeney* to be a help; something that Ulstermen of both persuasions could have some identity with. You see, the problem with translations from the Irish is that, on the whole they have been perceived—and *Sweeney* will too, of course— be perceived as a . . . declaration of Sinn Fein culture. But I think Sweeney's different because he's from the North, he's from Antrim, I did him, and he's got all these places. . . . In a hundred years' time . . . ideally *[Sweeney]* would be part of some united Ulster mythology" (quoted in Richtarik, *Acting between the Lines,* 150).

22. Heaney, "Earning a Rhyme," 68.

23. Ibid., 70.

24. See Russell, "Imagining a New Province," for an extended analysis of Heaney's attempt to develop a unifying Northern Irish regionalism through his early poetry and through a series of BBC Northern Ireland Radio broadcasts in the late 1960s and early 1970s.

25. Heaney, "Placeless Heaven," 5.

26. Heaney, "From Monaghan," 120.

27. Heaney, "Placeless Heaven," 5.

28. Heaney, "Edwin Muir," 269.

29. Heaney's continued immersion in Yeats's poetry also enabled him to conceive of the mind's unlimited potential. As he has recently noted in his introduction to a selection of Yeats's poetry, his reading of "A Dialogue of Self and Soul" led him to realize that "the expansiveness arises from a confidence

that the mind is its own place and within it great distances can be imagined and traversed at will" (Heaney, introduction to *W. B. Yeats*, xvi).

30. Heaney, "Placeless Heaven," 5.

31. Polanyi, *Tacit Dimension*, 4.

32. Ibid., 18.

33. Heaney, "Poet as a Christian," 604.

34. See Hart's discussion of how Catholic meditation techniques such as those found in the Spiritual Exercises of St. Ignatius Loyola and in St. Theresa of Avilla and St. John of the Cross have influenced Heaney's work and how Heaney has reinvigorated and personalized these practices (*Seamus Heaney*, 32–48). Although Hart's chapter focuses on the meditative qualities of poems from *Door into the Dark*, it nonetheless is helpful in delineating these Catholic meditative influences upon the poet, practices that he revisits again explicitly in *Station Island*.

35. Tobin, *Passage to the Center*, 177.

36. Hufstader, "Coming into Consciousness," 61–62.

37. Turner and Turner, *Image and Pilgrimage*, 34.

38. Ibid., 249–50.

39. See Molino's explication of the "Station Island" sequence for a detailed, thoughtful reading of the significance of the various ghosts and the implication of the sequence for Heaney himself, which Molino sees as a purgation of survivor's guilt "when violence and death befalls others around him" (*Questioning Tradition*, 146, 146–67).

40. Polanyi, *Tacit Dimension*, 23.

41. Vendler argues that "the poem both implicitly and explicitly asks, again and again, the question of male vocation. 'If you did not follow my path' (the young priest might ask), 'why not?' 'If you are like me' (a writer such as Joyce might say), 'why are you still in Ireland?' 'If you write poetry' (a victim might cry), 'what good is it to me?'" (*Seamus Heaney*, 94).

42. Joyce's multivocal influence on Heaney here gives some credence to Dillon Johnston's claim that in contemporary Irish poetry "Joyce leads the shift from a single point of view to a more dramatic form of narration in which the reader arrives at judgments formerly proclaimed by the narrator. As no insignificant byproduct of this narrative shift, Joyce suggests to the [subsequent] Irish poets a way of freeing their vision from historical determinism which has had a killing hold on the Irish consciousness" (*IP*, 33). As I have tried to make clear, though, and as my discussion of *Seeing Things* in the next chapter demonstrates, Heaney is also heavily influenced by Yeats, especially in his essentially liminal poetic stance.

43. Fussell, *Abroad*, 39.

44. Ibid., 39.

45. Ibid.

46. Greer, "Station Island," 118.

47. Bolton, "'Customary Rhythms,'" 209.

48. Heaney, "Writer at Work," 13.

49. Heaney, "God in the Tree," 189.

50. Ibid., 189.

51. Heaney, "Frontiers of Writing," 190.

52. Johnston, "Seamus Heaney and Violence," 126.

53. Heaney, "Place of Writing," 19.

54. Ibid., 20. Heaney employs language similar to that in his earlier essay "The Placeless Heaven: Another Look at Kavanagh": "When he writes about places now, they are luminous spaces within his mind . . . and exist instead as transfigured images, sites where the mind projects its own force" (5).

55. Heaney, "Place of Writing," 20.

56. For a specific discussion of "From the Frontier of Writing" as a particularly subversive type of postcolonial poem that partially accords with Heaney's argument in "The Place of Writing: W. B. Yeats and Thoor Ballylee" that "the poetic imagination in its strongest manifestation imposes its vision upon a place rather than accepts a vision from it," see Herron, "Spectaculars," 185–91. Herron finally argues that the concluding receding image of the soldiers in the windscreen of the speaker's car is manipulated subtly by the poet: he has, as it were, "posted" the soldiers "into circulation" so that "they, and the power invested in them, empty out onto the surface of the windscreen and the poem. They evaporate like specters; they dematerialize; they enter into the imaginary" (191). For an interesting theoretical discussion of the sense of place generally in Heaney's work using theoretical terms adopted from Jacques Derrida and Emanuel Levinas, see E. O'Brien, *Seamus Heaney*, passim.

EIGHT. **Redressing Reality**

1. Heaney, introduction to *Redress of Poetry*, xii. For an extended religious reading of Heaney's poetry that takes this statement as its inspiration, see Dau's "Seamus Heaney's Religious Redress." And for a powerfully sustained close reading of Heaney's conception of the redress of poetry, see McDonald, *Serious Poetry*, 85–94, in which he identifies poetry's verbal authority as Heaney's overriding concern: "The weight of emphasis which *The Redress of Poetry* places on

poetry as 'a process of language' means that Heaney's criticism brings along with it many assumptions and implications that repay questioning, especially those which shed some light on the nature, as Heaney sees it, of the language of poetry and the possibility of its answerable relation to the quotidian environment in which it is read as well as written" (88). McDonald praises Heaney for having "instincts about the power of poetic language [that] are sound" but criticizes him for "his sense of the specific dimensions of such language [that] can seem at times constrained by the pressing purposes of his own art" (91).

2. Heaney, "Connection."

3. The two poems are in Yeats, *Collected Poems*, 126 and 187 respectively. Heaney discusses "The Cold Heaven" in his essay "Joy or Night."

4. Ibid., 125.

5. Heaney, "Connection."

6. The passage is familiar, but I quote it to show how Heaney's conception of the individual mind is seemingly similar to, yet fundamentally different from, Yeats's concept of the *Anima Mundi*. Although Yeats articulates three doctrines of magic, the relevant one for our purposes is the first: "That the borders of our mind are ever shifting, and that many minds can flow into one another, as it were, and create or reveal a single mind, a single energy" ("Magic," 28).

7. Brown, "Northern Voice," 27.

8. Roe, "'Wordsworth at the Flax Dam,'" 169.

9. Heaney, preface to *Stations*, 3.

10. Heaney, "Seamus Heaney" [Murphy], " 89–90.

11. Ibid., 90.

12. For a penetrating discussion of Heaney's debt to Yeats's use of form, particularly the stanza, see McDonald, *Serious Poetry*, 149–52. McDonald's quotations from Heaney's introduction to W. B. Yeats in the *Field Day Anthology of Irish Literature* particularly support my contention that Heaney often tries to make himself a sound chamber for poetry and portrays this process in some of his poems, as well as illuminate my present purpose of showing how Heaney constructs a new space of potential in his later poetry: Heaney states that "poems like 'Among School Children' and 'A Dialogue of Self and Soul' go beyond the lyric's usual function of giving perfected form to a privileged state of mind and achieve an effulgent, oracular impersonality" and that "Yeats's essential gift is his ability to raise a temple in the ear, to make a vaulted space in language through the firmness, in-placeness and undislodgeableness of stanzaic form" (quoted in McDonald, *Serious Poetry*, 151).

13. Yeats, *Collected Poems*, 125.

14. Ibid. Albright makes the connection between the poem and *A Vision* in his notes on the poem (Yeats, *W. B. Yeats*, 543).

15. Jeffares's *Commentary on the Collected Poems,* 146, articulates these two glosses of "Out of all sense."

16. Donoghue, "Yeats," 43.

17. I was pleased to discover that Ron Schuchard, in his essay on Yeats's legacy to contemporary Irish poets, a group including Heaney, points out Heaney's approving mention of the Yeatsian gaze in an uncollected lecture entitled "Yeats's Nobility," delivered on January 28, 1989, at the Guildhall in Derry on the fiftieth anniversary of Yeats's death. Heaney recalls "the fortitude and composure of Yeats's *gaze* [which] is equal to the violence and danger of the historical disintegration which it witnesses" (quoted in Schuchard, "Legacy of Yeats," 300, Schuchard's emphasis). Although Schuchard discusses the "gaze" here in terms of Yeats's artistic courage in the face of historical violence, he also shows how enamored Heaney is of Yeatsian gazing generally, an interest that would enable Heaney as well to gaze deeply through his art and achieve a visionary state often in his later poetry.

18. Tobin, *Passage to the Center,* 252.

19. Ibid., 253.

20. McDonald, "Faiths and Fidelities," 68.

21. Heaney, *Place and Displacement,* 8.

22. See Wright's analysis of Heaney's poetry in terms used by the philosopher Martin Heidegger for a general discussion of poetic possibility. In discussing the poetry beginning with *Field Work,* Wright argues that Heaney "clearly exemplifies the power of poetry to liberate language and thought that is central to Heidegger's understanding of poetry and the poets. Heaney engages in what Heidegger has described as the 'saying' which brings the 'unsayable' into the world" ("Heidegger and Heaney," 398). For a more interesting study, employing a Derridean framework, of the potential engendered in Heaney's late poetry, see Eugene O'Brien's argument that Heaney's new notion of place as a "luminous emptiness" works to unpack "essentialist ideas of place and [acts as] an invitation to the imagination to reenvisage place as a form of possibility in the future as opposed to some form of hypostasized past" (*Seamus Heaney,* 159).

23. Brandes, "Secondary Sources," 77.

24. Heaney, "Further Language," 10.

25. Heaney, preface to *Stations,* 3.

26. Polanyi, *Tacit Dimension,* 23.

27. Ibid., 25.

28. Thornton, "Between Circle and Straight Line," 75.

29. Heaney, "For Liberation," 229.

30. Heaney, "In the Middle," n. pag.

31. Heaney, "Joy or Night," 159–60. See also the similar language he employs in "The Redress of Poetry," where he states, "If our given experience is a labyrinth, its impassibility can still be countered by the poet's imagining some equivalent of the labyrinth and presenting himself and us with a vivid experience of it. Such an operation does not intervene in the actual but by offering consciousness a chance to recognize its predicaments, *foreknow* its capacities and rehearse its comebacks in all kinds of venturesome ways, it does constitute a beneficent event, for poet and audience alike" (2, emphasis mine).

32. Yeats actively cultivated his sense of artistic liminality. He discusses his continued attempts to evoke a liminal state within himself through rhythm in his essay "The Symbolism of Poetry": "The purpose of rhythm, it has always seemed to me, is to prolong the moment of contemplation, the moment when we are both asleep and awake, which is the one moment of creation, by hushing us with an alluring monotony, while it holds us waking by variety, to keep us in that state of perhaps real trance, in which the mind liberated from the pressure of the will is unfolded in symbols. . . . I have heard in meditation voices that were forgotten the moment they had spoken, and I have been swept, when in more profound meditation, beyond all memory but of those things that came beyond the threshold of waking life" (159). This passage shows how Yeats comes to occupy this middle ground in which he is able to perceive elements beyond the grasp of the conscious mind, a liminal state akin to a trance — "the moment when we are both awake and asleep." Rhythm is the mantra that lulls him into this state of liminality, from which he is then able to interact with "those things that came from beyond the threshold of waking life." Yeats is detailing actual occasions on which he has accessed another dimension of reality through his position of liminality. Lest we have any doubts that liminality was a major aspect of Yeats's abiding interest in mysticism, his late essay "A General Introduction to My Work" affirms his interest in this concept. For example, he again describes a state of being that enables him to experience insights: "What moves me and my hearer is a vivid speech that has no laws except that it must not exorcise the ghostly voice. I am awake and asleep, at my moment of revelation, self-possessed in self-surrender; there is no rhyme, no echo of the beating drum, the dancing foot, that would overset my balance" (524).

33. Heaney, introduction to *Redress of Poetry*, xvi.

34. Heaney, "Frontiers of Writing," 190.

35. Andrews has pointed out (citing an interview with Brian Friel conducted by John Gray in *Linen Hall Review* 2 [Summer 1985]: 7) that "one of the central Field Day concepts is that of the 'Fifth Province'—'a place for dissenters, traitors to the prevailing ideologies in the other four provinces.' This is

the neutral realm of the imagination, where the symbol may mediate between subject and object, where actualities need not be so terribly insisted upon as they normally are in Ireland" ("Fifth Province," 30). For a full history of the provenance of the term, see Andrews's second note to this essay in Peacock, *Achievement of Brian Friel*, 242–43.

36. Muldoon, "'Welsh Incident,'" 395.

37. Heaney, "Learning from Eliot," 41.

38. Deane, "Famous Seamus," 66.

39. Heaney, introduction to *W. B. Yeats*, xviii.

40. Donoghue, *Speaking of Beauty*, 114.

41. Heaney, "Further Language," 15.

42. Ibid., 16.

43. Desmond, *Gravity and Grace*, 108.

44. Heaney, *Opened Ground*, 15.

45. Foster, "Crediting Marvels," 207.

46. Heaney, "Interview with Seamus Heaney" [Randall], 16.

47. Heaney, *Anything Can Happen*, 18.

48. Yeats, *Collected Poems*, 187.

49. Heaney, *Anything Can Happen*, 11.

50. Longenbach, *Resistance to Poetry*, 108.

51. Yeats, *Collected Poems*, 180, 182.

52. McDonald, *Serious Poetry*, 93, emphasis in original.

53. Peacock, "Mediations," 242.

54. Heaney, "Interview with Seamus Heaney" [Wylie and Kerrigan], 131.

55. Underhill, *Problem of Consciousness*, 15.

56. Hancock, "Seamus Heaney," 375.

57. Heaney, "Joy or Night," 159.

CODA. **Poetry and the Northern Irish Peace Process**

1. O'Driscoll, "Heaney in Public," 67.

2. Quoted in Buell, *Future of Environmental Criticism*, 50.

3. Batten, "Heaney's Wordsworth," 184.

4. M. Longley, "Q. and A.," 21.

5. Brearton, *Reading Michael Longley*, 200.

6. See the August 9, 1974, issue of *Hibernia*, suppl. "71—Internment—74," 1, cited in Brandes, *Seamus Heaney*, 443.

7. O'Driscoll, "Heaney in Public," 59.

8. The petition reads, "We the undersigned believe that there currently exists a real desire for a permanent solution in Ireland. We therefore urge the Irish and British governments to seize any opportunity for peace presented by the Hume-Adams initiative" (quoted in Brandes, *Seamus Heaney*, 446).

9. E. Longley, "Poetry and the Peace Process."

10. E. Longley, "Multi-culturalism and Northern Ireland," 42.

11. Spring, statement to the Irish Senate.

12. Bloomfield, "We Will Remember Them."

13. BBC Northern Ireland, "War" [Longley].

14. O Muiri, "Good Friday Agreement," 1.

15. Ibid., 2.

16. M. Longley, "Brendan Corcoran and Michael Longley," 116.

17. Ibid., 117.

18. McKittrick et al., *Lost Lives.*

19. BBC Northern Ireland, "Keane on Longley."

20. "Book on Nationalism."

21. See Northern Ireland Curriculum, "Growing Up in Northern Ireland."

22. BBC Northern Ireland, "War" [Heaney].

23. Heaney, "*Cure at Troy*: Production Notes," 177.

24. Ibid., 177–78. The editors of the volume of essays in which Heaney's appeared give two more appearances of the "hope and history" phrase from Heaney's translation of this play—in President Bill Clinton's 1997 book, *Between Hope and History: Meeting America's Challenges for the 21st Century,* and in South African Nobel Prize Winner Nadine Gordimer's 1999 essay collection, *Living in Hope and History* (180 n. 5).

25. See too Heaney's essay on Omagh, "Reciprocity of Tears," 7, in which he laments the great loss of life but also calls for a tentative optimism that matches the earlier such call in the by-then famous lines of his Greek chorus in *The Cure at Troy*: "As realists, we know that such a trust ['among ourselves,' from the previous sentence] will be constantly disappointed and that the atrocious will always be a threat; but as mourners, we have reason also to believe that we have reached some tragic conclusion, and that the whimper of exhausted grief just might turn into the cry of something vulnerable and new."

26. Quoted in McKay, *Northern Protestants*, 346.

27. "Year a Nation Drank."

28. Ibid.

29. See, for example, the quotation by Ray Davey, founder of one of the province's ecumenical Christian communities, Corrymeela, of Heaney's complete stanza on hope and history and all but the last two lines of the next stanza

beginning "So hope for a great sea-change" in his piece in the *Corrymeela News: The Journal of the Corrymeela Community,* Summer 1998, 5, cited in Wells, *People behind the Peace,* 80.

30. Kiberd, "Wilde and the Belfast Agreement," 443.

31. Edna Longley, "Poetry and the Peace Process."

32. M. Longley, "Interview with Michael Longley" [McDonald].

33. Heaney, "Unheard Melodies," 1.

34. Ibid.

35. Ibid.

36. Ibid.

37. See Heaney's continued recourse to poetry as musical harbinger of political rapprochement in his address upon receiving the Struga Prize in Macedonia in August 2001. Drawing on the myth of Orpheus, whom he terms "the archetypal poet," Heaney suggests that "Macedonian poets," like Orpheus, "are ready to lift their lyre and raise their voice and sing the song of the future. They will do what poets always do: they will listen to the music of what is actually happening, but they will answer it by playing the music of what might happen" ("Struga Address," 115).

38. Heaney, *Anything Can Happen,* 12.

39. Quoted in A. Roche, preface to *Senate Speeches of W. B. Yeats,* iii.

40. Ibid., iv.

Bibliography

Allen, Michael. "Bleak Afflatus! A Review by Michael Allen of *Poets from the North of Ireland*, ed. Frank Orsmby." *Threshold* 31 (Autumn-Winter 1980): 82–87.

———. "Longley's Long Line: Looking Back from *The Ghost Orchid*." In *The Poetry of Michael Longley*, edited by Alan J. Peacock and Kathleen Devine, 121–41. Gerrards Cross: Colin Smythe, 2000.

———. "The Normal Love of the Otherworldly." *Fortnight* 425 (May 2004). http://fortnight.org/allen425.html.

———. "Options: The Poetry of Michael Longley." *Eire-Ireland* 10 (Winter 1975): 129–36.

Anderson, Benedict. *Imagined Communities.* Rev. ed. 1991. Reprint, London: Verso, 1996.

Andrews, Elmer. [See also Kennedy-Andrews, Elmer.] "The Fifth Province." In *The Achievement of Brian Friel*, edited by Alan Peacock, 29–48. Gerrards Cross: Colin Smythe, 1993.

———. *The Poetry of Seamus Heaney: All the Realms of Whisper.* New York: St. Martin's Press, 1988.

———, ed. *Seamus Heaney: A Collection of Critical Essays.* London: Macmillan, 1992.

Arbery, Glenn C. *Why Literature Matters: Permanence and the Politics of Reputation.* Wilmington, DE: Intercollegiate Studies Institute Books, 2001.

Archibald, Douglas, ed. "The Michael Longley Issue." *Colby Quarterly* 39 (September 2003).

"The Artist's Conflict in Ulster." BBC Northern Ireland broadcast, October 1, 1973. Museum no. 301, BBC Northern Ireland Community Archive, Cultra, Northern Ireland.

Ashley, Renee. "Writing on the Brink: Peripheral Vision and the Personal Poem." *Writer's Chronicle* 39 (May-Summer 2007): 60–65.

Attridge, Derek. *The Singularity of Literature.* New York: Routledge, 2004.

Bakhtin, Mikhail. "Discourse in the Novel." In *The Dialogic Imagination: Four Essays by M. M. Bakhtin,* edited by Michael Holquist and translated by Caryl Emerson and Michael Holquist, 259–422. Austin: University of Texas Press, 1981.

Bardon, Jonathan. *A History of Ulster.* Belfast: Blackstaff Press, 1992.

Batten, Guinn. "Heaney's Wordsworth and the Poetics of Displacement." In *The Cambridge Companion to Seamus Heaney,* edited by Bernard O'Donoghue, 178–91. Cambridge: Cambridge University Press, 2009.

BBC Northern Ireland. "Keane on Longley." January 22, 2008. www.bbc.co.uk/ northernireland/tv/programmes/longley/.

———. "War [Michael Longley]." n.d. Northern Ireland Learning. www.bbc.co .uk/northernireland/schools/11_16/poetry/war3.shtml. Accessed June 19, 2008.

———. "War [Seamus Heaney]." n.d. Northern Ireland Learning. www.bbc.co .uk/northernireland/schools/11_16/poetry/war2.shtml. Accessed June 19, 2008.

"The Belfast Group: A Symposium." *Honest Ulsterman* 53 (November–December 1976): 53–63.

"The Belfast Group: Overview." n.d. Lewis H. Beck Center, Manuscript, Archives, and Rare Book Library, Emory University. http://chaucer.library .emory.edu/irishpoet/overview/. Accessed July 10, 2000.

Belknap, Robert. "The Literary List: A Survey of Its Uses and Deployments." *Literary Imagination* 2, no. 1 (2000): 35–54.

Bew, Paul, Peter Gibbon, and Henry Patterson. *Northern Ireland, 1921–1996: Political Forces and Social Classes.* Rev. ed. London: Serif, 1996.

Bew, Paul, and Gordon Gillespie. *Northern Ireland: A Chronology of the Troubles, 1968–1993.* Dublin: Gill and Macmillan, 1993.

Bloom, Harold. Introduction to *Seamus Heaney,* edited by Harold Bloom, 1–10. New York: Chelsea House, 1986.

Bloomfield, Sir Kenneth, Northern Ireland Victims Commissioner. "We Will Remember Them." April 1998. www.nio.gov.uk/bloomfield_report.pdf.

Boland, Eavan. "A Backward Look: An Interview with Eavan Boland." By Jody Allen Randolph. *Colby Quarterly* 35 (December 1999): 292–304.

Bolton, Jonathan. "'Customary Rhythms': Seamus Heaney and the Rite of Poetry." *Papers on Language and Literature* 37 (Spring 2001): 205–22.

Boly, John. "Beloved Mentors: Seamus Heaney's Poems of Vocation." *Genre* 38 (Spring-Summer 2005): 145–78.

"Book on Nationalism Wins Ewart Biggs Award." *Independent,* February 23, 2007. www.independent.ie/entertainment/news-gossip/book-on-nation-alism-wins-ewartbiggs-award-56354.html.

Bottum, Joseph. "Death and Politics." *First Things: The Journal of Religion, Culture, and Public Life,* June–July 2007. www.firstthings.com/article.php3?id_article=5917.

"The Boys of Mullaghbawn." December 20, 2000. Henry's Songbook. www.mysongbook.de/msb/songs/b/boysofmu.html.

"The Boys of Mullaghbawn: Traditional Ulster Ballad." n.d. Cantaria. www.chivalry.com/cantaria/lyrics/boys-mullaghbawn.html. Accessed on June 3, 2009.

Brandes, Rand. *Seamus Heaney: A Bibliography, 1959–2003.* London: Faber and Faber, 2008.

———. "Secondary Sources: A Gloss on the Critical Reception of Seamus Heaney, 1965–1993." *Colby Quarterly* 30, no. 1 (1994): 63–77.

Brearton, Fran. "Cenotaphs of Snow: Memory, Remembrance, and the Poetry of Michael Longley." *Irish Studies Review* 12, no. 2 (2004): 175–89.

———. *The Great War in Irish Poetry: W. B. Yeats to Michael Longley.* Oxford: Oxford University Press, 2000.

———. "Poetry of the 1960s: The 'Northern Ireland Renaissance.'" In *The Cambridge Companion to Contemporary Irish Poetry,* edited by Matthew Campbell, 94–112. Cambridge: Cambridge University Press, 2003.

———. "'The privilege / Of vertigo': Reading Michael Longley in the 1960s." *Colby Quarterly* 39 (September 2003): 198–214.

———. *Reading Michael Longley.* Newcastle: Bloodaxe, 2006.

———. "Snow Poet." Review of *Selected Poems* and *Broken Dishes,* by Michael Longley. *Thumbscrew* 12 (Winter 1998–99). www.poetrymagazines.org.uk/magazine/print.asp?id=12177.

Brewster, Scott. "Rites of Defilement: Abjection and the Body Politic in Northern Irish Poetry." *Irish University Review* 35 (Autumn–Winter 2005): 304–19.

Brogan, T. V. F., Peter Sacks, and Stephen F. Fogle. "Elegy." In *The New Princeton Encyclopedia of Poetry and Poetics,* edited by Alex Preminger and T. V. F. Brogan. New York: MJF Books, 1993.

Brooks, Cleanth. "The Uses of Literature." In *A Shaping Joy: Studies in the Writer's Craft,* 1–16. New York: Harcourt, Brace, Jovanovich, 1971.

Broom, Sarah. "Learning about Dying: Mutability and the Classics in the Poetry of Michael Longley." *New Hibernia Review* 6 (Spring 2002): 94–112.

Brown, Terence. "Mahon and Longley: Place and Placelessness." In *The Cambridge Companion to Contemporary Irish Poetry,* edited by Matthew Campbell, 133–48. Cambridge: Cambridge University Press, 2003.

———. "Michael Longley and the Irish Poetic Tradition." In *The Poetry of Michael Longley,* edited by Alan J. Peacock and Kathleen Devine, 1–12. Gerrards Cross: Colin Smythe, 2000.

———. "A Northern Voice." In *Seamus Heaney,* edited by Harold Bloom, 25–38. New York: Chelsea House, 1986.

———. "The Witnessing Eye and the Speaking Tongue." In *Seamus Heaney: A Collection of Critical Essays,* edited by Elmer Andrews, 182–92. New York: St. Martin's Press, 1992.

———. "W. R. Rodgers and John Hewitt." In *Two Decades of Irish Writing: A Critical Survey,* edited by Douglas Dunn, 81–97. Chester Springs, PA: Dufour, 1975.

Buckley, Vincent. *Poetry and the Sacred.* New York: Barnes and Noble, 1968.

Buell, Lawrence. *The Future of Environmental Criticism: Environmental Crisis and Literary Imagination.* Malden, MA: Blackwell, 2005.

Burris, Sidney. *The Poetry of Resistance: Seamus Heaney and the Pastoral Tradition.* Athens: Ohio University Press, 1990.

Cabot, David. "The Big Man." In *Love Poet, Carpenter: Michael Longley at Seventy,* edited by Robin Robertson, 23–25. London: Enitharmon Press, 2009.

Campbell, Julieann, and Tom Herron, eds. *Harrowing of the Heart: The Poetry of Bloody Sunday.* Derry: Guildhall Press, 2008.

Campbell, Matthew, ed. *The Cambridge Companion to Contemporary Irish Poetry.* Cambridge: Cambridge University Press, 2003.

Carson, Ciaran. "'Escaped from the Massacre'?" *Honest Ulsterman* 50 (Winter 1975): 183–86.

Cavanagh, Michael. *Professing Poetry: Seamus Heaney's Poetics.* Washington, DC: Catholic University of America Press, 2009.

Clark, Heather. *The Ulster Renaissance: Poetry in Belfast, 1962–1972.* Oxford: Oxford University Press, 2006.

Cleary, Joe. "'Fork-Tongued on the Border Bit': Partition and the Politics of Form in Contemporary Narratives of the Northern Irish Conflict." *South Atlantic Quarterly* 95 (Winter 1996): 227–76.

———. *Literature, Partition and the Nation-State: Culture and Conflict in Ireland, Israel and Palestine.* Cambridge: Cambridge University Press, 2002.

Corcoran, Neil. *After Yeats and Joyce: Reading Modern Irish Literature.* Oxford: Oxford University Press, 1997.

———. "My Botanical Studies: The Poetry of Natural History in Michael Longley." In *The Poetry of Michael Longley,* edited by Alan J. Peacock and Kathleen Devine, 101–19. Gerrards Cross: Colin Smythe, 2000.

———. *The Poetry of Seamus Heaney: A Critical Study.* London: Faber and Faber, 1998.

———. *A Student's Guide to Seamus Heaney.* London: Faber and Faber, 1986.

Craig, Patricia. "Michael Longley's Belfast." In *Love Poet, Carpenter: Michael Longley at Seventy,* edited by Robin Robertson, 33–36. London: Enitharmon Press, 2009.

Cuda, Anthony J. "The Use of Memory: Seamus Heaney, T. S. Eliot, and the Unpublished Epigraph to *North.*" *Journal of Modern Literature* 28, no. 4 (2005): 152–75.

Curtis, Tony, ed. *The Art of Seamus Heaney.* 1985. Reprint, Chester Springs, PA: Seren Books, 1994.

Dau, Duc. "Seamus Heaney's Religious Redress." *Literature and Theology* 17 (March 2003): 32–43.

Dawe, Gerald. "History Class: Northern Poetry, 1970–82." *New Hibernia Review* 7 (Spring 2003): 75–86.

———. "'Icons and Lares': Derek Mahon and Michael Longley." In *Across a Roaring Hill: The Protestant Imagination in Modern Ireland,* edited by Gerald Dawe and Edna Longley, 218–35. Belfast: Blackstaff Press, 1985.

———. "Just Images: On Regionalism." In *How's the Poetry Going? Literary Politics and Ireland Today,* 84–87. Belfast: Lagan Press, 1991.

———. "The Sound of the Shuttle." In *A Real Life Elsewhere,* 54–70. Belfast: Lagan Press, 1993.

Dawson, Graham. *Making Peace with the Past? Memory, Trauma, and the Irish Troubles.* Manchester: Manchester University Press, 2007.

Deane, Seamus. "The Artist and the Troubles." In *Ireland and the Arts* [special issue of *Literary Review*], edited by Tim Pat Coogan, 42–50. London: Namara Press, 1983.

———. *Celtic Revivals: Essays in Modern Irish Literature, 1880–1980.* Winston-Salem, NC: Wake Forest University Press, 1985.

———. "The Famous Seamus." *New Yorker,* March 20, 2000, 54–79.

———, gen. ed. *The Field Day Anthology of Irish Writing.* Vol. 2. Derry: Field Day Publications, 1991.

———. "Seamus Heaney: The Timorous and the Bold." In *Celtic Revivals: Essays in Modern Irish Literature, 1880–1980,* 174–86. Winston-Salem, NC: Wake Forest University Press, 1985.

Desmond, John. *Gravity and Grace: Seamus Heaney and the Force of Light.* Waco, TX: Baylor University Press, 2009.

Donoghue, Denis. "The Literature of Trouble." In *We Irish: Essays on Irish Literature and Society,* 182–94. New York: Knopf, 1986.

———. *The Practice of Reading.* New Haven: Yale University Press, 1998.

———. *The Sovereign Ghost: Studies in Imagination.* Berkeley: University of California Press, 1976.

———. *Speaking of Beauty.* New Haven: Yale University Press, 2003.

———. "Yeats: The Question of Symbolism." In *We Irish: Essays on Irish Literature and Society,* 34–51. New York: Knopf, 1986.

Drummond, Gavin. "The Difficulty of We: The Epistolary Poems of Michael Longley and Derek Mahon." *Yearbook of English Studies* 35 (2005): 31–42.

Dunn, Douglas. "Letter to Michael Longley." June 15, 1972. Michael Longley Collection, box 1, folder 8. Special Collections Department, Robert W. Woodruff Library, Emory University.

———. "Longley's Metric." In *The Poetry of Michael Longley,* edited by Alan J. Peacock and Kathleen Devine, 13–33. Gerrards Cross: Colin Smythe, 2000.

Eagleton, Terry. "Review of *Field Work.*" In *Seamus Heaney: Contemporary Critical Essays,* edited by Michael Allen, 102–6. New York: St. Martin's Press, 1997.

Eliade, Mircea. Trans. Willard R. Trask. *The Sacred and the Profane: The Nature of Religion.* New York: Harcourt Brace, 1959.

Eliot, T. S. "The Music of Poetry." In *On Poetry and Poets,* 26–38. London: Faber and Faber, 1957.

Elliott, Marianne. *The Catholics of Ulster: A History.* New York: Basic Books, 2001.

Felski, Rita. *Uses of Literature.* Malden, MA: Blackwell, 2008.

Flanagan, Thomas. "The Poetry of Seamus Heaney." In *Seamus Heaney: Poems and a Memoir,* ix–xvi. New York: Limited Editions Club, 1982.

Forrester, Duncan B. "Politics and Reconciliation." In *Reconciliation in Religion and Society,* edited by Michael Hurley, S.J., 111–22. Belfast: Institute of Irish Studies, 1994.

Foster, John Wilson. *The Achievement of Seamus Heaney.* Dublin: Lilliput Press, 1995.

———. "Crediting Marvels: Heaney after 50." In *The Cambridge Companion to Seamus Heaney,* edited by Bernard O'Donoghue, 206–23. Cambridge: Cambridge University Press, 2009.

———. "'A Lough Neagh Sequence': Sources and Motifs." In *Seamus Heaney: Modern Critical Views,* edited by Harold Bloom, 45–49. New Haven: Chelsea House, 1986.

———. "The Poetry of Seamus Heaney." In *Colonial Consequences: Essays in Irish Literature and Culture,* 81–96. Dublin: Lilliput Press, 1991.

———. "Post-war Ulster Poetry." In *Colonial Consequences: Essays in Irish Literature and Culture,* 60–80. Dublin: Lilliput Press, 1991.

Fox, Renee. "Michael Longley's Early Epitaphs." *New Hibernia Review* 13 (Summer 2009): 125–40.

Frazier, Adrian. "Anger and Nostalgia: Seamus Heaney and the Ghost of the Father." *Eire-Ireland* 36 (Fall–Winter 2001): 7–38.

Fussell, Paul. *Abroad: British Literary Traveling between the Wars.* New York: Oxford University Press, 1980.

Garratt, Robert F. *Modern Irish Poetry: Tradition and Continuity from Yeats to Heaney.* Berkeley: University of California Press, 1989.

Gebler, Carlo. *The Glass Curtain: Inside an Ulster Community.* London: Hamish Hamilton, 1991.

Girard, René. *Violence and the Sacred.* Baltimore: Johns Hopkins University Press, 1977.

"Good Morning Ulster." BBC Northern Ireland broadcast, June 17, 1993. Museum no. 6666, BBC Northern Ireland Community Archive, Cultra, Northern Ireland.

Grant, Patrick. *Breaking Enmities: Religion, Literature, and Culture in Northern Ireland, 1967–97.* New York: St. Martin's Press, 1999.

———. *Literature, Rhetoric, and Violence in Northern Ireland, 1968–1998: Hardened to Death.* New York: Palgrave, 2001.

Gray, Cecile. "Medbh McGuckian: Imagery Wrought to Its Uttermost." In *Learning the Trade: Essays on W. B. Yeats and Contemporary Poetry,* edited by Deborah Fleming, 165–77. West Cornwall, CT: Locust Hill Press, 1993.

Greer, Sammye Crawford. "'Station Island' and the Poet's Progress." In *Seamus Heaney: The Shaping Spirit,* edited by Catharine Malloy and Phyllis Carey, 106–19. Newark: University of Delaware Press.

Hall, Jason David. "Rhyme in Seamus Heaney's Group Poems." *ANQ: A Journal of Short Essays, Notes, and Queries* 17 (Summer 2004): 55–60.

Hancock, Tim. "Seamus Heaney: Poet of Tension or Poet of Conviction?" *Irish University Review* 29 (Autumn–Winter 1999): 358–75.

Harmon, Maurice. "'We Pine for Ceremony': Ritual and Reality in the Poetry of Seamus Heaney, 1965–75." In *Seamus Heaney: A Collection of Critical Essays,* edited by Elmer Andrews, 67–86. New York: St. Martin's Press, 1992.

Hart, Henry. *Seamus Heaney: Poet of Contrary Progressions.* Syracuse: Syracuse University Press, 1992.

Harte, Liam, and Michael Parker. Introduction to *Contemporary Irish Fiction: Themes, Tropes, Theories,* 1–12. New York: St. Martin's Press, 2000.

Heaney, Seamus. "Above the Brim." In *Homage to Robert Frost,* by Joseph Brodsky, Derek Wolcott, and Seamus Heaney, 60–88. New York: Farrar Straus Giroux, 1996.

———. *Among Schoolchildren.* John Malone Memorial Lecture, presented at the Queen's University of Belfast, June 9, 1983. Belfast: John Malone Memorial Committee, 1983.

———. *Anything Can Happen: A Poem and Essay by Seamus Heaney with Translations in Support of Art for Amnesty.* Dublin: Townhouse, 2004.

———. "Belfast." In *Preoccupations: Selected Prose, 1968–1978,* 28–37. London: Faber, 1980.

———. "Between North and South: Poetic Contours." Interview by Richard Kearney. In *States of Mind: Dialogues with Contemporary Thinkers on the European Mind,* 101–8. Manchester: Manchester University Press, 1995.

———. "Burns's Art Speech." In *Finders Keepers: Selected Prose, 1971–2001,* 347–63. New York: Farrar Straus Giroux, 2002.

———. *Commencement Address.* Presented at the University of North Carolina at Chapel Hill, May 12, 1996. Stinehour, VT: Lunenburg Press.

———. "'The Connection': Interview with Christopher Lydon." Audiotape. May 16, 1996. Henry C. Pearson Collection of Seamus Heaney, Rare Book Collection, University of North Carolina at Chapel Hill.

———. "The Conversation." In *Seamus Heaney in Conversation with Karl Miller,* 17–56. London: Between the Lines, 2000.

———. *Crediting Poetry.* Loughcrew, Ireland: Gallery Press, 1996.

———. *The Cure at Troy: A Version of Sophocles' Philoctetes.* New York: Noonday Press, 1991.

———. "*The Cure at Troy:* Production Notes in No Particular Order." In *Amid Our Troubles: Irish Versions of Greek Tragedy,* edited by Marianne McDonald and J. Michael Walton, 171–80. London: Methuen, 2003.

———. *Death of a Naturalist.* London: Faber and Faber, 1966.

———. *District and Circle.* London: Faber and Faber, 2006.

———. *Door into the Dark.* London: Faber and Faber, 1969.

———. "Earning a Rhyme." In *Finders Keepers: Selected Prose, 1971–2001,* 48–55. New York: Farrar Straus Giroux, 2002.

———. "Edwin Muir." In *Finders Keepers: Selected Prose, 1971–2001,* 269–80. New York: Farrar, Straus, Giroux, 2002.

———. "Englands of the Mind." In *Preoccupations: Selected Prose, 1968–1978,* 150–69. London: Faber, 1980.

———. "Faith, Hope and Poetry: Osip Mandelstam." In *Preoccupations: Selected Prose, 1968–1978,* 217–20. London: Faber, 1980.

———. "Feeling into Words." In *Preoccupations: Selected Prose, 1968–1978,* 41–60. London: Faber, 1980.

———. *Field Work.* New York: Noonday Press, 1979.

———. "For Liberation: Brian Friel and the Use of Memory." In *The Achievement of Brian Friel,* edited by Alan Peacock, 229–40. Gerrards Cross: Colin Smythe, 1993.

———. "From Monaghan to the Grand Canal: The Poetry of Patrick Kavanagh." In *Preoccupations: Selected Prose, 1968–1978*, 115–30. London: Faber, 1980.

———. "Frontiers of Writing." In *The Redress of Poetry: Oxford Lectures*, 186–203. London: Faber and Faber, 1995.

———. "Further Language." *Studies in the Literary Imagination* 30 (Fall 1997): 7–16.

———. "*Galway Echo* Interview with Des Kenny." Audiotape. April 1986. Henry C. Pearson Collection of Seamus Heaney, Rare Book Collection, University of North Carolina at Chapel Hill.

———. "The God in the Tree: Early Irish Nature Poetry." In *Preoccupations: Selected Prose, 1968–1978*, 181–89. London: Faber, 1980.

———. "The Government of the Tongue." In *The Government of the Tongue: Selected Prose, 1978–1987*, 91–108. New York: Noonday Press, 1988.

———. *The Haw Lantern*. London: Faber and Faber, 1987.

———. "In the Country of Convention: English Pastoral Verse." In *Preoccupations: Selected Prose, 1968–1978*, 173–80. London: Faber, 1980.

———. "In the Middle of the Field." Insert for brochure of "Henry Pearson" exhibit, Columbia, South Carolina Museum of Art, October 30, 1988–January 8, 1989. Henry C. Pearson Collection of Seamus Heaney, Rare Book Collection, University of North Carolina at Chapel Hill.

———. "The Interesting Case of Nero, Chekhov's Cognac and a Knocker." In *The Government of the Tongue: Selected Prose, 1978–1987*, xi–xxiii. New York: Noonday Press, 1988.

———. "Interview with Seamus Heaney." By Bel Mooney. *Nightwaves*, BBC Radio, September 16, 1998. www.bbc.co.uk/bbcfour/audiointerviews/profilepages/heaneys1.shtml.

———. "An Interview with Seamus Heaney." By James Randall. *Ploughshares* 5, no. 3 (1979): 7–22.

———. "An Interview with Seamus Heaney." By J. J. Wylie and John C. Kerrigan. *Nua: Studies in Contemporary Irish Writing* 2 (Autumn 1998–Spring 1999): 125–37.

———. Introduction to *The Redress of Poetry: Oxford Lectures*, xiii–xviii. London: Faber and Faber, 1995.

———. Introduction to *Sweeney Astray*. London: Faber and Faber, 1983.

———. Introduction to *W. B. Yeats: Poems Selected by Seamus Heaney*, xi–xxv. London: Faber and Faber, 2000.

———. "John Hume's Derry." *Hibernia*, November 21, 1969. Reprinted in *Irish Writing in the Twentieth Century: A Reader*, edited by David Pierce. Cork: Cork University Press, 2000. 766.

———. "Joy or Night: Last Things in the Poetry of W. B. Yeats and Philip Larkin." In *The Redress of Poetry: Oxford Lectures,* 146–63. London: Faber and Faber, 1995.

———. "Learning from Eliot." In *Finders Keepers: Selected Prose, 1971–2001,* 28–41. New York: Farrar, Straus, Giroux, 2002.

———. "Light Finally Enters the Black Hole." *Sunday Tribune,* September 4, 1994, A9.

———. "The Makings of a Music: Reflections on Wordsworth and Yeats." In *Preoccupations: Selected Prose, 1968–1978,* 61–78. London: Faber, 1980.

———. *Munro. Everyman: An Annual Religio-Cultural Review* 3 (1970): 58–65.

———. "Norman MacCaig, 1910–1996." In *Finders Keepers: Selected Prose, 1971–2001,* 433–36. New York: Farrar, Straus, Giroux, 2002.

———. *North.* London: Faber and Faber, 1975.

———. "Old Derry's Walls." *Listener,* October 24, 1968, 521–23.

———. *An Open Letter.* Derry: Field Day Publications, 1983.

———. *Opened Ground: Selected Poems, 1966–1996.* New York: Farrar, Straus, Giroux, 1998.

———. "Our Own Dour Way." *Hibernia,* April 1963, 15.

———. "Out of London's Troubles." *New Statesman,* July 1, 1966, 23–24.

———. "The Pathos of Things." *Guardian,* November 24, 2007, 20.

———. "The Peace of the Word Is Always with You." *Sunday Times* (London), January 17, 1999, 10–11.

———. *Place and Displacement: Recent Poetry of Northern Ireland.* Pete Laver Memorial Lecture. Grasmere: Trustees of Dove Cottage, August 2, 1984.

———. "The Place of Writing: W. B. Yeats and Thoor Ballylee." In *The Place of Writing.* Atlanta: Scholars Press, 1989.

———. "The Placeless Heaven: Another Look at Kavanagh." In *The Government of the Tongue: Selected Prose, 1978–1987,* 3–14. New York: Noonday Press, 1988.

———. "The Poems of the Dispossessed Repossessed." In *The Government of the Tongue: Selected Prose, 1978–1987,* 30–35. New York: Noonday Press, 1988.

———. "The Poet as a Christian." *Furrow* 29 (October 1978): 603–6.

———. Preface to *Seamus Heaney: Poems and a Memoir,* xvii–xviii. New York: Limited Editions Club, 1982.

———. Preface to *Stations,* 3. Belfast: Ulsterman Publications, 1975.

———. "The Pre-natal Mountain: Vision and Irony in Recent Irish Poetry." In *The Place of Writing,* 36–53. Atlanta: Scholars Press, 1989.

———. "The Reciprocity of Tears." *Irish Times,* August 22, 1998, 7.

————. "The Redress of Poetry." In *The Redress of Poetry: Oxford Lectures*, 1–16. London: Faber and Faber, 1995.

————. "The Road to Derry." Quoted in "Conferences Past," *IASIL Newsletter* 4 (March 1998). www.iasil.org/newsletter/archive/newsletter1998/05_conp.html.

————. "The Saturday Interview." By Caroline Walsh. *Irish Times*, December 6, 1975, 5.

————. "Seamus Heaney." In *Reading the Future: Irish Writers in Conversation with Mike Murphy*, edited by Cliodhna Ni Anluain, 80–97. Dublin: Lilliput Press, 2000.

————. *Seamus Heaney: Poems and a Memoir.* New York: Limited Editions Club, 1982.

————. "Seamus Heaney—Poetry International." BBC Northern Ireland broadcast, October 15, 1972. Museum no. 908, BBC Northern Ireland Community Archive, Cultra, Northern Ireland.

————. *Seeing Things.* London: Faber and Faber, 1991.

————. "The Sense of Place." In *Preoccupations: Selected Prose, 1968–1978*, 131–49. London: Faber, 1980.

————. "Something to Write Home About." *Princeton University Library Chronicle* 59 (Spring 1998): 621–32.

————. *The Spirit Level.* London: Faber and Faber, 1996.

————. *Station Island.* New York: Farrar, Straus, Giroux, 1985.

————. "The Staying Power of Poetry." Interview by Simone Kearney. *Irish Literary Supplement* 27 (Fall 2007): 14.

————. *Stepping Stones: Interviews with Seamus Heaney.* By Dennis O'Driscoll. New York: Farrar, Straus, Giroux, 2008.

————. "The Struga Address and Two Poems." *Irish Pages: A Journal of Contemporary Writing* 1 (Spring 2002): 114–16.

————. "Through-Other Places, Through-Other Times: The Irish Poet and Britain." In *Finders Keepers: Selected Prose, 1971–2001*, 396–415. New York: Farrar, Straus, Giroux, 2002.

————. "Tradition and an Individual Talent: Hugh MacDiarmid." In *Preoccupations: Selected Prose, 1968–1978*, 195–98. London: Faber, 1980.

————. "Unhappy and at Home: Interview with Seamus Heaney by Seamus Deane." *Crane Bag Book of Irish Studies* 1, no. 1 (1977): 66–72.

————. "Unheard Melodies." *Irish Times Supplement* April 11, 1998, 1.

————. "William Butler Yeats." In *The Field Day Anthology of Irish Literature*, general editor Seamus Deane, vol. 2, 783–90. Derry: Field Day Publications, 1991.

———. *Wintering Out.* London: Faber and Faber, 1972.

———. "Writer at Work." *Honest Ulsterman* 8 (December 1968): 13.

———. "Yeats as an Example." In *Preoccupations: Selected Prose, 1968–1978,* 98–114. London: Faber, 1980.

Heritage Lottery Fund. "Digging Deeper Speaker Summary" for the conference "Digging Deeper: Sharing Our Past, Sharing Our Future," November 15, 2007, Belfast, Northern Ireland. www.heritageandidentity.co.uk/ni/summary.asp.

Herron, Tom. "Spectaculars: Seamus Heaney and the Limits of Mimicry." *Irish Studies Review* 7 (August 1999): 183–91.

Hobsbaum, Philip. "The Belfast Group: A Recollection." *Eire-Ireland* 32 (Summer–Fall 1997): 173–82.

———. "Craft and Technique in *Wintering Out.*" In *The Art of Seamus Heaney,* edited by Tony Curtis, 35–43. 1985. Reprint, Chester Springs, PA: Seren Books, 1994.

———. "Creative Writing." BBC Northern Ireland broadcast, May 31, 1966. Museum no. 1951, BBC Northern Ireland Radio Community Archive, Cultra, Northern Ireland.

———. *Theory of Criticism.* Bloomington: Indiana University Press, 1970.

Homer. *The Odyssey.* Translated by Robert Fitzgerald. New York: Farrar, Straus, and Giroux, 1998.

Howard, Ben. "Why Did the Buddhadharma Come to Ireland? Buddhist Themes in Recent Irish Poetry." *An Sionnach: A Journal of Literature, Culture, and the Arts* 1 (Fall 2005): 65–75.

Hufstader, Jonathan. "Coming into Consciousness by Jumping in Graves: Heaney's Bog Poems and the Politics of *North.*" *Irish University Review* 26 (Spring–Summer 1996): 61–74.

———. *Tongue of Water, Teeth of Stones: Northern Irish Poetry and Social Violence.* Lexington: University Press of Kentucky, 1999.

Hughes, Eamonn. "Representation in Modern Irish Poetry." In *Seamus Heaney: Contemporary Critical Essays,* edited by Michael Allen, 78–94. New York: St. Martin's Press, 1997.

Jeffares, Norman. *A Commentary on the Collected Poems of W. B. Yeats.* Stanford: Stanford University Press, 1968.

Johnston, Dillon. *Irish Poetry after Joyce.* 2nd ed. Syracuse: Syracuse University Press, 1997.

———. "Seamus Heaney and Violence." In *The Cambridge Companion to Contemporary Irish Poetry,* edited by Matthew Campbell, 113–32. Cambridge: Cambridge University Press, 2003.

Johnstone, Robert. "Climate Control." In *Love Poet, Carpenter: Michael Longley at Seventy*, edited by Robin Robertson, 72–74. London: Enitharmon Press, 2009.

Kavanagh, Patrick. "The Parish and the Universe." In *Collected Pruse*, 281–83. London: Macgibbon and Kee, 1967.

Kennedy, David. "Mound-Dwellers and Mummers: Language and Community in Seamus Heaney's *Wintering Out*." *Irish Studies Review* 10 (December 2002): 303–13.

Kennedy, Edward. "Northern Ireland—A View from America." Tip O'Neill Memorial Lecture, presented in Derry, Northern Ireland, January 9, 1998, http://cain.ulst.ac.uk/events/peace/docs/ek9198.htm.

Kennedy-Andrews, Elmer. "Conflict, Violence and 'The Fundamental Interrelatedness of All Things.'" In *The Poetry of Michael Longley*, edited by Alan J. Peacock and Kathleen Devine, 73–99. Gerrards Cross: Colin Smythe, 2000. See also Andrews, Elmer.

———. *Fiction and the Northern Ireland Troubles since 1969: (De-) constructing the North*. Dublin: Four Courts Press, 2003.

———. *Writing Home: Poetry and Place in Northern Ireland, 1968–2008*. Cambridge: D. S. Brewer, 2008.

Kennelly, Brendan. "Letter to Michael Longley." November 23, 1973. Michael Longley Collection, box 1, folder 9. Special Collections Department, Robert W. Woodruff Library, Emory University.

Kersnowski, Frank. *The Outsiders: Poets of Contemporary Ireland*. Fort Worth: Texas Christian University Press, 1975.

Kertzer, Jon. "The Course of a Particular: On the Ethics of Literary Singularity." *Twentieth-Century Literature* 50 (Fall 2004): 207–38.

Kiberd, Declan. "Irish Literature and Irish History." In *The Oxford Illustrated History of Ireland*, edited by R. F. Foster, 275–337. Oxford: Oxford University Press, 1991.

———. "Wilde and the Belfast Agreement." *Textual Practice* 13, no. 3 (1999): 441–45.

King, Sophia Hillen, and Sean McMahon, eds. *Hope and History: Eyewitness Accounts of Life in Twentieth-Century Ulster*. Belfast: Friar's Bush Press, 1996.

Kirkland, Richard. *Literature and Culture in Northern Ireland since 1965: Moments of Danger*. London: Longman, 1996.

Lange, Karen E. "Tales from the Bog." *National Geographic*, September 2007, 80–93.

Langer, Lawrence L. *The Holocaust and the Literary Imagination*. New Haven: Yale University Press, 1975.

Lederach, John Paul. *The Moral Imagination: The Art and Soul of Building Peace.* Oxford: Oxford University Press, 2005.

Leggett, B. J. *Larkin's Blues: Jazz, Popular Music, and Poetry.* Baton Rouge: Louisiana State University Press, 1999.

Lensing, George. *Poetry, Senator McCarthy, and Me.* E. Maynard Adams Lecture, Program in the Humanities and Human Values, presented at the University of North Carolina at Chapel Hill, October 8, 2006. Chapel Hill: University of North Carolina Program in the Humanities and Human Values.

Levinson, Marjorie. "What Is New Formalism?" *PMLA* 122 (March 2007): 558–69.

Lewis, C. S. *An Experiment in Criticism.* 1961. Reprint, Cambridge: Cambridge University Press, 1995.

———. *A Preface to "Paradise Lost."* New York: Oxford University Press, 1961.

Ling, Ruth. "The Double Design of Michael Longley's Recent Elegies: *The Ghost Orchid* and *Broken Dishes.*" *Irish Studies Review* 10 (April 2002): 39–50.

Lipsitz, Solly. "Jazz." In *Causeway: The Arts in Ulster,* edited by Michael Longley, 131–37. Belfast: Arts Council of Northern Ireland, 1971.

Livingston, Paisley. "Literary Aesthetics and the Aims of Criticism." In *Theory's Empire: An Anthology of Dissent,* edited by Daphne Patai and Will H. Corral, 651–67. New York: Columbia University Press, 2004.

Longenbach, James. *The Resistance to Poetry.* Chicago: University of Chicago Press, 2004.

Longley, Edna. "'Atlantic's Premises': American Influences on Northern Irish Poetry in the 1960s." In *Poetry and Posterity,* 259–79. Newcastle: Bloodaxe, 2000.

———. "*Door into the Dark.*" *Phoenix* 6/7 (Summer 1970): 145–49.

———. "From Cathleen to Anorexia: The Breakdown of Irelands." In *The Living Stream: Literature and Revisionism in Ireland,* 173–95. Newcastle: Bloodaxe, 1994.

———. "Heaney's Hidden Ireland." *Phoenix* 10 (July 1973): 86–89.

———. "Introduction: Revising 'Irish Literature.'" In *The Living Stream: Literature and Revisionism in Ireland,* 9–68. Newcastle: Bloodaxe, 1994.

———. "Multi-culturalism and Northern Ireland: Making Differences Fruitful." In *Multi-culturalism: The View from the Two Irelands,* edited by Edna Longley and Declan Kiberd, 1–44. Cork: Cork University Press, 2001.

———. "*North:* 'Inner Émigré' or 'Artful Voyeur?'" In *The Art of Seamus Heaney,* edited by Tony Curtis, 65–95. 1985. Reprint, Chester Springs, PA: Seren Books, 1994.

———. "Northern Irish Poetry and the End of History." In *Poetry and Posterity,* 280–316. Newcastle: Bloodaxe, 2000.

———. "Opening Up: A New Pluralism." *Fortnight* 256 (1987): 24–25.
———. "Pastoral Theologies." In *Poetry and Posterity,* 90–133. Newcastle: Blood-axe, 2000.
———. "The Poetics of Celt and Saxon." In *Poetry and Posterity,* 52–89. New-castle: Bloodaxe, 2000.
———. "Poetry and Posterity." In *Poetry and Posterity,* 90–133. Newcastle: Bloodaxe, 2000.
———. "Poetry and the Peace Process." Speech presented at the Blue Metropolis Literary Festival, Montreal, Canada, July 2005. Transcript at "Books and Writing with Ramona Koval," Radio National (Canada), July 24, 2005. www.abc.net.au/rn/arts/bwriting/stories/s1419531.htm.
Longley, Michael. "Book Review." n.d. Michael Longley Collection, box 25, folder 27. Special Collections Department, Robert W. Woodruff Library, Emory University.
———. "Brendan Corcoran and Michael Longley: Interview." *An Sionnach: A Journal of Literature, Culture, and the Arts* 3 (Fall 2007): 102–20.
———, ed. *Causeway: The Arts in Ulster.* Belfast: Arts Council of Northern Ireland, 1971.
———. *Collected Poems.* Winston-Salem, NC: Wake Forest University Press, 2006.
———. "Contemporary Poetry." n.d. Michael Longley Collection, box 26, folder 9. Special Collections Department, Robert W. Woodruff Library, Emory University.
———. *The Echo Gate: Poems, 1975–1979.* London: Secker and Warburg, 1979.
———. *An Exploded View: Poems, 1968–1972.* London: Victor Gollancz, 1973.
———. "The Fire in the Window: A Response to the Paintings of David Crone." In *David Crone: Paintings, 1963–1999,* 7–8. Dublin: Four Courts Press, 1999.
———. *The Ghost Orchid.* London: Jonathan Cape, 1995.
———. *Gorse Fires.* Winston-Salem, NC: Wake Forest University Press, 1991.
———. "An Inner Adventure." *Phoenix* 5 (Summer 1969): 54–55.
———. "Interview: Michael Longley and Jody Allen Randolph." *Colby Quarterly* 39 (September 2003): 294–308.
———. "An Interview with Michael Longley." By Sarah Broom. *Metre: A Magazine of International Poetry* 4 (Spring–Summer 1998): 17–26.
———. "An Interview with Michael Longley." By Dermot Healy. *Southern Review* 31, no. 3 (1995): 557–61.
———. "An Interview with Michael Longley: *Au Revoir,* Oeuvre." By Peter McDonald. *Thumbscrew* 12 (Winter 1998–99). www.poetrymagazines.org.uk/magazine/print.asp?id=12172.

———. Introduction to *Causeway: The Arts in Ulster,* edited by Michael Longley, 7–9. Belfast: Arts Council of Northern Ireland, 1971.

———. Introduction to *Secret Marriages,* 2–3. Manchester: Phoenix Pamphlets Poets Press, 1968.

———. *A Jovial Hullabaloo: Inaugural Lecture as Ireland Professor of Poetry.* London: Enitharmon, 2008.

———. "Letter to David Highham." November 11, 1975. Michael Longley Collection, box 1, folder 11. Special Collections Department, Robert W. Woodruff Library, Emory University.

———. "Letter to the Editor." *Hibernia,* December 10, 1974. Michael Longley Collection, box 1, folder 10. Special Collections Department, Robert W. Woodruff Library, Emory University.

———. "Letter to Wason, 1973–74." *Belfast Telegraph.* Michael Longley Collection, box 1, folder 10. Special Collections Department, Robert W. Woodruff Library, Emory University.

———. "The Longley Tapes." Interview by Robert Johnstone. *The Honest Ulsterman* 78 (Summer 1985): 13–31.

———. "Man Lying on a Wall." Michael Longley Collection, box 25, folder 9. Special Collections Department, Robert W. Woodruff Library, Emory University.

———. "Medbh McGuckian's Poetry." n.d. Michael Longley Collection, box 25, folder 23. Special Collections Department, Robert W. Woodruff Library, Emory University.

———. "Memory and Acknowledgement." *Irish Review* 17–18 (Winter 1995): 153–59.

———. "Michael Longley." BBC Northern Ireland broadcast, date unknown. Museum no. 3948, BBC Northern Ireland Community Archive, Cultra, Northern Ireland.

———. "Michael Longley." In *Reading the Future: Irish Writers in Conversation with Mike Murphy,* edited by Cliodhna Ni Anluain, 118–35. Dublin: Lilliput Press, 2000.

———. "Michael Longley: An Interview with Margaret Mills Harper." *Five Points* 8, no. 3 (2004): 56–71.

———. "The Neolithic Night: A Note on the Irishness of Louis MacNeice." In *Two Decades of Irish Writing: A Critical Survey,* edited by Douglas Dunn, 98–104. Chester Springs, Pennsylvania: Dufour, 1975.

———. *No Continuing City: Poems, 1963–68.* Chester Springs, PA: Dufour, 1969.

———. "Observing the Sons of Ulster." Interview by Eileen Battersby. *Irish Times,* March 9, 2000, 13.

————. "Patrick Kavanagh." n.d. Michael Longley Collection, box 26, folder 17. Special Collections Department, Robert W. Woodruff Library, Emory University.

————. "A Perpetual One-Night Stand: Some Thoughts on Jazz and Poetry." *Writing Ulster* 5 (1998): 91–98.

————. "Playing Football in No-Man's Land." Interview by Paul Keen. *Books in Canada* 28 (March 1999): 9–10.

————. "Playthings for the Soul: The Art of Felim Egan." Halloween 1995. www.felimegan.ie/longley.html.

————. *Poems, 1963–1983.* Winston-Salem, NC: Wake Forest University Press, 1987.

————. "A Poet at Work." BBC Northern Ireland broadcast, February 29, 1989. Museum no. 5671, BBC Northern Ireland Community Archive, Cultra, Northern Ireland.

————. "Poetry." In *Causeway: The Arts in Ulster,* edited by Michael Longley, 95–109. Belfast: Arts Council of Northern Ireland, 1971.

————. "Propertius." n.d. Michael Longley Collection, box 25, folder 29. Special Collections Department, Robert W. Woodruff Library, Emory University.

————. "A Provocation of Orchids." n.d. Michael Longley Collection, box 25, folder 27. Special Collections Department, Robert W. Woodruff Library, Emory University.

————. "Q. and A.: Michael Longley." Interview by Dillon Johnston. *Irish Literary Supplement* 10 (Fall 1986): 20–22.

————. "Reading Notes." n.d. Michael Longley Collection, box 25, folder 22. Special Collections Department, Robert W. Woodruff Library, Emory University.

————. "Reading Notes." n.d. Michael Longley Collection, box 25, folder 30. Special Collections Department, Robert W. Woodruff Library, Emory University.

————. "Reading Notes." n.d. Michael Longley Collection, box 25, folder 31. Special Collections Department, Robert W. Woodruff Library, Emory University.

————. "Review of Arts Funding Arrangements." n.d. Michael Longley Collection, box 25, folder 35. Special Collections Department, Robert W. Woodruff Library, Emory University.

————. *Selected Poems.* Winston-Salem, NC: Wake Forest University Press, 1999.

————. "Sketches of Britain—Letter from Ulster." BBC Northern Ireland broadcast, September 29, 1987. Museum no. 6018, BBC Northern Ireland Community Archive, Cultra, Northern Ireland.

———. *Snow Water.* Winston-Salem, NC: Wake Forest University Press, 2004.

———. "Strife and the Ulster Poet." *Hibernia,* November 7, 1969. Reprinted in *Irish Writing in the Twentieth Century: A Reader,* edited by David Pierce, 765. Cork: Cork University Press, 2000.

———. "Thought for the Day: 'A Favourite Reading.'" BBC Northern Ireland Radio broadcast, September 21, 1970. Michael Longley Collection, box 30, folder 12. Special Collections Department, Robert W. Woodruff Library, Emory University.

———. "A Tongue at Play." In *How Poets Work,* edited by Tony Curtis, 111–21. Bridgend, UK: Seren Books, 1996.

———. *Tuppenny Stung: Autobiographical Chapters.* Belfast: Lagan Press, 1994.

———. "Walking Forwards into the Past." Interview by Fran Brearton. *Irish Studies Review* 6 (Spring 1997): 35–39.

———. *The Weather in Japan.* Winston-Salem, NC: Wake Forest University Press, 2000.

———. ["Yeats."] n.d. Michael Longley Collection, box 25, folder 17. Special Collections Department, Robert W. Woodruff Library, Emory University.

Lucas, John. "Seamus Heaney and the Possibilities of Poetry." In *Seamus Heaney: A Collection of Critical Essays,* edited by Elmer Andrews, 117–38. New York: St. Martin's Press, 1992.

Lyon, John. "Michael Longley's Lists." *English* 45 (Autumn 1996): 228–46.

Lyotard, Jean-Francois. *Heidegger and the Jews.* Translated by Andreas Michel and Mark Roberts. Minneapolis: University of Minnesota Press, 1990.

MacNeice, Louis. *The Collected Poems of Louis MacNeice,* edited by E. R. Dodds. London: Faber, 1966.

———. *The Poetry of W. B. Yeats.* New York: Oxford University Press, 1941.

Mahon, Derek. "Letter to the Editor." *New Statesman,* December 7, 1971. Michael Longley Collection, box 1, folder 7. Special Collections Department, Robert W. Woodruff Library, Emory University.

———. "Personal Letter to Michael Longley." December 1971. Michael Longley Collection, box 1, folder 7. Special Collections Department, Robert W. Woodruff Library, Emory University.

———. "Poetry in Northern Ireland." *Twentieth Century Studies* 4 (November 1970): 92–93.

McCarthy, Conor. *Seamus Heaney and Medieval Poetry.* Cambridge: D. S. Brewer, 2008.

McCormack, W. J. "Irish Gothic and After." In *The Field Day Anthology of Irish Writing,* general editor Seamus Deane, vol. 2, 831–54. Derry: Field Day Publications, 1991.

McDonagh, Oliver. *States of Mind: A Study of Anglo-Irish Conflict, 1780–1980.* London: Unwin-Hyman, 1983.

McDonald, Peter. "Cold Comfort." Review of *Snow Water,* by Michael Longley. *Guardian,* May 22, 2004. http://books.guardian.co.uk/review/story/ 0,12084,1221327,00.html.

———. "Faiths and Fidelities: Heaney and Longley at Mid-career." In *The Tabla Book of New Verse,* edited by Stephen James, 63–72. Bristol: Tabla, 1999.

———. "Lapsed Classics: Homer, Ovid, and Michael Longley's Poetry." In *The Poetry of Michael Longley,* edited by Alan J. Peacock and Kathleen Devine, 35–50. Gerrards Cross: Colin Smythe, 2000.

———. *Mistaken Identities: Poetry and Northern Ireland.* Oxford: Oxford University Press, 1997.

———. *Serious Poetry: Form and Authority from Yeats to Hill.* Oxford: Oxford University Press, 2002.

McFadden, Grania. "Reporting the Arts." In *Stepping Stones: The Arts in Ulster 1971–2001,* edited by Mark Carruthers and Stephen Douds, 237–60. Belfast: Blackstaff, 2001.

McGinn, Colin. "The Meaning and Morality of *Lolita.*" *Philosophical Forum* 30 (March 1999): 31–42.

McGuckian, Medbh. "Michael Longley as a Metaphysical." *Colby Quarterly* 39 (September 2003): 215–20.

McKay, Susan. *Northern Protestants: An Unsettled People.* Belfast: Blackstaff Press, 2002.

McKittrick, David, Seamus Kelters, Brian Feeney, Chris Thornton, and David McVea. *Lost Lives: The Stories of the Men, Women and Children Who Died as a Result of the Northern Ireland Troubles.* 1999. Reprint, Edinburgh: Mainstream, 2001.

Miller, J. Hillis. *On Literature.* London: Routledge, 2002.

Milroy, James. "Social Variation in Belfast Speech." In *Regional Accents of English: Belfast,* 82–103. Belfast: Blackstaff Press, 1981.

Molino, Michael. *Questioning Tradition, Language, and Myth: The Poetry of Seamus Heaney.* Washington, DC: Catholic University of America Press, 1994.

Montague, John. "Letter to Michael Longley." May 1980. Michael Longley Collection, box 2, folder 3. Special Collections Department, Robert W. Woodruff Library, Emory University.

Moriarty, Gerry. "Writers Pay Tribute at Michael Longley's 70th Birthday." *Irish Times,* June 26, 2009. www.irishtimes.com/newspaper/ireland/2009/ 0626/1224249575155_pf.html.

Morrison, Blake. *Seamus Heaney.* London: Methuen, 1982.

Muldoon, Paul. "'Welsh Incident,' by Robert Graves; 'A Failure,' by C. Day Lewis; 'Keeping Going,' by Seamus Heaney." In *The End of the Poem: Oxford Lectures,* 368–95. New York: Farrar, Straus Giroux, 2006.

Murray, W. H. *The Hebrides.* London: Heinemann, 1966.

The New Testament in Modern English. Translated by J. B. Phillips. New York: Macmillan, 1964.

Ni Anluain, Cliodhna, ed. *Reading the Future: Irish Writers in Conversation with Mike Murphy.* Dublin: Lilliput Press, 2000.

Nobel Foundation. "The Nobel Prize in Literature 1995: Seamus Heaney." News release, October 5, 1995. http://nobelprize.org/nobel_prizes/literature/laureates/1995/press.html.

Northern Ireland Curriculum. "Growing up in Northern Ireland: 'A Plague on Both Your Houses.'" n.d. www.nicurriculum.org.uk/connected_learning/thematic_units/citizenship/english.asp. Accessed June 19, 2008.

Northern Ireland Executive. "McGuinness Announces Honour for Poet Michael Longley." News release, September 6, 2007. www.northernireland.gov.uk/news/news-ofmdfm/new-ofmdfm-september-2007/news-ofmdfm-060907-mcguinness-announces-honour-htm.

O'Brien, Conor Cruise. "A Slow North-East Wind." *Listener,* September 25, 1975, 404–5.

O'Brien, Eugene. "*North*: The Politics of Plurality." *Nua: Studies in Contemporary Irish Writing* 2 (Autumn 1998–Spring 1999): 1–19.

———. *Seamus Heaney and the Place of Writing.* Gainesville: University Press of Florida, 2002.

O'Donoghue, Bernard, ed. *The Cambridge Companion to Seamus Heaney.* Cambridge: Cambridge University Press, 2009.

O'Driscoll, Dennis. "Heaney in Public." In *The Cambridge Companion to Seamus Heaney,* edited by Bernard O'Donoghue, 56–72. Cambridge: Cambridge University Press, 2009.

O'Muiri, Pol. "The Good Friday Agreement: An Irishman's Diary." *Irish Times,* October 6, 1998. BBC Northern Ireland, www.bbc.co.uk/northernireland/schools/agreement/culture/support/cul2_n031.shtml.

Owen, Wilfred. *The Poems of Wilfred Owen,* edited by Jon Stallworthy. New York: Norton, 1986.

Parker, David. *Ethics, Theory and the Novel.* Cambridge: Cambridge University Press, 1994.

Parker, Michael. "From *Winter Seeds* to *Wintering Out*: The Evolution of Heaney's Third Collection." *New Hibernia Review* 11 (Summer 2007): 130–41.

———. "The Imprint of History: John Boyd's *The Flats,* Its Cultural and Political Contexts." *Essays in Theatre/Etudes Theatrales* 20 (May 2002): 137–56.

———. *Northern Irish Literature: The Imprint of History.* Vol. 1. *1956–1975.* New York: Palgrave, 2007.

———. *Northern Irish Literature: The Imprint of History.* Vol. 2. *1975–2006.* New York: Palgrave, 2007.

———. "Reckonings: The Political Contexts for Northern Irish Literature, 1965–68." *Irish Studies Review* 10, no. 2 (2002): 133–58.

———. *Seamus Heaney: The Making of the Poet.* Iowa City: University of Iowa Press, 1993.

Paterson, T. G. F. *Harvest Home: The Last Sheaf,* edited by E. Estyn Evans. Dundalk, Ireland: Dundalgan Press, 1975.

Paulin, Tom. Foreword to *Rhyming Weavers and Other Country Poets of Antrim and Down,* edited by John Hewitt, vii–xii. Belfast: Blackstaff, 2004.

———. "Northern Protestant Oratory and Writing, 1791–1985." In *The Field Day Anthology of Irish Literature,* general editor Seamus Deane, vol. 3, 314–18. Derry: Field Day Publications, 1991.

———. "Paisley's Progress." *Writing to the Moment: Selected Critical Essays, 1980–1996,* 28–47. London: Faber and Faber, 1996.

———. "Political Verse." In *Writing to the Moment: Selected Critical Essays, 1980–1996,* 101–39. London: Faber and Faber, 1996.

Peacock, Alan, ed. *The Achievement of Brian Friel.* Gerrards Cross: Colin Smythe, 1993.

———. "'How Do You Sew the Night?': *The Weather in Japan.*" In *The Poetry of Michael Longley,* edited by Alan J. Peacock and Kathleen Devine, 143–67. Gerrards Cross: Colin Smythe, 2000.

———. "Mediations: Poet as Translator, Poet as Seer." In *Seamus Heaney: A Collection of Critical Essays,* edited by Elmer Andrews, 233–54. New York: St. Martin's Press, 1992.

———. "Michael Longley: Poet between Worlds." In *Poetry in Contemporary Irish Literature,* edited by Michael Kenneally, 263–79. Gerrards Cross: Colin Smythe, 1995.

Peacock, Alan J., and Kathleen Devine, eds. *The Poetry of Michael Longley.* Gerrards Cross: Colin Smythe, 2000.

Peters, Pauline. "Interfaith." December 2005. Friends in Meditation. www.friendsinmeditation.com/testimonials_interfaith3.html.

Pocock, J. G. A. "British History: A Plea for a New Subject." *Journal of Modern History* 47 (December 1975): 601–28.

———. "The Limits and Divisions of British History: In Search of the Unknown Subject." *American Historical Review* 87 (April 1982): 311–36.

Polanyi, Michael. *The Tacit Dimension.* Garden City, NY: Anchor, 1967.
Porter, Norman. *The Elusive Quest: Reconciliation in Northern Ireland.* Belfast: Blackstaff Press, 2003.
Post, Gregory, and Charles Turner. *The Feast: Reflections on the Bread of Life.* San Francisco: HarperCollins, 1992.
"Radio Two Arts Programme." BBC Northern Ireland broadcast, September 28, 1990. Museum nos. 6687/6688, BBC Northern Ireland Community Archive, Cultra, Northern Ireland.
Ramazani, Jahan. *Poetry of Mourning: The Modern Elegy from Hardy to Heaney.* Chicago: University of Chicago Press, 1994.
Richtarik, Marilynn J. *Acting between the Lines: The Field Day Theatre Company and Irish Cultural Politics, 1980–1984.* Oxford: Oxford University Press, 1984.
Robertson, Robin, ed. *Love Poet, Carpenter: Michael Longley at Seventy.* London: Enitharmon Press, 2009.
Robinson, Alan. *Instabilities in Contemporary British Poetry.* London: Macmillan, 1988.
Robinson, Tim. *Setting Foot on the Shores of Connemara and Other Writings.* Dublin: Lilliput Press, 1996.
Roche, Anthony. Preface to *The Senate Speeches of W. B. Yeats,* edited by Donald R. Pearce, iii–xix. London: Prendeville, 2001.
Roche, Mark William. *Why Literature Matters in the 21st Century.* New Haven: Yale University Press, 2004.
Roe, Nicholas. "'Wordsworth at the Flax Dam': An Early Poem by Seamus Heaney." In *Critical Approaches to Anglo-Irish Literature,* edited by Michael Allen and Angela Wilcox, 166–70. Totowa, NJ: Barnes and Nobles Books, 1989.
Rushdie, Salman. "Is Nothing Sacred?" In *Imaginary Homelands: Essays and Criticism 1981–1991,* 415–29. New York: Granta/Viking Penguin, 1991.
Russell, Richard Rankin. "Imagining a New Province: Seamus Heaney's Creative Work for BBC Northern Ireland Radio, 1968–1971." *Irish Studies Review* 15 (Spring 2007): 137–62.
———. "Inscribing Cultural Corridors: Michael Longley's Poetic Contribution to Reconciliation in Northern Ireland." *Colby Quarterly* 39 (September 2003): 221–40.
———. "The Liberating Fictional Truth of Community in Brian Friel's *The Freedom of the City.*" *South Atlantic Review* 71 (Winter 2006): 42–73.
———. "Of Flowers and Fighting: Michael Longley's *Selected Poems.*" *Carolina Quarterly* 52 (Spring 2000): 74–79.
———. "Poems without Frontiers: Poetic Reception and Political Possibility in the Work of Seamus Heaney." In *Seamus Heaney: Poet, Critic, Translator,*

edited by Jason David Hall and Bland Crowder, 26–41. Basingstoke: Palgrave Macmillan, 2007.

———. Review of *Reading Michael Longley*, by Fran Brearton. *Irish Studies Review* 16 (May 2008): 226–28.

———. Review of *Snow Water*, by Michael Longley. *New Hibernia Review* 9 (Autumn 2005): 151–52.

———. "Seamus Heaney's Regionalism." *Twentieth-Century Literature* 54 (Spring 2008): 47–74.

———. "The Yeatsian Refrain in Paul Muldoon's *Moy Sand and Gravel*." *ANQ: A Journal of Short Essays, Notes, and Queries* 19 (Summer 2006): 51–57.

Scarry, Elaine. *On Beauty and Being Just*. Princeton: Princeton University Press, 1999.

Schmidt, Michael. *Reading Modern Poetry*. New York: Routledge, 1989.

Schuchard, Ronald. "The Legacy of Yeats in Contemporary Irish Poetry." *Irish University Review* 34 (Autumn–Winter 2004): 291–314.

Schwarz, Daniel R. *Imagining the Holocaust*. New York: St. Martin's Press, 1999.

Scott, Nathan, Jr. *The Poetics of Belief: Studies in Coleridge, Arnold, Pater, Santayana, Stevens, and Heidegger*. Chapel Hill: University of North Carolina Press, 1985.

———. *The Wild Prayer of Longing: Poetry and the Sacred*. New Haven: Yale University Press, 1971.

Sontag, Susan. *Regarding the Pain of Others*. New York: Farrar Straus Giroux, 2003.

Spring, Dick. Statement to the Irish Senate on the Opsahl Report. July 13, 1993. http://historical-debates.oireachtas.ie/S/0137/S.0137.199307130004.html.

Steiner, George. *Grammars of Creation*. New Haven: Yale University Press, 2002.

———. *Real Presences*. Chicago: University of Chicago Press, 1989.

Strickland, Geoffrey. "F. R. Leavis and 'English.'" In *The New Pelican Guide to English Literature: 8. The Present*, edited by Boris Ford, 175–92. New York: Penguin, 1983.

Tannahill, Anne. "More Than Just a Day Job." In *Love Poet, Carpenter: Michael Longley at Seventy*, edited by Robin Robertson, 115–17. London: Enitharmon Press, 2009.

Taylor, Peter. *Loyalists*. London: Bloomsbury, 1999.

Thornton, Weldon. "Between Circle and Straight Line: A Pragmatic View of W. B. Yeats and the Occult." *Studies in the Literary Imagination* 14 (Spring 1981): 61–75.

Tobin, Daniel. *Passage to the Center: Imagination and the Sacred in the Poetry of Seamus Heaney*. Lexington: University Press of Kentucky, 1999.

Turner, Victor, and Edith Turner. *Image and Pilgrimage in Christian Culture.* New York: Columbia University Press, 1978.

Underhill, Hugh. *The Problem of Consciousness in Modern Poetry.* Cambridge: Cambridge University Press, 1992.

Vendler, Helen. *Seamus Heaney.* Cambridge, MA: Harvard University Press, 1998.

Viney, Michael. "Michael in Mayo." In *Love Poet, Carpenter: Michael Longley at Seventy,* edited by Robin Robertson, 121–23. London: Enitharmon Press, 2009.

Wall, Richard. "A Dialect Glossary for Seamus Heaney's Works." *Irish University Review* 28, no. 1 (1998): 68–86.

Warman, April. "Precision and Suggestion: The Role of the Self in Michael Longley's Public Elegies." *English* 56 (Spring 2007): 41–56.

Watson, George. "The Narrow Ground: Northern Poets and the Northern Irish Crisis." In *Irish Writers and Society at Large,* edited by Marasu Sekine, 207–24. Totowa, NJ: Barnes and Noble, 1985.

Weeks, Jerome. "Nobel Winner Seamus Heaney Digs into the Rural Irish Peat and Unearths Poetic Gold." *Dallas Morning News,* May 6, 2001, 1C, 6C.

Welch, Robert. "Michael Longley and the West." In *The Poetry of Michael Longley,* edited by Alan J. Peacock and Kathleen Devine, 51–64. Gerrards Cross: Colin Smythe, 2000.

———. "Sacrament and Significance: Some Reflections on Religion and the Irish." *Religion and Literature* 28 (Summer–Autumn 1996): 101–13.

Wells, Ronald A. *People behind the Peace: Community and Reconciliation in Northern Ireland.* Grand Rapids, MI: Eerdmans, 1999.

"Whatever You Say Say Nothing." BBC Northern Ireland broadcast of round-table discussion, July 24, 1994. Museum no. 4010, BBC Northern Ireland Community Archive, Cultra, Northern Ireland.

Wheatley, David. "'That Blank Mouth': Secrecy, Shibboleths, and Silence in Northern Irish Poetry." *Journal of Modern Literature* 25 (Fall 2001): 1–16.

Wright, Terrence C. "Heidegger and Heaney: Poetry and Possibility." *Philosophy Today* 38 (Winter 1994): 390–99.

"The Year a Nation Drank from the Healing Well." *Independent,* January 1, 2008. www.independent.co.uk/opinion/leading-articles/leading-article-the-year-a-nation-drank-from-the-healing-well-767547.html.

Yeats, William Butler. *The Collected Poems of W. B. Yeats: A New Edition.* Edited by Richard Finneran. New York: Macmillan, 1989.

———. "A General Introduction to My Work." In *Essays and Introductions,* 509–26. New York: Macmillan, 1961.

———. "Magic." In *Essays and Introductions,* 28–52. New York: Macmillan, 1961.

———. "The Symbolism of Poetry." In *Essays and Introductions,* 153–64. New York: Macmillan, 1961.

———. *A Vision.* London: Macmillan, 1937.

———. *W. B. Yeats: The Poems.* Edited by Daniel Albright. London: Everyman's Library, 1992.

Index

Richard Rankin Russell

is associate professor of English at Baylor University.

He is the author of *Bernard MacLaverty* and *Martin McDonagh: A Casebook.*